Readings in Educational Psychology

Second Edition

Anita E. Woolfolk
The Ohio State University

Allyn and Bacon
Boston • London • Toronto • Sydney • Tokyo • Singapore

Library of Congress Cataloging-in-Publication Data

Readings in educational psychology / [edited by] Anita E. Woolfolk.—
    2nd ed.
        p.   cm.
    Rev. ed. of: Readings and cases in educational psychology. c1993.
    Includes bibliographical references.
    ISBN 0-205-27889-2
    1. Educational psychology.   2. Educational psychology—Case studies   I. Woolfolk, Anita.   II. Readings and cases in educational psychology.
    LB1051.R386   1998
    370.15—dc21   97-31589
                                                                  CIP

CREDITS

1. Gage, N. L. (1991). The obviousness of social and educational research results. *Educational Researcher, 20*(1), 10–16. Copyright 1991 by the American Educational Research Association. Reprinted by permission of the publisher.

2. Epstein, J. L. (1995). School/family/community partnerships: Caring for the children we share. *Phi Delta Kappan, 76,* 701–712. Reprinted by permission of Joyce L. Epstein.

3. Vygodskaia, G. L. (1995). Remembering father. *Educational Psychology, 30,* 57–59. Reprinted by permission of Lawrence Erlbaum Associates, Inc.

4. Flavell, J. H. (1996). Piaget's legacy. *Psychological Science, 7*(4), 200–203. Reprinted by permission of John H. Flavell.

5. Canfield, J. (1990). Improving students' self-esteem. *Educational Leadership, 46*(6), 19–23. Reprinted by permission of Jack Canfield, co-author of Chicken Soup for the Soul Series.

6. Reprinted with permission from *The Harvard Education Letter,* July/August 1990 (vol. VI, No. 4, pages 5–7), Girls at 11: An interview with Carol Gilligan. Copyright 1990 by the President and Fellows of Harvard College. All rights reserved.

Credits continue on page 265, which constitutes an extension of the copyright page.

Printed in the United States of America

10 9 8 7 6 5 4 3 2   COU 04 03 02 01 00 99

Contents

Preface

TO THE READER

Many of you reading this book are studying educational psychology for the first time. Others may be taking an advanced course or a graduate seminar. To all of you, welcome to some interesting reading and exciting ideas. I have been teaching and learning about educational psychology for almost 30 years and have witnessed many developments. But of all the times to study educational psychology, this is the most fascinating. The field has been changing rapidly. There is renewed interest in how the mind works, how children and adults learn, what motivates students, and how excellent teaching happens. Educational psychologists have more useful information for teachers than ever before, as you will see in the coming pages.

This volume is a collection of readings selected from professional journals and magazines. Some of the articles are reviews of research on important topics prepared for practicing teachers and administrators. Others articles take a position or make an argument for a particular approach to teaching or testing.

TO THE INSTRUCTOR

This book is a collection of articles chosen from professional journals and magazines. Many of the articles are summaries of research in a given area—some written for researchers and others for practicing teachers and administrators. Other articles take a position on a controversial issue. These reviews and position papers are taken from the *Educational Researcher, Review of Educational Research, Phi Delta Kappan, Educational Leadership, The Harvard Education Letter, Current Directions in Psychological Science, The Elementary School Journal,* and the *Journal of Educational Psychology.*

Most of the readings in this volume are cited in my educational psychology textbook (*Educational Psychology,* Seventh Edition, published by Allyn and Bacon). But I have chosen the articles to complement any text, even if these sources are not directly cited. The articles are grouped by topics and these topics are consistently found in most educational psychology books.

I am interested in hearing about how you use these readings in your teaching and about your students' reactions. Please send any comments or suggestions to:

Anita Woolfolk
Allyn and Bacon
160 Gould Street
Needham Heights, MA 02194

Chapter 1: Teachers, Teaching, and Educational Psychology

The Obviousness of Social and Educational Research Results

N. L. GAGE

Highly estimable writers have averred that well nigh all of the results of social and educational research are obvious, that is, could have been predicted without doing the research. To examine the justifiability of this allegation, one should examine its accord with actual research results. Thus, is it a "truism" that higher achievement comes about when students spend more time with the subject matter? That smaller groups are easier to control than larger groups? Do judges regard actual results as more obvious and statements of their opposites as nonobvious? Both the century-old research results of Joseph Mayer Rice and recent results throw light on these issues.

—Educational Researcher, Vol. 20, no. 1, pp. 10–16

Is what we find out in social and educational research old hat, stale, platitudinous? Are the results of such research mere truisms that any intelligent person might know without going to the trouble of doing social or educational research?

THE IMPORTANCE OF THE OBVIOUSNESS QUESTION

The obviousness question has important ramifications. It can influence the motivation of any person who is thinking about doing social or educational research. Why do research if you are not going to find anything new, anything not already known? Obviousness also relates to the justification of social science departments and schools of education in expecting or requiring their faculties and graduate students to do social and educational research. It also concerns government funding policies, such as those

N. L. Gage is at the School of Education, Stanford University, Stanford, California 94305.

of the National Science Foundation and the National Institute of Mental Health that support social research, and those of the U.S. Department of Education, particularly the Office of Educational Research and Improvement, that support educational research. Foundations, school boards, state legislatures, and Congressional committees need to be convinced, before they put up the money, that social and educational research will produce something that any intelligent adult might not already know.

So, the issue of obviousness, apart from piquing our intellectual curiosity, has tremendous practical importance. Unless social and educational researchers face that issue, they may lack motivation to do research and lose societal support expressed in dollars.

THE CHARGE OF OBVIOUSNESS

Does anyone really hold that social and educational research yields only the obvious? I begin with an old joke attributed to James T. Farrell, the novelist who became famous in the 1930s for *Studs Lonigan*. Farrell was quoted in those days as having defined a sociologist as someone who will spend $10,000 to discover the location of the nearest house of ill fame. He actually used a less polite term, and nowadays he would have said a quarter of a million dollars. I also remember a fellow graduate student who could always get a laugh by referring to the content of some of his textbooks as "unctuous elaborations of the obvious."

Schlesinger's Critique

The first serious piece of writing that I know of that made the same charge appeared in 1949 in *The Partisan Review*. It was in a review by Arthur Schlesinger, Jr., of the two volumes of *The American Soldier*, which had just been published. *The American Soldier* was written by a group led by Samuel A. Stouffer, who later became a professor of sociology at Harvard. It reported on the work done by sociologists and other social scientists in surveying, with questionnaires and interviews, the attitudes of American soldiers during World War II. The first volume, subtitled "Adjustment During Army Life," dealt with soldiers' attitudes during training, and the second, subtitled "Combat and Its Aftermath," dealt with soldiers' attitudes while they were engaged with the enemy and risking their lives. As a young assistant professor, I found the two books impressive for their methodological thoroughness, sophisticated interpretation, and theoretical formulations of such concepts as "relative deprivation."

So I was taken aback after some months when I discovered a review of those two volumes by Arthur Schlesinger, Jr., the distinguished historian. Then a young professor at Harvard University, Schlesinger had just won a Pulitzer Prize for his *Age of Jackson*. Witty and vituperative, Schlesinger's review also denounced what he considered the pretensions of social scientists. Schlesinger wrote:

> *Does this kind of research yield anything new? . . . [T]he answer . . . is easy. Most of* The American Soldier *is a ponderous demonstration in Newspeak of such facts as these: New recruits do not like noncoms; front-line troops resent rear-echelon troops; combat men manifest a high level of anxiety as compared to other soldiers; married privates are more likely than single privates to worry about their families back home. Indeed, one can find little in the 1,200 pages of*

> *text and the innumerable surveys which is not described more vividly and compactly and with far greater psychological insight, in a small book entitled* Up Front *by Bill Mauldin. What Mauldin may have missed will turn up in the pages of Ernie Pyle. (p. 854)*

Lazarsfeld's Examples

At about the same time as Schlesinger, Paul Lazarsfeld, a professor of sociology at Columbia University, also reviewed *The American Soldier*. Lazarsfeld (1949) was dearly aware of the same problem of obviousness. He wrote:

> [I]t is hard to find a form of human behavior that has not already been observed somewhere. Consequently, if a study reports a prevailing regularity, many readers respond to it by thinking "of course, that is the way things are." Thus, from time to time, the argument is advanced that surveys only put into complicated form observations which are already obvious to everyone.
>
> Understanding the origin of this point of view is of importance far beyond the limits of the present discussion. The reader may be helped in recognizing this attitude if he looks over a few statements which are typical of many survey findings and carefully observes his own reaction. A short list of these, with brief interpretive comments, will be given here in order to bring into sharper focus probable reactions of many readers.
>
> 1. *Better educated men showed more psychoneurotic symptoms than those with less education. (The mental instability of the intellectual as compared to the more impassive psychology of the man-in-the-street has often been commented on.)*
> 2. *Men from rural backgrounds were usually in better spirits during their Army life than soldiers from city backgrounds. (After all, they are more accustomed to hardships.)*
> 3. *Southern soldiers were better able to stand the climate in the hot South Sea Islands than Northern soldiers. (Of course. Southerners are more accustomed to hot weather.)*
> 4. *White privates were more eager to become noncoms than Negroes. ([Because of their having been deprived of opportunity for so many years], the lack of ambition among Negroes was [quite understandable].)*

5. *Southern Negroes preferred Southern to Northern white officers [because Southerners were much more experienced in having interpersonal interactions with Negroes than Northern officers were].*

6. *As long as the fighting continued, men were more eager to be returned to the States than they were after the Germans surrendered [because during the fighting, soldiers were in danger of getting killed, but after the surrender there was no such danger]. (pp. 379–380)*

Keppel's Position

For a later sample of the worry about obviousness, we can turn to an essay by Frank Keppel, titled "The Education of Teachers," which appeared in 1962 in a volume of talks on American education by American scholars that had been broadcast by radio to foreign audiences. Keppel had left the deanship of the Harvard Graduate School of Education to serve as U.S. Commissioner of Education under President Kennedy. As Commissioner he led the movement that resulted in the Elementary and Secondary Education Act of 1965, the first major effort in the U.S. to improve the education of children from low-income families. In his article, Keppel (1962) indicated that some people question the principles that have emerged from psychological studies of teaching and learning. Without committing himself as to whether he agreed, he summed up the critics' arguments this way:

> *The efforts to use scientific methods to study human behavior seem to them [the critics] ridiculous if not impious. The result is a ponderous, pseudo-scientific language which takes ten pages to explain the obvious or to dilute the wisdom long ago learned in humanistic studies. . . . To build an art of teaching on the basis of the "behavioral sciences," they suggest, is to build on sand. (p. 91)*

Conant's Position

The very next year, obviousness was mentioned again, by another prestigious educator, namely, James Bryant Conant, who had been president of Harvard University for 20 years, and then the U.S. High Commissioner (and eventually the U.S. ambassador) in West Germany. During World War II, he had been a member of the highest scientific advisory committees, including the one that led to the production of the atom bomb. When he returned from Germany, he devoted himself almost exclusively to educational problems. In 1963, he published a book titled *The Education of American Teachers*, in which he reported on his studies of teacher education programs and schools—studies made through much interviewing, reading, and visiting. His book gained extremely wide and respectful attention. Yet, when I looked into it, as an educational psychologist, I couldn't help being dismayed by Conant's assertion that educational psychology largely gives us merely common-sense generalizations about human nature—generalizations that are "for the most part highly limited and unsystematized generalizations, which are the stock in trade of every day life for all sane people" (p. 133).

Phillips's Critique

These references to obviousness take us only into the 1960s. Did the attacks disappear after that? Or are there more recent statements on the obviousness of educational and social research results? In 1985, a volume of papers appeared on the subject of instructional time, which had been central in a variety of formulations, such as John B. Carroll's model of school learning, Benjamin Bloom's mastery approach to teaching, and the concept of academic engaged time developed by Charles Fisher and David Berliner. All of these writers seemed to agree that the more time students spent in studying, practicing, and being engaged with the content or skills to be learned, the greater the related learning they achieved. The correlations between academic engaged time and achievement were not perfect, of course, because outside of the laboratory, correlations are never perfect, even in the natural sciences and certainly not in the social and behavioral sciences.

The subject of instructional time thus received a lot of attention in many articles and several books, including the edited volume, *Perspectives on Instructional Time*, to which the philosopher of the social sciences, Denis Phillips (1985), contributed a chapter entitled "The Uses and Abuses of Truisms." Here Phillips first cited Hamlyn, also a philosopher, who had criticized the work of Piaget. Hamlyn had asked his readers to try to imagine a world in which Piaget's main ideas were untrue:

> *a world where children mastered abstract and complex tasks before concrete and simple ones,*

for example. Such a world would differ crazily from our own, and one gets the sense that many of Piaget's views are unsurprising and necessarily (if not trivially) true. (p. 311)

Phillips then raised the same kind of question about the research on instructional time: "What sort of world would it be if children learned more the *less* time they spent on a subject? If achievement were not related to the time spent engaged on a topic?" (p. 311). So, just as with Piaget's major findings, "one [senses] that these findings [about instructional time] are almost necessarily (and perhaps even trivially) true" (p. 311). "Indeed, it suddenly seems strange to dress up these truisms as 'findings' " (p. 312).

Phillips then went on to make a distinction between truisms and statements that are trivially true. "[T]he latter are, in effect, a subgroup of the former. A truism is a statement the truth of which is self-evident or obvious . . . whereas a trivially true statement is one that is true by virtue of the meaning of the terms involved (e.g., 'All colored objects are colored,' or 'All bachelors are unmarried')" (p. 312). He went on to say that "'It is easier to keep a small group of children working on a task than it is a large group' is a truism, for it is obviously true, but it is not true by virtue of the meanings of the terms involved" (p. 312). Phillips also pointed out that:

> *truisms and statements that are trivially true are not thereby* trivial. *The terms* truism *and* trivially true *refer to the patentness of the truth of statements, whereas* trivial *refers to their degree of value or usefulness. The two do not automatically go together; many a statement the truth of which is far from obvious is of no practical use . . . and many truisms are vitally important and even theoretically significant ("The sky is dark at night" [this truism bears on the theory of the expanding universe]). (p. 313)*

Furthermore,

> *truisms uncovered by researchers, then, are not necessarily trivial. But on the other hand truisms do not require research in order to be uncovered. Agencies would be wasting money if they awarded grants to researchers who wanted to determine if all bachelors in the United States were unmarried, or if the sky is dark at night, or if small groups are easier to control than large groups. (p. 313, emphasis added)*

In Short

Let me summarize the argument so far. I have presented a series of opinions quite damaging to the notion that social and educational research yields results that would not already be known to any intelligent and thoughtful citizen. These opinions are hard to ignore. Extremely estimable people—Farrell, Schlesinger, Keppel, Conant, Lazarsfeld, and Phillips—all have made statements that might well give pause to any sensible person considering the pursuit of social and educational research or any organization being asked to part with money to support such research. I have presented these statements in chronological order extending from novelist James T. Farrell in the mid-1930s to philosopher Denis Phillips in the mid-1980s.

EMPIRICAL EXAMINATION OF OBVIOUSNESS

One noteworthy characteristic of all of these criticisms is that they were what might be called nonempirical or, at least, not systematically and formally empirical. Informal and personal, the appraisals were not made with any great specificity, detail, explicitness, or exactitude. Presumably, Schlesinger had not actually compared the statements of results reported in *The American Soldier* with statements made by Bill Mauldin or Ernie Pyle. He did not perform a content analysis of the two kinds of reports about soldiers to show in any literal way that the sociologists' statements of results had been anticipated by the insights of the cartoonist and the journalist. The same point can be made about what was said by Keppel and Conant: They did not go into any detail, or become at all specific, to support their allegations. However, the sociologist Lazarsfeld did go into detail and referred to specific results, namely, soldiers' attitudes of various kinds. Phillips referred to specific findings about instructional time, or time on task, and also findings about size of group or class size.

Rice's Studies

Now I should like to go back and look at some empirical efforts that seem to me to bear upon the whole issue of obviousness. I begin with what may be the first process–outcome study in the history of research on teaching. The results of this investigation were published by Joseph Mayer Rice (1897/1913) under the title "The Futility of the Spelling Grind." Rice reported, after studying tests on 33,000 school children, that there was no correlation worth noticing between amount of time devoted to spelling homework and classwork and competence in spelling.

Rice's evidence is still being cited in support of the argument that spelling competence results from "incidental" learning, rather than from any "systematic" teaching; that is, spelling is "caught" rather than "taught." So far as instructional time or "academic engaged time" is concerned, the issue does not appear to be the open-and-shut case implied by Phillips (1985) when he asked, "What kind of world would it be if achievement were not related to the time spent engaged on a topic?" (p. 311). As Rice (1897/1913) put it, "concerning the amount of time devoted to spelling . . . an increase of time . . . is not rewarded by better results. . . . The results obtained by forty or fifty minutes' daily instruction were not better than those obtained where not more than ten or fifteen minutes had been devoted to the subject" (pp. 86–87).

Apparently, showing a relationship between time on task and achievement was not as easy as falling off a log, as it should have been if the relationship between time-on-task and achievement were necessarily true, that is, a truism. At least in one subject matter, namely, spelling, the relationship between time-on-task and achievement was fragile, perhaps even nonexistent. So perhaps the relationship depended on the subject matter. Perhaps other factors also made a difference. Things may be more complicated than we should expect if the relationship were a truism.

Similarly, if smaller groups were always easier to control, a relationship that Phillips assumed to be a truism, then they should show higher time-on-task and thus higher achievement. However, the trickiness of the relationship between class size and achievement is by now well established. Reducing class size from 40 to 20 does not improve achievement with any consistency at all. Glass (1987) reported that it required an "exhaustive and quantitative integration of the research" to refute well-nigh unanimous older assessments (e.g., Goodlad, 1960) that class size made no difference in achievement, student attention, and discipline. Even then Glass found that the relationship of class size to achievement appeared only probabilistically (in 111 of 160 instances, or 69%) when classes of

approximately 18 and 28 pupils were compared. Moreover, the duration of the instruction made a big difference: the relationship was stronger in studies of pupils taught for more than 100 hours. In addition, the class size had to be reduced dramatically to make a major improvement: "Bringing about even a 10 percentile rank improvement in the average pupil's achievement . . . may entail cutting class size (and, hence, increasing schooling costs) by a third to a half" (p. 544).

Alleging that a relationship (e.g., the size-of-group relationship to the ease of control) is a truism implies that it should always be found and that no exceptions should occur. Thus, all bachelors without exception are unmarried, all colored objects without exception are colored. By the same reasoning, if the group size-controllability relationship were a truism, all smaller groups should be easier to control than all larger groups. If the age-reasoning ability relationship were a truism, all older children should be capable of more abstract and valid reasoning than all younger children. But, of course, the last two examples are untrue. If a truism is "an undoubted or self-evident truth, especially one too obvious or unimportant for mention" (*Webster's New Collegiate Dictionary,* 1979), then these relationships are not truisms because they are not always "undoubted" or "self-evident."

Suppose we change the "truism" to a probabilistic statement (e.g., children *tend* to learn more, the more time they spend on a subject; time on task is positively but *imperfectly* correlated with achievement). Now the research aims to determine the strength of the tendency, or the magnitude of the positive correlation. Does the r equal .05, .25, .45, .65, or .85? It seems to be a truism that the size of the time-on-task versus achievement correlation depends on many factors: the reliability of the achievement measure, the variabilities of the two variables, perhaps the subject matter, and so on. Is the research to answer these important and specific practical questions still unnecessary?

Here may lie one key to the problem: To enhance the truism with the specifics that make it have value for theory and practice, the research does become necessary. Even if the broad generalization is a truism, the specifics of its actualization in human affairs—to determine the magnitude of the probability and the factors that affect that magnitude—require research. Even if "smaller groups tend to be more easily controlled" were a truism, we would ask, how much difference in group size is needed to produce a given difference in controllability? How do other factors—age and gender of group members, task difficulty, and the like—affect the difference in controllability resulting from changes in group size? Similar questions would apply to all the other seemingly truistic findings. Even if intelligent people could always (without any research) predict the direction (positive or negative) of a relationship between two variables, they could not predict its size and its contingencies without research-based knowledge.

Lazarsfeld's Examples

Let us go back now to Lazarsfeld's examples of obvious results from the World War II studies of *The American Soldier*. Recall his examples of the "obvious" conclusions from that study: better educated men showed more psychoneurotic symptoms; men from rural backgrounds were usually in better spirits than those from cities; Southern soldiers were better able than Northerners to stand the climate in the South Sea Islands; White privates were more eager to become noncoms than Black privates were; Southern Negroes preferred Southern to Northern White officers; and men were more eager to be returned to the States during the fighting than they were after the Germans surrendered.

Lazarsfeld (1949) asked, "Why, since they are so obvious, is so much money given to establish such findings?" However, he then revealed that

> Every one of these statements is the direct opposite of what was actually found. *Poorly educated soldiers were more neurotic than those with high educations; Southerners showed no greater ability than Northerners to adjust to a tropical climate; Negroes were more eager for promotion than whites, and so on. . . . If we had mentioned the actual results of the investigation first, the reader would have labelled these "obvious" also. Obviously something is wrong with the entire argument of obviousness. It should really be turned on its head. Since every kind of human reaction is conceivable, it is of great importance to know which reactions actually occur most frequently and under what conditions. . . . (p. 380)*

Lazarsfeld's rhetorical ploy has always impressed me as fairly unsettling for those who make the allegations of obviousness, but its force depends on whether we are willing to grant him his assumption

that we accepted the first version of the research results as valid, so that he could then startle us with his second presentation, which gave the true findings: the results that were actually obtained. It might be argued that Lazarsfeld's assumption was unwarranted and that most of us would not have believed that first set of statements that he later revealed were spurious.

The Mischels' Study

So I took notice when I heard about investigations that made no assumptions of the kind that Lazarsfeld's exercise required. The first of these (Mischel, 1981; Mischel & Mischel, 1979) consisted of giving fourth- and sixth-grade children (Ns = 38 and 49, respectively) items presenting psychological principles stated in both their actual form and the opposite of the actual forms. For example, the first item dealt with the finding by Solomon Asch that college students would respond contrarily to the evidence of their senses about which of three lines had the same length as a comparison line when the students first heard four other students (confederates of the investigator) misidentify the same-length line. The second item concerned Harry Helson's finding that the same water temperature feels cooler on a hot day than on a cool day. In all, there were 17 such items, some of which were presented to only one of the two grade-level groups. The children circled the one of the two to four choices that they thought described what would happen in each situation.

Of the 29 opportunities for either the fourth graders or the sixth graders to select the actual research result to a statistically significant degree, the groups did so on 19, or 66%. One group or the other was wrong to a statistically significant degree on five opportunities, and there was no statistically significant correctness or incorrectness on 5 opportunities. Clearly, the children had substantial success, but far from the perfect record that would support the allegation of almost universal obviousness.

But these were only children. What about college students and adults? And what happens when the research results are presented as flat statements rather than as multiple-choice items requiring the selection of the actual result from two or more alternatives?

Baratz's Study

Baratz (1983) selected 16 social research findings from various studies, and then did an experiment. She manipulated, for each of the findings, whether the statement concerning that finding was the true finding or the opposite of the true finding. She also presented each finding, either the true one or the opposite one, with or without an explanation of the finding. That second manipulation was intended to "explore the possibility that adding explanations to the findings may render the findings more obvious" (p. 20). Thus, each of her subjects—85 male and female undergraduates enrolled in introductory psychology at Stanford University—evaluated 16 findings: four statements with a true finding plus explanation, four statements with the opposite finding plus explanation, four statements with a true finding without explanation, and four statements of an opposite finding without an explanation. Each finding was presented in the same format: first, the question addressed by the study, such as "a study sought to determine whether people spend a larger proportion of their income during *prosperous* times or during a *recession*." And for this study the reported finding was "In prosperous times people spend a larger proportion of their income than during a recession." The statement of the opposite finding differed from that of the true finding only in the order of the critical terms, and half of the findings were followed at the time by a short explanation, which was presented as the "explanation given by our subject."

Here are two sample pairs of the true and opposite findings used by Baratz in her experiment: "People who go to church regularly tend to have more children than people who go to church infrequently" versus "People who go to church infrequently tend to have more children than people who go to church regularly" and "Single women express more distress over their unmarried status than single men do" versus "Single men express more distress over their unmarried status than single women do."

For each of the 16 findings presented to each student, the students were asked how readily predictable or obvious the finding was and were instructed to choose one of the responses on the following four-point scale:

1. I am *certain* that I would have predicted the result obtained rather than the opposite result.
2. I *think* that I would have predicted the result obtained rather than the opposite result, but I am *not certain*.
3. I *think* that I would have predicted the opposite to the obtained result, but I am *not certain*.
4. I am *certain* that I would have predicted the *opposite to* the obtained result.

The subjects were asked to express their "initial impressions of the relevant findings, i.e., the kind of impression that you might form if you read a brief article about the research in your daily newspaper" (p. 25).

In a summary table, Baratz presented the mean percentage of subjects who marked either "I am *certain* that I would have predicted the reported outcome" or "I *think* I would have predicted the reported outcome" for pairs of opposite findings. When the reported outcome was "A," 80% of her students claimed they would have predicted that outcome. When the reported outcome was "B," 66% of her subjects claimed they would have predicted that outcome. Thus, as Baratz put it, "It is clear that findings that contradict each other were both retrospectively judged 'obvious'. . . . These results show clearly that reading a result made that result appear obvious. No matter which result was presented, the majority of the subjects thought that they would have predicted it" (p. 26).

I considered Baratz's experiment and her findings to be persuasive. They seemed to provide evidence against the argument that social research yields only obvious findings. Her results indicated that intelligent people, namely, Stanford undergraduates, tend to regard any result they read, whether it is the true one or the opposite of the true one, as obvious. This tendency to say results are obvious was, of course, only a tendency; not all of her subjects followed that tendency, but it was a majority tendency.

Wong's Study

Baratz's research on obviousness dealt with results from a fairly wide range of the social sciences, but I had been focusing on research on teaching, and particularly on one area within that field: process-outcome research. That kind of research seeks relationships between classroom processes (what teachers and students do or what goes on in the classroom) and outcomes (what students acquire by way of knowledge, understanding, attitude, appreciation, skill, etc.). Would such research results elicit obvious reactions similar to those obtained by Baratz?

A few years ago, Lily Wong, a Stanford graduate student from Singapore, replicated and extended Baratz's experiments, but with findings from process-outcome research on teaching. Wong chose her respondents from four different categories of persons who differed on the dimension of how much they might be expected to know about classroom teaching. At the low end of that dimension were undergraduates in engineering; next, undergraduates majoring in psychology; next, teacher trainees; and at the high end, experienced teachers. Each of these four groups of respondents was sampled both from Singaporeans and from Americans residing either at Stanford University or in the neighboring area. In total, Wong used 862 Singaporeans and 353 Americans. For the research findings, she used 12 statements based on results of process-outcome research carried out in the elementary grades, results that had been cited in the third edition of the *Handbook of Research on Teaching* (Wittrock, 1986) and in textbooks of educational psychology. Her items came from the results of research by Anderson, Evertson, and Brophy; Brophy and Evertson; Good and Grouws; Soar and Soar; and Stallings and Kaskowitz. Here is the first of her 12 items: "When first-grade teachers work on reading with a small group of children, some attend closely to just the children in the small group, whereas others monitor children's activities throughout the classroom. The class's reading achievement is higher *when teachers monitor the entire classroom*" versus " *. . . when teachers attend to just the children in the small group.*" Here is the second item: "When first-grade teachers work on reading with a small group of children, some call on the children in a fixed order, whereas others call on children in a random order. Reading achievement is higher *when children are called on in a fixed order*" versus " *. . . when children are called on in a random order.*"

Wong had five forms of questionnaires: Form A, Forms B_1 and B_2, and Forms C_1 and C_2. Subjects completing Form A had to select in each item the true finding between two options—one stating an actual finding of research on teaching at the primary-grade level and the other stating the opposite of the actual finding. The subject then rated the chosen statement on a 4-point scale from 1, "extremely obvious" to 4, "extremely unobvious."

Subjects completing Forms B_1 or Form B_2 were required to rate the obviousness of each of 12 single statements presented as actual research findings. In fact, 6 were true findings and 6 were the opposite of true findings. Each of the 24 statements from Form A thus appeared in either Form B_1 or Form B_2.

Form C subjects were given the same purported findings as Form B subjects, but in Form C, each statement was accompanied by a possible explana-

tion. Subjects in Form C had to rate not only the obviousness of the findings but also the clarity of the explanations.

Wong's results on Form A showed that her respondents chose both actual findings and opposite findings. On 4 of the 12 items, her subjects chose the actual finding more often, but on the other 8, they chose the false finding more often. The r between percentage choosing a finding and the mean obviousness rating of the finding was .66. The respondents to Forms B and C rated about half of the opposite findings as obvious. Wong concluded that

> *judging by the smaller proportions of respondents choosing the actual findings as the real findings, and the mean rating of obviousness on the presented (both actual and opposite) finding statements, we can say reasonably that people cannot distinguish true findings from their opposites. (p. 86)*

The Singaporeans rated most of the items as more obvious than the American subjects did in all conditions. There were few gender differences in the average responses to the various forms. Teachers were no more accurate, on the average, than the other groups in the selection of true findings: "In the rating of obviousness of items, knowledge and experience [in teaching] were found to have some significant effect on several items. This does not mean that teachers and trainees rated true findings more obvious or opposite findings less obvious than the psychology undergraduates and the engineering undergraduates" (Wong, 1987, p. 87).

Wong concluded that her results "clearly confirmed the idea that knowledge of outcome increases the feeling of obviousness. Thus, when people claim to have known it all along when an event is reported to them, their claim is often not warranted" (p. 88).

WHERE THE ISSUE STANDS

From the work of Baratz and Wong we can conclude that the feeling that a research result is obvious is untrustworthy. People tend to regard as obvious almost any reasonable statement made about human behavior. A recent example comes from the *Arizona Daily Star* of March 8, 1988, in an article about the booklet entitled *What Works*, compiled by the U.S. Department of Education. The booklet contains brief discussions, with references to the research, of 41 research findings considered potentially helpful to schools and teachers. The headline read, "Restating the Obvious."

My most recent example comes from the June 1990 issue of *The Atlantic* (Murphy, 1990): "A recent survey (by me) of recent social-science findings . . . turned up no ideas or conclusions that can't be found in Bartlett's or any other encyclopedia of quotations" (p. 22).

As suggested by an anonymous referee for this article, the results of Baratz and Wong are consistent with the conclusions of Nisbett and Wilson (1977): "[T]here may be little or no direct introspective access to higher order cognitive processes" (p. 231). Thus the cognitive processes that lead one to regard a research result as obvious are probably nonveridical unless, as Ericsson and Simon (1980) argued, the response is based on (a) short-term memory leading to verbalization of information that (b) would have been attended to even without the instructions given. It is questionable whether judging the obviousness of research results always meets these requirements.

The same reviewer also suggested that these results do not belie the fact that most adults' generalizations about human interactions are at least functional. I agree; otherwise human society would be impossible.

Another issue arose in a conversation between Robert D. Hess and me. Upon being apprised of judges' tendency to regard as obvious both actual research results and their opposites, Hess asked about the frequency with which the results had been confirmed through replications. His question calls for research in which the "obviousness" of research results frequently confirmed with high consistency would be compared with that of research relationships frequently studied with results of only low consistency. Examples of both high-consistency and low-consistency results can be found in the synthesis of results of research on teaching by Walberg (1986). His Table 7.2 (pp. 218–219) contains results whose "percentage positive" across replications ranges from very low (where 50% is completely inconsistent) to very high (where 0% and 100% are completely consistent).

An investigator could administer questionnaires similar to those of Baratz (1983) and Wong (1987), but using items representing both (a) frequently studied with highly consistent results and (b) frequently studied with highly inconsistent results. It would then be possible to determine the difference, if any, in the mean obviousness rating of these two types of research results. It may turn out that only items of Type b would be rated obvious in both their actual and opposite forms. A frequently replicated and highly consistent result—for example, the "result" that auto drivers in England stay to the left side of the road whereas auto drivers in the United States stay to the right side of the road—will almost certainly be rated highly obvious in its actual form and highly nonobvious in its opposite form. Here the requisite knowledge is widely possessed, and the "obvious" reaction will not occur. Much depends on the relationship between the content of the research result and the background knowledge of the judge of the result's obviousness. Both Baratz and Wong may have studied results whose relationship to their judges' background knowledge was tenuous. Even Wong's experienced teachers, who probably had never thought about or encountered the phenomena dealt with in the research results used by Wong, had too little background knowledge to be able to detect the nonobviousness of the opposite-to-actual results.

Thus, the obvious reaction may be hypothesized to occur only when the judge's background knowledge in relation to the judged research result is weak. If the hypothesis is borne out, the question might be raised, How does a representative sample of social and educational research results fare, as to their obviousness in actual and opposite forms, when presented to a representative sample of the persons who might be expected to encounter or be concerned with those results? That is, research on obviousness now needs to be aimed at maximal external validity, or the degree to which the obviousness research is relevant to real life.

The issue joined by Schlesinger when he attacked students of human affairs who use scientific methods has its roots in the old controversy that C. P. Snow (1964) examined later in *The Two Cultures: And a Second Look*. Snow was concerned with the mutual disregard and disrespect of natural scientists and scholars in the humanities. Snow regretted this condition, but it still exists. Schlesinger's denunciation of social research reflected what Karl Popper called the antinaturalist position: the position that the scientific method useful for studying the natural world is inappropriate for the study of human affairs. The response of Paul Lazarsfeld reflects the position, held by Karl Popper and many others, that scientific method is appropriate for the study of human affairs.

Scientific method need not be used, in my opinion, only for the construction of a social science—where such a science is defined as a network of laws that will hold over whole eras and in many different cultural contexts, just as the laws of mechanics hold in different historical periods and in contexts as different as planetary motion and the motion of a pendulum. Rather, scientific method can be used for what Popper called "piecemeal social engineering," a more modest enterprise aimed at improving human affairs by applying scientific methods to the development and evaluation of new "treatments"—in education, in social welfare projects, or in fighting against drugs.

I have speculated (Gage, 1989) that people gravitate toward one or the other of Snow's two cultures—toward science (natural or social) or toward humanistic insight and sensibility—because their upbringing and intellectual experience have inclined them toward one or the other. The wars between the several paradigms in social and educational research may result from temperamentally different (i.e., not entirely rational) intellectual predilections, often developed during the secondary school years. If so, improved education may someday produce scholars and educational researchers who experience no conflict between their scientific and humanistic orientations.

In any case, the allegation of obviousness may now be countered with the research result that people tend to regard even contradictory research results as obvious. Perhaps even that result will henceforth be regarded as obvious.

This article is based in part on the Maycie K. Southall Lecture at George Peabody College, Vanderbilt University, on February 27, 1990.

I am grateful to my daughter, Sarah Gage, for calling the Murphy (1990) article to my attention.

REFERENCES

Baratz, D. (1983). How justified is the "obvious" reaction. *Dissertation Abstracts International, 44/02B,* 644B. (University Microfilms No. DA 8314435.)

Conant, J. B. (1963). *The education of American teachers.* New York: McGraw-Hill.

Ericsson, K. A., & Simon, H. A. (1980). Verbal reports as data. *Psychological Review, 87,* 215–251.

Gage, N. L. (1989). The paradigm wars and their aftermath: A "historical" sketch of research on teaching since 1989. *Teachers College Record, 91,* 135–150.

Glass, G. V. (1987). Class size. In M. J. Dunkin (Ed.), *The international encyclopedia of teaching and teacher education* (pp. 540–545). Oxford: Pergamon.

Goodlad, J. I. (1960). Classroom organization. In C. W. Harris (Ed.), *Encyclopedia of education research* (3rd ed., p. 224). New York: Macmillan.

Keppel, F. (1962). The education of teachers. In H. Chauncey (Ed.), *Talks on American education: A series of broadcasts to foreign audiences by American scholars* (pp. 83–94). New York: Bureau of Publications, Teachers College, Columbia University.

Lazarsfeld, P. F. (1949). The American soldier—An expository review. *Public Opinion Quarterly, 13,* 377–404.

Mischel, W. (1981). Metacognition and the rules of delay. In J. H. Flavell & L. Ross (Eds.), *Social cognitive development: Frontiers and possible futures.* New York: Cambridge University Press.

Mischel, W., & Mischel, H. (1979). *Children's knowledge of psychological principles.* Unpublished manuscript.

Murphy, C. (1990). New findings: Hold on to your hat. *The Atlantic, 265*(6), 22–23.

Nisbett, R. E., & Wilson, T. D. (1977). Telling more than we can know: Verbal reports on mental processes. *Psychological Review, 84,* 231–259.

Phillips, D. C. (1985). The uses and abuses of truisms. In C. W. Fisher & D. C. Berliner (Eds.), *Perspectives on instructional time* (pp. 309–316). New York: Longman.

Rice, J. M. (1913). *Scientific management in education.* New York: Hinds, Noble & Eldredge. (Original work published 1897.)

Schlesinger, Jr., A. (1949). The statistical soldier. *Partisan Review, 16,* 852–856.

Snow, C. P. (1964). *The two cultures: And a second look.* New York: Cambridge University Press.

Walberg, H. J. (1986). Syntheses of research on teaching. In M. C. Wittrock (Ed.), *Handbook of research on teaching* (3rd ed., pp. 214–229). New York: Macmillan.

Wittrock, M. C. (Ed.). (1986). *Handbook of research on teaching* (3rd ed.). New York: Macmillan.

Wong, L. (1987). Reaction to research findings: Is the feeling of obviousness warranted? *Dissertation Abstracts International, 48112,* 3709B. (University Microfilms No. DA 8801059.)

School/Family/
Community Partnerships

Caring for the Children We Share

JOYCE L. EPSTEIN

The way schools care about children is reflected in the way schools care about the children's families. If educators view children simply as *students*, they are likely to see the family as separate from the school. That is, the family is expected to do its job and leave the education of children to the schools. If educators view students as *children*, they are likely to see both the family and the community as partners with the school in children's education and development. Partners recognize their shared interests in and responsibilities for children, and they work together to create better programs and opportunities for students.

There are many reasons for developing school, family, and community partnerships. They can improve school programs and school climate, provide family services and support, increase parents' skills and leadership, connect families with others in the school and in the community, and help teachers with their work. However, the main reason to create such partnerships is to help all youngsters succeed in school and in later life. When parents, teachers,

Joyce L. Epstein is co-director of the Center on Families, Communities, Schools, and Children's Learning and co-director of the Schools, Family, and Community Partnerships Program in the Center for Research on the Education of Students Placed at Risk, Johns Hopkins University, Baltimore. The research reported in this article was supported by grants from the Office of Educational Research and Improvement of the U.S. Department of Education and the Lilly Endowment. However, the perspectives and opinions are the author's own.

students, and others view one another as partners in education, a caring community forms around students and begins its work.

What do successful partnership programs look like? How can practices be effectively designed and implemented? What are the results of better communications, interactions, and exchanges across these three important contexts? These questions have challenged research and practice, creating an interdisciplinary field of inquiry into school, family, and community partnerships with "caring" as a core concept.

The field has been strengthened by supporting federal, state, and local policies. For example, the Goals 2000 legislation sets partnerships as a voluntary national goal for all schools; Title I specifies and mandates programs and practices of partnership in order for schools to qualify for or maintain funding. Many states and districts have developed or are preparing policies to guide schools in creating more systematic connections with families and communities. These policies reflect research results and the prior successes of leading educators who have shown that these goals are attainable.

Underlying these policies and programs are a theory of how social organizations connect; a framework of the basic components of school, family, and community partnerships for children's learning; a growing literature on the positive and negative results of these connections for students, families, and schools; and an understanding of how to organize good programs. In this article I summarize the theory, framework, and guidelines that have assisted the schools in our research projects in building partnerships and that should help any elementary, middle, or high school to take similar steps.

OVERLAPPING SPHERES OF INFLUENCE: UNDERSTANDING THE THEORY

Schools make choices. They might conduct only a few communications and interactions with families and communities, keeping the three spheres of influence that directly affect student learning and development relatively separate. Or they might conduct many high-quality communications and interactions designed to bring all three spheres of influence closer together. With frequent interactions between schools, families, and communities, more students are more likely to receive common messages from various people about the importance of school, of working hard, of thinking creatively, of helping one another, and of staying in school.

The *external model* of overlapping spheres of influence recognizes that the three major contexts in which students learn and grow—the family, the school, and the community—may be drawn together or pushed apart. In this model, there are some practices that schools, families, and communities conduct separately and some that they conduct jointly in order to influence children's learning and development. The *internal* model of the interaction of the three spheres of influence shows where and how complex and essential interpersonal relations and patterns of influence occur between individuals at home, at school, and in the community. These social relationships may be enacted and studied at an *institutional* level (e.g., when a school invites all families to an event or sends the same communications to all families) and at an *individual* level (e.g., when a parent and a teacher meet in conference or talk by phone). Connections between schools or parents and community groups, agencies, and services can also be represented and studied within the model.[1]

The model of school, family, and community partnerships locates the student at the center. The inarguable fact is that students are the main actors in their education, development, and success in school. School, family, and community partnerships cannot simply produce successful students. Rather, partnership activities may be designed to engage, guide, energize, and motivate students to produce their own successes. The assumption is that, if children feel cared for and encouraged to work hard in the role of student, they are more likely to do their best to learn to read, write, calculate, and learn other skills and talents and to remain in school.

Interestingly and somewhat ironically, studies indicate that students are also crucial for the success of school, family, and community partnerships. Students are often their parents' main source of information about school. In strong partnership programs, teachers help students understand and conduct traditional communications with families (e.g., delivering memos or report cards) and new communications (e.g., interacting with family members about homework or participating in parent/teacher/student conferences). As we gain more information about the role of students in partnerships, we are developing a more complete understanding of how schools, families, and communities must work with students to increase their chances for success

How Theory Sounds in Practice

In some schools there are still educators who say, "If the family would just do its job, we could do our job." And there are still families who say, "I raised this child; now it is your job to educate her." These words embody the theory of "separate spheres of influence." Other educators say, "I cannot do my job without the help of my students' families and the support of this community." And some parents say, "I really need to know what is happening in school in order to help my child." These phrases embody the theory of "overlapping spheres of influence."

In a partnership, teachers and administrators create more *family-like* schools. A family-like school recognizes each child's individuality and makes each child feel special and included. Family-like schools welcome all families, not just those that are easy to reach. In a partnership, parents create more *school-like* families. A school-like family recognizes that each child is also a student. Families reinforce the importance of school, homework, and activities that build student skills and feelings of success. Communities, including groups of parents working together, create school-like opportunities, events, and programs that reinforce, recognize, and reward students for good progress, creativity, contributions, and excellence. Communities also create *family-like* settings, services, and events to enable families to better support their children. *Community-minded* families and students help their neighborhoods and other families. The concept of a community school is re-emerging. It refers to a place where programs and services for students, parents, and others are offered before, during, and after the regular school day.

Schools and communities talk about programs and services that are "family-friendly"—meaning that they take into account the needs and realities of family life in the 1990s, are feasible to conduct, and are equitable toward all families. When all these concepts combine, children experience *learning communities* or *caring communities*.[2]

All these terms are consistent with the theory of overlapping spheres of influence, but they are not abstract concepts. You will find them daily in conversations, news stories, and celebrations of many kinds. In a family-like school, a teacher might say, "I know when a student is having a bad day and how to help him along." A student might slip and call a teacher "mom" or "dad" and then laugh with a mixture of embarrassment and glee. In a school-like family, a parent might say, "I make sure my daughter knows that homework comes first." A child might raise his hand to speak at the dinner table and then joke about acting as if he were still in school. When communities reach out to students and their families, youngsters might say, "This program really made my schoolwork make sense!" Parents or educators might comment, "This community really supports its schools."

Once people hear about such concepts as family-like schools or school-like families, they remember positive examples of schools, teachers, and places in the community that were "like a family" to them. They may remember how a teacher paid individual attention to them, recognized their uniqueness, or praised them for real progress, just as a parent might. Or they might recall things at home that were "just like school" and supported their work as a student, or they might remember community activities that made them feel smart or good about themselves and their families. They will recall that parents, siblings,

and other family members engaged in and enjoyed educational activities and took pride in the good schoolwork or homework that they did, just as a teacher might.

How Partnerships Work in Practice

These terms and examples are evidence of the *potential* for schools, families, and communities to create caring educational environments. It is possible to have a school that is excellent academically but ignores families. However, that school will build barriers between teachers, parents, and children—barriers that affect school life and learning. It is possible to have a school that is ineffective academically but involves families in many good ways. With its weak academic program, that school will shortchange students' learning. Neither of these schools exemplifies a caring educational environment that requires academic excellence, good communications, and productive interactions involving school, family, and community.

Some children succeed in school without much family involvement or despite family neglect or distress, particularly if the school has excellent academic and support programs. Teachers, relatives outside of the immediate family, other families, and members of the community can provide important guidance and encouragement to these students. As support from school, family, and community accumulates, significantly more students feel secure and cared for, understand the goals of education, work to achieve to their full potential, build positive attitudes and school behaviors, and stay in school. The shared interests and investments of schools, families, and communities create the conditions of caring that work to "overdetermine" the likelihood of student success.[3]

Any practice can be designed and implemented well or poorly. And even well-implemented partnership practices may not be useful to all families. In a caring school community, participants work continually to improve the nature and effects of partnerships. Although the interactions of educators, parents, students, and community members will not always be smooth or successful, partnership programs establish a base of respect and trust on which to build. Good partnerships withstand questions, conflicts, debates, and disagreements; provide structures and processes to solve problems;

and are maintained—even strengthened—after differences have been resolved. Without this firm base, disagreements and problems that are sure to arise about schools and students will be harder to solve.

What Research Says

In surveys and field studies involving teachers, parents, and students at the elementary, middle, and high school levels, some important patterns relating to partnerships have emerged.[4]

- Partnerships tend to decline across the grades, *unless* schools and teachers work to develop and implement appropriate practices of partnership at each grade level.
- Affluent communities currently have more positive family involvement, on average, *unless* schools and teachers in economically distressed communities work to build positive partnerships with their students' families.
- Schools in more economically depressed communities make more contacts with families about the problems and difficulties their children are having, *unless* they work at developing balanced partnership programs that include contacts about positive accomplishments of students.
- Single parents, parents who are employed outside the home, parents who live far from the school, and fathers are less involved, on average, at the school building, *unless* the school organizes opportunities for families to volunteer at various times and in various places to support the school and their children.

Researchers have also drawn the following conclusions.

- Just about all families care about their children, want them to succeed, and are eager to obtain better information from schools and communities so as to remain good partners in their children's education.
- Just about all teachers and administrators would like to involve families, but many do not know how to go about building positive and productive programs and are consequently fearful about trying. This creates a "rhetoric rut," in which educators are stuck, expressing support for partnerships without taking any action.

- Just about all students at all levels—elementary, middle, and high school—want their families to be more knowledgeable partners about schooling and are willing to take active roles in assisting communications between home and school. However, students need much better information and guidance than most now receive about how their schools view partnerships and about how they can conduct important exchanges with their families about school activities, homework, and school decisions.

The research results are important because they indicate that caring communities can be built, on purpose; that they include families that might not become involved on their own; and that, by their own reports, just about all families, students, and teachers believe that partnerships are important for helping students succeed across the grades.

Good programs will look different in each site, as individual schools tailor their practices to meet the needs and interests, time and talents, ages and grade levels of students and their families. However, there are some commonalities across successful programs at all grade levels. These include a recognition of the overlapping spheres of influence on student development; attention to various types of involvement that promote a variety of opportunities for schools, families, and communities to work together; and an Action Team for School, Family, and Community Partnerships to coordinate each school's work and progress.

SIX TYPES OF INVOLVEMENT; SIX TYPES OF CARING

A framework of six major types of involvement has evolved from many studies and from many years of work by educators and families in elementary, middle, and high schools. The framework (summarized in the accompanying tables) helps educators develop more comprehensive programs of school and family partnerships and also helps researchers locate their questions and results in ways that inform and improve practice.[5]

Each type of involvement includes many different *practices* of partnership (see Table 1). Each type presents particular *challenges* that must be met in order to involve all families and needed *redefinitions* of some basic principles of involvement (see Table 2 [on page 16]). Finally, each type is likely to

TABLE 1   Epstein's Framework of Six Types of Involvement and Sample Practices

Type 1 Parenting	Type 2 Communicating	Type 3 Volunteering	Type 4 Learning at Home	Type 5 Decision Making	Type 6 Collaborating with Community
Help all families establish home environments to support children as students.	Design effective forms of school-to-home and home-to-school communications about school programs and children's progress.	Recruit and organize parent help and support.	Provide information and ideas to families about how to help students at home with homework and other curriculum-related activities, decisions, and planning.	Include parents in school decisions, developing parent leaders and representatives.	Identify and integrate resources and services from the community to strengthen school programs, family practices, and student learning and development.
Sample Practices	**Sample Practices**	**Sample Practices**	**Sample Practices**	**Sample Practices**	**Sample Practices**
Suggestions for home conditions that support learning at each grade level.	Conferences with every parent at least once a year, with follow-ups as needed.	School and classroom volunteer program to help teachers, administrators, students, and other parents.	Information for families on skills required for students in all subjects at each grade.	Active PTA/PTO or other parent organizations, advisory councils, or committees (e.g., curriculum, safety, personnel) for parent leadership and participation.	Information for students and families on community health, cultural, recreational, social support, and other programs or services.
Workshops, videotapes, computerized phone messages on parenting and child rearing at each age and grade level.	Language translators to assist families as needed.	Parent room or family center for volunteer work, meetings, resources for families.	Information on homework policies and how to monitor and discuss schoolwork at home.	Independent advocacy groups to lobby and work for school reform and improvements.	Information on community activities that link to learning skills and talents, including summer programs for students.
Parent education and other courses or training for parents (e.g., GED, college credit, family literacy).	Weekly or monthly folders of student work sent home for review and comments.	Annual postcard survey to identify all available talents, times, and locations of volunteers.	Information on how to assist students to improve skills on various class and school assessments.	District-level councils and committees for family and community involvement.	Service integration through partnerships involving school; civic, counseling, cultural, health, recreation, and other agencies and organizations; and businesses.
Family support programs to assist families with health, nutrition, and other services.	Parent/student pickup of report card, with conferences on improving grades.	Class parent telephone tree, or other structures to provide all families with needed information.	Regular schedule of homework that requires students to discuss and interact with families on what they are learning in class.	Information on school or local elections for school representatives.	Service to the community by students, families, and schools (e.g., recycling, art, music, drama, and other activities for seniors or others).
Home visits at transition points to preschool, elementary, middle, and high school. Neighborhood meetings to help families understand schools and to help schools understand families.	Regular schedule of useful notices, memos, phone calls, newsletters, and other communications.	Parent patrols or other activities to aid safety and operation of school programs.	Calendars with activities for parents and students at home.	Networks to link all families with parent representatives.	Participation of alumni in school programs for students.
	Clear information on choosing schools or courses, programs, and activities within schools.		Family math, science, and reading activities at school.		
	Clear information on all school policies, programs, reforms, and transitions.		Summer learning packets or activities.		
			Family participation in setting student goals each year and in planning for college or work.		

lead to different *results* for students, for parents, for teaching practice, and for school climate (see Table 3 [on page 17]). Thus schools have choices about which practices will help achieve important goals.

The tables provide examples of practices, challenges for successful implementation, redefinitions for up-to-date understanding, and results that have been documented and observed.

TABLE 2   **Challenges and Redefinitions for the Six Types of Involvement**

Type 1 Parenting	Type 2 Communicating	Type 3 Volunteering	Type 4 Learning at Home	Type 5 Decision Making	Type 6 Collaborating with Community
Challenges	**Challenges**	**Challenges**	**Challenges**	**Challenges**	**Challenges**
Provide information to *all* families who want it or who need it, not just to the few who can attend workshops or meetings at the school building. Enable families to share information with schools about culture, background, children's talents and needs. Make sure that all information for and from families is clear, usable, and linked to children's success in school.	Review the readability, clarity, form, and frequency of all memos, notices, and other print and nonprint communications. Consider parents who do not speak English well, do not read well, or need large type. Review the quality of major communications (newsletters, report cards, conference schedules, and so on). Establish clear two-way channels for communications from home to school and from school to home.	Recruit volunteers widely so that *all* families know that their time and talents are welcome. Make flexible schedules for volunteers, assemblies, and events to enable parents who work to participate. Organize volunteer work; provide training; match time and talent with school, teacher, and student needs; and recognize efforts so that participants are productive.	Design and organize a regular schedule of interactive homework (e.g., weekly or bimonthly) that gives *students* responsibility for discussing important things they are learning and helps families stay aware of the content of their children's classwork. Coordinate family-linked homework activities, if students have several teachers. Involve families and their children in all important curriculum-related decisions.	Include parent leaders from all racial, ethnic, socioeconomic, and other groups in the school. Offer training to enable leaders to serve as representatives of other families, with input from and return of information to all parents. Include students (along with parents) in decision-making groups.	Solve turf problems of responsibilities, funds, staff, and locations for collaborative activities. Inform families of community programs for students, such as mentoring, tutoring, business partnerships. Assure equality of opportunities for students and families to participate in community programs or to obtain services. Match community contributions with school goals; integrate child and family services with education.
Redefinitions	**Redefinitions**	**Redefinitions**	**Redefinitions**	**Redefinitions**	**Redefinitions**
"Workshop" to mean more than a *meeting* about a topic held at the school building at a particular time. "Workshop" may also mean making information about a topic available in a variety of forms that can be viewed, heard, or read anywhere, any time, in varied forms.	"Communications about school programs and student progress" to mean two-way, three-way, and many-way channels of communication that connect schools, families, students, and the community.	"Volunteer" to mean anyone who supports school goals and children's learning or development in any way, at any place, and at any time—not just during the school day and at the school building.	"Homework" to mean not only work done alone, but also interactive activities shared with others at home or in the community, linking schoolwork to real life. "Help" at home to mean encouraging, listening, reacting, praising, guiding, monitoring, and discussing—not "teaching" school subjects.	"Decision making" to mean a process of partnership, of shared views and actions toward shared goals, not just a power struggle between conflicting ideas. Parent "leader" to mean a real representative, with opportunities and support to hear from and communicate with other families.	"Community" to mean not only the neighborhoods where students' homes and schools are located but also any neighborhoods that influence their learning and development. "Community" rated not only by low or high social or economic qualities, but by strengths and talents to support students, families, and schools. "Community" means all who are interested in and affected by the quality of education, not just those with children in the schools.

TABLE 3 **Expected Results of the Six Types of Involvement for Students, Parents, and Teachers**

Type 1 Parenting	Type 2 Communicating	Type 3 Volunteering	Type 4 Learning at Home	Type 5 Decision Making	Type 6 Collaborating with Community
Results for Students	**Results for Students**	**Results for Students**	**Results for Students**	**Results for Students**	**Results for Students**
Awareness of family supervision; respect for parents. Positive personal qualities, habits, beliefs, and values, as taught by family. Balance between time spent on chores, on other activities, and on homework. Good or improved attendance. Awareness of importance of school.	Awareness of own progress and of actions needed to maintain or improve grades. Understanding of school policies on behavior, attendance, and other areas of student conduct. Informed decisions about courses and programs. Awareness of own role in partnerships, serving as courier and communicator.	Skill in communicating with adults. Increased learning of skills that receive tutoring or targeted attention from volunteers. Awareness of many skills, talents, occupations, and contributions of parents and other volunteers.	Gains in skills, abilities, and test scores linked to homework and classwork. Homework completion. Positive attitude toward schoolwork. View of parents as more similar to teacher and of home as more similar to school. Self-concept of ability as learner.	Awareness of representation of families in school decisions. Understanding that student rights are protected. Specific benefits linked to policies enacted by parent organizations and experienced by students.	Increased skills and talents through enriched curricular and extracurricular experiences. Awareness of careers and of options for future education and work. Specific benefits linked to programs, services, resources, and opportunities that connect students with community.
For Parents	**For Parents**	**For Parents**	**For Parents**	**For Parents**	**For Parents**
Understanding of and confidence about parenting, child and adolescent development, and changes in home conditions for learning as children proceed through school. Awareness of own and others' challenges in parenting. Feeling of support from school and other parents.	Understanding school programs and policies. Monitoring and awareness of child's progress. Responding effectively to students' problems. Interactions with teachers and ease of communication with school and teachers.	Understanding teacher's job, increased comfort in school, and carry-over of school activities at home. Self-confidence about ability to work in school and with children or to take steps to improve own education. Awareness that families are welcome and valued at school. Gains in specific skills of volunteer work.	Know how to support, encourage, and help student at home each year. Discussions of school, classwork, and homework. Understanding of instructional program each year and of what child is learning in each subject. Appreciation of teaching skills. Awareness of child as a learner.	Input into policies that affect child's education. Feeling of ownership of school. Awareness of parents' voices in school decisions. Shared experiences and connections with other families. Awareness of school, district, and state policies.	Knowledge and use of local resources by family and child to increase skills and talents or to obtain needed services. Interactions with other families in community activities. Awareness of school's role in the community and of community's contributions to the school.
For Teachers	**For Teachers**	**For Teachers**	**For Teachers**	**For Teachers**	**For Teachers**
Understanding families' backgrounds, cultures, concerns, goals, needs, and views of their children. Respect for families' strengths and efforts. Understanding of student diversity. Awareness of own skills to share information on child development.	Increased diversity and use of communications with families and awareness of own ability to communicate clearly. Appreciation for and use of parent network for communications. Increased ability to elicit and understand family views on children's programs and progress.	Readiness to involve families in new ways, including those who do not volunteer at school. Awareness of parents' talents and interests in school and children. Greater individual attention to students, with help from volunteers.	Better design of homework assignments. Respect of family time. Recognition of equal helpfulness of single-parent, dual-income, and less formally educated families in motivating and reinforcing student learning. Satisfaction with family involvement and support.	Awareness of parent perspectives as a factor in policy development and decisions. View of equal status of family representatives on committees and in leadership roles.	Awareness of community resources to enrich curriculum and instruction. Openness to and skill in using mentors, business partners, community volunteers, and others to assist students and augment teaching practice. Knowledgeable, helpful referrals of children and families to needed services.

Charting the Course

The entries in the tables are illustrative. The sample practices displayed in Table 1 are only a few of hundreds that may be selected or designed for each type of involvement. Although all schools may use the framework of six types as a guide, each school must chart its own course in choosing practices to meet the needs of its families and students.

The challenges shown (Table 2) are just a few of many that relate to the examples. There are challenges—that is, problems—for every practice of partnership, and they must be resolved in order to reach and engage all families in the best ways. Often, when one challenge is met, a new one will emerge.

The redefinitions (also in Table 2) redirect old notions so that involvement is not viewed solely as or measured only by "bodies in the building." As examples the table calls for redefinitions of workshops, communication, volunteers, homework, decision making, and community. By redefining these familiar terms, it is possible for partnership programs to reach out in new ways to many more families.

The selected results (Table 3) should help correct the widespread misperception that any practice that involves families will raise children's achievement test scores. Instead, in the short term, certain practices are more likely than others to influence students' skills and scores, while other practices are more likely to affect attitudes and behaviors. Although students are the main focus of partnerships, the various types of involvement also promote various kinds of results for parents and for teachers. For example, the expected results for parents include not only leadership in decision making, but also confidence about parenting, productive curriculum-related interactions with children, and many interactions with other parents and the school. The expected results for teachers include not only improved parent/teacher conferences or school/home communications, but also better understanding of families, new approaches to homework, and other connections with families and the community.

Most of the results noted in Table 3 have been measured in at least one research study and observed as schools conduct their work. The entries are listed in positive terms to indicate the results of well-designed and well-implemented practices. It should be fully understood, however, that results may be negative if poorly designed practices exclude families or create greater barriers to communication and exchange. Research is still needed on the results of specific practices of partnership in various schools, at various grade levels, and for diverse populations of students, families, and teachers. It will be important to confirm, extend, or correct the information on results listed in Table 3 if schools are to make purposeful choices among practices that foster various types of involvement.

The tables cannot show the connections that occur when one practice activates several types of involvement simultaneously. For example, volunteers may organize and conduct a food bank (Type 3) that allows parents to pay $15 for $30 worth of food for their families (Type 1). The food may be subsidized by community agencies (Type 6). The recipients might then serve as volunteers for the program or in the community (perpetuating Type 3 and Type 6 activities). Or consider another example. An after-school homework club run by volunteers and the community recreation department combines Type 3 and Type 6 practices. Yet it also serves as a Type 1 activity, because the after-school program assists families with the supervision of their children. This practice may also alter the way homework interactions are conducted between students and parents at home (Type 4). These and other connections are interesting, and research is needed to understand the combined effects of such activities.

The tables also simplify the complex longitudinal influences that produce various results over time. For example, a series of events might play out as follows. The involvement of families in reading at home leads students to give more attention to reading and to be more strongly motivated to read. This in turn may help students maintain or improve their daily reading skills and then their reading grades. With the accumulation over time of good classroom reading programs, continued home support, and increased skills and confidence in reading, students may significantly improve their reading achievement test scores. The time between reading aloud at home and increased reading test scores may vary greatly, depending on the quality and quantity of other reading activities in school and out.

Or consider another example. A study by Seyong Lee, using longitudinal data and rigorous statistical controls on background and prior influences, found important benefits for high school students' attitudes and grades as a result of continuing several types of family involvement from the middle school into the high school. However, achievement test scores were not greatly affected by partnerships at the high school level. Longitudinal studies and practical experiences that are monitored over time are needed to increase our understanding of the complex patterns of results that can develop from various partnership activities.[6]

The six types of involvement can guide the development of a balanced, comprehensive program of partnerships, including opportunities for family involvement at school and at home, with potentially important results for students, parents, and teachers. The results for students, parents, and teachers will depend on the particular types of involvement that are implemented, as well as on the quality of the implementation.

ACTION TEAMS FOR SCHOOL, FAMILY, AND COMMUNITY PARTNERSHIPS

Who will work to create caring school communities that are based on the concepts of partnership? How will the necessary work on all six types of involvement get done? Although a principal or a teacher may be a leader in working with some families or with groups in the community, one person cannot create a lasting, comprehensive program that involves all families as their children progress through the grades.

From the hard work of many educators and families in many schools, we have learned that, along with clear policies and strong support from state and district leaders and from school principals, an Action Team for School, Family, and Community Partnerships in each school is a useful structure. The action team guides the development of a comprehensive program of partnership, including all six types of involvement, and the integration of all family and community connections within a single, unified plan and program. The trials and errors, efforts and insights of many schools in our projects have helped to identify five important steps that any school can take to develop more positive school/family/community connections.[7]

Step 1: Create an Action Team

A team approach is an appropriate way to build partnerships. The Action Team for School, Family, and Community Partnerships can be the "action arm" of a school council, if one exists. The action

team takes responsibility for assessing present practices, organizing options for new partnerships, implementing selected activities, evaluating next steps, and continuing to improve and coordinate practices for all six types of involvement. Although the members of the action team lead these activities, they are assisted by other teachers, parents, students, administrators, and community members.

The action team should include at least three teachers from different grade levels, three parents with children in different grade levels, and at least one administrator. Teams may also include at least one member from the community at large and, at the middle and high school levels, at least two students from different grade levels. Others who are central to the school's work with families may also be included as members, such as a cafeteria worker, a school social worker, a counselor, or a school psychologist. Such diverse membership ensures that partnership activities will take into account the various needs, interests, and talents of teachers, parents, the school, and students.

The leader of the action team may be any member who has the respect of the other members, as well as good communication skills and an understanding of the partnership approach. The leader or at least one member of the action team should also serve on the school council, school improvement team, or other such body, if one exists.

In addition to group planning, members of the action team elect (or are assigned to act as) the chair or co-chair of one of six subcommittees for each type of involvement. A team with at least six members (and perhaps as many as 12) ensures that responsibilities for leadership can be delegated so that one person is not overburdened and so that the work of the action team will continue even if members move or change schools or positions. Members may serve renewable terms of two to three years, with replacement of any who leave in the interim. Other thoughtful variations in assignments and activities may be created by small or large schools using this process.

In the first phase of our work in 1987, projects were led by "project directors" (usually teachers) and were focused on one type of involvement at a time. Some schools succeeded in developing good partnerships over several years, but others were thwarted if the project director moved, if the principal changed, or if the project grew larger than one person could handle. Other schools took a team approach in order to work on many types of involvement simultaneously. Their efforts demonstrated how to structure the program for the next set of schools in our work. Starting in 1990, this second set of schools tested and improved on the structure and work of action teams. Now, all elementary, middle, and high schools in our research and development projects and in other states and districts that are applying this work are given assistance in taking the action team approach.

Step 2: Obtain Funds and Other Support

A modest budget is needed to guide and support the work and expenses of each school's action team. Funds for state coordinators to assist districts and schools and funds for district coordinators or facilitators to help each school may come from a number of sources. These include federal, state, and local programs that mandate, request, or support family involvement, such as Title I, Title II, Title VII, Goals 2000, and other federal and similar state funding programs. In addition to paying the state and district coordinators, funds from these sources may be applied in creative ways to support staff development in the area of school, family, and community partnerships; to pay for lead teachers at each school; to set up demonstration programs; and for other partnership expenses. In addition, local school/ business partnerships, school discretionary funds, and separate fund-raising efforts targeted to the schools' partnership programs have been used to support the work of their action teams. At the very least, a school's action team requires a small stipend (at least $1,000 per year for three to five years, with summer supplements) for time and materials needed by each subcommittee to plan, implement, and revise practices of partnership that include all six types of involvement.

The action team must also be given sufficient time and social support to do its work. This requires explicit support from the principal and district leaders to allow time for team members to meet, plan, and conduct the activities that are selected for each type of involvement. Time during the summer is also valuable—and may be essential—for planning new approaches that will start in the new school year.

Step 3: Identify Starting Points

Most schools have some teachers who conduct some practices of partnership with some families some of

the time. How can good practices be organized and extended so that they may be used by all teachers, at all grade levels, with all families? The action team works to improve and systematize the typically haphazard patterns of involvement. It starts by collecting information about the school's present practices of partnership, along with the views, experiences, and wishes of teachers, parents, administrators, and students.

Assessments of starting points may be made in a variety of ways, depending on available resources, time, and talents. For example, the action team might use formal questionnaires[8] or telephone interviews to survey teachers, administrators, parents, and students (if resources exist to process, analyze, and report survey data). Or the action team might organize a panel of teachers, parents, and students to speak at a meeting of the parent/teacher organization or at some other school meeting as a way of initiating discussion about the goals and desired activities for partnership. Structured discussions may be conducted through a series of principal's breakfasts for representative groups of teachers, parents, students, and others; random sample phone calls may also be used to collect reactions and ideas, or formal focus groups may be convened to gather ideas about school, family, and community partnerships at the school.

What questions should be addressed? Regardless of how the information is gathered, some areas must be covered in any information gathering.

- *Present strengths.* Which practices of school/family/community partnerships are now working well for the school as a whole? For individual grade levels? For which types of involvement?
- *Needed changes.* Ideally, how do we want school, family, and community partnerships to work at this school three years from now? Which present practices should continue, and which should change? To reach school goals, what new practices are needed for each of the major types of involvement?
- *Expectations.* What do teachers expect of families? What do families expect of teachers and other school personnel? What do students expect their families to do to help them negotiate school life? What do students expect their teachers to do to keep their families informed and involved?
- *Sense of community.* Which families are we now reaching, and which are we not yet reaching?

Who are the "hard-to-reach" families? What might be done to communicate with and engage these families in their children's education? Are current partnership practices coordinated to include all families as a school community? Or are families whose children receive special services (e.g., Title I, special education, bilingual education) separated from other families?

- *Links to goals.* How are students faring on such measures of academic achievement as report card grades, on measures of attitudes and attendance, and on other indicators of success? How might family and community connections assist the school in helping more students reach higher goals and achieve greater success? Which practices of school, family, and community partnerships would directly connect to particular goals?

Step 4: Develop a Three-Year Plan

From the ideas and goals for partnerships collected from teachers, parents, and students, the action team can develop a three-year outline of the specific steps that will help the school progress from its starting point on each type of involvement to where it wants to be in three years. This plan outlines how each subcommittee will work over three years to make important, incremental advances to reach more families each year on each type of involvement. The three-year outline also shows how all school/family/community connections will be integrated into one coherent program of partnership that includes activities for the whole school community, activities to meet the special needs of children and families, activities to link to the district committees and councils, and activities conducted in each grade level.

In addition to the three-year outline of goals for each type of involvement, a detailed one-year plan should be developed for the first year's work. It should include the specific activities that will be implemented, improved, or maintained for each type of involvement; a time line of monthly actions needed for each activity; identification of the subcommittee chair who will be responsible for each type of involvement; identification of the teachers, parents, students, or others (not necessarily action team members) who will assist with the implementation of each activity; indicators of how the implementation and results of each major activity will be assessed; and other details of importance to the action team.

The three-year outline and one-year detailed plan are shared with the school council and/or parent organization, with all teachers, and with the parents and students. Even if the action team makes only one good step forward each year on each of the six types of involvement, it will take 18 steps forward over three years to develop a more comprehensive and coordinated program of school/family/community partnerships.

In short, based on the input from the parents, teachers, students, and others on the school's starting points and desired partnerships, the action team will address these issues.

- *Details.* What will be done each year, for three years, to implement a program on all six types of involvement? What, specifically, will be accomplished in the first year on each type of involvement?
- *Responsibilities.* Who will be responsible for developing and implementing practices of partnership for each type of involvement? Will staff development be needed? How will teachers, administrators, parents, and students be supported and recognized for their work?
- *Costs.* What costs are associated with the improvement and maintenance of the planned activities? What sources will provide the needed funds? Will small grants or other special budgets be needed?
- *Evaluation.* How will we know how well the practices have been implemented and what their effects are on students, teachers, and families? What indicators will we use that are closely linked to the practices implemented to determine their effects?

Step 5: Continue Planning and Working

The action team should schedule an annual presentation and celebration of progress at the school so that all teachers, families, and students will know about the work that has been done each year to build partnerships. Or the district coordinator for school, family, and community partnerships might arrange an annual conference for all schools in the district. At the annual school or district meeting, the action team presents and displays the highlights of accomplishments on each type of involvement. Problems are discussed and ideas are shared about improvements, additions, and continuations for the next year.

Each year, the action team updates the school's three-year outline and develops a detailed one-year plan for the coming year's work. It is important for educators, families, students, and the community at large to be aware of annual progress, of new plans, and of how they can help.

In short, the action team addresses the following questions. How can it ensure that the program of school/family/community partnership will continue to improve its structure, processes, and practices in order to increase the number of families who are partners with the school in their children's education? What opportunities will teachers, parents, and students have to share information on successful practices and to strengthen and maintain their efforts?

Characteristics of Successful Programs

As schools have implemented partnership programs, their experience has helped to identify some important properties of successful partnerships.

- *Incremental progress.* Progress in partnerships is incremental, including more families each year in ways that benefit more students. Like reading or math programs, assessment programs, sports programs, or other school investments, partnership programs take time to develop, must be periodically reviewed, and should be continuously improved. The schools in our projects have shown that three years is the minimum time needed for an action team to complete a number of activities on each type of involvement and to establish its work as a productive and permanent structure in a school.

  The development of a partnership is a process, not a single event. All teachers, families, students, and community groups do not engage in all activities on all types of involvement all at once. Not all activities implemented will succeed with all families. But with good planning, thoughtful implementation, well-designed activities, and pointed improvements, more and more families and teachers can learn to work with one another on behalf of the children whose interests they share. Similarly, not all students instantly improve their attitudes or achievements when their families become in-

volved in their education. After all, student learning depends mainly on good curricula and instruction and on the work completed by students. However, with a well-implemented program of partnership, more students will receive support from their families, and more will be motivated to work harder.

- *Connection to curricular and instructional reform.* A program of school/family/community partnerships that focuses on children's learning and development is an important component of curricular and instructional reform. Aspects of partnerships that aim to help more students succeed in school can be supported by federal, state, and local funds that are targeted for curricular and instructional reform. Helping families understand, monitor, and interact with students on homework, for example, can be a clear and important extension of classroom instruction, as can volunteer programs that bolster and broaden student skills, talents, and interests. Improving the content and conduct of parent/teacher/student conferences and goal-setting activities can be an important step in curricular reform; family support and family understanding of child and adolescent development and school curricula are necessary elements to assist students as learners.

  The connection of partnerships to curriculum and instruction in schools and the location of leadership for these partnership programs in district departments of curriculum and instruction are important changes that move partnerships from being peripheral public relations activities about parents to being central programs about student learning and development.

- *Redefining staff development.* The action team approach to partnerships guides the work of educators by restructuring "staff development" to mean colleagues working together and with parents to develop, implement, evaluate, and continue to improve practices of partnership. This is less a "dose of inservice education" than it is an active form of developing staff talents and capacities. The teachers, administrators, and others on the action team become the "experts" on this topic for their school. Their work in this area can be supported by various federal, state, and local funding programs as a clear investment in staff development for overall school reform. Indeed, the action team approach as outlined can be applied to any or all important topics on a school improvement agenda. It need not be restricted to the pursuit of successful partnerships.

It is important to note that the development of partnership programs would be easier if educators came to their schools prepared to work productively with families and communities. Courses or classes are needed in preservice teacher education and in advanced degree programs for teachers and administrators to help them define their professional work in terms of partnerships. Today, most educators enter schools without an understanding of family backgrounds, concepts of caring, the framework of partnerships, or the other "basics" I have discussed here. Thus most principals and district leaders are not prepared to guide and lead their staffs in developing strong school and classroom practices that inform and involve families. And most teachers and administrators are not prepared to understand, design, implement, or evaluate good practices of partnership with the families of their students. Colleges and universities that prepare educators and others who work with children and families should identify where in their curricula the theory, research, policy, and practical ideas about partnerships are presented or where in their programs these can be added.[9]

Even with improved preservice and advanced coursework, however, each school's action team will have to tailor its menu of practices to the needs and wishes of the teachers, families, and students in the school. The framework and guidelines offered in this article can be used by thoughtful educators to organize this work, school by school.

THE CORE OF CARING

One school in our Baltimore project named its partnerships the "I Care Program." It developed an I Care Parent Club that fostered fellowship and leadership of families, an *I Care Newsletter,* and many other events and activities. Other schools also gave catchy, positive names to their programs to indicate to families, students, teachers, and everyone else in the school community that there are important relationships and exchanges that must be developed in order to assist students.

Interestingly, synonyms for *caring* match the six types of involvement: Type 1, parenting: supporting, nurturing, and rearing; Type 2, communicating: relating, reviewing, and overseeing; Type 3, volunteering: supervising and fostering; Type 4, learning at home: managing, recognizing, and rewarding; Type 5, decision making: contributing, considering, and judging; and Type 6, collaborating with the community: sharing and giving.

Underlying all six types of involvement are two defining synonyms of caring: *trusting* and *respecting.* Of course, the varied meanings are interconnected, but it is striking that language permits us to call forth various elements of caring associated with activities for the six types of involvement. If all six types of involvement are operating well in a school's program of partnership, then all of these caring behaviors could be activated to assist children's learning and development.

Despite real progress in many states, districts, and schools over the past few years, there are still too many schools in which educators do not understand the families of their students; in which families do not understand their children's schools; and in which communities do not understand or assist the schools, families, or students. There are still too many states and districts without the policies, departments, leadership, staff, and fiscal support needed to enable all their schools to develop good programs of partnership. Yet relatively small financial investments that support and assist the work of action teams could yield significant returns for all schools, teachers, families, and students. Educators who have led the way with trials, errors, and successes provide evidence that any state, district, or school can create similar programs.[10]

Schools have choices. There are two common approaches to involving families in schools and in their children's education. One approach emphasizes conflict and views the school as a battleground. The conditions and relationships in this kind of environment guarantee power struggles and disharmony. The other approach emphasizes partnership and views the school as a homeland. The conditions and relationships in this kind of environment invite power sharing and mutual respect and allow energies to be directed toward activities that foster student learning and development. Even when conflicts rage, however, peace must be restored sooner or later, and the partners in children's education must work together.

NEXT STEPS: STRENGTHENING PARTNERSHIPS

Collaborative work and thoughtful give-and-take among researchers, policy leaders, educators, and parents are responsible for the progress that has been made over the past decade in understanding and developing school, family, and community partnerships. Similar collaborations will be important for future progress in this and other areas of school reform. To promote these approaches, I am establishing a national network of Partnership-2000 Schools to help link state, district, and other leaders who are responsible for helping their elementary, middle, and high schools implement programs of school, family, and community partnerships by the year 2000. The state and district coordinators must be supported for at least three years by sufficient staff and budgets to enable them to help increasing numbers of elementary, middle, and high schools in their districts to plan, implement, and maintain comprehensive programs of partnership.

Partnership-2000 Schools will be aided in putting the recommendations of this article into practice in ways that are appropriate to their locations. Implementation will include applying the theory of overlapping spheres of influence, the framework of six types of involvement, and the action team approach. Researchers and staff members at Johns Hopkins will disseminate information and guidelines, send out newsletters, and hold optional annual workshops to help state and district coordinators learn new strategies and share successful ideas. Activities for leaders at the state and district levels will be shared, as will school-level programs and successful partnership practices.

The national network of Partnership-2000 Schools will begin its activities in the fall of 1995 and will continue until at least the year 2000. The goal is to enable leaders in all states and districts to assist all their schools in establishing and strengthening programs of school/family/community partnership.[11]

NOTES

1. Joyce L. Epstein, "Toward a Theory of Family–School Connections: Teacher Practices and Parent Involvement," in Klaus Hurrelmann, Frederick Kaufmann, and Frederick Losel, eds., *Social Intervention: Potential and Constraints* (New York: DeGruyter, 1987), pp. 121–36; idem, "School and Family Partnerships," in Marvin Alkin, ed., *Encyclopedia of Educational Research*, 6th ed. (New York: Macmillan, 1992), pp. 1139–51; idem, "Theory to Practice: School and Family Partnerships Lead to School Improvement and Student Success," in Cheryl L. Fagnano and Beverly Z. Werber, eds., *School, Family, and Community Interaction: A View from the Firing Lines* (Boulder, CO: Westview Press, 1994), pp. 39–52; and idem, *School and Family Partnerships: Preparing Educators and Improving Schools* (Boulder, CO: Westview Press, forthcoming).

2. Ron Brandt, "On Parents and Schools: A Conversation with Joyce Epstein," *Educational Leadership*, October 1989, pp. 24–27; Epstein, "Toward a Theory"; Catherine C. Lewis, Eric Schaps, and Marilyn Watson, "Beyond the Pendulum: Creating Challenging and Caring Schools," *Phi Delta Kappan*, March 1995, pp. 547–54; and Debra Viadero, "Learning to Care," *Education Week*, 26 October 1994, pp. 31–33.

3. A. Wade Boykin, "Harvesting Culture and Talent: African American Children and Educational Reform," in Robert Rossi, ed., *Schools and Students at Risk* (New York: Teachers College Press, 1994), pp. 116–39.

4. For references to studies by many researchers, see the following literature reviews: Epstein, "School and Family Partnerships"; idem, *School and Family Partnerships*; and idem, "Perspectives and Previews on Research and Policy for School, Family, and Community Partnerships," in Alan Booth and Judith Dunn, eds., *Family-School Links: How Do They Affect Educational Outcomes?* (Hillsdale, NJ: Erlbaum, forthcoming). Research that reports patterns of involvement across the grades, for families with low and high socioeconomic status, for one- and two-parent homes, and on schools' programs of partnership includes: Carol Ames, with Madhab Khoju and Thomas Watkins, "Parents and Schools: The Impact of School-to-Home Communications on Parents' Beliefs and Perceptions," Center on Families, Communities, Schools, and Children's Learning, Center Report 15, Johns Hopkins University, Baltimore, 1993; David P. Baker and David L. Stevenson, "Mothers' Strategies for Children's School Achievement: Managing the Transition to High School," *Sociology of Education*, vol. 59, 1986, pp. 156–66; Patricia A. Bauch, "Is Parent Involvement Different in Private Schools?," *Educational Horizons*, vol. 66, 1988, pp. 78–82; Henry J. Becker and Joyce L. Epstein, "Parent Involvement: A Study of Teacher Practices," *Elementary School Journal*, vol. 83, 1982, pp. 85–102; Reginald M. Clark, *Family Life and School Achievement: Why Poor Black Children Succeed or Fail* (Chicago: University of Chicago Press, 1983); Susan L. Dauber and Joyce L. Epstein, "Parents' Attitudes and Practices of Involvement in Inner-City Elementary and Middle Schools," in Nancy Chavkin, ed., *Families and Schools in a Pluralistic Society* (Albany: State University of New York Press, 1993), pp. 53–71; Sanford

M. Dornbusch and Philip L. Ritter, "Parents of High School Students: A Neglected Resource," *Educational Horizons*, vol. 66, 1988, pp. 75–77; Jacquelynne S. Eccles, "Family Involvement in Children's and Adolescents' Schooling," in Booth and Dunn, op. cit.; Joyce L. Epstein, "Parents' Reactions to Teacher Practices of Parent Involvement," *Elementary School Journal*, vol. 86, 1986, pp. 277–94; idem, "Single Parents and the Schools: Effects of Marital Status on Parent and Teacher Interactions," in Maureen Hallinan, ed., *Change in Societal Institutions* (New York: Plenum, 1990), pp. 91–121; Joyce L. Epstein and Seyong Lee, "National Patterns of School and Family Connections in the Middle Grades," in Bruce A. Ryan and Gerald R. Adams, eds., *The Family-School Connection: Theory, Research, and Practice* (Newbury Park, CA: Sage, forthcoming); Annette Lareau, *Home Advantage: Social Class and Parental Intervention in Elementary Education* (Philadelphia: Falmer Press, 1989); and Diane Scott-Jones, "Activities in the Home That Support School Learning in the Middle Grades," in Barry Rutherford, ed., *Creating Family/School Partnerships* (Columbus, OH: National Middle School Association, 1995), pp. 161–81.

5. The three tables update earlier versions that were based on only five types of involvement. For other discussions of the types, practices, challenges, redefinitions, and results, see Epstein, "School and Family Partnerships"; Lori Connors Tadros and Joyce L. Epstein, "Parents and Schools," in Marc H. Bornstein, ed., *Handbook of Parenting* (Hillsdale, NJ: Erlbaum, forthcoming); Joyce L. Epstein and Lori Connors Tadros, "School and Family Partnerships in the Middle Grades," in Rutherford, op. cit.; and idem, "Trust Fund: School, Family, and Community Partnerships in High Schools," Center on Families, Communities, Schools, and Children's Learning, Center Report 24, Johns Hopkins University, Baltimore, 1994. Schools' activities with various types of involvement are outlined in Don Davies, Patricia Burch, and Vivian Johnson, "A Portrait of Schools Reaching Out: Report of a Survey on Practices and Policies of Family–Community–School Collaboration," Center on Families, Communities, Schools, and Children's Learning, Center Report 1, Johns Hopkins University, Baltimore, 1992.

6. Seyong Lee, "Family-School Connections and Students' Education: Continuity and Change of Family Involvement from the Middle Grades to High School" (Doctoral dissertation, Johns Hopkins University, 1994). For a discussion of issues concerning the results of partnerships, see Epstein, "Perspectives and Previews." For various research reports on results of partnerships for students and for parents, see Joyce L. Epstein, "Effects on Student Achievement of Teacher Practices of Parent Involvement," in Steven Silvern, ed., *Literacy Through Family, Community, and School Interaction* (Greenwich, CT: JAI Press, 1991), pp. 261–276; Joyce L. Epstein and Susan L. Dauber, "Effects on Students of an Interdisciplinary Program Linking Social Studies, Art, and Family Volunteers in the Middle Grades," *Journal of Early Adolescence*, vol. 15, 1995, pp. 237–266; Joyce L. Epstein and Jill Jacobsen, "Effects of School Practices to Involve Families in the Middle Grades: Parents' Perspectives," paper presented at the annual meeting of the American Sociological Association, Los Angeles, 1994; Joyce L. Epstein and Seyong Lee, "Effects of School Practices to Involve Families on Parents and Students in the Middle Grades: A View from the Schools," paper presented at the annual meeting of the American Sociological Association, Miami, 1993; and Anne T. Henderson and Nancy Berla, *A New Generation of Evidence: The Family Is Critical to Student Achievement* (Washington, DC: National Committee for Citizens in Education, 1994).

7. Lori Connors Tadros and Joyce L. Epstein, "Taking Stock: The Views of Teachers, Parents, and Students on School, Family, and Community Partnerships in High Schools," Center on Families, Communities, Schools, and Children's Learning, Center Report 25, Johns Hopkins University, Baltimore, 1994; Epstein and Tadros, "Trust Fund"; Joyce L. Epstein and Susan L. Dauber, "School Programs and Teacher Practices of Parent Involvement in Inner-City Elementary and Middle Schools," *Elementary School Journal*, vol. 91, 1991, pp. 289–303; and Joyce L. Epstein, Susan C. Herrick, and Lucretia Coates, "Effects of Summer Home Learning Packets on Student Achievement in Language Arts in the Middle Grades," *School Effectiveness and School Improvement*, in press. For other approaches to the use of action teams for partnerships, see Patricia Burch and Ameetha Palanki, "Action Research on Family–School–Community Partnerships," *Journal of Emotional and Behavioral Problems*, vol. 1, 1994, pp. 16–19; Patricia Burch, Ameetha Palanki, and Don Davies, "In Our Hands: A Multi-Site Parent-Teacher Action Research Project," Center on Families, Communities, Schools, and Children's Learning, Center Report 29, Johns Hopkins University, Baltimore, 1995; Don Davies, "Schools Reaching Out: Family, School, and Community Partnerships for Student Success," *Phi Delta Kappan*, January 1991, pp. 376–82; idem, "A More Distant Mirror: Progress Report on a Cross-National Project to Study Family–School–Community Partnerships," *Equity and Choice*, vol. 19, 1993, pp. 41–46; and Don Davies, Ameetha Palanki, and Patricia D. Palanki, "Getting Started: Action Research in Family–School–Community Partnerships," Center on Families, Communities, Schools, and Children's Learning, Center Report 17, Johns Hopkins University, Baltimore, 1993. For an example of an organizing mechanism for action teams, see Vivian R. Johnson, "Parent Centers in Urban Schools: Four Case Studies," Center on Families, Communities, Schools, and Children's Learning, Center Report 23, Johns Hopkins University, Baltimore, 1994.

8. Surveys for teachers and parents in the elementary and middle grades and for teachers, parents, and students in high school, developed and revised in 1993 by Joyce L. Epstein, Karen Clark Salinas, and Lori Connors Tadros,

are available from the Center on Families, Communities, Schools, and Children's Learning at Johns Hopkins University.

9. Mary Sue Ammon, "University of California Project on Teacher Preparation for Parent Involvement, Report I: April 1989 Conference and Initial Follow-up," mimeo, University of California, Berkeley, 1990; Nancy F. Chavkin and David L. Williams, "Critical Issues in Teacher Training for Parent Involvement," *Educational Horizons*, vol. 66, 1988, pp. 87–89; and Lisa Hinz, Jessica Clarke, and Joe Nathan, "A Survey of Parent Involvement Course Offerings in Minnesota's Undergraduate Preparation Programs," Center for School Change, Humphrey Institute of Public Affairs, University of Minnesota, Minneapolis, 1992. To correct deficiencies in the education of educators, I have written a course text or supplementary reader based on the theory, framework, and approaches described in this article. See Epstein, *School and Family Partnerships*. Other useful readings for a university course include Sandra L. Christenson and Jane Close Conoley, eds., *Home–School Collaboration: Enhancing Children's Academic Competence* (Silver Spring, Md.: National Association of School Psychologists, 1992); Fagnano and Werber, op. cit.;

Norman Fruchter, Anne Galletta, and J. Lynne White, *New Directions in Parent Involvement* (Washington, DC: Academy for Educational Development, 1992); William Rioux and Nancy Berla, eds., *Innovations in Parent and Family Involvement* (Princeton Junction, N.J.: Eye on Education, 1993); and Susan McAllister Swap, *Developing Home–School Partnerships: From Concepts to Practice* (New York: Teachers College Press, 1993).

10. See, for example, Gary Lloyd, "Research and Practical Application for School, Family, and Community Partnerships," in Booth and Dunn, op cit.; Wisconsin Department of Public Instruction. *Sharesheet: The DPI Family–Community–School Partnership Newsletter*, August/ September 1994; and the special section on parent involvement in the January 1991 *Phi Delta Kappan*.

11. For more information about the national network of Partnership-2000 Schools, send the name, position, address, and phone and fax numbers of the contact person/coordinator for partnerships for your state or district to Joyce Epstein, Partnership-2000 Schools, CRESPAR/ Center on Families, Communities, Schools, and Children's Learning, Johns Hopkins University, 3505 N. Charles St., Baltimore, MD 21218.

Chapter 2: Cognitive Development and Language

Remembering Father

GITA L. VYGODSKAIA

And I thought: it cannot be
That I would ever forget this
—Anna Akhmatova

J. P. Das has asked me to write briefly about Lev Semenovich Vygotsky. Understandably, I have willingly agreed.

It may seem strange, but this has turned out to be not so simple. On the one hand, it is easy and a pleasure for me to write about him. He was one of the dearest people, with whom I was very close. We loved each other very much. And that is natural—he was my father.

On the other hand, I experienced certain difficulties: There has been so much written about him (alas, not always objectively—even, not always truthfully), and I do not want my voice to drown in the general chorus of many voices.

It is true that analysis of his work, either in its entirety or of its individual aspects, prevails in the literature on L. S. Vygotsky. But even when his personality is discussed in the books and articles devoted to him, then, as a rule, it is only in passing. And yet, I believe, discussion of his personality is no less interesting than a debate about his scientific achievements. He was, after all, an interesting, extraordinary person and deserves, without any doubt, that his personality and fate be known. Furthermore, in an article written right after my father's death, A. N. Leontiev wrote that knowledge

of his personality is necessary to an understanding of his work.

And so I decided that I can tell about what nobody knows better than me. I will try to share my recollections about Lev Semenovich in everyday life, with his family. I will tell about the last years of his life, as I lived those years beside him and closely witnessed this period of his life.

From 1924 to 1934, Lev Semenovich lived in Moscow. These were the years when science was the main part of his life and scientific work, his main activity.

After living the first year and a half in the basement of the Institute of Psychology, he and his family moved into an apartment in the early autumn of 1925 on Bolshaia Serpukhovskaia Street. The building we lived in was not big (it included only 18 flats), it had three stories, and it was on the corner of a street that was then very lively and a quite peaceful side street.

Lev Semenovich did not live in that building long, only 9 years (he passed away in 1934), but it was well-known to all those who were in touch with him during those years. His students who would later become famous scientists would remember till the end of their days the flat on Serpukhovskaia, where, ignoring the cramped conditions, they would gather regularly to debate questions that were then exciting them. This is how A. R. Luria writes about it: "We—L. S. Vygotskii, A. N. Leontiev and myself—began to meet in L. S. Vygotskii's flat once

Gita L. Vygodskaia can be reached at Russia Moscow 103045, Bol'shaia Sukharevskaia Ploshchad', d.16/18, KV 70.

or twice a week, to work on plans for further research." It was there, to Serpukhovskaia, that students began coming, the famous "five," as they called L. I. Bozhovich, P. E. Levina, L. S. Slavina, N. G. Morozova, and A. V. Zaporozhets. They all, till the end of their days, remained faithful to Lev Semenovich's memory, continuing to consider him their teacher despite their own advanced age and scientific achievements.

Many knew the address during those years—Serpukhovskaia, 17. Letters from other cities and other countries would arrive there. That's where his close friends, colleagues, students, and people not well-known to him (even people not known to him at all till then) would come—teachers, scientists, writers, even foreign scientists. (I remember well how Professor Kurt Levin came to our house, how he had unending debates with Lev Semenovich, hotly debating something. The conversation was in German—not the only reason I did not understand it.) People would come for advice, for support, and to evaluate some of their problems.

Yes, the house on Bolshaia Serpukhovskaia was known to many during those years. Regretfully, it does not exist anymore: It was demolished during the construction of another line of the underground, and in the spot where it stood, there is the entrance to the station Serpukhovskaia. None of the passersby or those descending into the underground would even suspect what interesting and intensive life stormed in this place at the end of the 1920s and beginning of the 1930s.

Our flat was on the second floor. It was a corner one; some of its windows faced the lively street, but the windows in my immediate family's room faced the narrow side street. Lev Semenovich did not have a separate room to work and rest. (Throughout his life, he never had a separate room of his own.) His living conditions were the least suited for scientific study. All of those colleagues and friends who dropped by were astonished how he could concentrate on his work while there were other people in the room—someone entering, someone leaving, conversations going on, children playing. All the while, he worked without interruption.

There were four of us living in the room: my parents, my sister, and I. The room was quite cramped: There was a big writing desk by the window. By the walls (beside our sleeping places), from the floor up to the ceilings, there were stands with books and bookcases. Only the center of the room was free, and we used it for our games. The only

thing Lev Semenovich owned was his writing desk, behind which he would spend most of his time when at home. And he lost part of his ownership when I went to school. In order for me to have a permanent place to study, he gave me the left half of the desk. We would often be neighbors, sitting side by side at the desk—I with my homework, he with his work.

In addition to ourselves, Lev Semenovich's parents (my grandfather and grandmother), four of his unmarried sisters, and his older sister with her husband and son, lived in our apartment. The family in which I spent my childhood was very big and friendly. I do not recall one instance, in all those years of living together, that anyone in the family quarreled with somebody else, expressed or somehow showed dissatisfaction with somebody else, or even raised his or her voice. All were attentive to one another and related with understanding to the interests and wishes of everybody. The family was ruled by a spirit of love and mutual respect. This tone was started by my grandmother during the years when her own children were little, and it persevered through all the years of our family's life together.

Lev Semenovich loved his parents very much; he showed great respect for his father, and he was, without fail, tender, attentive, and helpful to his mother. I cannot recall his addressing her as anything other than "mamochka" (diminutive for *mom*). When his father died, Lev Semenovich shouldered all of the responsibility for the family and surrounded his mother with even more attention. He made sure that all doctor's orders were strictly observed (my grandmother was quite ill), and he would administer injections himself. I remember well how he would send me to grandmother, to stay with her and entertain her: "Go to your grandmother. Read something to her; she would enjoy it." I would go, of course, and read. I remember it was then that I read to her Gogol's *Evenings in a Hamlet Near Dikanka* and *Mirgorod,* and she would listen and correct me when I used incorrect accents in those words I did not know.

In the evenings, the family would always gather in grandmother's room (or, as the family called it, the dining room) around a big table. After obligatory tea, some would remain seated by the table, while others would move to the warm stove (the flat was always cool). Then the most interesting things would begin. Someone would read aloud, and everybody else would listen. There would be debates about new plays, reciting of poems, joking.

When Lev Semenovich came home alone, he always took part before going to our room to work. In those hours, he liked to stand, his back to the masonry of the stove, his hands behind his back. Even now I remember distinctly his kind smile, and it's as if I hear him, joking merrily with one of his sisters or reciting poems. He knew very many poems, loved them very much, and was always ready to recite—usually, the classics. From contemporary poetry, he would most often recite Pasternak, an especially favorite poet of his, whose poems he knew well. He could recite poems literally for hours, and everybody, having fallen silent and seated themselves comfortably, listened to him with pleasure. He would recite excellently.

We, the children, would be right there in the room (there were three of us in the family—my sister and I and our cousin, dad's sister's son), but we never thought of making noise or otherwise upsetting the adults. We could silently play right there, or listen to general conversation, or leave when we felt bored. Nobody would order us or force us to stay, but I cannot recall a single time when I would voluntarily leave that room—there was such an unusual atmosphere of emotional closeness there. I still remember well how I was always sad when mom sent me to go to sleep.

Right there, by the stove, Lev Semenovich would demonstrate to us his ability to remember large numbers of words. We would, working together, compile a list of 100 words (I took part, I remember) and hand it over to Lev Semenovich. He would slowly read each word, return the list, and then offer to recite it in any order. To our amazement and joy, he would, without mistake, repeat all the words on the list from beginning to end, and then repeat them in the reverse order. Then we would ask him to reproduce the 17th, 43rd, 61st, 7th, and so on, word, and he, without difficulty and without any mistakes, would do it. I remember, at my sister's request, he explained the mechanics of remembering and told us how he did it.

But this would be only when Lev Semenovich came home alone. If he were joined by any of his colleagues, students, or coworkers, they would be given tea and then allowed to go to our room to work. (The rest of us would spend the evening without my father.) That's where I would find them, in debates, when I would come to sleep. Their debates seemed to be boring, uninteresting, because, of course, I did not understand anything. While they were talking, I would make my bed; while they were talking, I would lie down; while they were talking, I would

usually fall asleep. Late at night, I would wake up to find the room silent, the top lamp turned off, little sister breathing in her sleep, mom sleeping quietly. And by the desk, under the desk lamp light, there sat, working, Lev Semenovich. Sometimes, I would whisper to call him, and he, right away, alarmed, would come to me. He would carefully look at my face, touch my forehead (checking for fever), ask whether I had a bad dream or if I needed anything, and tenderly touch my head. I would tell him quietly, so as not to wake anybody, "Daddy, go to sleep; it's late at night already." "Yes, yes," he would answer. "I'll lie down soon. I still have to work a bit. But you, please do sleep." He would kiss me, pet my head, and go sit by the desk again. When did he rest?

He was attentive and nice to us children without fail, always interested in what we were doing, seriously watching our games, never interfering, only supporting. When we needed something for a game, he would try to help us.

My sister was still little at this time, and we and my cousin would permanently be father's test subjects. We liked it when he introduced us to his experiments. I can see it as if it were today: On the floor at the center of the room, there would be objects forming a labyrinth, with a mandarin orange at its center. It's Lev Semenovich, repeating Keler's experiments with us. We would very much like to get the mandarin orange as a reward, so we're trying hard.

My father always talked to us peacefully, kindly, but when we did something bad, he would never accept that. He did not give us long talks on manners, did not rip into us, did not demand that we beg forgiveness and promise we would never do that again. He would simply tell us we had misbehaved and show us with his look how it saddened him, how he felt it was unpleasant. That, I can assure you, was the toughest punishment! One philosopher who was coming to the apartment was very absentminded and had a bad vision, too. Once, dad's guest was trying to break into the closet in the hallway, thinking this was the door to the washroom and assuring Lev Semenovich he knew perfectly well what he was doing. Of course, we snickered, but my father gave us a strict look, and we fell silent. When the guest left, Lev Semenovich told us he could not understand what was so funny about a person who cannot see absentmindedly mixing up things. He said he was very disappointed that we did not understand it was indecent and cruel to make fun of the weaknesses and shortcomings of others, that he was ashamed of us. Having said that, he quickly left the room and left us there alone. Believe me, this was a lesson for the rest of my life. I still can remember how I was ashamed and how I suffered, trying to get back into my father's good graces.

We loved each other very much. Perhaps it is not even necessary to say how I cherished our relationship. We were connected by real friendship. Our relationship was open, sincere; we always felt it interesting and good to be together. And it is perfectly natural that I always tried to be beside him. He, it seemed, also was pleased with my company and never made a secret of it. Despite his workload and lack of time, he would always be there for me when I needed help.

We very much loved going out for walks, but in Moscow, thanks to Lev Semenovich's lack of time, this did not happen too often. But in the summer, out of the city, when he was on vacation, we would go for long walks. On occasion, mom would join us, and that's when Lev Semenovich would be at his happiest. When we were walking through forests, just the two of us, he would recite poems for me, and then we would sing. The problem was, Lev Semenovich did not have a musical ear, and he could not sing well even the simplest melody. He, of course, knew this, and he would never sing in front of anybody; he would be even more embarrassed in front of mom, who was very musically talented. I was the only person who would hear him sing. He would not be embarrassed in front of me, and because it would bring me joy, he would sing poems by Lermontov and Nekrasov to melodies that he would think of himself. These melodies would be extraordinarily simple and monotonous, but we liked them, and I would sing with him. I have no doubt that our singing must have sounded terrible, but because we liked the process itself, we never thought of the result, of the sound of it. (Thank God, nobody ever

heard us.) So many years have passed, but I still recall the melody to which Lev Semenovich would sing *The Airship (Vozhdushnyi Korablj)*, Lermontov's lullaby, or *White Day (Belyi Denji)* and *Kallistrata* by Nekrasov. For me, these melodies are still alive, and they sound in my soul even now.

Lev Semenovich was not at all an ascetic, uninterested in anything but his science, who would not notice anything around him. He was a very lively, emotional person who knew well the entire scale of human emotions. He, like nobody else, could empathize and share a person's sorrow, but he was also very happy and lively with friends. He had a wonderful sense of humor, loved and appreciated a joke, could make jokes himself. And yet, at the same time, he was always a very modest, extremely delicate human being. He was very unassuming, never demanded special conditions for himself, never oppressed anybody. Not only would he let me bring in kids from our yard, but sometimes he would insist on it. When kids would drop by, we would start playing right there beside him, while he would sit at his desk, working and from time to time turning around and looking with a smile as we played before immersing himself in his work again. One has to wonder how he managed, under such conditions, to achieve so much.

Lev Semenovich worked very much, way too much. And when he died, his relatives did not have to ponder long what to bury him in: He had only one suit.

To us, his children, he left the most important, dearest thing parents can leave to their children: good memories of him and a good, spotlessly clean name.

Soon, it will be 60 years since he has been with us. Yet the interest in his name, his personality, his ideas, and the thoughts he spelled out has not abated.

This collection of articles is proof.

Piaget's Legacy

JOHN H. FLAVELL

There have been many published assessments of Jean Piaget's work over the years, both during his lifetime and since his death in 1980. One has only to look in any introductory textbook on developmental psychology or cognitive development to find examples. Most of these assessments mention both praiseworthy and criticizable aspects of his work, but often give more space to the latter than to the former. This is understandable. In most cases, identified weaknesses in his work are proxies for important scientific discoveries made by subsequent researchers. That is, we learn that some Piagetian developmental story is probably wrong by doing research that points to some alternative, more correct-seeming story. Naturally, it is important for the people who write about cognitive development to communicate both the weaknesses and the scientific discoveries that revealed them and took us the next step forward.

In the present assessment, I take a different tack, however. Useful though it is to examine the criticizable in Piagetiana, I focus entirely on the praiseworthy in this article. My objective is to summarize what I believe to be Piaget's contributions to what we know about cognitive development and how we think about it. Everyone knows that Piaget was the most important figure the field has known; the purpose of this article is simply to explain why.

Address correspondence to John H. Flavell, Department of Psychology, Stanford University, Stanford, CA 94305-2130.

PIAGET'S CONTRIBUTIONS

1. Piaget's greatest contribution was to found the field of cognitive development as we currently know it. As Miller (1993) explained:

> *Piaget transformed the field of developmental psychology. If a developmental psychologist were somehow plucked out of the 1950's and set down today, he would be bewildered by the talk around him. He would hear psychologists discussing strategies, rule-governed behaviors, cognitive structures, schemes, plans, and representations, instead of stimulus generalization, mean length of utterance, mental age, conditioning, discrimination learning, and learning set. To a great extent Piaget was responsible for this change. He altered the course of psychology by asking new questions that made developmentalists wonder why they had ever asked the old questions in the first place. Once psychologists looked at development through Piaget's eyes, they never saw children in quite the same way. (p. 81)*

As a developmental psychologist who began his career in the 1950s, I can attest to the accuracy of Miller's characterization. Piaget provided the field with an entirely new vision of the nature of children, and of the what, when, and how of their cognitive growth. This vision invaded the field during the 1960s and 1970s and largely supplemented the rather limited and uninteresting visions that were already there. The result was that "almost everything people think and do in this field has some connection with questions that Piaget raised" (Flavell & Markman, 1983, p. viii). Thus, Piaget's role in cognitive development was similar to Chomsky's role in language development: He created and shaped a new field of inquiry.

2. Piaget's *assimilation-accommodation* model of cognitive growth correctly emphasizes the active, constructive nature of the child. This model allows us to view cognitive development as a gradual, step-by-step process of structural acquisition and change, with each new mental structure growing out of its predecessor through the continuous operation of assimilation and accommodation. It is largely due to Piaget that we now take for granted that

> *children are clearly not blank slates that passively and unselectively copy whatever the environment presents to them. Rather, the cognitive structures and processing strategies available to them at that point in their development lead them to select from the input what is meaningful to them and to represent and transform what is selected in accordance with their cognitive structures. As Piaget correctly taught us, children's cognitive structures dictate both what they accommodate to (notice) in the environment and how what is accommodated to is assimilated (interpreted). The active nature of their intellectual commerce with the environment makes them to a large degree the manufacturers of their own development. (Flavell, 1992, p. 998)*

Views similar to Piaget's constructivist conception are widely held by present-day cognitive psychologists as well as by cognitive developmentalists. As Halford (1989, p. 326) has pointed out, Piaget's conception also anticipated schema theory and the concept of constraints on learning. Bates and Elman (1993) even went so far as to predict that

> *we will soon see a revival of Piagetian theory within a connectionist framework—not a mindless reinterpretation of the old theory in modern jargon, but a return to Piaget's program of genetic epistemology, instantiating his principles of equilibration and adaptation in concrete systems that really work—and really change. (p. 17)*

3. Piaget helped us to accept the idea that children's cognitive behavior is intrinsically rather than extrinsically motivated. Although social and other reinforcements may influence children's curiosity and cognitive explorations to some degree, basically children think and learn because they are built that way. For Piaget, cognitive adaptation to the environment via the mechanisms of assimilation and accommodation is a form of biological adaptation, and adaptation is something organisms have evolved to do. Cognitive functioning, and cognitive-structural change through repeated cognitive functioning, have their own internal power source and are certain to occur in every human child. It might be objected that everyone has always believed this, but that is not the case. In the 1950s, psychologists were just beginning to play with such notions as curiosity, competence, exploratory, and sensory motives and drives, and in the early 1960s it was natural to write, "It seems less improbable today than it once did to imagine that the Piagetian infant really does need to look at, listen to, and otherwise assimilate stimuli, even (perhaps especially) when he is not hungry" (Flavell, 1963, p. 410).

4. Piaget saw that to characterize human cognitive development adequately, one needs something less general than the functional invariants of assimilation and accommodation, co-present in all cognitive activity, but also more general than an endless list of specific acquired concepts. For Piaget, that something was cognitive structure:

> *There has to be some* tertium quid: *something which changes with age, as the functional invariants do not; but also something more general than individual contents, something which will pull diverse contents together into a single chunk. Piaget realized this early and wisely resisted what we think was the guiding spirit of the 1930's: to move upward towards function (the child "learns" more and more things as he grows, but the mind which learns is homogeneous throughout) and to move downward toward content (as he grows, the child acquires this, and this, and this, and this—period). However critical one may be of the particular structural analysis Piaget has made, we are much in his debt for seeing so clearly, and so early, the necessity for making one. (Flavell, 1963, pp. 409–410)*

Although developmental psychologists have indeed criticized the particular structures Piaget proposed in the years since those lines were written, most continue to see the need for structural analyses of one kind or another. Thus, we continue to read about grammars, schemas, scripts, rules, systems, central conceptual structure, and other structural concepts. Similarly structural in nature are characterizations of cognitive development as the acquisition of naive theories within specific domains (Wellman & Gelman, 1992). One would not be licensed to describe the child's knowledge about the mind as a theory of mind unless one thought it consisted of a set of interrelated concepts—and thus a knowledge structure—rather than a set of unrelated ones.

5. In elaborating his *equilibration* model, Piaget was one of the first psychologists to make a serious try at explaining as well as describing cognitive development. He argued that all significant intellectual advances are made through an equilibration process consisting of three major steps: first, cognitive equilibrium at a lower developmental level; then, cognitive disequilibrium, induced by awareness of puzzling, contradictory, discrepant, or otherwise unassimilable phenomena not previously noticed; and finally, cognitive equilibration (or reequilibration) at a higher developmental level, as the result of reconceptualizing the problem in such a way as to make sense of the previously nonassimilable phenomena. Although this model clearly has its problems (lack of clarity and specificity, apparent inapplicability to certain types of developmental change), we are only now beginning to see attempts at explanations of cognitive-developmental changes that appear to be more promising (Siegler, 1996). Moreover, recent explanations of naive theory development in children feature a change process very reminiscent of Piaget's equilibration model (e.g., Bartsch & Wellman, 1995; Gopnik & Wellman, 1992).

6. Piaget proposed many insightful concepts and ideas in the course of his extensive theorizing about cognitive development. The Piagetian concept of *scheme* (or *schema*) is one such. The image of children searching for objects to assimilate to their developing action schemes—for example, searching for countables with which to exercise their newly minted counting scheme—seems very true to life (Gelman, 1979). Similarly, his concept of *vertical décalage* captures the possibility that there are hidden

similarities or recursions in children's functioning across different stages of development. "Development in the Piagetian mode has a cyclic character which buttresses the feeling that it is somehow all of one cloth" (Flavell, 1963, p. 408). Neo-Piagetian theorists such as Case and Fischer have also found it necessary to build such recursiveness into their stage theories. For example, Case et al. (1991) proposed that the three substages of *unifocal, bifocal,* and *elaborated* coordination are found within each of four major stages of development. Piaget's belief that images are active internal imitations rather than passive copies of external objects and events anticipated the concept of mental rotation (Shepard & Metzler, 1971). The concepts of *egocentrism, centration,* and *decentration* have proven to be very useful in understanding the development of both social and nonsocial thinking. Piaget's idea that a person's own point of view tends to be more salient and available to him or her than the points of view of other people finds its modern counterpart in Tversky and Kahneman's (1973) availability heuristic. Piaget's concepts of *reflective abstraction* and *formal operations,* involving the idea of cognition about cognition, live on in Karmiloff Smith's (1992) developmental theory and in the large developmental and nondevelopmental literature on metacognition.

Gelman (1979) described another insight thusly:

> *Piaget was the first to point out the role of transformations in a theory of cognition. The world is known not only in terms of static representations of it; we "know" how transformations will affect objects or classes of objects. Likewise our representations include knowledge of those transformations that do and do not change certain properties of an object or class of objects. How such knowledge develops is a central concern of Piagetian theory. Since I cannot imagine anyone denying the central role of transformations in a theory of cognition, I think we will continue to be influenced by Piaget's ideas and related observations on the object concept, conservation, etc. (p. 5)*

Finally, although we often think of Piaget as focused on developmental discontinuities from one age to the next (qualitatively different stages, etc.), his emphasis on invariant developmental sequences strongly highlights underlying continuities in development. He emphasized the idea that, despite their novel features, later structures grow out of and build upon earlier ones:

> *He at once shows us wherein a new structure is really new, is a true emergent, and at the same time shows us wherein it is not new, is not something inexplicable in terms of antecedent events. In Piaget's scheme of things, all structures are emergents but no structures are emergents* ex nihilo. *(Flavell, 1963, p. 416)*

7. Piaget contributed importantly to our stock of research methods for studying children's intellectual growth (Beilin, 1992). He pioneered the use of a clinical method, in which the researcher probes for the child's underlying understanding and knowledge through repeated questioning. Most of us still use variants of this method in our research, especially in the pilot-testing phases. A related contribution is that early in his career he had the insight—novel at that time—that one can learn more about children's thought by noting and querying their incorrect answers than by just tallying their correct ones. That is, he recognized that "the 'wrong' or 'cute' notions that preschool children have about the world are the symptom of a complex, probing intellectual system that is trying to understand reality" (Miller, 1993, p. 84).

8. For many people, of course, Piaget's most important contributions have been his remarkable empirical discoveries, far too numerous to summarize here:

> *What may well be one of Piaget's most important and enduring legacies to the field is simply that he has revealed the development of cognition to be a thing of unsuspected and extraordinary richness. Piaget has systematically ploughed his way through most of the principal modes of human experience and knowledge—space, time, number, and the rest. And in each case he has laid bare a complex succession of preforms and precursors for the most mundane and obvious of cognitions, cognitions we had no reason to assume needed a prehistory, let alone such an involved one. It is an uncommon experience to find out something about children's behavior which really surprises, which produces a sense of shock and even disbelief; after all, people have been child-watching for a long time. But Piaget may have discovered more things about children*

> *which shock and surprise than anyone else, and this alone is an immense accomplishment. (Flavell, 1963, p. 411)*

Gelman (1979) further noted that Piaget gave us "some of the most reliable phenomena in psychology" and that "they are amongst the phenomena that make it possible to claim there is a field of cognitive development" (p. 6). Clearly, Piaget had the greenest thumb ever for unearthing fascinating and significant developmental progressions. Just compare what Piaget discovered in his career with what the rest of us have discovered in ours (considered singly or—it sometimes almost seems—even collectively!).

9. Piaget's descriptions give us a highly memorable and at least fairly true picture of how children at different ages think. The qualitative thought of the preschooler, the more quantitative and logical thought of the elementary school child, the more abstract and metacognitive thought of the adolescent—although these pictures are not wholly accurate, they do capture much of the essence of the child's mental tendencies during these age periods. Siegler (1991) expressed this point well:

> *What explains the longevity of Piaget's theory? Perhaps the basic reason is that Piaget's theory conveys an almost tangible sense of what children's thinking is like. His descriptions feel right. Many of his individual observations are quite surprising, but the general trends that he detects appeal to our intuitions and to our memories of childhood. (p. 18)*

10. Piaget's work has had important influences on fields other than cognitive-developmental psychology. For example, his ideas and tasks have been used extensively in the fields of educational psychology, special education, socioemotional development, childhood psychopathology, and comparative psychology. His ideas have also influenced the thinking of professionals (e.g., Brazelton) who provide advice about parenting practices to the general public. His conception of children as active, constructive thinkers who learn only what they are structurally ready to learn has had an especially profound influence on educational thinking and practice. Indeed, it is hard to see how the contemporary field of instructional psychology would have developed as it did had there been no Piaget.

11. Ultimately, Piaget's most important and enduring legacy may not be his theory and research findings as much as the deep questions and issues he raised: What development-making cognitive equipment is the child born with? What role do interactions with the environment play in the child's development? How can we diagnose the child's competencies accurately, without either overestimating or underestimating them? What would it mean to claim that cognitive development is stagelike, and how stagelike is it in fact? Are there invariant developmental sequences and, if so, why are they invariant? What are the mechanisms or processes that cause cognitive development to occur? And so on and on. Piaget got us started, and by continuing to wrestle with the issues he bequeathed us, we will continue to learn more about children's intellectual development (Siegler, 1991).

CONCLUSION

This description of Piaget's contributions has been very laudatory. Has it been too laudatory? Some readers may think so, but I do not. I think we are in more danger of underappreciating Piaget than of overappreciating him, for much the same reason that fish are said to underappreciate the virtues of water. That is, many of Piaget's contributions have become so much a part of the way we view cognitive development nowadays that they are virtually invisible. The invisible would quickly become more visible if one were to examine a child psychology textbook written in the 1950s and compare what the field was like then to what it is like now. A footnote in Beilin's (1992) article on "Piaget's enduring contribution to developmental psychology" says it all:

An anonymous reviewer of a draft of this article . . . observed that "assessing the impact of Piaget on developmental psychology is like assessing the impact of Shakespeare on English or Aristotle on philosophy—impossible. The impact is too monumental to embrace and at the same time too omnipresent to detect." I agree. (p. 191, fn. 1)

Me too.

REFERENCES

Bartsch, K., & Wellman, H. M. (1995). *Children talk about the mind.* New York: Oxford University Press.

Bates, E. H., & Elman, J. L. (1993). Connectionism and the study of change. In M. H. Johnson (Ed.), *Brain development and cognition: A reader* (pp. 2–23). Oxford, England: Blackwell.

Beilin, H. (1992). Piaget's enduring contribution to developmental psychology. *Developmental Psychology, 28,* 191–204.

Case, R., Bruchkowsky, M., Capodilupo, A. M., Crammond, J., Dennis, S., Fiati, T. A., Goldberg-Reitman, J., Griffin, S., Marini, Z., McKeough, A., Okamoto, Y., Porath, M., Reid, D. T., & Sandieson, R. (1991). *The mind's staircase: Exploring the conceptual underpinnings of children's thought and knowledge.* Hillsdale, NJ: Erlbaum.

Flavell, J. H. (1963). *The developmental psychology of Jean Piaget.* New York: D. Van Nostrand.

Flavell, J. H. (1992). Cognitive development: Past, present, and future. *Developmental Psychology, 28,* 998–1005.

Flavell, J. H., & Markman, E. M. (1983). Preface. In P. H. Mussen (Series Ed.) & J. H. Flavell & E. M. Markman (Vol. Eds.), *Handbook of child psychology: Vol. 3. Cognitive development* (pp. viii–x). New York: Wiley.

Gelman, R. (1979, March). *Why we will continue to read Piaget.* Paper presented at the meeting of the Society for Research in Child Development, San Francisco.

Gopnik, A., & Wellman, H. M. (1992). Why the child's theory of mind really is a theory. *Mind and Language, 7,* 145–171.

Halford, G. S. (1989). Reflections on 25 years of Piagetian cognitive developmental psychology, 1963–1988. *Human Development, 32,* 325–357.

Karmiloff-Smith, A. (1992). *Beyond modularity: A developmental perspective on cognitive science.* Cambridge, MA: MIT Press.

Miller, P. H. (1993). *Theories of developmental psychology* (3rd ed.). New York: Freeman.

Shepard, R. N., & Metzler, J. (1971). Mental rotation of three-dimensional objects. *Science, 171,* 701–703.

Siegler, R. S. (1991). *Children's thinking* (2nd ed.). Englewood Cliffs, NJ: Prentice-Hall.

Siegler, R. S. (1996). *Emerging minds: The process of change in children's thinking.* New York: Oxford University Press.

Tversky, A., & Kahneman, D. (1973). Availability: A heuristic for judging frequency and probability. *Cognitive Psychology, 5,* 207–232.

Wellman, H. M., & Gelman, S. A. (1992). Cognitive development: Foundational theories of core domains. *Annual Review of Psychology, 43,* 337–375.

Chapter 3: Personal, Social, and Emotional Development

Improving Students' Self-Esteem

JACK CANFIELD

Teachers intuitively know that when kids feel better about themselves, they do better in school. The simple fact is, though, that youngsters today are not receiving enough positive, nurturing attention from adults, either at home or at school. The reasons are numerous and complex, but the result is that more and more students have low levels of self-esteem.

To raise the self-esteem of students, you must start with the school staff. The main way students learn is through modeling and imitation. If teachers have low self-esteem, they are likely to pass it on to their students. We must ensure, through preservice and inservice training, that teacher-student interactions are positive, validating, affirming, and encouraging.[1]

The challenge facing schools is great, but there are day-to-day things educators can do to increase children's self-esteem and, in so doing, improve their prospects for success (see "Does Self-Esteem Affect Achievement?"). I use a 10-step model to help students become winners in life.[2]

1. *Assume an aptitude of 100 percent responsibility.* I introduce the following formula: E (events) + R (your response to them) = O (outcomes). When people don't get the outcomes they want, I urge them not to blame external events and other people but to take responsibility for changing *their* responses. For example, if I ask a class how many of them think it

will raise Peter's self-esteem if I tell him he is the biggest idiot I ever met in my whole life, very few of them will raise their hands. I then tell them that it is not what I say to Peter but what Peter says to *himself* afterward that ultimately affects his self-esteem. If Peter says, "Mr. Canfield has only known me for a few days, how did he find out so fast?", his self-esteem will probably go down. But if he says to himself, "Mr. Canfield just picked me out for his example because he knows I can take a little kidding," then his self-esteem will not be damaged.

I also emphasize that we are responsible for our behavioral responses. For example, hit someone who yells at you, and you go to the principal's office. Respond with humor or by ignoring the person, and you stay out of trouble. Surprisingly, most kids don't understand that they have choices, let alone what those different choices are.

2. *Focus on the positive.* In order to feel successful, you have to have experienced success. Many students, because they feel they have never done anything successful, need to be coached. Often this is because they equate "success" with, say, winning a medal or getting rich. I spend a lot of time having students recall, write about, draw, and share their past achievements. With some probing and discussion, students often identify successful aspects of their lives that they have not recognized before.

3. *Learn to monitor your self-talk.* Each of us thinks 50,000 thoughts per day, and many of them are about ourselves. We all need to learn to replace negative thoughts—I can't dance, I'm not smart, I don't like my face—with positive self-talk: I can learn to do anything I want, I am smart, I love and

---

[1]For more information about raising self-esteem of faculty in a school, contact the resources listed in the box on p. 38.

[2]The 10-step model is spelled out in greater detail and with many examples in *Self-Esteem in the Classroom: A Curriculum Guide,* which is available from the author at the address given below.

Jack Canfield is president of Self-Esteem Seminars, 6035 Bristol Pkwy., Culver City, CA 90230.

Does Self-Esteem Affect Achievement?

Let's see what happens when a school makes a concerted effort in the area of self-esteem. One of the most detailed studies ever done was conducted by Gail Dusa (current president of the National Council for Self-Esteem) and her associates at Silver Creek High School in San Jose, California. (For more information, contact Gail Dusa, NCSE, 6641, Leyland Park Dr., San Jose, CA 95120.)

She divided the freshman class into three groups. The self-esteem group (93 students) was taught by teachers who adhered to three operating principles.

They (1) treated all students with unconditional positive regard, (2) encouraged all students to be all they could be, and (3) encouraged all students to set and achieve goals. In addition, the group participated in a 40-minute activity to build self-esteem every second Friday throughout their freshman year. The control group (also 93 students) received no treatment but was monitored along with the self-esteem group for four years. The third group was not involved in the study. At the end of four years, Dusa's findings were as follows:

	Self-Esteem Group	Control Group
Days of absenteeism per semester	1	16
Percentage of students who completed 90 percent or more of their homework	75%	25%
Percentage of students who participated in 20 or more extracurricular activities	25%	2%
Percentage of class offices held by groups between freshman and senior years	75%	0
Percentage of students who graduated from high school	83%	50%

Jack Canfield

accept myself the way I am. I teach students to say, "Cancel, cancel," when they hear themselves or another person saying something negative about them and to replace the negative remark with a positive one. This technique takes time and practice, but it really makes a difference. Also, whenever others put them down, they are to repeat the following "antidote" sentence. "No matter what you say or do to me, I'm still a worthwhile person."

4. *Use support groups in the classroom.* It's possible for a kid to come to school for a whole day and never once be the center of positive attention. "Sharing dyads" and "support groups" help overcome this alienation. Each day teachers might ask their students to find a partner (preferably a different partner each day) and then give them one or two minutes each of uninterrupted time to talk about a specific topic; for example, *Who is your best friend and why? What is your favorite thing to do on the weekend? If you won a million dollar lottery, what would you do with the money?* Topics such as these can also be discussed in "buddy groups" of six kids with three sets of buddies. Sometimes youngsters meet with their buddies and sometimes with their whole group. They learn that it is a positive,

healing experience to talk about their feelings, and they become bonded to their fellow students.

5. *Identify your strengths and resources.* An important part of expanded self-esteem is the broadened awareness of one's strengths and resources. One technique is to have students in their support groups write down and tell each other what they see as their positive qualities and strengths. Because their assessments need to be realistic as well as positive, it is also important to help students note those areas that need more development if they are to achieve their goals.

6. *Clarify your vision.* Without a clear vision, there is no motivation. Questions such as the following help students clarify their visions: *If you had only one year left to live, how would you spend your time? If a genie granted you three wishes, what would you wish for? If you were guaranteed success in anything you attempted, and money were not a limiting factor, what would you do when you grow up?* I also use extended guided visualizations in which students construct, for example, their "perfect life"—complete with their ideal house, job, and marriage partner—and share it with their support groups.

Resources for Increasing Students' Self-Esteem

The Alliance for Invitational Education, Room 216, Curry Building, University of North Carolina, Greensboro, NC 27412. The alliance publishes a comprehensive newsletter on self-esteem and invitational education and sponsors one national conference and several regional conferences yearly.

The California Task Force to Promote Self-Esteem and Personal and Social Responsibility, 1130 K St., Suite 300, Sacramento, CA 95814. This 25-member task force was appointed by the California governor and legislature to determine how to raise the self-esteem of at-risk groups in the state. Hawaii, Maryland, and Virginia have also created or begun to create similar task forces. For a copy of California's final report, *Toward a State of Esteem* (January 1990), send $4.50 to the Bureau of Publications, California State Department of Education, P.O. Box 271, Sacramento, CA 95802-0271. A 200-page *Appendix,* which includes an extensive bibliography on self-esteem and personal and social responsibility, is also available for $7.50.

The Center for Self-Esteem, P.O. Box 1532, Santa Cruz, CA 95060; 426-6850. The center sponsors an annual conference; publishes a free newsletter; distrib-

utes curriculums, books, and tapes; and provides consultants and workshop leaders.

The Foundation for Self-Esteem, 6035 Bristol Pkwy., Culver City, CA 90230; (213) 568-1505. The foundation has published The GOALS Program, a three-and-a-half hour video training program being used in adult schools, correctional facilities, and with welfare recipients. It also sponsors an annual conference, provides consultants and workshop leaders, and distributes curriculums, books, and tapes.

The National Council for Self-Esteem, c/o Gail Dusa, President, 6641 Leyland Park Dr., San Jose, CA 95120. The council publishes a newsletter and a resource packet and sponsors a national conference and about 20 regional conferences yearly. Write for a free copy of the newsletter and an information packet. Annual dues, $25.

Self-Esteem Seminars, 6035 Bristol Pkwy., Culver City, CA 90230; (213) 337-9222. The organization conducts inservice training, offers an intensive Facilitators' Training Course, conducts weekend workshops for personal and professional growth, publishes a free quarterly newsletter, and offers a broad spectrum of books, tapes, and curriculum guides. Write for a free copy of their newsletter/catalogue.

---

7. *Set goals and objectives.* Until our visions are broken down into specific and measurable goals—with timelines and deadlines—we are not likely to move forward very quickly. I teach students how to set measurable goals and objectives for self, family, school, and community. They then share their goals with the rest of the class, support one another as they work toward them, and celebrate any completed goals.

8. *Use visualization.* The most powerful yet underutilized tool in education is visualization. When we hold a clear vision of our goals as if they were already achieved, the action releases creativity, increases motivation, and actually alters our perceptions of ourselves and our environments. I ask students to spend five minutes per day visualizing each of their goals and objectives as if it were already achieved. This can produce radical results very quickly.

9. *Take action.* To be successful, you yourself have to "do the doing." I often cite the following example: you cannot hire someone else to do your push-ups for you and expect to develop your muscles. I constantly work with students to stretch into more and more action steps—doing things they previously did not think possible.

10. *Respond to feedback—and persevere.* I try to inspire students with stories of people like themselves who have gone on to do great things, often by working against the odds; for example, Wilma Rudolph, the great track star who was told as a youth that she would never walk again. I show them how to use mistakes for growth, to employ positive as well as negative feedback to their advantage, and to persevere until they accomplish their goals.

When teachers use these 10 steps in their classrooms, the improvements in students' self-esteem and achievement are rewarding. A comment from a teacher who participated in one of my workshops sums up the dramatic change that can occur in a child's life:

I used to think all I needed to do was to teach mathematics well. Now I teach children, not math. . . . The youngster who really made me understand this was Eddie. When I asked him one day why he thought he was doing so much better than last year, he replied, "It's because I like myself now when I'm with you."

Girls at 11

An Interview with Carol Gilligan

Since the publication of her widely acclaimed book In a Different Voice *(1982), Carol Gilligan, a professor at Harvard University, has conducted and encouraged research on the development of girls. Her new project, "Strengthening Healthy Resistance and Courage in Preadolescent Girls," involves her in interviewing fourth- and sixth-grade girls in public and private schools, observing them in their classrooms, and participating with them in an afterschool club.*

HEL: Girls of 10 and 11 years old have the reputation of being somewhat bossy, or recalcitrant. Is there any contradiction between this and the intriguing title of your new project?

CG: Girls at that age are sometimes called bossy. Based on our studies of development we prefer to think of them as astute observers of the human social world and stalwart resisters of outside pressure to relinquish their own perceptions and judgment.

They seem to carry around a kind of "field guide"—a naturalist's guide to human feelings—not summarized or abstracted, but detailed: how a person feels after this or that event; and of course sequences, narratives of relationships. If so-and-so does something to so-and-so, what happens.

My colleague Lyn Mikel Brown recently analyzed the narratives told by 7-to-16-year-old girls and discovered a key shift just around the age of 11. At this point, girls describe an internal struggle between what they value and what is "good" for them—as defined by their mothers, teachers, or others with greater experience and recognized authority.

In the face of this conflict, girls may begin to feel guilty about attending to their own needs and wants. But 11-year-old girls still value their experiences and knowledge. And they will speak out publicly. If a teacher misinterprets a sixth-grade girl's statement, the girl is likely to insist "That is not what I meant," rather than acquiesce or say "never mind."

HEL: So why does this resistance need strengthening?

CG: Sometime between the ages of 11 and 12, there is a change. I used to ask, "When responsibility to self and others conflicts, how should one choose?" Eleven-year-olds said, "Can you give me an example? That never happens." As one told me, "I am in all my relationships."

Girls a year older would ponder at length over whether it was better to act in terms of yourself or the relationship. In other words, they had begun to separate "self" from relationship—to accept damaging conventions like defining care in terms of self-sacrifice.

In the face of these conventions, it's hard for girls to hold on to their own knowledge about caring and relationships. The clarity and outspokenness disappear. They equivocate, and sometimes even take desperate action to preserve a relationship or meet the expectations of others. They may, for example, risk pregnancy to please a boyfriend or ride in a car with a drunk driver rather than offend a friend.

HEL: What happens to their previous knowledge?

CG: By mid-adolescence, many girls come to question the validity of their own perceptions or feelings and, as a result, become deeply confused about what constitutes truth or trust in relationships. In a sense they withdraw their real selves from their relationships.

Adolescence poses a crisis of connection to a girl coming of age in this culture. What she can say is not what she deeply knows—except when she is in a carefully checked-out, private place. The dilemma is very real, and her solution—I think of it as brilliant, but highly costly—is to take that which she values most and remove it from the situation. It's an incredible price to pay. She loses her voice and connection with others. She is at risk psychologically, in danger of drowning or going underground.

HEL: Isn't adolescence a difficult stage for both boys and girls? Are adolescent girls more at risk?

CG: Adolescent boys come of age in a world "prepared" for them, or "like" them in a very real sense. Conventional norms and values strengthen male voices at adolescence. This is not as true for girls.

Lyn Brown has documented the ways girls struggle over whether to articulate their perceptions. They wonder: "Will I be taken seriously?" "Will I damage my relationships?" If girls resist the conventions, they must continually struggle to authorize their own voices with very little support from the social system or from institutions like the schools.

I think there may be a greater asymmetry than any of us have ever imagined between girls' and boys' development—in other words, a real difference. I do not mean one is better, one is worse. To understand this you have to put away the usual assumption about child development—that there is a parallel, lockstep progression, with boys and girls marching side by side, stage by stage, toward adulthood.

Adolescence, particularly early adolescence, may be a watershed in girls' development, comparable in some respects to early childhood for boys. There is evidence in the research literature for this theory. For example, Glen Elder and Avshalom Caspi studied families under stress—children of the Great Depression, and families during World War II—and found that the most vulnerable children were boys in early childhood and adolescent girls.

When boys experience psychological difficulties in adolescence, there's usually a history that goes back to childhood. Whereas girls tend to experience these difficulties for the first time in adolescence. They become depressed; by the age of 17 they feel significantly worse about themselves than boys do.

HEL: What implications does this have for educators?

CG: The dilemma of girls' education tends to come to crisis in early adolescence. Girls are encouraged to give up their own experience and tune into the way other people want them to see things. They replace their detailed knowledge of the social world with an idealized, stereotyped notion of relationships and of the type of girl people admire. This nice or perfect girl isn't angry or selfish, and she certainly doesn't disagree in public.

At a faculty meeting in one school we studied, an experienced teacher said. "How can we help the girls to deal with disagreement in public when we can't do it ourselves?" The women then began to talk about how they discussed conflict privately, on the telephone at night, in the bathroom after meetings—but not in public. Girls learn a lot about what is acceptable behavior for women from observing the adults around them.

HEL: It's interesting to think about the role of women teachers. Often girls' problems in high school have been talked about in terms of the insensitivity of male teachers.

CG: Relationships between girls and adult women may be particularly critical during the transition into adolescence. Preadolescents seek out and listen attentively to advice from women; they observe how we treat one another and how we negotiate relationships; they note inconsistencies and discrepancies, and they want to talk about them.

In our studies we have noted that girls often feel abandoned or betrayed by women: they see that mothers on whom they have relied for support can all but disappear in the world. They also become confused about the messages and behaviors of women teachers.

In one school where we did interviews, the younger girls—in the lower school—thought of their teachers as extremely knowledgeable. They could do such essential things as help children learn to read, and you could talk to them about important questions such as "If I have to choose someone for my team and I have two friends, how do I do it without losing a friend?"

But the upper-school teachers did not credit their lower-school colleagues with knowing a great deal. They talked about their colleagues as "nice," or "good with children"—the kinds of things people say about mothers and elementary school teachers. You could predict that girls would have trouble in the middle grades, because their passage to the culture of the upper school was going to involve a kind of betrayal.

HEL: Girls at this age can also betray or be mean to each other. Why are cliques so common?

CG: Last summer Annie Rogers and I started the "Strengthening Healthy Resistance" project with a writing, outings, and theater club. Every time we got on a bus, every time we walked, the most important question among the girls was who would be with whom. Everything else paled in intensity.

One way to think about a clique is as an experiment in inclusion and exclusion, a way of gaining information about how it feels to be left out or taken in, and how it feels to include or exclude others. If you take relationships seriously, these are enormously weighty questions. Cliques are an awkward and often extremely painful way in which girls begin to deal with some of these questions.

I also think cliques are a dark mirroring of what girls see in relationships among women. It's not surprising that when cliques start to form, women freeze. We reexperience our own helplessness, and either tell girls they can't act this way or don't engage with them around the issue because it's just too painful. Our selective or ineffective response is part of a tacit agreement that this is how life among women goes.

HEL: Have you found ways to create a different kind of interaction?

CG: The project is premised on our belief that preadolescent girls can benefit from particular kinds of relationships with one another and with adult women. We believe that girls, in order to strengthen their capacities for resistance, courage, and creativity, have to learn to face fears of displeasing others, to feel the genuine risks that are an inevitable part of important relationships, and to sustain their disagreements.

The central activities of the club are journal writing, theater projects, field trips, and group discussion. We want the girls to have opportunities to observe the world and to sort out discrepancies between what they see and what they believe they're supposed to think. The goal is to help them hold on to the veracity of their own perceptions and feelings, even in the face of contradictory norms, and thus to be in real rather than fraudulent relationships with themselves, with others, and with the world.

We also try to provide a safe place for them to explore disagreements. The group discussions become experiments for the girls in speaking publicly about what they know, in being honest with one another and with two adult women.

As the adults, we have to be willing to confront ourselves honestly as well: that is, to consider our own experiences and assumptions about being female in this society at this time and about what it means for women to foster the education and development of girls.

On Our Changing Family Values

A Conversation with David Elkind

MARGE SCHERER

Most of us are familiar with the term "nuclear family." And we are also aware that the demographics have changed, that there are many more nontraditional families today. You take the idea further and introduce the idea of the postmodern family. Would you explain that concept?

The modern nuclear family—two parents, two and one-half children, with one parent at home with the children—is fast disappearing. We now have the postmodern family, what I call the permeable family—two parents working; single-parent families; adoptive families; remarried families; and so on. The permeable family is more fluid, more flexible, and more obviously vulnerable to pressures from outside itself. It mirrors the openness, complexity, and diversity of our contemporary lifestyles.

In Ties That Stress you explain some of the historical forces that have shaped families of the past and families today. Would you give us a capsule history?

Around the '50s, most of us lived in nuclear families. We operated under the assumptions that women should stay home, men should be the

providers, and the children were to be protected. Then many events changed us, like World War II, the atomic bomb, the Holocaust, then later the Women's Rights movement, the Civil Rights movement, Watergate. These events and their consequences challenged our basic ideas about how the world works. For example, we began to doubt the notion that after World War II, there would never be another major war; that everyday and in every way, we're getting better and better.

And how has this new, more pessimistic thinking about the world changed family values?

As a consequence of these events, we began to see the sentiments of the modern nuclear family as overly idealized and blind to the dark side of human behavior. For example, couples used to believe in romantic love—that there was just one person in the whole world for you and once you found that person you would live happily ever after, without having to work at the relationship. Our divorce rate contradicts the notion.

Second, there was the notion of maternal love, the belief that women possessed a maternal instinct to be with their children all the time, and make a nest, and that if they didn't, something was wrong with them. When the maternal love notion became very prominent, husbands began to think that they should be included within that maternal love and should be looked after in the manner of children. It

David Elkind is Professor of Child Study at Tufts University, 105 College Ave., Medford, MA 02155. He is the author of many books, including *Ties That Stress: The New Family Imbalance,* (Cambridge: Harvard University Press, 1994). Marge Scherer is Managing Editor of *Educational Leadership.*

put a heavy burden on women. Today we talk more about shared parenting than maternal instinct.

A third sentiment of the nuclear family was domesticity and the idea that the home was the center of one's life. That really grew out of the movement into cities and industrialization. The factory was a cold hard place, and the factory worker was a cog in a machine. In contrast, the home was a warm, welcoming place in a heartless world. And in that home, the mother was the center. She had had—up until the turn of the century—creative outlets such as quilting, canning, cooking, and baking. The industrialization of home products robbed women of creative outlets. Women were told not to grind their own coffee because they could buy it vacuum-packed, not to bake their own bread because they could buy Wonder Bread, not to make their own clothes because factory-made clothes were much cheaper. Women were turned into consumers, which eventually contributed in a very important way to the women's movement.

Those were the three major sentiments of the nuclear family, and they've been supplanted with new sentiments, those of consensual love, shared parenting, and urbanity.

We talk a lot about family values. The real family value that grew out of the nuclear family sentiments was that of togetherness. It's the notion that the family is the most important relationship in one's life. Parents don't divorce because family is more important than personal needs or happiness. In the same way, business comes after, not before the family. Obviously all families didn't live by these rules, but togetherness was the ideal.

And these notions are gradually being eroded and replaced with new sentiments that are not idealistic?

I want to make it very clear. I'm not arguing that the nuclear family was good and the postmodern, permeable family, bad, or vice versa. There is a lot of misunderstanding about postmodernism. Some identify it with trendy fads in literature and the arts. But it is a more general movement that argues that the modern beliefs—for example, the belief in progress—have to be modified in light of world events. Postmodernism really challenges some of the ideas of modernity, but it also tries to incorporate what is good from the past, just as postmodern architecture takes what it sees as good from the past but also discards what doesn't work.

What happened to the family was thanks to the sexual revolution and new contraceptive methods,

premarital sex became socially acceptable. And that had the effect of making virginity lose its value. That's a significant point because it means that relationships are very different today. The implicit contract based on an exchange of virginity for commitment no longer exists. The basis of the contract has become consensual. Marriage is an agreement between two equals, with the idea that we'll stay in the relationship as long as it serves our purposes and needs. It's more egalitarian, and it gives adults many more options.

Talk more about the family values of today that supplant the old values, like autonomy replacing togetherness.

Instead of togetherness, we have a new focus on autonomy. The individual becomes more important than the family, not because of egocentrism or narcissism, but rather because of a rapidly changing society and economy. We hear about layoffs everyday. Occupations that never even existed before are invented, and whole other occupations disappear. It's a difficult time for people occupationally.

When I lived in Rochester, generations had worked for Eastman Kodak. Your parents worked there, you were working there, your kids were going to work there. The company—they called it Mother Kodak—had recreation centers, health centers. And you bought stock and you had security. All of that has changed.

Parents today have to protect themselves first, much as in an airplane they must put the breathing mask on themselves before they put it on their child. To make sure that their children are provided for, they devote tremendous time to working and refurbishing their skills. So, too often, parents are focused on their own activities, forcing kids to be autonomous as well—to be much more independent, to be home alone, to get their own meals, to organize their own time.

The notion of autonomy is that each person should be free to follow his or her own trajectory. The family meal has gone by the board. It used to be a gathering place for the nuclear family. Today soccer practice or a business meeting takes precedence over dinner because personal needs are more important than the family.

You don't urge people to have the family meal anymore, or do you?

If possible, it's wonderful but increasingly difficult in today's world. Rituals are, nonetheless, very important for children, and even if you don't have a family meal, at least you should have certain rituals on birthdays or holidays. They may not be every day or every week, but it's important to have a time when the family can come together.

We talk a lot about quality time, but it's not really the quality of the time that is important. What is critical is that the children feel that they are important enough in their parents' lives that the parents are going to sacrifice something for them. Real quality time is when parents say, "Look, I know I have this meeting but you are more important, and I am going to come to your recital." Children need to know they are important in their parents' lives.

Children used to be thought of as innocent. But our TV shows today often depict kids as smarter than their parents. You've even said that **Home Alone** *is the perfect metaphor for our concept of childhood. Did the concept of competent children come out of popular culture or child psychology?*

It didn't come from any new discoveries in child development. We have no data indicating that children are more competent today than we knew them to be in another time in history. The perception of child competence comes directly from social changes and from our need as parents and adults to have competent children. As society has changed, we can no longer protect children in the way we once did. So now we believe we have to prepare them by exposing them to everything and anything.

Television is the prime culprit, but not the only one. We can no longer control the information flow to children. When we were dealing with print media, children had to have a certain level of intellectual ability and skill to decipher words. With television, even young children can get information visually. After the tragedy in South Carolina when a mother drowned her children, a woman called me and said, "What do I say to my 5-year-old? She saw the news on TV and she is asking, 'Mommy, are you going to kill me?' " It's a whole different world today. As a result, parents and society have to see children as competent. It's a way for us to stay sane to say, "Well, you know, they are seeing all this stuff, but they can handle it. It will prepare them for the real world."

You don't think that children today are more savvy than they used to be?

We overestimate their competence. As I travel and lecture across the country, teachers tell me routinely that they see much more aggressive behavior and much more hostility on the playgrounds. We see many more learning problems. We see much more depression in children. These are all the stress symptoms of kids who are expected to be more competent in handling all sorts of experiences than they really are.

You call this the new morbidity, all the stress-related illnesses that affect children and families.

Right. The pediatrician Robert Haggerty and his colleagues called it that. Up until mid-century, most young people died from polio, tuberculosis—from disease. Fortunately, medical science conquered these illnesses, but today we lose as many young people through stress-related causes as we once lost through disease. We lose 10,000 youngsters a year in substance abuse-related automobile accidents. We lose 5,000 kids a year in suicide. We have two million alcoholic teenagers. All of these are stress-related problems arising from the fact that in our society the needs of children and youth are simply weighted less heavily than the needs of adults. A few decades ago, women consumed millions of pounds of tranquilizers because their needs were not being met. Today children and adolescents are reacting to stress in equally self-destructive ways.

If we really want to attack this problem, we can't just talk about drug and sex education. They are important, but we have to talk about how we can better meet the needs of children and youth. Their needs for love and care and adult supervision and guidance. Their need for more space for activities. More age-appropriate curricula. More sense that they are important in their parents' lives and in the life of society.

I was watching a documentary program last night. The reporters were asking a group of kids about stealing and lying. These kids had no strong moral sense about doing these things. They didn't worry about whether the person would be hurt or damaged by taking something from them. It's not true for all of our children, but I think that to the extent we don't really care about kids, kids are not going to care about other people.

Are they a lost generation?

No, not entirely. The question is, Can a society survive when the number of kids who are lost gets larger than the number of kids who are not?

Returning to the idea of the competent child, do schools buy into that notion, too? Are there prac-

tices at school that might be creating too much stress?

One of the most serious examples of schools buying into the notion of childhood competence is the whole early childhood issue. Up until the '60s, fewer than half of children had been in early childhood programs prior to kindergarten. Today 85 percent of children enter kindergarten with some preschool experience. As a result, administrators tend to believe that a child entering 1st grade should know letters and numbers. If children don't have those literacy and numeracy skills, they are held back or put in transition classes. Nationally, we are retaining 10 to 20 percent of kids; in some communities, 50 percent. The average age in many of the suburban 1st grades now is 7.

You are saying that children this age shouldn't be retained because they might just need a few more years to develop?

Right. What people don't recognize is that the 4–7 age period is one of very rapid intellectual growth, much like the period of rapid physical growth in early adolescence. Children grow at different rates, quite independently of their intellectual potential. If a 6-year-old isn't able to read, it may have nothing to do with his or her motivation or ability and everything to do with intellectual immaturity. And we punish children simply for having different growth rates.

Pushing the curriculum down to lower grade levels is another example. The decimal fractions that used to be taught at 6th grade in a week or two are now being taught at 4th grade. It takes 4th graders a month and they still don't understand it. There are a great many things that children can learn in 4th grade. They don't have to learn decimal fractions. We should have them learning things that are challenging at their level but not so daunting that they feel frustrated.

I hear the same thing at the high school level. One instructor used to teach organic chemistry at 12th grade. Parents pushed the school to teach it at 10th grade. Many 10th graders were in tears over that course. Yet we hold to the idea that somehow anything can be taught at any time and kids can learn it.

At the same time schools are being criticized for not challenging students or for not having high standards.

There isn't sufficient individualization in the schools. High standards are best met by individualization.

Most of the printed curriculum material makes little provision for wide differences in learning styles. It's not that we shouldn't have expectations and standards, but we need to recognize that children don't all learn in the same way at the same rate.

One of the most important findings of the Tennessee study (STAR) is that class size makes a difference. It's the amount of one-on-one time between teacher and child that has the most impact.

Of course, it's easier for us to have a one-size-fits-all curriculum. And it's economically easier to have larger classes. But those concerns speak to the adult issues, not to child issues. If you reduced class size to 18, did just that one thing across the country, you'd see a remarkable improvement in education across the board.

In this issue of **Educational Leadership**, *several articles point out that there is increasing division among what parents want from schools. Some parents object to cooperative learning and call for a back-to-basics approach, prayer in the schools. Other parents want to build their child's self-esteem and have a multicultural curriculum. How can schools please parents with such different values?*

We must start from the truism that most parents want to do what's best for their children. They want schools to provide a safe place for kids. They want teachers who are trained and knowledgeable. Everybody believes that kids should know how to read, do math, and use a computer. Parents may differ over other things, but schools can't serve all needs. If parents feel strongly about religious faith, hold classes after school. We have become very secular and our society has a need for spirituality, but there is an established principle of separation of church and state. Schools can only do certain things.

A problem I see with some parents is that they want to go back to an earlier, less complicated time. But we will not get the postmodern genie back in the bottle.

If you are a teacher and you see children in your classroom who aren't receiving much attention from their parents, what do you do?

One of the things I tell our student teachers is that children want to be loved, as we all do, by the people whom they love. If that love is not reciprocated, we can't replace it. Certainly loving and caring teachers are important, but they cannot fulfill the parental role. Teachers cry out for these children, but they have to recognize there are limits to their role as providers of the kind of affection and love that kids need.

How can schools help families feel more connected to a larger community?

Many schools already are reaching out to families by providing the quality child care that is so difficult for parents to find and afford.

Another important thing schools can do is to provide parenting classes. There is a wonderful program (Parents as Teachers) in 14 midwestern states where the school systems send trainers on home visits to help young mothers engage in developmentally appropriate activities with their infants.

A lot of other things can be done—schools are bringing grandparents in, using tutors, bringing social services and health services into the school.

We have to recognize, however, that we are a very, very diverse society, not a homogeneous one. You can go to Brownsville, Texas, where 98 percent of the kids speak Spanish. You can go to some towns in California, where the kids speak eight different languages. In Groton, Connecticut, most fathers are in the Navy, and get transferred out of town every three years. The result is that no child both starts and finishes the elementary school. In communities around Pittsburgh, kids still walk to school and go home for lunch. You could lift those neighborhoods out of the '20s or '30s.

We don't sufficiently appreciate the extraordinary diversity of our society. It's one of our great strengths. There is no one way to interact with the community. Schools have to work with the community in ways that are meaningful in their particular miniature world.

One last question. Some of us have grown up in nuclear families and are experiencing all the stresses of postmodern families today. What's next for families?

I am hopeful that we will move beyond the permeable family to a *vital* family that meets the needs of both parents and children. The problem with the postmodern permeable family was that it went to extremes. Erik Erikson once said something to the effect that to be heard in our society, you have to take an extreme position and shout it loudly. Once your position is heard and taken seriously, then you can move back to a middle ground. I hope that we are moving back toward a more balanced family. I see some signs of it, especially in our concern with community.

Statistics show that young people are marrying later and are having fewer children. They are trying in their own lives not to make the mistakes their parents made. They don't want to go through divorce. When they do get into a relationship, they want to make it work. This bodes well for the family. At schools, there is a new excitement about change. Hopefully, we will individualize more and begin to place the needs of teachers and children on a par with political and economic considerations. That's the most significant way schools can help families.

Teaching Themes of Care

NEL NODDINGS

Some educators today—and I include myself among them—would like to see a complete reorganization of the school curriculum. We would like to give a central place to the questions and issues that lie at the core of human existence. One possibility would be to organize the curriculum around themes of care—caring for self, for intimate others, for strangers and global others, for the natural world and its nonhuman creatures, for the human-made world, and for ideas.[1]

A realistic assessment of schooling in the present political climate makes it clear that such a plan is not likely to be implemented. However, we can use the rich vocabulary of care in educational planning and introduce themes of care into regular subject-matter classes. In this article, I will first give a brief rationale for teaching themes of care; second, I will suggest ways of choosing and organizing such themes; and, finally, I'll say a bit about the structures required to support such teaching.

WHY TEACH CARING?

In an age when violence among schoolchildren is at an unprecedented level, when children are bearing children with little knowledge of how to care for them, when the society and even the schools often concentrate on materialistic messages, it may be unnecessary to argue that we should care more genuinely for our children and teach them to care.

Nel Noddings is Lee Jacks Professor of Child Education at Stanford University and author of *The Challenge to Care in Schools* (Teachers College Press, 1992).

However, many otherwise reasonable people seem to believe that our educational problems consist largely of low scores on achievement tests. My contention is, first, that we should want more from our educational efforts than adequate academic achievement and, second, that we will not achieve even that meager success unless our children believe that they themselves are cared for and learn to care for others.

There is much to be gained, both academically and humanly, by including themes of care in our curriculum. First, such inclusion may well expand our students' cultural literacy. For example, as we discuss in math classes the attempts of great mathematicians to prove the existence of God or to reconcile a God who is all good with the reality of evil in the world, students will hear names, ideas, and words that are not part of the standard curriculum. Although such incidental learning cannot replace the systematic and sequential learning required by those who plan careers in mathematically oriented fields, it can be powerful in expanding students' cultural horizons and in inspiring further study.

Second, themes of care help us to connect the standard subjects. The use of literature in mathematics classes, of history in science classes, and of art and music in all classes can give students a feeling of the wholeness in their education. After all, why should they seriously study five different subjects if their teachers, who are educated people, only seem to know and appreciate one?

Third, themes of care connect our students and our subjects to great existential questions. What is the meaning of life? Are there gods? How should I live?

Fourth, sharing such themes can connect us person-to-person. When teachers discuss themes of care, they may become real persons to their students and so enable them to construct new knowledge. Martin Buber put it this way:

> *Trust, trust in the world, because this human being exists—that is the most inward achievement of the relation in education. Because this human being exists, meaninglessness, however hard pressed you are by it, cannot be the real truth. Because this human being exists, in the darkness the light lies hidden, in fear salvation, and in the callousness of one's fellow-man the great love.*[2]

Finally, I should emphasize that caring is not just a warm, fuzzy feeling that makes people kind and likable. Caring implies a continuous search for competence. When we care, we want to do our very best for the objects of our care. To have as our educational goal the production of caring, competent, loving, and lovable people is not anti-intellectual. Rather, it demonstrates respect for the full range of human talents. Not all human beings are good at or interested in mathematics, science, or British literature. But all humans can be helped to lead lives of deep concern for others, for the natural world and its creatures, and for the preservation of the human-made world. They can be led to develop the skills and knowledge necessary to make positive contributions, regardless of the occupation they may choose.

CHOOSING AND ORGANIZING THEMES OF CARE

Care is conveyed in many ways. At the institutional level, schools can be organized to provide continuity and support for relationships of care and trust.[3] At the individual level, parents and teachers show their caring through characteristic forms of attention: by cooperating in children's activities, by sharing their own dreams and doubts, and by providing carefully for the steady growth of the children in their charge. Personal manifestations of care are probably more important in children's lives than any particular curriculum or pattern of pedagogy.

However, curriculum can be selected with caring in mind. That is, educators can manifest their care in the choice of curriculum, and appropriately chosen curriculum can contribute to the growth of children as carers. Within each large domain of care, many topics are suitable for thematic units: in the domain of "caring for self," for example, we might consider life stages, spiritual growth, and what it means to develop an admirable character; in exploring the topic of caring for intimate others, we might include units on love, friendship, and parenting; under the theme of caring for strangers and global others, we might study war, poverty, and tolerance; in addressing the idea of caring for the human-made world, we might encourage competence with the machines that surround us and a real appreciation for the marvels of technology. Many other examples exist. Furthermore, there are at least two different ways to approach the development of such themes: units can be constructed by interdisciplinary teams, or themes can be identified by individual teachers and addressed periodically throughout a year's or semester's work.

The interdisciplinary approach is familiar in core programs, and such programs are becoming more and more popular at the middle school level. One key to a successful interdisciplinary unit is the degree of genuinely enthusiastic support it receives from the teachers involved. Too often, arbitrary or artificial groupings are formed, and teachers are forced to make contributions that they themselves do not value highly. For example, math and science teachers are sometimes automatically lumped together, and rich humanistic possibilities may be lost. If I, as a math teacher, want to include historical, biographical, and literary topics in my math lessons, I might prefer to work with English and social studies teachers. Thus it is important to involve teachers in the initial selection of broad areas for themes, as well as in their implementation.

Such interdisciplinary arrangements also work well at the college level. I recently received a copy of the syllabus for a college course titled "The Search for Meaning," which was co-taught by an economist, a university chaplain, and a psychiatrist.[4] The course is interdisciplinary, intellectually rich, and aimed squarely at the central questions of life.

At the high school level, where students desperately need to engage in the study and practice of caring, it is harder to form interdisciplinary teams. A conflict arises as teachers acknowledge the intensity of the subject-matter preparation their students need for further education. Good teachers often wish there were time in the day to co-teach unconventional topics of great importance, and they even admit that their students are not getting what they need for full personal development. But they feel constrained by the requirements of a highly competitive world and the structures of schooling established by that world.

Is there a way out of this conflict? Imaginative, like-minded teachers might agree to emphasize a particular theme in their separate classes. Such themes as war, poverty, crime, racism, or sexism can be addressed in almost every subject area. The teachers should agree on some core ideas related to caring that will be discussed in all classes, but beyond the central commitment to address themes of care, the topics can be handled in whatever way seems suitable in a given subject.

Consider, for example, what a mathematics class might contribute to a unit on crime. Statistical information might be gathered on the location and number of crimes, on rates for various kinds of crime, on the ages of offenders, and on the cost to society; graphs and charts could be constructed. Data on changes in crime rates could be assembled. Intriguing questions could be asked: Were property crime rates lower when [the] penalties were more severe—when, for example, even children were hanged as thieves? What does an average criminal case cost by way of lawyers' fees, police investigation, and court processing? Does it cost more to house a youth in a detention center or in an elite private school?

None of this would have to occupy a full period every day. The regular sequential work of the math class could go on at a slightly reduced rate (e.g., fewer textbook exercises as homework), and the work on crime could proceed in the form of interdisciplinary projects over a considerable period of time. Most important would be the continual reminder in all classes that the topic is part of a larger theme of caring for strangers and fellow citizens. It takes only a few minutes to talk about what it means to live in safety, to trust one's neighbors, to feel secure in greeting strangers. Students should be told that metal detectors and security guards were not part of their parents' school lives, and they should be encouraged to hope for a safer and more open future. Notice the words I've used in this paragraph: caring, trust, safety, strangers, hope. Each could be used as an organizing theme for another unit of study.

English and social studies teachers would obviously have much to contribute to a unit on crime. For example, students might read *Oliver Twist,* and they might also study and discuss the social condi-

tions that seemed to promote crime in 19th-century England. Do similar conditions exist in our country today? The selection of materials could include both classic works and modern stories and films. Students might even be introduced to some of the mystery stories that adults read so avidly on airplanes and beaches, and teachers should be engaged in lively discussion about the comparative value of the various stories.

Science teachers might find that a unit on crime would enrich their teaching of evolution. They could bring up the topic of social Darwinism, which played such a strong role in social policy during the late 19th and early 20th centuries. To what degree are criminal tendencies inherited? Should children be tested for the genetic defects that are suspected of predisposing some people to crime? Are females less competent than males in moral reasoning? (Why did some scientists and philosophers think this was true?) Why do males commit so many more violent acts than females?

Teachers of the arts can also be involved. A unit on crime might provide a wonderful opportunity to critique "gangsta rap" and other currently popular forms of music. Students might profitably learn how the control of art contributed to national criminality during the Nazi era. These are ideas that pop into my mind. Far more various and far richer ideas will come from teachers who specialize in these subjects.

There are risks, of course, in undertaking any unit of study that focuses on matters of controversy or deep existential concern, and teachers should anticipate these risks. What if students want to compare the incomes of teachers and cocaine dealers? What if they point to contemporary personalities from politics, entertainment, business, or sports who seem to escape the law and profit from what seems to be criminal behavior? My own inclination would be to allow free discussion of these cases and to be prepared to counteract them with powerful stories of honesty, compassion, moderation, and charity.

An even more difficult problem may arise. Suppose a student discloses his or her own criminal activities? Fear of this sort of occurrence may send teachers scurrying for safer topics. But, in fact, any instructional method that uses narrative forms or encourages personal expression runs this risk. For example, students of English as a second language who write proudly about their own hard lives and new hopes may disclose that their parents are illegal immigrants. A girl may write passages that lead her teacher to suspect sexual abuse. A boy may brag about objects he has "ripped off." Clearly, as we use these powerful methods that encourage students to initiate discussion and share their experiences, we must reflect on the ethical issues involved, consider appropriate responses to such issues, and prepare teachers to handle them responsibly.

Caring teachers must help students make wise decisions about what information they will share about themselves. On the one hand, teachers want their students to express themselves, and they want their students to trust in and consult them. On the other hand, teachers have an obligation to protect immature students from making disclosures that they might later regret. There is a deep ethical problem here. Too often educators assume that only religious fundamentalists and right-wing extremists object to the discussion of emotionally and morally charged issues. In reality, there is a real danger of intrusiveness and lack of respect in methods that fail to recognize the vulnerability of students. Therefore, as teachers plan units and lessons on moral issues, they should anticipate the tough problems that may arise. I am arguing here that it is morally irresponsible to simply ignore existential questions and themes of care; we must attend to them. But it is equally irresponsible to approach these deep concerns without caution and careful preparation.

So far I have discussed two ways of organizing interdisciplinary units on themes of care. In one, teachers actually teach together in teams; in the other, teachers agree on a theme and a central focus on care, but they do what they can, when they can, in their own classrooms. A variation on this second way—which is also open to teachers who have to work alone—is to choose several themes and weave them into regular course material over an entire semester or year. The particular themes will depend on the interests and preparation of each teacher.

For example, if I were teaching high school mathematics today, I would use religious/existential questions as a pervasive theme because the biographies of mathematicians are filled with accounts of their speculations on matters of God, other dimensions, and the infinite—and because these topics fascinate me. There are so many wonderful stories to be told: Descartes' proof of the existence of God, Pascal's famous wager, Plato's world of forms, Newton's attempt to verify Biblical chronology, Leibnitz' detailed theodicy, current attempts to describe a divine domain in terms of metasystems, and mystical speculations on the infinite.[5] Some of these stories can be told as rich "asides" in five minutes or

less. Others might occupy the better part of several class periods.

Other mathematics teachers might use an interest in architecture and design, art, music, or machinery as continuing themes in the domain of "caring for the human-made world." Still others might introduce the mathematics of living things. The possibilities are endless. In choosing and pursuing these themes, teachers should be aware that they are both helping their students learn to care and demonstrating their own caring by sharing interests that go well beyond the demands of textbook pedagogy.

Still another way to introduce themes of care into regular classrooms is to be prepared to respond spontaneously to events that occur in the school or in the neighborhood. Older teachers have one advantage in this area: they probably have a greater store of experience and stories on which to draw. However, younger teachers have the advantage of being closer to their students' lives and experiences; they are more likely to be familiar with the music, films, and sports figures that interest their students.

All teachers should be prepared to respond to the needs of students who are suffering from the death of friends, conflicts between groups of students, pressure to use drugs or to engage in sex, and other troubles so rampant in the lives of today's children. Too often schools rely on experts—"grief counselors" and the like—when what children really need is the continuing compassion and presence of adults who represent constancy and care in their lives. Artificially separating the emotional, academic, and moral care of children into tasks for specially designated experts contributes to the fragmentation of life in schools.

Of course, I do not mean to imply that experts are unnecessary, nor do I mean to suggest that some matters should not be reserved for parents or psychologists. But our society has gone too far in compartmentalizing the care of its children. When we ask whose job it is to teach children how to care, an appropriate initial response is "Everyone's." Having accepted universal responsibility, we can then ask about the special contributions and limitations of various individuals and groups.

SUPPORTING STRUCTURES

What kind of schools and teacher preparation are required, if themes of care are to be taught effectively?

First, and most important, care must be taken seriously as a major purpose of schools; that is, educators must recognize that caring for students is fundamental in teaching and that developing people with a strong capacity for care is a major objective of responsible education. Schools properly pursue many other objectives—developing artistic talent, promoting multicultural understanding, diversifying curriculum to meet the academic and vocational needs of all students, forging connections with community agencies and parents, and so on. Schools cannot be single-purpose institutions. Indeed, many of us would argue that it is logically and practically impossible to achieve that single academic purpose if other purposes are not recognized and accepted. This contention is confirmed in the success stories of several inner-city schools.[6]

Once it is recognized that school is a place in which students are cared for and learn to care, that recognition should be powerful in guiding policy. In the late 1950s, schools in the U.S., under the guidance of James Conant and others, placed the curriculum at the top of the educational priority list. Because the nation's leaders wanted schools to provide high-powered courses in mathematics and science, it was recommended that small high schools be replaced by efficient larger structures complete with sophisticated laboratories and specialist teachers. Economies of scale were anticipated, but the main argument for consolidation and regionalization centered on the curriculum. All over the country, small schools were closed, and students were herded into larger facilities with "more offerings." We did not think carefully about schools as communities and about what might be lost as we pursued a curriculum-driven ideal.

Today many educators are calling for smaller schools and more family-like groupings. These are good proposals, but teachers, parents, and students should be engaged in continuing discussion about what they are trying to achieve through the new arrangements. For example, if test scores do not immediately rise, participants should be courageous in explaining that test scores were not the main object of the changes. Most of us who argue for caring in schools are intuitively quite sure that children in such settings will in fact become more competent learners. But, if they cannot prove their academic competence in a prescribed period of time, should we give up on caring and on teaching them to care? That would be foolish. There is more to life and learning than the academic proficiency demonstrated by test scores.

In addition to steadfastness of purpose, schools must consider continuity of people and place. If we are concerned with caring and community, then we must make it possible for students and teachers to stay together for several years so that mutual trust can develop and students can feel a sense of belonging in their "schoolhome."[7]

More than one scheme of organization can satisfy the need for continuity. Elementary school children can stay with the same teacher for several years, or they can work with a stable team of specialist teachers for several years. In the latter arrangement, there may be program advantages; that is, children taught by subject-matter experts who get to know them well over an extended period of time may learn more about the particular subjects. At the high school level, the same specialist teachers might work with students throughout their years in high school. Or, as Theodore Sizer has suggested, one teacher might teach two subjects to a group of 30 students rather than one subject to 60 students, thereby reducing the number of different adults with whom students interact each day.[8] In all the suggested arrangements, placements should be made by mutual consent whenever possible. Teachers and students who hate or distrust one another should not be forced to stay together.

A policy of keeping students and teachers together for several years supports caring in two essential ways: it provides time for the development of caring relations, and it makes teaching themes of care more feasible. When trust has been established, teacher and students can discuss matters that would be hard for a group of strangers to approach, and classmates learn to support one another in sensitive situations.

The structural changes suggested here are not expensive. If a high school teacher must teach five classes a day, it costs no more for three of the classes to be composed of continuing students than for all five classes to comprise new students—i.e., strangers. The recommended changes come directly out of a clear-headed assessment of our major aims and purposes. We failed to suggest them earlier because we had other, too limited, goals in mind.

I have made one set of structural changes sound easy, and I do believe that they are easily made. But the curricular and pedagogical changes that are required may be more difficult. High school textbooks rarely contain the kinds of supplementary material I have described, and teachers are not formally prepared to incorporate such material. Too often, even the people we regard as strongly prepared in a liberal arts major are unprepared to discuss the history of their subject, its relation to other subjects, the biographies of its great figures, its connections to the great existential questions, and the ethical responsibilities of those who work in that discipline. To teach themes of care in an academically effective way, teachers will have to engage in projects of self-education.

At present, neither liberal arts departments nor schools of education pay much attention to connecting academic subjects with themes of care. For example, biology students may learn something of the anatomy and physiology of mammals but nothing at all about the care of living animals; they may never be asked to consider the moral issues involved in the annual euthanasia of millions of pets. Mathematics students may learn to solve quadratic equations but never study what it means to live in a mathematicized world. In enlightened history classes, students may learn something about the problems of racism and colonialism but never hear anything about the evolution of childhood, the contributions of women in both domestic and public caregiving, or the connection between the feminization of caregiving and public policy. A liberal education that neglects matters that are central to a fully human life hardly warrants the name,[9] and a professional education that confines itself to technique does nothing to close the gaps in liberal education.

The greatest structural obstacle, however, may simply be legitimizing the inclusion of themes of care in the curriculum. Teachers in the early grades have long included such themes as a regular part of their work, and middle school educators are becoming more sensitive to developmental needs involving care. But secondary schools—where violence, apathy, and alienation are most evident—do little to develop the capacity to care. Today, even elementary teachers complain that the pressure to produce high test scores inhibits the work they regard as central to their mission: the development of caring and competent people. Therefore, it would seem that the most fundamental change required is one of attitude. Teachers can be very special people in the lives of children, and it should be legitimate for them to spend time developing relations of trust, talking with students about problems that are central to their lives, and guiding them toward greater sensitivity and competence across all the domains of care.

NOTES

1. For the theoretical argument, see Nel Noddings, *The Challenge to Care in Schools* (New York: Teachers College Press, 1992); for a practical example and rich documentation, see Sharon Quint, *Schooling Homeless Children* (New York: Teachers College Press, 1994).

2. Martin Buber, *Between Man and Man* (New York: Macmillan, 1965), p. 98.

3. Noddings, chap. 12.

4. See Thomas H. Naylor, William H. Willimon, and Magdalena R. Naylor, *The Search for Meaning* (Nashville, Tenn.: Abingdon Press, 1994).

5. For many more examples, see Nel Noddings, *Educating for Intelligent Belief and Unbelief* (New York: Teachers College Press, 1993).

6. See Deborah Meier, "How Our Schools Could Be," *Phi Delta Kappan*, January 1995, pp. 369–73; and Quint, op. cit.

7. See Jane Roland Martin, *The Schoolhome: Rethinking Schools for Changing Families* (Cambridge, Mass.: Harvard University Press, 1992).

8. Theodore Sizer, *Horace's Compromise: The Dilemma of the American High School* (Boston: Houghton Mifflin, 1984).

9. See Bruce Wilshire, *The Moral Collapse of the University* (Albany: State University of New York Press, 1990).

Chapter 4: Learning Abilities and Learning Problems

Myths, Countermyths, and Truths about Intelligence

ROBERT J. STERNBERG

Ten myths and countermyths about intelligence are considered, as well as what is currently our best account of the truth. We need to be circumspect in our claims for tests of intelligence and for what intelligence can tell us about people in general.

Educational Researcher, *Vol. 25, No. 2, pp. 11–16*

Is intelligence one thing or many? Is it modifiable or not? Is it inherited or is it environmental? Are there differences between racial and ethnic groups or aren't there? Educators, laypersons, and even psychologists are confused about these issues as never before, in part because of the conflicting claims that have arisen out of *The Bell Curve* (Herrnstein & Murray, 1994) and various responses to it (e.g., Fraser, 1995; Jacoby & Glauberman, 1995), and in part because many of these issues have never been satisfactorily resolved, regardless of what has been written in the most recent in a long series of skirmishes between believers in alternative views about intelligence.

A major thesis of this article is that in the desire for simplicity and, perhaps, for the greater publicity that accompanies extreme rather than moderate statements, psychologists and others writing about intelligence have sometimes taken strong positions that are not justified by either the current state of theory or recent data. Reporters from the various media are often more interested in controversy than in sci-

entific truth, because it is controversy that sells newspapers, magazines, or whatever. Moreover, the lay public often wants simplicity, not qualifications like "the answer depends on a number of factors, including how you define the construct." But what sells magazines or books is often not what best reflects the state of our scientific knowledge. Pendulum shifts from one extreme to another may appeal to the public, but may retard the progress of both science and education, as we find that the extremes that may capture people's fancies do not work in practice.

The goal of this article is to raise some of the main questions that are being asked about intelligence and to indicate our current state of knowledge about their answers. The structure of the article is shown in Table 1 [on page 54], which lists a series of myths, countermyths, and, I believe, truths about human intelligence.

1. Is intelligence one thing or many? On no question about intelligence has there been greater disagreement among psychologists than on the question of its structure (see Sternberg, 1990, for a discussion of many alternative views). At one extreme, theorists from Spearman (1904) to Herrnstein and Murray (1994) have argued for the primacy of a

Robert J. Sternberg is IBM Professor of Psychology and Education, Department of Psychology, Yale University, P.O. Box 208205, New Haven, CT 06520-8205. He specializes in educational theory and measurement.

TABLE 1   **Myths, Mythical Countermyths, and Truths about Intelligence**

Myth	Mythical Countermyth	Truth
1. Intelligence is one thing, g (or IQ).	Intelligence is so many things you can hardly count them.	Intelligence is multidimensional but scientifically tractable.
2. The social order is a natural outcome of the IQ pecking order.	Tests wholly create a social order.	The social order is partially but not exclusively created by tests.
3. Intelligence cannot be taught to any meaningful degree.	We can perform incredible feats in teaching individuals to be more intelligent.	We can teach intelligence in at least some degree, but cannot effect radical changes at this point.
4. IQ tests measure virtually all that's important for school and job success.	IQ tests measure virtually nothing that's important for school and job success.	IQ tests measure skills that are of moderate importance in school success and of modest importance in job success.
5. We are using tests too little, losing valuable information.	We're overusing tests and should abolish them.	Tests, when properly interpreted, can serve a useful but limited function, but often they are not properly interpreted.
6. We as a society are getting stupider because of the dysgenic effects of stupid superbreeders.	We have no reason at all to fear any decline in intellectual abilities among successive generations.	We have some reason to fear loss of intellectual abilities in future generations, but the problem is not stupid superbreeders.
7. Intelligence is essentially all inherited except for trivial and unexplainable variance.	Intelligence is essentially all environmental except for trivial and unexplainable variance.	Intelligence involves substantial heritable and environmental components in interaction.
8. Racial differences in IQ clearly lead to differential outcomes.	Racial differences in IQ have nothing to do with differential environmental outcomes.	We don't really understand the relationships among race, IQ, and environmental outcomes.
9. We should write off stupid people.	There's no such thing as a stupid person. Everyone is smart.	We need to rethink what we mean by "stupid" and "smart."

general factor of intelligence; at the other extreme, theorists such as Guilford (1982) have argued for as many as 150 factors of intelligence. At the same time, we have theorists such as Gardner (1983) who argue that intelligence is not one thing but many, theorists such as Perkins (1995) who argue that intelligence is not only multiple but includes aspects of values and personality as well as cognitive skills, and theorists such as Neisser (1979) who argue that intelligence is merely a cultural invention having no existence outside our invention of it as a prototype of what we value as a culture.

The most widely accepted view at the current time is probably a hierarchical one, such as that of Carroll (1993), according to which abilities can be laid out in a hierarchy, with general ability at the top and successively more specific abilities at successively lower levels of the hierarchy. But the consensus is by no means unanimous, and in any case, scientific truth is not decided by plurality (or even majority) vote (see Sternberg & Lubart, 1995). The weight of the evidence at the present time is that

intelligence is multidimensional, and that the full range of these dimensions is not completely captured by any single general ability (Sternberg, 1994). For example, practical aspects of abilities seem to be theoretically and empirically rather distinct from more academic ones (Sternberg, 1985; Sternberg, Wagner, Williams, & Horvath, 1995).

We need to be much more cautious than we have been in trumpeting as truths our views on the nature of intelligence. In this respect, psychologists have been less than circumspect. Almost all psychologists agree, at the level of definition, that intelligence involves adaptation to the environment (see "Intelligence and Its Measurement," 1921; Sternberg & Detterman, 1986). What is left unclear is just what environment is being talked about.

If we are talking about cultural environment, it is quite clear that the overwhelming majority of theories and tests have been tailored to Western environments and might not apply as well in nonwestern ones (see Cole, 1990; Laboratory of Comparative Human Cognition, 1982). Indeed, non-Western tests might look quite different from Western ones and might create a rank-ordering different from the one we are comfortable creating.

If we are talking about biological adaptation, species other than the human one might get the last laugh. Although humans are quick to put themselves at the top of the evolutionary scale in intelligence, even evaluating dogs and other species in terms of the kinds of skills that we, as humans, value (Coren, 1994), our view may be rather species-specific. For example, if the devastation wrought by the HIV virus were attributed to extraterrestrial aliens who attacked Earth and devised weapons and counterweapons that so far always outwitted our own, we might view the aliens as smarter than we are. And if we read of some other species that was unique in the history of all species in devising the weapons of its own mass destruction, we might not necessarily conclude that this species was the most intelligent of all. The question of what is intelligent in a long-term evolutionary perspective, therefore, is wide open.

2. Is the social order a natural result of people's differing levels of intelligence? A central and particularly controversial claim of Herrnstein and Murray's (1994) is that differences in intelligence across people have resulted in the formation of a "cognitive elite." According to these authors, "no one decreed that occupations should sort us out by our cognitive abilities, and no one enforces the process. It goes on beneath the surface, guided by its own invisible hand" (p. 52).

This somewhat glib and modernized version of social Darwinism is belied by the fact, recognized by Herrnstein and Murray, that at different points in the history of civilization, different factors have sorted people into different social classes. During the Middle Ages, one's social status was completely determined by one's parentage. If you were born a noble, a noble you remained. If you were born a serf, so you remained.

Even as late as the 1950s in the United States, scores on standardized tests of cognitive abilities counted for far less in society than they do now. As Herrnstein and Murray point out, in 1950, only 55% of high school graduates in the top IQ quartile went directly to college (compared with 80% in 1980), and the mean SAT-verbal score at Harvard was a mere 583 (on the older SAT scale), compared with 678 in 1960.

The point is that societies choose their bases for sorting, and abilities measured by current cognitive tests are simply one of many bases for sorting. The abilities for which societies sort change: They have

changed in the United States over the past several decades, and they have changed in Russia over just the past several years, causing social upheaval.

We should not overestimate the importance of the fact, pointed out by Herrnstein and Murray (1994), that people in higher prestige occupations in the United States have higher IQs. Of course they do: Their passage through the gates that enable them to enter these occupations generally requires that they take cognitive tests—the SAT or ACT for college, the GRE for graduate school, the LSAT for law school, the GMAT for business school, the MCAT for medical school, and so on. If you do not score well on these tests, your ability to pass through the gates for entry into the more prestigious occupations is severely curtailed. If you do not test reasonably well, you are likely to find that you can't even get the training, much less the high-prestige job, that you well might want.

We might have chosen to focus on other attributes. For example, one could argue that creativity—which is not measured by any of the widely used cognitive tests, is at least as important for job success as are the kinds of memory and analytical abilities measured by the conventional tests (see Sternberg, 1988; Sternberg & Lubart, 1995). As a different kind of example, if we decided only to admit tall people to selective colleges, and very tall ones to graduate, law, business, and medical schools, we would notice some years after our decision that people in high-prestige occupations tend to be tall. Lest this sorting procedure sound silly, we should keep in mind that there is, in fact, a correlation between height and various kinds of success (CEOs, for example, tend to be well above average in height).

At the same time, it would be foolish to dismiss altogether the role of psychometrically measured intelligence in societal success. For better or worse, we have created a society in which such intelligence does matter, a fact amply documented by Hunter and Schmidt (Hunter & Hunter, 1984; Schmidt & Hunter, 1981, 1993). And the same skills may well matter in greater or lesser degree in other societies. Our own social order, then, is partially a function of the kinds of cognitive abilities measured by psychometric tests, but the proportions of variation accounted for in job placement, usually in the order of .1 to .3, are far from a complete explanation of what leads some people to high-prestige and others to low-prestige jobs.

3. Can intelligence be taught to any meaningful degree? Herrnstein and Murray (1994), like Jensen (1969) before them, have argued that intelligence cannot be modified to any meaningful degree. This claim is a bit strange in view of the results of one highly successful program directed by Herrnstein himself (Herrnstein, Nickerson, De Sanchez, & Swets, 1986) and of the documented success (in refereed journals) of other programs as well (e.g., Ramey, 1994). A comprehensive review of programs for teaching cognitive skills (Nickerson, Perkins, & Smith, 1985) shows that intellectual skills can be taught to at least some of the people, some of the time. Our own research is consistent with these results (Davidson & Sternberg, 1984; Gardner, Krechevsky, Sternberg, & Okagaki, 1994; Sternberg, Okagaki, & Jackson, 1990).

Whether one views the history of attempts to teach children to think and learn better as successful or not depends in part on what one's expectations are. Certainly, we have not been able to achieve dramatic gains consistently, and overblown claims have soured some by raising their expectations beyond what we can achieve. But to say that "taken together, the story of attempts to raise intelligence is one of high hopes, flamboyant claims, and disappointing results" (Herrnstein & Murray, 1994, p. 389) is an exaggeration. Disappointment is in the mind of the beholder, and in fact, many people working in the field have been cautious rather than flamboyant in their claims.

We need to keep in mind that contemporary attempts to raise intellectual abilities really date back only to the 1960s—to the Head Start program. We can scarcely expect programs in their first 10, 20, or even 30 years to have the kind of stunning success that some might have hoped for. Imagine if we judged medicine by the accomplishments of its first years in ancient Greece, or anywhere else. Moreover, our understanding of cognitive abilities has increased greatly since the 1960s, although of course there is still much to be learned. Certainly it is too early to come to the conclusion that attempts to raise intelligence have been, and will continue in the near term to be, unsuccessful. At the same time, we are in no position to claim that dramatic successes can be achieved on a regular basis.

4. Do intelligence tests measure pretty much all it takes for success in school and on the job? We discussed above the role of psychometrically measured intelligence in sorting people into various educational and job streams. How well do such tests account for success, once people are in those streams?

Again, the work of Hunter and Schmidt, cited above, as well as the work of many others, shows correlations between scores on psychometric tests of in-

telligence and both school and job performance (see, e.g., Hunt, 1995; Jensen, 1980; Ree & Earles, 1993). The cause of these correlations is unclear: Amount of schooling, for example, may affect IQ at least as much as IQ affects amount of schooling (see Ceci, 1990).

During recent years, it has also become amply clear that there is more to the cognitive abilities required for various kinds of school and job success than is measured by IQ and related constructs (such as scores on SATs and ACTs). For example, Ceci and Liker (1986) have shown that men who are successful in making bets at the race track and who use highly complex mental algorithms for predicting winners may have only average IQs. Nunes and her colleagues (Nunes, Schliemann, & Carraher, 1993) have shown that Brazilian street children who can successfully do the math to run a school business may be failing math. And Lave, Murtaugh, and de la Roche (1984) have shown that housewives who can choose better buys by computing unit prices in a supermarket cannot do comparable mathematical operations in a paper-and-pencil arithmetic-operations test.

In our own work, we have shown that measures of practical intelligence that predict success in school as well as measures of practical intelligence that predict performance on the job do not correlate meaningfully with psychometrically measured intelligence (Sternberg & Wagner, 1993; Sternberg, Wagner, & Okagaki, 1993; Sternberg et al., 1995). We have also found, however, that psychometrically measured intelligence predicts these kinds of performances independently of our own tests. In other words, psychometrically measured intelligence is a reasonable predictor of various kinds of success; it is, however, far from being the only one. Thus, it is not true that tests of constructs other than psychometric intelligence "that predict well do so largely because they happen themselves to be correlated with tests of general ability" (Herrnstein & Murray, 1994, p. 70).

5. Are we underusing, or overusing, intelligence tests? Herrnstein and Murray (1994) are not alone in their view that we are losing valuable information by not paying sufficient attention to the results of psychometric tests. Indeed, Herrnstein and Murray make these claims largely on the basis of the Hunter-Schmidt work cited above.

From the standpoint of the organization, there may indeed be economic or other gains to be had by paying more attention to scores on tests. We need to ensure that these gains are there to be had, though. For example, we found that for 10 years' worth of matriculants into our psychology graduate program at Yale, scores on the GRE, although predictive of lst-year grades in the graduate program, were not predictive of professors' ratings of students' analytical, creative, practical, research, or teaching abilities, or of dissertation ratings. When the middle 50% or even 80% of the distribution was eliminated in order greatly to increase the standard deviation of the distribution, prediction of grades shot up, but prediction of the more meaningful kinds of graduate performance did not (Sternberg & Williams, 1994).

If we are going to increase our use of tests, however, we might well wish to consider whether we should broaden the sphere of abilities tested, for example, to include important creative and practical as well as analytical abilities of the kinds measured by conventional tests (Sternberg, 1985). Moreover, we need to remember that what works well, on average, may be disastrous for certain individuals. Those who do not test well may be consistently disadvantaged by heavy reliance on tests, as may be those who are tested under inappropriate circumstances. For example, my own son was moved from the top reading group in one school to the bottom reading group in another, comparable school solely on the basis of a reading-test score obtained in his 1st day in the new school. And some gifted programs still classify children as gifted solely on the basis of a single score on a psychometric test of intelligence or related constructs.

Ultimately, the problem is not with tests, per se, but with how we use them. Tests were originally intended to level the playing field—to increase fairness by reducing the subjectivity of judgments about children. Tests can still serve this purpose, when they are used in conjunction with other predictors and when they measure diverse abilities rather than only unitary aspects of abilities.

6. Are we becoming stupider as a society as a result of the dysgenic effects of higher rates of reproduction among those with lower psychometric intelligence? Herrnstein and Murray (1994) argue that the national level of intelligence in the United States, not to mention other countries, is imperiled by the higher reproduction rates of less intelligent as compared with more intelligent individuals. A fact that they never quite successfully deal with is the so-called "Flynn effect" (Flynn, 1984, 1987)—the fact that intelligence as measured by conventional tests has been rising over a period of a number of years (at least since the 1930s), not only in the United States but in other nations as well.

Of course, it is possible and indeed likely that some influences lead to increases and others to de-

creases in psychometrically measured intelligence and that the forces leading to increase have been winning out to date, but may not continue to do so. Certainly, higher levels of education would be one of the forces leading to increases (Ceci, 1990).

It is not clear what effect differential rates of reproduction are having on national IQs, nor is it clear what we would do if it did indeed turn out that such differential rates of reproduction were lowering IQs. For one thing, they might be lowering IQs at the same time that they raised levels of other attributes that are important for adaptation. For another thing, it is not clear that IQ should serve as the basis, or even an important basis, for the valuing of a person. And perhaps most importantly, it is not clear that if our goal is to improve societal productivity and well-being in general, reproduction rates are where we should be turning our attention.

In my own view, there is a far greater source of alarm, and a far more manageable one, than differential reproduction rates. It is is the dumbing down of textbooks in the United States, which has been amply demonstrated by Reis and Renzulli (1992). The same phenomenon may be occurring elsewhere as well. One has only to compare current texts at a given grade level with the texts of 10, 20, or 30 years ago to see a progressive deterioration in our standards for what constitutes an acceptable level of reading difficulty for students of a given grade level. If one looks back at the old McGuffey Readers, one may become thoroughly depressed, so much higher were the expectations early in U.S. history than they are at present. And anyone who has written a college text, as I have, knows that the same issues that apply at the elementary and secondary levels apply at the college level as well. The pressure is to keep reading level low, not high.

Some would like to blame the publishers, but really, we have only ourselves to blame, because publishers merely produce what they find will sell. And what they have discovered is that people talk about high standards, but then buy books that meet only low ones. As it is said, educators talk out of both sides of their mouths. If we really want to help our children, we have not only to talk about high standards, but to enforce them, and a good place to start would be in our choice of texts.

7. Is intelligence essentially inherited or essentially environmental? Probably no one today would claim that individual differences in intelligence are due wholly to heredity, nor are many psychologists familiar with the data available in 1995 likely to echo the claims of Kamin (1974) that there is no credible evidence for any hereditary effects at all. The heritability of intelligence will depend, of course, on how intelligence is defined (and thus what is inherited) as well as the population about which we are talking. Available data, for example, suggest that heritability in the United States is higher for Whites than for Blacks (Scarr, in press), and that heritability increases with age (Plomin, in press).

To my knowledge, every investigator who actually studies the behavior genetics of human intelligence believes that there is some role both for heredity and for environment in intelligence (see essays in Sternberg & Grigorenko, in press). I personally am not enthusiastic about attempts to assign percentages to heredity and environment because what percentages are assigned depend on so many factors, including geographic, temporal, and other factors. Perhaps more important from an educational point of view is to realize that the heritability of intelligence is a question entirely distinct from that of the modifiability of intelligence. Intelligence could be partially or even highly heritable and, at the same time, partially or highly modifiable. The two issues are simply distinct, as shown, for example, by the fact that certain highly heritable traits are also highly modifiable. For example, height has a heritability coefficient in excess of .9, but heights have gone up in recent generations both in the United States and elsewhere. Phenylketonuria has a heritability of 1 (i.e., it is completely heritable), but its symptoms (such as mental retardation) can be alleviated by a wholly environmental intervention (withholding of phenylalanine from the diet from the time of birth). Our ability to modify intelligence, therefore, is not determined in the least by the heritability of intelligence.

8. Are there racial and ethnic group differences in intelligence, and if so, what causes them and what are their implications for societal outcomes? The difference of about 1 standard deviation between Blacks and Whites in the United States on psychometric tests of intelligence has been documented many times (Jensen, 1980), although there is also quite credible evidence that the difference has been shrinking (Nisbett, 1995), and the difference may well continue to shrink. Contrary to the claims of Herrnstein and Murray, the preponderance of evidence, reviewed by Nisbett (1995), is that the difference is environmental rather than genetic in origin. But given the probable environmental origins of the difference, we really have very little idea of what the

factors are that lead to the difference. We also need to remember that the difference is on tests that many scholars believe measure only certain aspects of intelligence, but by no means the whole thing.

Whatever the origins of the current difference between Blacks and Whites on psychometric tests, it is clear that much more is going on in terms of differences in societal outcomes than is caused by IQ differences. Herrnstein and Murray (1994) themselves point out that of Blacks and Whites with the same average IQ, Blacks are twice as likely as Whites to be in poverty (p. 326), five times more likely to be born out of wedlock (p. 331), three times more likely to be on welfare (p. 332), more than twice as likely to have lived in poverty during the first 3 years of their life (p. 335), and twice as likely to have had low birth weight (p. 334). Given that IQ was equated for Blacks and Whites, it is clear that much more is contributing to differences in societal outcomes than just IQ.

One of the greatest temptations we face, whether in education or otherwise, is that of falling victim to confirmation bias. We have a bias, whatever it may be, and then seek out or interpret evidence to support that bias. Such bias is particularly dangerous when it comes to differences between groups in levels of intelligence. One of the easiest ways to fall victim to this bias is to interpret correlational differences as causal in a direction that is consistent with one's prior expectations. Thus, suppose there are differences between groups, on average, in IQ, and also differences, on average, in societal outcomes, and suppose one believes, deep down, that the IQ differences between the groups cause the differences in outcomes. It is easy to fall into the trap of interpreting the correlational data as supporting one's causal hypothesis, when in fact one knows that correlations do not permit causal inference. IQ differences between groups may lead to differences in societal outcomes; differences in societal outcomes may lead to IQ differences; both may be dependent on some third factor. Or any combination of these three mechanisms may be at work. Moreover, we need to remember that we cannot draw conclusions about individuals from data that apply only to groups.

9. Should we write off stupid people as not having much hope of contributing much of value to society? Perhaps the most pernicious conclusions that come out of the Herrnstein-Murray book are those of the last chapters, which basically argue that we should not expect much from people with low IQs and should treat them accordingly, forming a "custodial state" that will take care of the "underclass" (Herrnstein and Murray's terms).

An alternative perspective would be that we need to rethink what we mean by intelligence, recognizing that there is more to intelligence than IQ and, more importantly, that we need not get caught in the ancient human trap of conflating some attribute of humans that we may happen to value with human worth. Somewhere, some time, it may have been noble birth; at another time or place, sheer wealth; at yet another time or place, hunting or gathering skills, physical prowess, physical attractiveness, or whatever. At any given time, we probably consider a combination of these and other attributes in assessing people. But none of these attributes is tantamount to human worth—to our values as human beings. Nor is the economic value of a person's labor, whether predicted from IQ or from something else.

It is always tempting to value most what we ourselves possess—and, in the process, to scapegoat other groups. It is happening in ethnic wars around the world. And one might argue it happens when Herrnstein and Murray (1994) cheerfully note that most readers of their book are members of the cognitive elite (p. 47) and other elite groups. We need to remember that over time and space, those at the higher rather than the lower end of the various intellectual spectra have been those most likely to be persecuted or scapegoated. However it is defined, intelligence is only one attribute of human beings and one attribute leading to certain kinds of success, but tests of intelligence can at best provide measures of certain cognitive skills (Keating, 1984); they are not measures of human worth.

The work reported herein was supported under the Javits Act program (Grant #R206R50001) as administered by the Office of Educational Research and Improvement, U.S. Department of Education. The findings and opinions expressed in this report do not reflect the positions or policies of the Office of Educational Research and Improvement or the U.S. Department of Education. Support was also provided by contracts from the Army Research Institute.

REFERENCES

Carroll, J. B. (1993). *Human cognitive abilities*. New York: Cambridge University Press.

Ceci, S. J. (1990). *On intelligence . . . more or less: A bio-ecological treatise on intellectual development*. Englewood Cliffs, NJ: Prentice-Hall.

Ceci, S. J., & Liker, J. (1986). Academic and nonacademic intelligence: An experimental separation. In R. J. Sternberg & R. K. Wagner (Eds.), *Practical intelligence: Nature and origins of competence in the everyday world* (pp. 119–142). New York: Cambridge University Press.

Cole, M. (1990). *Mind as a cultural achievement: Implications for IQ testing*. Unpublished manuscript. Hokkaido University, Sapporo, Japan.

Coren, S. (1994). *Intelligence in dogs*. New York: Macmillan.

Davidson, J. E., & Sternberg, R. J. (1984). The role of insight in intellectual giftedness. *Gifted Child Quarterly, 28*, 58–64.

Flynn, J. R. (1984). The mean IQ of Americans: Massive gains 1932 to 1978. *Psychological Bulletin, 95*, 29–51.

Flynn, J. R. (1987). Massive IQ gains in 14 nations: What IQ tests really measure. *Psychological Bulletin, 101*, 171–191.

Fraser, S. (Ed.). (1995) *The bell curve wars: Race, intelligence and the future of America*. New York: Basic Books.

Gardner, H. (1983). *Frames of mind: The theory of multiple intelligences*. New York: Basic.

Gardner, H., Krechevsky, M., Sternberg, R. J., & Okagaki, L. (1994). Intelligence in context: Enhancing students' practical intelligence for school. In K. McGilly (Ed.), *Classroom lessons: Integrating cognitive theory and classroom practice* (pp. 105–127). Cambridge, MA: Bradford Books.

Guilford, J. P. (1982). Cognitive psychology's ambiguities: Some suggested remedies. *Psychological Review, 89*, 48–59.

Herrnstein, R., & Murray, C. (1994). *The bell curve*. New York: Free Press.

Herrnstein, R. J., Nickerson, R. S., de Sanchez, M., & Swets, J. A. (1986). Teaching thinking skills. *American Psychologist, 41*, 1279–1289.

Hunt, E. (1995). The role of intelligence in modern society. *American Scientist, 83*, 356–368.

Hunter, J. E., & Hunter, R. F. (1984). Validity and utility of alternative predictors of job performance. *Psychological Bulletin, 96*, 72–98.

Intelligence and its measurement. (1921). *Journal of Educational Psychology*.

Jacoby, R., & Glauberman, N. (Eds.). (1995). *The bell curve debate*. New York: Times Books.

Jensen, A. R. (1969). How much can we boost IQ and scholastic achievement? *Harvard Educational Review, 39*(1), 1–123.

Jensen, A. R. (1980). *Bias in mental testing*. New York: Free Press.

Kamin, L. (1974). *The science and politics of IQ*. Hillsdale, NJ: Erlbaum.

Keating, D. P. (1984). The emperor's new clothes: The "new look" in intelligence research. In R. J. Sternberg, (Ed.), *Advances in the psychology of human intelligence* (Vol. 2, pp. 1–45). Hillsdale, NJ: Erlbaum.

Laboratory of Comparative Human Cognition. (1982). Culture and intelligence. In R. J. Sternberg (Ed.), *Handbook of human intelligence* (pp. 642–719). New York: Free Press.

Lave, J., Murtaugh, M., & de la Roche, O. (1984). The dialectic of arithmetic in grocery shopping. In B. Rogoff & J. Lave (Eds.), *Everyday cognition: Its development in social context* (pp. 67–94). Cambridge, MA: Harvard University Press.

Neisser, U. (1979). The concept of intelligence. In R. J. Sternberg & D. K. Detterman (Eds.), *Human intelligence: Perspectives on its theory and measurement* (pp. 179–189). Norwood, NJ: Ablex.

Nickerson, R. S., Perkins, D. N., & Smith, E. E. (1985). *The teaching of thinking.* Hillsdale, NJ: Erlbaum.

Nisbett, R. (1995). Race, IQ, and scientism. In S. Fraser (Ed.), *The bell curve wars: Race, intelligence and the future of America* (pp. 36–57). New York: Basic Books.

Nunes, T., Schliemann, A. D., & Carraher, D. W. (1993). *Street mathematics and school mathematics.* New York: Cambridge University Press.

Perkins, D. N. (1995). Insight in minds and genes. In R. J. Sternberg & J. E. Davidson (Eds.), *The nature of insight* (pp. 495–534). Cambridge, MA: MIT Press.

Plomin, R. (in press). Identifying genes for cognitive abilities and disabilities. In R. J. Sternberg & E. L. Grigorenko (Eds.), *Intelligence, heredity, and environment.* New York: Cambridge University Press.

Ramey, C. (1994). Abecedarian project. In R. J. Sternberg (Ed.), *Encyclopedia of human intelligence* (Vol. 1, pp. 1–3). New York: Macmillan.

Ree, M. J., & Earles, J. A. (1993). *g* is to psychology what carbon is to chemistry: A reply to Sternberg and Wagner, McClelland, and Calfee, *Current Directions in Psychological Science, 1,* 11–12.

Reis, S. M., & Renzulli, J. S. (1992). Using curriculum compacting to challenge the above-average. *Educational Leadership, 50*(3), 51–57.

Scarr, S. (in press). Behavior genetic and socialization theories of intelligence: Truce and reconciliation. In R. J. Sternberg & E. L. Grigorenko (Eds.), *Intelligence, heredity, and environment.* New York: Cambridge University Press.

Schmidt, F. L., & Hunter, J. E. (1981). Employment testing: Old theories and new research findings. *American Psychologist, 36,* 1128–1137.

Schmidt, F. L., & Hunter, J. E. (1993). Tacit knowledge, practical intelligence, general mental ability, and job knowledge. *Current Directions in Psychological Science, 1,* 8–9.

Spearman, C. E. (1904). 'General intelligence' objectively determined and measured. *American Journal of Psychology, 15,* 201–293.

Sternberg, R. J. (1985). *Beyond IQ: A triarchic theory of human intelligence.* New York: Cambridge University Press.

Sternberg, R. J. (Ed.). (1988). *The nature of creativity: Contemporary psychological perspectives.* New York: Cambridge University Press.

Sternberg, R. J. (1990). *Metaphors of mind: Conceptions of the nature of intelligence.* New York: Cambridge University Press.

Sternberg, R. J. (1994). The triarchic theory of human intelligence. In R. J. Sternberg (Ed.), *Encyclopedia of human intelligence* (Vol. 2, pp. 1087–1091). New York: Macmillan.

Sternberg, R. J., & Detterman, D. K. (Eds.). (1986). *What is intelligence? Contemporary viewpoints on its nature and definition.* Norwood, NJ: Ablex.

Sternberg, R. J., & Grigorenko, E. L. (Eds.). (in press). *Intelligence, heredity, and environment.* New York: Cambridge University Press.

Sternberg, R. J., & Lubart, T. I. (1995). *Defying the crowd: Cultivating creativity in a culture of conformity.* New York: Free Press.

Sternberg, R. J., Okagaki, L., & Jackson, A. (1990). Practical intelligence for success in school. *Educational Leadership, 48,* 35–39.

Sternberg, R. J., & Wagner, R. K. (1993). The *g*-ocentric view of intelligence and job performance is wrong. *Current Directions in Psychological Science, 2*(1), 1–4.

Sternberg, R. J., Wagner, R. K., & Okagaki, L. (1993). Practical intelligence: The nature and role of tacit knowledge in work and at school. In H. Reese & J. Puckett (Eds.), *Advances in lifespan development* (pp. 205–227). Hillsdale, NJ: Erlbaum.

Sternberg, R. J., Wagner, R. K., Williams, W. M., & Horvath, J. A., (1995). Testing common sense. *American Psychologist, 50*(11), 912–927.

Sternberg, R. J., & Williams, W. M. (1994). *Does the Graduate Record Examination predict meaningful success in psychology?* Unpublished manuscript, Yale University, New Haven, CT.

Reflections on Multiple Intelligences

Myths and Messages

HOWARD GARDNER

A silence of a decade's length is sometimes a good idea. I published *Frames of Mind*, an introduction to the theory of multiple intelligences (MI theory) in 1983.[1] Because I was critical of current views of intelligences within the discipline of psychology, I expected to stir controversy among my fellow psychologists. This expectation was not disappointed.

I was unprepared for the large and mostly positive reaction to the theory among educators. Naturally I was gratified by this response and was stimulated to undertake some projects exploring the implications of MI theory. I also took pleasure from—and was occasionally moved by—the many attempts to institute an MI approach to education in schools and classrooms. By and large, however, except for a few direct responses to criticisms,[2] I did not speak up about new thoughts concerning the theory itself.

In 1993 my self-imposed silence was broken in two ways. My publisher issued a 10th-anniversary edition of *Frames of Mind*, to which I contributed a short, reflective introductory essay. In tandem with that release, the publisher issued *Multiple Intelligences: The Theory in Practice*, a set of articles chronicling some of the experiments undertaken in the wake of MI theory—mostly projects pursued by colleagues at Harvard Project Zero, but also other MI initiatives.[3] This collection gave me the opportunity to answer some other criticisms leveled against MI theory and to respond publicly to some of the most frequently asked questions.

In the 12 years since *Frames of Mind* was published, I have heard, read, and seen several hundred different interpretations of what MI theory is and how it can be applied in the schools.[4] Until now, I have been content to let MI theory take on a life of its own. As I saw it, I had issued an "ensemble of ideas" (or *memes*) to the outer world, and I was inclined to let those memes fend for themselves.[5] Yet, in light of my own reading and observations, I believe that the time has come for me to issue a set of new memes of my own.

In the next part of this article, I will discuss seven myths that have grown up about multiple intelligences and, by putting forth seven complementary "realities," I will attempt to set the record straight. Then, in the third part of the article, reflecting on my observations of MI experiments in the schools, I will describe three primary ways in which education can be enhanced by a multiple intelligences perspective.

Howard Gardner is a professor of education and co-director of Project Zero at the Harvard Graduate School of Education and an adjunct professor of neurology at the Boston University School of Medicine. For their comments on an earlier draft of this article, he wishes to thank Melissa Brand, Patricia Bolanos, Thomas Hatch, Thomas Hoerr, Mara Krechevsky, Mindy Kornhaber, Jerome Murphy, Bruce Torff, Julie Viens, and Ellen Winner. Preparation of this article was supported by the MacArthur Foundation and the Spencer Foundation.

In what follows, I make no attempt to isolate MI theory from MI practice. "Multiple intelligences" began as a theory but was almost immediately put to practical use. The commerce between theory and practice has been ready, continuous, and, for the most part, productive.

MYTHS OF MULTIPLE INTELLIGENCES

Myth 1. Now that seven intelligences have been identified, one can—and perhaps should—create seven tests and secure seven scores.

Reality 1. MI theory represents a critique of "psychometrics-as-usual." A battery of MI tests is inconsistent with the major tenets of the theory.

Comment. My concept of intelligences is an outgrowth of accumulating knowledge about the human brain and about human cultures, not the result of a priori definitions or of factor analyses of test scores. As such, it becomes crucial that intelligences be assessed in ways that are "intelligent-fair," that is, in ways that examine the intelligence directly rather than through the lens of linguistic or logical intelligence (as ordinary paper-and-pencil tests do).

Thus, if one wants to look at spatial intelligence, one should allow an individual to explore a terrain for a while and see whether she can find her way around it reliably. Or if one wants to examine musical intelligence, one should expose an individual to a new melody in a reasonably familiar idiom and see how readily the person can learn to sing it, recognize it, transform it, and the like.

Assessing multiple intelligences is not a high priority in every setting. But when it is necessary or advisable to assess an individual's intelligences, it is best to do so in a comfortable setting with materials (and cultural roles) that are familiar to that individual. These conditions are at variance with our general conception of testing as a decontextualized exercise using materials that are unfamiliar by design, but there is no reason in principle why an "intelligence-fair" set of measures cannot be devised. The production of such useful tools has been our goal in such projects as Spectrum, Arts PROPEL, and Practical Intelligence for School.[6]

Myth 2. An intelligence is the same as a domain or a discipline.

Reality 2. An intelligence is a new kind of construct, and it should not be confused with a domain or a discipline.

Comment. I must shoulder a fair part of the blame for the propagation of the second myth. In writing *Frames of Mind,* I was not as careful as I should have been in distinguishing intelligences from other related concepts. As I have now come to understand, largely through my interactions with Mihaly Csikszentmihalyi and David Feldman,[7] an *intelligence* is a biological and psychological potential; that potential is capable of being realized to a greater or lesser extent as a consequence of the experiential, cultural, and motivational factors that affect a person.

In contrast, a *domain* is an organized set of activities within a culture, one typically characterized by a specific symbol system and its attendant operations. Any cultural activity in which individuals participate on more than a casual basis, and in which degrees of expertise can be identified and nurtured, should be considered a domain. Thus, physics, chess, gardening, and rap music are all domains in Western culture. Any domain can be realized through the use of several intelligences; thus the domain of musical performance involves bodily-kinesthetic and personal as well as musical intelligences. By the same token, a particular intelligence, like spatial intelligence, can be put to work in a myriad of domains, ranging from sculpture to sailing to neuroanatomical investigations.

Finally, a *field* is the set of individuals and institutions that judge the acceptability and creativity of products fashioned by individuals (with their characteristic intelligences) within established or new domains. Judgments of quality cannot be made apart from the operation of members of a field, though it is worth noting that both the members of a field and the criteria that they employ can and do change over time.

Myth 3. An intelligence is the same as a *learning style,* a *cognitive style,* or a *working style.*

Reality 3. The concept of *style* designates a general approach that an individual can apply equally to every conceivable content. In contrast, an *intelligence* is a capacity, with its component processes, that is geared to a specific content in the world (such as musical sounds or spatial patterns).

Comment. To see the difference between an intelligence and a style, consider this contrast. If a person is said to have a "reflective" or an "intuitive" style, this designation assumes that the individual will be reflective or intuitive with all manner of content, ranging from language to music to social analysis. However, such an assertion reflects an empirical assumption that actually needs to be investigated. It might well be the case that an individual is reflective with music but fails to be reflective in a domain that requires mathematical thinking or that a person is highly intuitive in the social domain but not in the least intuitive when it comes to mathematics or mechanics.

In my view, the relation between my concept of intelligence and the various conceptions of style needs to be worked out empirically, on a style-by-style basis. We cannot assume that *style* means the same thing to Carl Jung, Jerome Kagan, Tony Gregoric, Bernice McCarthy, and other inventors of stylistic terminology.[8] There is little authority for assuming that an individual who evinces a style in one milieu or with one content will necessarily do so with other diverse contents—and even less authority for equating styles with intelligences.

Myth 4. MI theory is not empirical. (A variant of Myth 4 alleges that MI theory is empirical but has been disproved.)

Reality 4. MI theory is based wholly on empirical evidence and can be revised on the basis of new empirical findings.

Comment. Anyone who puts forth Myth 4 can not have read *Frames of Mind*. Literally hundreds of empirical studies were reviewed in that book, and the actual intelligences were identified and delineated on the basis of empirical findings. The seven intelligences described in *Frames of Mind* represented my best-faith effort to identify mental abilities of a scale that could be readily discussed and critiqued.

No empirically based theory is ever established permanently. All claims are at risk in the light of new findings. In the last decade, I have collected and reflected on empirical evidence that is relevant to the claims of MI theory, 1983 version. Thus work on the development in children of a "theory of mind," as well as the study of pathologies in which an individual loses a sense of social judgment, has provided fresh evidence for the importance and independence of interpersonal intelligence.[9] In contrast, the finding of a possible link between musical and spatial thinking has caused me to reflect on the possible relations between faculties that had previously been thought to be independent.[10]

Many other lines of evidence could be mentioned here. The important point is that MI theory is constantly being reconceptualized in terms of new findings from the laboratory and from the field (see also Myth 7).

Myth 5. MI theory is incompatible with *g* (general intelligence),[11] with hereditarian accounts, or with environmental accounts of the nature and causes of intelligence.

Reality 5. MI theory questions not the existence but the province and explanatory power of *g*. By the same token, MI theory is neutral on the question of heritability of specific intelligences, instead underscoring the centrality of genetic/environmental interactions.

Comment. Interest in *g* comes chiefly from those who are probing scholastic intelligence and those who traffic in the correlations between test scores. (Recently people have become interested in the possible neurophysiological underpinnings of *g*[12] and, sparked by the publication of *The Bell Curve*,[13] in the possible social consequences of "low *g*.") While I have been critical of much of the research in the *g* tradition, I do not consider the study of *g* to be scientifically improper, and I am willing to accept the utility of *g* for certain theoretical purposes. My interest, obviously, centers on those intelligences and intellectual processes that are not covered by *g*.[14]

While a major animating force in psychology has been the study of the heritability of intelligence(s), my inquiries have not been oriented in this direction. I do not doubt that human abilities—and human differences—have a genetic base. Can any serious scientist question this at the end of the twentieth century? And I believe that behavioral genetic studies, particularly of twins reared apart, can illuminate certain issues.[15] However, along with most biologically informed scientists, I reject the "inherited versus learned" dichotomy and instead stress the interaction, from the moment of conception, between genetic and environmental factors.

Myth 6. MI theory so broadens the notion of intelligence that it includes all psychological constructs and thus vitiates the usefulness, as well as the usual connotation, of the term.

Reality 6. This statement is simply wrong. I believe that it is the standard definition of intelligence that narrowly constricts our view, treating a certain form of scholastic performance as if it encompassed the range of human capacities and leading to disdain for those who happen not to be psychometrically bright. Moreover, I reject the distinction between talent and intelligence; in my view, what we call *intelligence* in the vernacular is simply a certain set of *talents* in the linguistic and/or logical-mathematical spheres.

Comment. MI theory is about the intellect, the human mind in its cognitive aspects. I believe that a treatment in terms of a number of semi-independent intelligences presents a more sustainable conception of human thought than one that posits a single "bell curve" of intellect.

Note, however, that MI theory makes no claims whatsoever to deal with issues beyond the intellect. MI theory is not, and does not pretend to be, about personality, will, morality, attention, motivation, and other psychological constructs. Note as well that MI theory is not connected to any set of morals or values. An intelligence can be put to an ethical or an antisocial use. Poet and playwright Johann Wolfgang von Goethe and Nazi propagandist Joseph Goebbels were both masters of the German language, but how different were the uses to which they put their talents!

Myth 7. There is an eighth (or ninth or tenth) intelligence.

Reality 7. Not in my writings so far. But I am working on it.

Comment. For the reasons suggested above, I thought it wise not to attempt to revise the principal claims of MI theory before the 1983 version of the theory had been debated. But recently, I have turned my attention to possible additions to the list. If I were to rewrite *Frames of Mind* today, I would probably add an eighth intelligence—the intelligence of the naturalist. It seems to me that the individual who is able readily to recognize flora and fauna, to make other consequential distinctions in the natural world, and to use this ability productively (in hunting, in farming, in biological science) is exercising an important intelligence and one that is not adequately encompassed in the current list. Individuals like Charles Darwin or E. O. Wilson embody the naturalist's intelligence, and, in our consuming culture, youngsters exploit their naturalist's intelligence as they make acute discriminations among cars, sneakers, or hairstyles.

I have read in several secondary sources that there is a spiritual intelligence and, indeed, that I have endorsed a spiritual intelligence. That statement is not true. It is true that I have become interested in understanding better what is meant by "spirituality" and by "spiritual individuals"; as my understanding improves, I expect to write about this topic. Whether or not it proves appropriate to add "spirituality" to the list of intelligences, this human capacity certainly deserves discussion and study in nonfringe psychological circles.

MESSAGES ABOUT MI IN THE CLASSROOM

If one were to continue adding myths to the list, a promising candidate would read: There is a single educational approach based on MI theory.

I trust that I have made it clear over the years that I do not subscribe to this myth.[16] On the contrary, MI theory is in no way an educational prescription. There is always a gulf between psychological claims about how the mind works and educational practices, and such a gulf is especially apparent in a theory that was developed without specific educational goals in mind. Thus, in educational discussions, I have always taken the position that educators are in the best position to determine the uses to which MI theory can and should be put.

Indeed, contrary to much that has been written, MI theory does not incorporate a "position" on tracking, gifted education, interdisciplinary curricula, the layout of the school day, the length of the school year, or many other "hot button" educational issues. I have tried to encourage certain "applied MI efforts," but in general my advice has echoed the traditional Chinese adage "Let a hundred flowers bloom." And I have often been surprised and delighted by the fragrance of some of these fledgling plants—for example, the use of a "multiple intelligences curriculum" in order to facilitate communication between youngsters drawn from different cultures or the conveying of pivotal principles in biology or social studies through a dramatic performance designed and staged by students.

I have become convinced, however, that while there is no "right way" to conduct a multiple intelligences education, some current efforts go against the spirit of my formulation and embody one or more of the myths sketched above. Let me mention a few applications that have jarred me.

- *The attempt to teach all concepts or subjects using all the intelligences.* As I indicate below, most topics can be powerfully approached in a number of ways. But there is no point in assuming that every topic can be effectively approached in at least seven ways, and it is a waste of effort and time to attempt to do this.
- *The belief that it suffices, in and of itself, just to go through the motions of exercising a certain intelligence.* I have seen classes in which children are encouraged simply to move their arms or to run

around, on the assumption that exercising one's body represents in itself some kind of MI statement. Don't read me as saying that exercise is a bad thing; it is not. But random muscular movements have nothing to do with the cultivation of the mind . . . or even of the body!

- *The use of materials associated with an intelligence as background.* In some classes, children are encouraged to read or to carry out math exercises while music is playing in the background. Now I myself like to work with music in the background. But unless I focus on the performance (in which case the composition is no longer serving as background), the music's function is unlikely to be different from that of a dripping faucet or a humming fan.

- *The use of intelligences primarily as mnemonic devices.* It may well be the case that it is easier to remember a list if one sings it or even if one dances while reciting it. I have nothing against such aids to memory. However, these uses of the materials of an intelligence are essentially trivial. What is not trivial—as I argue below—is to think musically or to draw on some of the structural aspects of music in order to illuminate concepts like biological evolution or historical cycles.

- *The conflating of intelligences with other desiderata.* This practice is particularly notorious when it comes to the personal intelligences. Interpersonal intelligence has to do with understanding other people, but it is often distorted as a license for cooperative learning or applied to individuals who are extroverted. Intrapersonal intelligence has to do with understanding oneself, but it is often distorted as a rationale for self-esteem programs or applied to individuals who are loners or introverted. One receives the strong impression that individuals who use the terms in this promiscuous way have never read my writings on intelligence.

- *The direct evaluation (or even grading) of intelligences, without regard to context or to content.* Intelligences ought to be seen at work when individuals are carrying out productive activities that are valued in a culture. And that is how reporting of learning and mastery in general should take place. I see little point in grading individuals in terms of how "linguistic" or how "bodily-kinesthetic" they are; such a practice is likely to introduce a new and unnecessary form of tracking and labeling. As a parent (or as a supporter of education living in the community), I am interested in the *uses* to which children's intelligences are put; reporting should have this focus.

Note that it is reasonable, for certain purposes, to indicate that a child seems to have a relative strength in one intelligence and a relative weakness in another. However, these descriptions should be mobilized in order to help students perform better in meaningful activities and perhaps even to show that a label was premature or erroneous.

Having illustrated some problematic applications of MI theory, let me now indicate three more positive ways in which MI can be—and has been—used in the schools.

1. *The cultivation of desired capabilities.* Schools should cultivate those skills and capacities that are valued in the community and in the broader society. Some of these desired roles are likely to highlight specific intelligences, including ones that have usually been given short shrift in the schools. If, say, the community believes that children should be able to perform on a musical instrument, then the cultivation of musical intelligence toward that end becomes a value of the school. Similarly, emphasis on such capacities as taking into account the feelings of others, being able to plan one's own life in a reflective manner, or being able to find one's way around an unfamiliar terrain are likely to result in an emphasis on the cultivation of interpersonal, intrapersonal, and spatial intelligences respectively.

2. *Approaching a concept, subject matter, or discipline in a variety of ways.* Along with many other school reformers, I am convinced that schools attempt to cover far too much material and that superficial understandings (or nonunderstandings) are the inevitable result. It makes far more sense to spend a significant amount of time on key concepts, generative ideas, and essential questions and to allow students to become thoroughly familiar with these notions and their implications.

Once the decision has been made to dedicate time to particular items, it then becomes possible to approach those topics or notions in a variety of ways. Not necessarily seven ways, but in a number of ways that prove pedagogically appropriate for the topic at hand. Here is where MI theory comes in. As I argue in *The Unschooled Mind,* nearly every topic can be approached in a variety of ways, ranging from the telling of a story, to a formal argument, to an artistic exploration, to some kind of "hands-on" experiment or simulation. Such pluralistic approaches should be encouraged.[17]

When a topic has been approached from a number of perspectives, three desirable outcomes ensue. First, because children do not all learn in the same way, more children will be reached. I term this desirable state of affairs "multiple windows leading into the same room." Second, students secure a sense of what it is like to be an expert when they behold that a teacher can represent knowledge in a number of different ways and discover that they themselves are also capable of more than a single representation of a specified content. Finally, since understanding can also be demonstrated in more than one way, a pluralistic approach opens up the possibility that students can display their new understandings—as well as their continuing difficulties—in ways that are comfortable for them and accessible to others. Performance-based examinations and exhibitions are tailor-made for the foregrounding of a student's multiple intelligences.

3. *The personalization of education.* Without a doubt, one of the reasons that MI theory has attracted attention in the educational community is because of its ringing endorsement of an ensemble of propositions: we are not all the same; we do not all have the same kinds of minds; education works most effectively for most individuals if these differences in mentation and strengths are taken into account rather than denied or ignored. I have always believed that the heart of the MI perspective—in theory and in practice—inheres in taking human differences seriously. At the theoretical level, one acknowledges that all individuals cannot be profitably arrayed on a single intellectual dimension. At the practical level, one acknowledges that any uniform educational approach is likely to serve only a minority of children.

When I visit an "MI school," I look for signs of personalization: evidence that all involved in the educational encounter take such differences among human beings seriously; evidence that they construct curricula, pedagogy, and assessment insofar as possible in the light of these differences. All the MI posters, indeed all the references to me personally, prove to be of little avail if the youngsters continue to be treated in homogenized fashion. By the same token, whether or not members of the staff have even heard of MI theory, I would be happy to send my children to a school with the following characteristics: differences among youngsters are taken seriously, knowledge about differences is shared with children and parents, children gradually assume responsibility for their own learning, and materials that are worth knowing are presented in ways that afford each child the maximum opportunity to master those materials and to show others (and themselves) what they have learned and understood.

CLOSING COMMENTS

I am often asked for my views about schools that are engaged in MI efforts. The implicit question may well be: "Aren't you upset by some of the applications that are carried out in your name?"

In truth, I do not expect that initial efforts to apply any new ideas are going to be stunning. Human experimentation is slow, difficult, and filled with zigs and zags. Attempts to apply any set of innovative ideas will sometimes be half-hearted, superficial, even wrongheaded.

For me the crucial question concerns what has happened in a school (or class) two, three, or four years after it has made a commitment to an MI approach. Often, the initiative will be long since forgotten—the fate, for better or worse, of most educational experiments. Sometimes, the school has gotten stuck in a rut, repeating the same procedures of the first days without having drawn any positive or negative lessons from this exercise. Needless to say, I am not happy with either of these outcomes.

I cherish an educational setting in which discussions and applications of MI have catalyzed a more fundamental consideration of schooling—its overarching purposes, its conceptions of what a productive life will be like in the future, its pedagogical methods, and its educational outcomes, particularly in the context of the values of that specific community. Such examination generally leads to more thoughtful schooling. Visits with other schools and more extended forms of networking among MI enthusiasts (and critics) constitute important parts of this building process. If, as a result of these discussions and experiments, a more personalized education is the outcome, I feel that the heart of MI theory has been embodied. And if this personalization is fused with a commitment to the achievement of worthwhile (and attainable) educational understandings for all children, then the basis for a powerful education has indeed been laid.

The MI endeavor is a continuing and changing one. There have emerged over the years new thoughts about the theory, new understandings and misunderstandings, and new applications, some very inspired, some less so. Especially gratifying to me has been the demonstration that this process is dynamic and interactive: no one, not even its creator, has a monopoly on MI wisdom or foolishness. Practice is enriched by theory, even as theory is transformed in the light of the fruits and frustrations of practice. The burgeoning of a community that takes MI issues seriously is not only a source of pride to me but also the best guarantor that the theory will continue to live in the years ahead.

NOTES

1. Howard Gardner, *Frames of Mind: The Theory of Multiple Intelligences* (New York: Basic Books, 1983). A 10th-anniversary edition, with a new introduction, was published in 1993.

2. Howard Gardner, "On Discerning New Ideas in Psychology," *New Ideas in Psychology*, 3, 1985, pp. 101–4; and idem, "Symposium on the Theory of Multiple Intelligences," in David N. Perkins, Jack Lochhead, and John C. Bishop, eds., *Thinking: The Second International Conference* (Hillsdale, N.J.: Erlbaum, 1983), pp. 77–101.

3. Howard Gardner, *Multiple Intelligences: The Theory in Practice* (New York: Basic Books, 1993).

4. For a bibliography through 1992, see the appendices to Gardner, *Multiple Intelligences*.

5. The term "memes" is taken from Richard Dawkins, *The Selfish Gene* (Oxford: Oxford University Press, 1976).

6. See Gardner, *Multiple Intelligences*.

7. Mihaly Csikszentmihalyi, "Society, Culture, and Person: A Systems View of Creativity," in Robert J. Sternberg, ed., *The Nature of Creativity* (New York: Cambridge University Press, 1988), pp. 325–39; idem, *Creativity* (New York: HarperCollins, forthcoming); David H. Feldman, "Creativity: Dreams, Insights, and Transformations," in Sternberg, op. cit., pp. 271–97; and David H. Feldman,

Mihaly Csikszentmihalyi, and Howard Gardner, *Changing the World: A Framework for the Study of Creativity* (Westport, Conn.: Greenwood, 1994).

8. For a comprehensive discussion of the notion of cognitive style, see Nathan Kogan, "Stylistic Variation in Childhood and Adolescence," in Paul Mussen, ed., *Handbook of Child Psychology*, vol. 3 (New York: Wiley, 1983), pp. 630–706.

9. For writings pertinent to the personal intelligences, see Janet Astington, *The Child's Discovery of the Mind* (Cambridge, Mass.: Harvard University Press, 1993); and Antonio Damasio, *Descartes' Error* (New York: Grosset/Putnam, 1994).

10. On the possible relation between musical and spatial intelligence, see Frances Rauscher, G. L. Shaw, and X. N. Ky, "Music and Spatial Task Performance," *Nature*, 14 October 1993, p. 611.

11. The most thorough exposition of *g* can be found in the writings of Arthur Jensen. See, for example, *Bias in Mental Testing* (New York: Free Press, 1980). For a critique, see Stephen J. Gould, *The Mismeasure of Man* (New York: Norton, 1981).

12. Interest in the neurophysiological bases of *g* is found in Arthur Jensen, "Why Is Reaction Time Correlated with Psychometric 'G'?," *Current Directions of Psychological Science*, vol. 2, 1993, pp. 53–56.

13. Richard Herrnstein and Charles Murray, *The Bell Curve* (New York: Free Press, 1994).

14. For my view on intelligences not covered by *g*, see Howard Gardner, "Review of Richard Herrnstein and Charles Murray, *The Bell Curve*," *The American Prospect*, Winter 1995, pp. 71–80.

15. On behavioral genetics and psychological research, see Thomas Bouchard and P. Propping, eds., *Twins as a Tool of Behavioral Genetics* (Chichester, England: Wiley, 1993).

16. On the many approaches that can be taken in implementing MI theory, see Mara Krechevsky, Thomas Hoerr, and Howard Gardner, "Complementary Energies: Implementing MI Theory from the Lab and from the Field," in Jeannie Oakes and Karen H. Quartz, eds., *Creating New Educational Communities: Schools and Classrooms Where All Children Can Be Smart: 94th NSSE Yearbook* (Chicago: National Society for the Study of Education, University of Chicago Press, 1995), pp. 166–86.

17. Howard Gardner, *The Unschooled Mind: How Children Learn and How Schools Should Teach* (New York: Basic Books, 1991).

Teaching Tommy

A Second-Grader with Attention Deficit Hyperactivity Disorder

KATHARINA FACHIN

When Tommy walked into my second-grade classroom on the first day of school, I was happy to see a familiar face. I looked at him with sympathy and hope, wanting to make the year one of learning and of building self-esteem.

Tommy was coming to my class with a difficult year behind him. He had spent first grade in a highly structured classroom, and he had not conformed to its behavioral standards. The behavior modification used with him in that class had included the removal of rewards, and Tommy had experienced little success in keeping the rewards he earned. He was often in trouble, and everyone in the school knew his name. He was three-fourths of a year behind his peers in reading and writing. These experiences led Tommy to believe that he was stupid and bad. I was determined to replace his negative self-image with a positive one based on academic and social success.

Tommy and I already had a history before that first day of school, for I had tutored him once a week from May through July. Originally, Tommy had qualified for home tutoring because of a myringotomy and an adenoidectomy. In preparation for

Katharina Fachin is a doctoral candidate in the Department of Curriculum and Instruction, University of New Hampshire, Durham. She was previously a second-grade teacher in a New Jersey public school. She wishes to thank Stefne Sears for untiring personal and professional support and Michael Driscoll for his thorough and caring advocacy for children's needs.

teaching Tommy at home, I talked to his first-grade teacher to find out about his capabilities and to see if she could recommend any materials. I was disappointed when I talked to her because she seemed so negative about him, yet she lacked any precise descriptions of his learning. I met Tommy with the impression that he had had a tough break—a little child facing a teacher who had no hope in him and who lacked the flexibility to meet his needs. Tommy's mother reaffirmed this impression when she described how the teacher wanted him tested and how she was afraid that they just wanted to drug her child so he would be easier to handle.

Tommy snacked on cupcakes and soda as we worked at the kitchen counter. The phone would ring, and siblings would be preparing to go to after-school activities. Tommy wiggled and slid about on the chair, and he would often take bathroom breaks. By remaining firm, I was able to get Tommy to read and write with me. We talked about his interests, and I got to know him. He had a very limited sight vocabulary and could not predict vowel sounds. He could identify most consonants but could not identify the correct vowels, nor was he familiar with how to spell common endings. Although Tommy did not like to read and write because it was such a struggle, he loved math. Using his fingers, he could calculate all first-grade-level addition and subtraction problems quickly and accurately. Tommy felt very confident of his mathematical abilities.

I became attached to this rough-and-tumble boy with the blue eyes and the big smile. He told me about his daredevil biking stunts and about jumping out of tree houses. Grass stains on his jeans, scrapes on his knees and elbows, and dirty hands were his hard-won war wounds. Tommy struck me as very inquisitive. He spoke of such experiments as creating a pocket of air under water with a bucket. I wondered how I could tap into his creativity in the classroom. Tommy was a very active boy who had trouble maintaining eye contact and concentration, but I attributed these characteristics to his personality, immaturity, diet, and environment. I couldn't understand why a teacher would be so negative about handling him in the classroom.

Over the course of the next school year, I found out why. But I also discovered the joys of teaching Tommy.

SECOND GRADE

Because of my experience tutoring Tommy and my hands-on teaching style, Tommy was placed in my class for second grade. By the third day, I had contacted Dr. Mitchell, our school psychologist. Tommy was singing and making loud noises throughout lessons. He crawled on the floor during transitions and sometimes even during class. As he laughed and shoved his way through the class to line up, he injured other children. He was playful and destructive at the same time. Instead of picking up the blocks when it was time to clean up, he would scatter them wildly with flailing arms and a big grin. Just when a bucket was filled with blocks, Tommy would dump it.

Throughout that first month I used "time out" with Tommy and had him write about his behavior—to no avail. Positive reinforcement, coupled with ignoring Tommy as a negative consequence, also did not increase Tommy's on-task behavior. Indeed, the research shows that these methods are commonly insufficient for children with Attention Deficit Hyperactivity Disorder (ADHD).[1] I think that ignoring Tommy not only didn't work to improve his behavior but was actually harmful to him. When I made it clear that I was ignoring him, he would feel unloved and bad about himself. On one occasion Tommy curled up in fetal position behind the computer. I had to be careful to let him know that I loved him and believed that he was a good and smart boy. When he needed to be reprimanded, I used a firm monotone voice to correct him succinctly. Still, I felt I had to find a way to help Tommy achieve more success in school.

TOKEN ECONOMY

At the suggestion of Dr. Mitchell, I instituted a token economy system of rewards for Tommy. Tangible rewards coupled with positive verbal reinforcement have been shown to be much more effectual than praise alone.[2] From the very beginning, though, Dr. Mitchell made it clear that I needed to document Tommy's behavior. In late September I explained the program to Tommy and then later to his mother over the telephone. He could earn play money in $5 bills for raising his hand, keeping his hands to himself, and being a model student. I would not take away any money that he earned. We would count it up at the end of the day and chart it. At the end of the week, Tommy could use the money to purchase time on the computer, time to play with the math manipulatives, or time for drawing in his journal.

As soon as the system was in effect, Dr. Mitchell observed Tommy in the classroom and charted his behavior at one-minute intervals for 30 minutes. Tommy was out of his seat 76.6% of the observed time, he rolled on the rug 16.6% of the time, and he spoke out of turn 63.3% of the time. Moreover, he exhibited aggressive behavior toward property or individuals 26.6% of the time. For example, he crushed some science material on a shelf, and he also tried to throw an object. Only 3.3% of the time were Tommy's eyes on the teacher while he listened and followed directions. For 86.6% of the time Tommy exhibited excessive or incidental movement, and he was off-task 93.3% of the observed time.

Dr. Mitchell called a meeting that included Tommy's father, Dr. Mitchell, the acting principal, and me. I offered specific examples of Tommy's impulsivity, distractibility, and motoric overflow. His father was upset when he heard about Tommy's behavior and acknowledged that he had wanted Tommy tested last year. He even supported the idea of the token economy and said he would have Tommy use his classroom money to purchase television time, dessert, and video-game time at home. In the coming months Tommy's father very consistently reinforced the token economy at home and signed the papers for Tommy to be tested.

When we began the token economy in September, Tommy averaged $18 a day for the remainder of that month. During October, he averaged $27 a day, with $10 as the lowest amount and $65 as the highest. For November Tommy averaged $31 a day, with a range from $5 to $110. During December Tommy averaged $51 a day, with a range from $15 to $105. With his parents' support for the system at home and Tommy's own interest in the token economy, I was pleased with the improvement.

Although Tommy was somewhat less disruptive, he would still step on other children as we sat on the rug, make intermittent loud noises, call out to other children, fall out of his chair on purpose, and get up from his desk during lessons. When we used blocks for mathematics, he would play with them and knock them off his desk unless I remained right beside him. If he raised his hand and I didn't call on him immediately, he would get angry and within a minute would be off task. His pencil and notebook could be found anywhere in the room but inside his desk. The situation was most difficult during whole-class times and transitions.

On the other hand, Tommy wanted very much to please me, and he would write me apologies and notes about how he loved me. After the fact, he felt bad about hurting other children and disrupting the class, so I tried to show him affection at every good opportunity.

Despite these difficult times, Tommy also showed his potential to succeed in school. Three days a week for 45 minutes, my instructional support teacher, Mrs. DeVito, worked with Tommy in a small reading group while I worked with two other groups. The fit between Mrs. DeVito's teaching style and Tommy's needs was perfect. Mrs. DeVito enthusiastically and dramatically offered her students positive reinforcement, and Tommy would glow from her praise. She also used a fast-paced, question-and-answer format for lessons that would not allow Tommy to lose focus. He looked forward to his time with Mrs. DeVito and showed great progress in reading. His sight vocabulary and word-attack skills were improving steadily.

ADHD AS A MOTIVATIONAL DISORDER

This disparity between Tommy's highly distractible and impulsive behavior during whole-class activities and his focused and appropriate behavior in the small reading group was very disconcerting for me. Throughout the year I analyzed and reanalyzed my teaching. I too am a lively and interactive teacher who uses a variety of visual and tactile methods. I made modifications for Tommy so that he could take breaks, vary his tasks more frequently, and stand up while working. I reorganized the classroom so that he was surrounded by calmer children and was seated directly in front of me as I taught. Why couldn't I achieve the same attending behavior as Mrs. DeVito could?

Russell Barkley explains this discrepancy in behavior by characterizing ADHD as a motivational disorder.[3] A child with ADHD can attend well in a highly motivating situation, such as while watching a favorite television program or playing a video game. When the situation is less intrinsically motivating or when there is delayed rather than immediate feedback, the child will display the characteristics of ADHD. This is why the token economy was somewhat successful during whole-class times when Tommy would not be called on as frequently as in a small group.

After seven months, Tommy continued to exhibit frequently every one of the 14 characteristics that the American Psychiatric Association lists as diagnostic criteria for ADHD. (For a list of these characteristics and a brief description of how they can be used in diagnosis, see Anna M. Thompson, "Attention Deficit Hyperactivity Disorder: A Parent's Perspective," page 433, [*Phi Delta Kappan, 77*].)

INTERVENTIONS

At the classification meeting in December, I found out that Tommy was classified as perceptually impaired because of the discrepancy between his general cognitive ability and his specific achievement in reading and language arts. Although the neurologist had diagnosed Tommy as exhibiting ADHD, this condition was not included in his individualized education program (IEP) in January because the psychologist explained that there was no separate classification in education for ADHD. In January 1995 an IEP was written that allowed Tommy three half-hour sessions in the resource room for language arts and provided an in-class aide each day from 1:30 p.m. to 2:30 p.m.

Resource room. The resource room teacher, Miss Steven, focused on Tommy's spelling. She created an individualized list for him using words from the

Dolch list as well as words that exhibited a regular spelling pattern. She scrambled the letters in the words for him to correct, asked him to write his homework sentences in the resource room, and let him write words with colored glue on cards. Using the glue was very motivating for Tommy. When it dried, Miss Steven instructed him to trace over it with his finger. The success of this use of colored glue is consistent with research that suggests that ADHD students "selectively attend to novelty such as color, changes in size, and movement."[4] Tommy went from getting at least 50% wrong on every spelling test to getting all but one word correct. His journal writing also reflected this change.

In-class aide. Tommy was assigned an aide, Mrs. Hellwell, in the last week of February. I gave Mrs. Hellwell a list of appropriate behaviors, inappropriate behaviors, and interventions. She reinforced Tommy's appropriate behavior and provided one-on-one tutoring in the classroom. When he was highly disruptive, she also provided alternative activities. At the end of the day, Mrs. Hellwell monitored Tommy as he counted and charted his earned money. This was a tremendous help to me because it was simply exhausting to manage Tommy and the token economy all day while trying to teach and pay attention to the needs of the rest of the class.

To help with transitions, particularly the transition from lunch recess to afternoon classroom activities, I employed relaxation techniques.[5] I walked the children in from the school yard and asked them to sit at their desks. One row at a time, I called them to lie or sit on the rug. (This usually helped keep Tommy from stepping on anyone.) Then I turned out the lights and talked the children through a breathing exercise; cued them to tense, hold, and relax their muscles; and used guided imagery of peaceful places and activities. Sometimes I encouraged them to think of themselves doing something challenging and achieving success.

At first Tommy wouldn't hold still for these techniques, so I began to sit knee to knee in front of him on the floor as I led the class. After some experience with relaxation, he gradually became able to participate without my sitting with him. As I led the class from a chair, I could see him following my cues for breathing in and out and witnessed his body growing still. Tommy also displayed some enthusiasm for the practices. One day, after I asked the children to try thinking of their own images of succeeding, Tommy told us about how he imagined himself winning a karate match he was nervous

about that evening. My long-range goal was to be able to suggest to Tommy that he use the techniques on his own during the day to relax himself. As we walked down the hall, I would say to him, "Tommy, do you notice how you are making loud noises or knocking into the walls? Try breathing like we do after lunch. Can you breathe in a color?" Sometimes he used my suggestions independently, and sometimes I had to take the time to help him use the techniques before we continued walking.

Peer tutoring. At the beginning of the year, the other children in the class thought Tommy was funny and enjoyed his daring and his flouting of classroom rules. Then they became jealous of the extra attention he got from me and tried to imitate his behavior or to win my attention in other ways. Eventually, though, they began to grow angry with him for hurting them or for not waiting his turn or for disrupting class. I felt I had to find a role for the other children in the class.

All through the year I had talked to the whole class about how I was responding to Tommy and had discussed how everyone should act and why. One day, Tommy pulled a chair out from another child, causing her to hit her head hard as she fell. He stared in horror as she cried. A couple of days later, I talked about how we sometimes think of our conscience as a devil on one shoulder and an angel on the other. Tommy called out, "I think my devil killed my angel," and "I'm evil." I asked, "How did you feel when Susan hit her head? A bad person would not feel sad. You have an angel. It just talks to you too late. We need to teach your angel to give you advice before you do something." I had never seen such a look of relief and peace on Tommy's face. I could have cried.

Then I was able to enlist the help of the other students. Each day, a different student, alternating boys and girls, would be a peer tutor and help Tommy's angel "talk." I got an empty desk to put next to Tommy's for his peer tutor. I coached the peer tutor to remind him of proper classroom behavior in a nice way, to set a good example, and to accompany him when he used his money for rewards. Attitudes toward Tommy improved as the other students saw themselves as his helpers and saw Tommy as not a bad kid. Of course, not every match worked, and the boys especially found it difficult not to incite Tommy's off-task behavior and then to goof off with him.

Modifying the behavior modification. After using the token economy for five months, I felt as if Tommy was hitting a plateau. His behavior in whole-class situations was still unacceptable. I decided to buy a digital timer to help him set goals. I would set the timer for five minutes, and he could earn $5 only if he raised his hand before speaking and generally acted appropriately for the full five minutes. I discovered that he tried very hard but could make five minutes only about 60% of the time. He never made it to six minutes.

It was February, and Tommy was getting into a lot of trouble on the bus and during recess. He often found himself in the principal's office. His mother was being called every day. I had tried so hard, and yet his year in my class was turning out just like the previous year. The art and physical education teachers came to me out of frustration about his behavior, and we talked about assertive discipline and about ways to manage Tommy. In a letter to Dr. Mitchell, they expressed their concerns about how Tommy was detracting from the learning experiences of the other students in the class.

Changing placement. What else could we try? Dr. Mitchell said that our last resort would be to explore different placement options for Tommy next year. A regular classroom might be inappropriate. Since our district did not have a special education classroom, that would mean an out-of-district placement. Based on my feelings of loyalty to Tommy and his parents, I asked that I be the one to discuss this with his parents.

I called Tommy's father at the beginning of March and described the situation. I told him that we needed to explore other school placement options if Tommy's behavior did not change. During our telephone conversation I also mentioned that perhaps he and his wife might reconsider taking Tommy to his pediatrician and trying medication. We met two weeks later at parent/teacher conferences to discuss the situation in more depth. I came to the meeting with a prepared presentation detailing Tommy's behavior, the interventions that had been tried, an analysis of his progress, and the options for the future. Tommy's father informed me at that time that they would be taking Tommy to the pediatrician to try medication. They had already reached a decision before our meeting.

Medication. Tommy was on Ritalin for the last month of school. For five days he would take a dose of five milligrams before school, and it would wear off around noon. The first day he was on the medication, he earned the most money he had ever earned in a day, $110. He behaved appropriately for

15-minute intervals. He never lost his sense of humor or energy or bubbliness.

The difference was remarkable. I would see him begin to call out and then stop himself to raise his hand. He would set the timer and look at it to monitor himself. All his behaviors seemed to indicate that he was more receptive to reinforcers. The entire class responded to Tommy with spontaneous encouragement and praise, though they didn't know he was taking medication. On the first day, one beaming student told me, "This is such a good day!" Tommy was riding so high from the morning that his general sense of feeling good about himself helped him make it through the afternoon. Although he would lose his pencil constantly in the afternoon and rush from one thing to another, he tried successfully to follow classroom rules.

Even on the medication, though, the daily variation in Tommy's behavior remained. Some days he was simply more active than others. For example, on the third morning after he began taking medication, Tommy was still shaking his leg and foot the whole time he was leading the pledge.

Every day I talked to his father after school on the phone to inform him of Tommy's reaction to the medication. His father was so relieved to hear of Tommy's success. He said that he would contact the pediatrician about an afternoon dose.

Tommy continued until the end of the school year with both a morning and an afternoon dose of Ritalin. There were days when I questioned whether or not he was given the dose before he came to school, but I didn't voice these concerns. We also had some difficulty establishing exactly when the second dose should be administered, and I had difficulty remembering to send him to the nurse's office before he exhibited severe off-task behavior.

I do not mean to argue for the use of medication to address the needs of all ADHD students. I see medication as a last resort and one that should be used in combination with a comprehensive behavioral and academic program. I offered Tommy an activities-based curriculum to tap into his energy and creativity. I taught abstract ideas concretely and contextually. I consistently used and adapted behavior modification techniques and tried other techniques like relaxation exercises. I let Tommy know that I thought he was a great kid and a talented person, too. I had the class support Tommy as peer tutors and as members of project teams, literature study groups, and cooperative learning groups. The district provided instructional and non-instructional support. But Tommy needed something more to enable him to benefit from these interventions. Tommy's ADHD was severe, and the medication helped him achieve success in the classroom.

From my experience with Tommy and his family, I have come to believe even more strongly that it is vital to gain the trust of parents. Their faith in our efforts and concern for their child must be the basis for communication and teamwork between home and school. I also realize how painful it can be for parents to accept that their child might need extra help and even medication. By fielding my colleagues' complaints about Tommy's behavior, I got a small taste of what parents must feel when they are told by friends, family members, and doctors that they don't know how to discipline their children. More painful than the frustration of trying to deal with the condition of ADHD itself is enduring the criticism and condemnation that come from oth-

ers. I think that this holds true for the student, the parents, and the teacher.

NOTES

1. Lee A. Rosen et al., "The Importance of Prudent Negative Consequences for Maintaining the Appropriate Behavior of Hyperactive Students," *Journal of Abnormal Child Psychology,* vol. 12, 1984, pp. 581–604.

2. Linda J. Pfiffner, Lee A. Rosen, and Susan G. O'Leary, "The Efficacy of an All-Positive Approach to Classroom Management," *Journal of Applied Behavior Analysis,* vol. 18, 1985, pp. 257–61.

3. Russell A. Barkley, *Attention Deficit Hyperactivity Disorder: A Handbook for Diagnosis and Treatment* (New York: Guilford Press, 1990).

4. Sydney F. Zentall, "Research on the Educational Implications of Attention Deficit Hyperactivity Disorder," *Exceptional Children,* vol. 60, 1993, p. 143.

5. Sandra F. Rief, *How to Reach and Teach ADD/ADHD Children* (New York: Center for Applied Research in Education, 1993).

Chapter 5: The Impact of Culture and Community

Cognitive Approaches to Teaching Advanced Skills to Educationally Disadvantaged Students

BARBARA MEANS and MICHAEL S. KNAPP

Once again, we are in a period of widespread concern about the education of the students regarded as least likely to succeed in school. Variously labeled "at risk," "disadvantaged," or "educationally deprived," these students come disproportionately from poor families and from ethnic and linguistic minority backgrounds.

In decades past, various diagnoses of school failure for these students focused on what they lacked—exposure to print outside of school, family support for education, and so on. Based on these diagnoses, the most widely accepted prescriptions for compensatory education sought to remedy the students' deficiencies by teaching "the basics" through curricula organized around discrete skills taught in a linear sequence—much like the academic program these students had previously encountered in their regular classrooms.

New evidence, however, suggests that more "advanced" skills can—and should—be taught to those who are at a disadvantage in today's schools. From this perspective, the sources of disadvantage and school failure lie as much with what schools do

as with what the children bring to the schoolhouse door. By reconceiving what is taught to disadvantaged youngsters and by rethinking how it is taught, schools stand a better chance of engaging students from impoverished and minority backgrounds in an education that will be of use to them in their lives outside school.

A fundamental assumption underlying much of the curriculum in America's schools is that certain skills are "basic" and so must be mastered before students are given instruction in more "advanced" skills, such as reading comprehension, written composition, and mathematical reasoning. For many students, particularly those most at risk of school failure, one consequence of adherence to this assumption is that the instruction focuses on these so-called basics (such as phonetic decoding and arithmetic operations) to the exclusion of reasoning activities, of reading for meaning, or of communicating in written form. Demonstrated success on basic skills measures becomes a hurdle that must be overcome before the student receives instruction in comprehension, reasoning, or composition.

The findings of research in cognitive science question this assumption and lead to quite a different view of the way children learn. By discarding assumptions about skill hierarchies and by attempting to understand children's competencies as constructed and evolving both within and outside of school,

Barbara Means is director of education and human services research at SRI International, Menlo Park, Calif. Michael S. Knapp, formerly program manager of the Education Policy Studies Program at SRI International, is an associate professor of education leadership and policy studies at the University of Washington, Seattle.

researchers are developing models of intervention that start with what children know and expose them to explicit applications of what has traditionally been thought of as higher-order thinking.

The research on which these models are based has provided a critical mass of evidence that students regarded as educationally disadvantaged can profit from instruction in comprehension, composition, and mathematical reasoning from the very beginning of their education. In what follows, we highlight a set of instructional principles that have evolved from this research and provide some concrete examples of the kinds of instruction that have been developed as a result.[1] To provide a context for this discussion, we first offer a brief description of the kind of teaching that most educationally disadvantaged students are receiving today.[2]

CONVENTIONAL APPROACHES

Classroom studies document the fact that disadvantaged students receive less instruction in higher-order skills than do their more advantaged peers.[3] Their curriculum is less challenging and more repetitive. Their teachers are typically more directive, breaking each task down into smaller pieces, walking the students through procedures step by step, and leaving them with less opportunity to engage in higher order thinking. As a consequence, disadvantaged students receive less exposure to problem-solving tasks in which there is more than one possible answer and in which they have to structure problems for themselves.[4]

The majority of efforts to provide at-risk students with compensatory education have tended to increase the differences between the kinds of instruction provided to the "haves" and to the "have nots." Children who score lower than their peers on standardized tests of reading and on teacher evaluations of their reading abilities—many of them from poor backgrounds and/or from cultural or linguistic minorities—are given special practice in reading, most often in a special pullout room, sometimes in the regular classroom.[5] In these settings, children in compensatory programs typically receive drill on phonics, vocabulary, and word decoding. Each of these is taught as a separate skill, with little or no integration. Often there is little or no coordination between the compensatory and regular classroom teachers and no congruence between the content of the two classes.

Similarly, compensatory programs in mathematics tend to have students practice basic arithmetic operations using workbooks or dittos. On the assumption that they cannot be expected to do even simple math-related problem solving until they have mastered the basics of computation, students are drilled on the same numerical operations year after year.

The results of state and national testing programs suggest that this kind of instruction has had some positive (though not dramatic) effects on student scores on measures of basic skills, especially in the early years of elementary school. What has been disheartening, however, is the fact that comparable gains have not been seen on measures of more advanced skills. In fact, despite years of back-to-basics curricula, minimum competency testing, and compensatory education, the majority of educationally disadvantaged children appear to fall ever farther behind their more advantaged peers as they progress through school and the emphasis increases on advanced skills in comprehension, problem solving, and reasoning.

For too long, there has been a tendency to blame this situation on the students. Tacitly or explicitly, it was assumed that they lacked the capability to perform complex academic tasks. Recently, however, there has been a reexamination of the premises underlying the instruction provided to educationally disadvantaged students. Critics have pointed out that we have decried these students' failure to demonstrate advanced skills even as we have failed to provide them with instruction designed to instill those skills.[6] There is a growing understanding that the failures lie both in the dominant approaches to compensatory education and in the regular classrooms in which educationally disadvantaged students receive the rest of their instruction.

A recent summary of critiques of conventional approaches to teaching academic skills to at-risk students, offered by a group of national experts in reading, writing, and mathematics education, concluded that such approaches tend to:

- underestimate what students are capable of doing;
- postpone more challenging and interesting work for too long—in some cases, forever; and
- deprive students of a meaningful or motivating context for learning or for employing the skills that are taught.[7]

THE ALTERNATIVE VIEW

Cognitive psychologists who study learning and the process of instruction point out that we have been too accepting of the assumption that learning certain skills must take place before learning others. In particular, they single out the assumption that mastery of those skills traditionally designated as "basic" is an absolute prerequisite for learning the skills that we regard as "advanced."

Consider the case of reading comprehension. Cognitive research on comprehension processes has shown the importance of trying to relate what you read to what you already know, of checking to see that your understanding of new information fits with what you have already read, and of setting up expectations for what is to follow and seeing whether those expectations are fulfilled.[8] Research on the reciprocal teaching approach demonstrates clearly that students can acquire comprehension skills—which we have traditionally called advanced—well before they are good decoders of the printed word.[9] Children can learn to reason about new information, to relate information from different sources, to ask questions, and to summarize by using orally presented text before they have mastered all the so-called basics.

Similarly, recent research on children's understanding of math concepts shows that, using modeling and counting, first-graders can solve a wide variety of math problems before they have memorized the computational algorithms that are traditionally regarded as prerequisites.[10] Likewise, Robert Calfee quotes two young children as an illustration of the fact that children can perform sophisticated composition tasks before they have acquired the mechanics of writing.

> *What you have to do with a story is, you analyze it, you break it into parts. You figure out the characters, how they're the same and different. And the plot, how it begins with a problem and goes on until it is solved. Then you understand the story better, and you can even write your own.* —First-Grader, Los Angeles

> *We started out the play by finding a theme, something really important to us personally. A lot of us come from broken homes, so we made the play about that. We did a web [a semantic map] on home; that gave us lots of ideas. Then we talked about how things are now and how we would like them to be. It's pretty lonely when you don't have a daddy, or maybe not even a mommy. So the play began with nothing on the stage, and one of us came out, sat down, and said, "My life is broke." We thought that would get the theme across. It worked pretty good.* —Second-Grader, Los Angeles[11]

In the early school years, children's achievement is typically measured in terms of their ability to perform basic skills in an academic context. The skills are formally assessed, and children are asked to perform independently and to execute the skills for their own sake, not as part of any task they're trying to accomplish. Children from impoverished and linguistic-minority backgrounds often perform poorly on these assessments. Their performance leads many educators to conclude that they are severely deficient academically, a conclusion predicated on the assumption that the skills being tested are the necessary foundation for all later learning.

Ironically, the decontextualized measures of discrete skills that we've come to regard as basic offer less opportunity for connecting with anything children know from their past experiences than would more complex exercises emphasizing the skills we regard as advanced. To prepare them for writing, children from different linguistic backgrounds are drilled on the conventions of standard written English. These will be harder for them than for other children because the conventions often conflict with the children's spoken language.[12] On the other hand, a task that focuses on higher-level issues of communication—e.g., formulating a message that will be persuasive to other people—is perfectly consistent with many of these children's out-of-school experiences. At the level of language mechanics and communication formats, there are many inconsistencies between the backgrounds of many disadvantaged children and the conventions of the schoolhouse, but at the level of the goals of communication, there is much more common ground.

A similar argument can be made about reading instruction. Young readers deemed at risk of school failure are subjected to more drill and tighter standards regarding correct pronunciation in oral reading.[13] These children must struggle with a pronunciation system that often differs from that of their spoken language or dialect at the same time that they're trying to master basic reading.

When it comes to comprehension skills, however, we have every indication that disadvantaged children can make use of their past experiences to help them understand a story. Annemarie Palincsar and Laura Klenk provide examples of how young children regarded as academically "at risk" apply their background knowledge to make inferences about text.[14] They show how a first-grade girl uses her prior knowledge about seasons to make inferences while listening to a story about a baby bear who played too roughly with his sister and fell from a tree into the water: "You know, it kind of told you what time of year it was because it told you it went 'splash,' because if it was this time of year [February], I don't think he'd splash in the water, I think he'd crack." This inference making is exactly the kind of comprehension-enhancing strategy that we regard as advanced. Real-life experiences and skills are relevant to these higher-level academic skills. Instruction in advanced skills offers opportunities for children to use what they already know in the process of developing and refining academic skills.

Educators and psychologists have been developing and studying new models, based on cognitive theory and research, that enable them to teach educationally disadvantaged students advanced skills in mathematics reasoning, reading comprehension, problem solving, and composition. These models represent a new attitude toward learners who have been labeled "at risk" and lead to a fundamental rethinking of the content of the curriculum. They have also made it possible to develop instructional strategies that allow the children to be active learners and that do not require them to work in isolation. Although the research encompasses a wide range of academic content and involves different grade levels, we can extract a set of major themes and principles from this work.

A NEW ATTITUDE TOWARD DISADVANTAGED LEARNERS

The instructional models coming out of cognitive psychology reflect a new attitude toward educationally disadvantaged learners. These researchers do not start with a list of academic skills, administer formal assessments, and catalogue children's deficits. Instead, they start with the conviction—bolstered by years of research in cognitive psychology and linguistics—that children from all kinds of backgrounds come to school with an impressive set of intellectual accomplishments. When we analyze what it means to understand numbers, what it takes

to master the grammar of a language, what is required to be able to categorize and recategorize objects, we can appreciate the magnitude of young children's intellectual accomplishments. When we look closely at how these kinds of understandings are achieved, we begin to understand that concepts are not "given" to the child by the environment but rather are constructed by the child through interactions with the environment.

Children from impoverished and affluent backgrounds alike come to school with important skills and knowledge. They have mastered the receptive and expressive skills of their native language. (The particular language or dialect the children have acquired may or may not match that of the classroom, but the intellectual feat is equivalent in any case.) They have learned basic facts about quantity—e.g., the fact that rearranging objects does not change their number. They have learned much about social expectations, such as the need to take turns talking when participating in a conversation. Moreover, they have a vast collection of knowledge about the world: grocery stores are places where you pay money for food; new flowers bloom in the spring; nighttime is for sleeping.

Instead of taking a deficit view of the educationally disadvantaged learner, cognitive researchers developing alternative models of instruction focus on the knowledge, skills, and abilities that the children possess. Early accomplishments, attained before coming to school, demonstrate that disadvantaged children can do serious intellectual work. What we need to do is design curricula and instructional methods that will build on that prior learning and complement rather than contradict the child's experiences outside of school.

RESHAPING THE CURRICULUM

Once the conventional assumption about a necessary hierarchy of skills has been abandoned, a new set of curricular principles follows.

Focus on Complex, Meaningful Problems
The dominant curricular approach over the last two decades has broken academic content down into small skills, with the idea that each piece would be easy to acquire. An unfortunate side effect is that, by the time we break something down into its smallest parts, the vision of the whole is often totally obscured. Children drill themselves on the spellings

and definitions of long lists of words, often without understanding what the words mean or without any motivation to use them. High school students practice computations involving logarithms, but most of them leave school with no idea of what the purpose of logarithms is or how they might aid in solving practical problems.[15]

The alterative is to keep tasks at a level high enough that the purpose of the task is apparent and makes sense to students. Thus children might write to their city council in support of a public playground. In the course of the exercise, they might need to acquire new vocabulary (*alderman, welfare, and community*), but each word would be acquired in a context that gave it meaning. At the same time, children would be attending to higher-level skills. What are the arguments in favor of a good playground? Which of these arguments would be most persuasive to a politician? What counter-arguments can be expected? How can these be refuted?

Allan Collins, Jan Hawkins, and Sharon Carver describe a math and science curriculum organized around the problem of understanding motion.[16] Students engage in extended investigations of such topics as the physical principles of motion underlying an amusement park ride of their own design or a foul shot in basketball. The Instructional Technology Group at Vanderbilt University has been developing programs that use interactive video to present students with complex problem situations, such as moving a wounded eagle to a distant veterinarian by the safest and fastest route. A whole series of rate, fuel consumption, and distance problems must be identified and solved in the process of devising a plan.[17]

Certainly these tasks are more complex than performing simple computations or phonics exercises, but there are instructional techniques that can lessen the burden on any individual student. Moreover, as we argued above, these more complex tasks build on things that students already know.

Embed Basic Skills Instruction in the Context of More Global Tasks

Teaching advanced skills from the beginning of a child's education does not mean failing to teach those skills traditionally called basic. Instead, these alternative approaches advocate using a complex, meaningful task as the context for instruction in both advanced and basic skills. In place of constant drill on basic addition and subtraction, these skills are practiced in the context of trying to solve real problems. Penelope Peterson, Elizabeth Fennema, and Thomas Carpenter have described the pedagogical use of problems stemming from daily classroom activities—for example, figuring out how many hot lunches and how many cold lunches are ordered each day.[18] Children can practice addition, subtraction, record-keeping, and the use of fractions in the course of this authentic classroom activity.

There are multiple advantages to this approach. First, the more global task provides a motivation for acquiring the knowledge and skills needed to accomplish it. The conventions of written English are worth learning if that will enable you to communicate with a distant friend. Word decoding is much more palatable if the words are part of a message you care about.

Second, embedding basic skills in more complex contexts means that students receive practice in executing a given skill in conjunction with other skills. One of the findings of cognitive research on learning is that it is possible to be able to perform all the subskills of a task without being able to coordinate them in any type of coherent performance. Cognitive psychologists call this the problem of orchestration. The ability to orchestrate discrete skills into the performance of a complex task is critical. After all, the desired outcome of schooling is not students who can perform arithmetic calculations on an arithmetic test but students who can use these skills to complete real-world tasks, and this requires that the calculations be performed in conjunction with the higher-level skills of problem recognition and formulation.

Finally, teaching basic skills in the context of meaningful tasks will increase the probability that the skills will transfer to real-world situations. The decontextualized academic exercises within which many basic skills have been taught are so different from what any of us encounter in the everyday world that it is little wonder that students question the relevance of much of what they learn in school. Some students come to accept the idea of performing academic exercises for their own sake; others reject the whole enterprise. Neither group could be expected to use what they have learned in school when they encounter problems in their everyday lives.

Moreover, much classroom instruction focuses on how to execute a skill without giving adequate attention to when to execute it. Students learn how to make three different kinds of graphs, but they receive no instruction or practice in deciding which kind of graph is most useful for a specific purpose. The matter of deciding which skill to apply and when doesn't come up when skills are taught in isolation; it is unavoidable when skills are taught in a complex, meaningful context.

Make Connections with Students' Out-of-School Experience and Culture

Implicit in the argument above is the notion that in-school instruction will be more effective if it both builds on what children have already learned out of school and makes connections to situations outside of school. Lauren Resnick and her colleagues have found positive effects for a program in which disadvantaged elementary children are not only given realistic problems to solve with arithmetic in class, but are also encouraged to bring in their own real-life problems for their classmates to solve.[19]

At the same time, it is important to recognize that the great cultural diversity in the U.S. means that many children in compensatory education come from homes with languages, practices, and beliefs that are at variance with some of those assumed in "mainstream" classrooms. Luis Moll argues that the strengths of a child's culture should be recognized, and instruction should capitalize on them.[20] He describes an intricate network for sharing practical knowledge and supporting the acquisition of English skills in a Hispanic community. This cultural practice of knowledge sharing can become an effective model for cooperative learning and problem solving in classrooms.

In addition, curriculum materials can be adapted to children's cultures. Thus typical mathematics problems involving figuring out how to obtain five liters of liquid, given only a three-liter and a seven-liter container, were converted to a Haitian story involving children using calabashes to obtain water from a spring.[21] This technique encouraged participation from the Haitian students in a culturally mixed classroom.

Peg Griffin and Michael Cole describe another example. They had black students compose rap lyrics in collaborative sessions using computers.[22] Although rap songs are not a form of literature found in many standard textbooks, they are no different from the sonnet in terms of having a structure and a set of conventions. When working with this form, which was both relevant to their culture and motivating, black students from low-income homes demonstrated a high degree of sophistication in their composition and revision skills.

NEW INSTRUCTIONAL STRATEGIES

The rethinking of the curriculum described above must be matched by a change in the methods that are employed to impart that curriculum. The approaches reviewed here stress teaching methods that are quite different from the structured drill and practice that typify most compensatory education.

Model Powerful Thinking Strategies

Research in cognitive psychology has long been concerned with making the thinking of expert performers manifest. A key goal of this effort has been to understand the processes that expert performers use in addressing complex tasks and solving novel problems and to model these processes explicitly for novice learners. Great strides have been made in understanding the strategies that accomplished readers use to monitor and enhance their understanding, that mathematicians use when faced with novel problems, and that skilled writers employ. The research on instructional approaches that provide models of expert thinking confirms the instructional value of making these strategies explicit for learners.

Cognitive psychologists recommend that teachers explicitly and repeatedly model the higher-order intellectual processes that they are trying to instill. This means thinking aloud while reading a text and trying to understand how the information in it fits with previously known facts; it means externalizing the thought processes that go into an effort to solve a mathematical puzzle; it means demonstrating the planning and revision processes involved in composition. For too long we have shown students the product that they are supposed to achieve (e.g., the right answer to a math problem or a polished essay) without demonstrating the critical processes required to achieve it.

Encourage Multiple Approaches to Academic Tasks

The alternative programs differ from the instruction conventionally provided in most classrooms in their encouragement of teaching multiple strategies for solving problems. Rather than try to teach the one right way to solve a problem, these programs seek to foster students' ability to invent strategies for solving problems.

In some cases, this kind of thinking is elicited by providing students with open-ended questions to which there is no single right answer. For example, given the assignment to develop a description of one's city that would entice other people to live there, students are free to follow very different paths and to produce different kinds of solutions. In other cases, such as elementary mathematics, problems do have one correct solution. Still, there may well be more than one way to reach that solution, and one of the clearest demonstrations of real understanding of mathematical concepts is the ability to use those concepts to invent solution strategies on one's own.

To support the development of this essential component of problem solving, innovative programs are inviting students to think of their own ways to address a problem. In the classroom described in the box on page 81, titled "Cognitively Guided Instruction," individuals or small groups of students are given mathematics problems to solve. As each child finds an answer, the teacher asks him or her to describe how the solution was reached. When all students have finished, the students' different paths to the answer are compared and discussed so students can see alternative approaches modeled and come to realize that there is no single right way to find the answer.

Provide Scaffolding to Enable Students to Accomplish Complex Tasks

On reading our recommendation that disadvantaged students be presented with authentic, complex tasks from the outset of their education, a reader's natural reaction might be concern about how the students will handle the demands of such tasks. We need to be sensitive to the fact that many of the components of the task will be difficult and will require mental resources. How is the disadvantaged student, particularly the young student, to handle all of this?

A key instructional concept is that of scaffolding—enabling the learner to handle a complex task by taking on parts of the task. For example, the instructor can perform all the computations required when first introducing students to algebra problems, or the instructor can use cue cards to remind novice writers to do things such as consider alternative arguments.[23] The reciprocal teaching approach alluded to above uses many kinds of scaffolding.[24] In the early stages of teaching, the teacher cues the student to employ various comprehension-enhancing strategies, leaving students free to concentrate on executing those strategies. A more extensive form of scaffolding can be provided for students who have yet to master decoding skills: the teacher reads the text orally, allowing students to practice comprehension strategies before they have fully mastered word decoding.

Like the physical scaffolding that permits a worker to reach higher places than would otherwise be possible, instructional scaffolding makes it possible for students to accomplish tasks with special materials or with assistance from the teacher or other students. The ultimate goal, of course, is for the student to be able to accomplish the task without assistance. This requires the judicious removal of the support as the student gains more skill.

Make Dialogue the Central Medium for Teaching and Learning

In conventional modes of instruction, the key form of communication is transmission: the teacher has the knowledge and transmits it to the students. Just as a television viewer cannot change the content of a program transmitted to his or her home, the student is a passive recipient of the message the teacher chooses to deliver. The student can pay attention or not, but the message will be the same.

A dialogue is a very different form of communication. It is an interchange in which two parties are full-fledged participants, both with significant influence on the nature of the exchange. This concept of dialogue is central to the cognitive approaches to instruction. Reciprocal teaching occurs through dialogue initially between the teacher and a small group of students, later among the students themselves.

The specifics of the instructional content emerge in the back-and-forth interchange. In their description of an innovative math/science program in a Harlem secondary school, Allan Collins, Jan Hawkins, and Sharon Carver provide an example of the value of student-to-student dialogue: students who had developed hypermedia information displays found that students from another school were bored by the work they had regarded as exemplary.[25] This experience led the student developers to look at their work from an audience's perspective and to undertake design changes to make their product better.

The instructional principles described here show that much more can be done in teaching comprehension, composition, and mathematical reasoning to educationally disadvantaged students than has generally been attempted—whether in compensatory programs or in regular classrooms. It is time to rethink our assumptions about the relationship between basic and advanced skills and to examine

Cognitively Guided Instruction

While most of the children in this first-grade class are solving word problems independently or in small groups, Ms. J. is sitting at a table with three students, Raja, Erik, and Ernestine (Ern). Each child has plastic cubes that can be connected together, a pencil, and a big sheet of paper on which are written the same word problems.

Ms. J.: Okay. Who wants to read the first one?

All: Me!

Ms. J.: Well, let's read them together.

All: [Reading] Raja made 18 clay dinosaurs. Ernestine has nine clay dinosaurs. How many more clay dinosaurs does Raja have than Ernestine?

Ms. J.: Okay. [Reads the problem again as the students listen.]

The students work on the problem in different ways. Raja puts together 18 cubes. She removes nine of them and counts the rest. She gets 11. She writes the answer down, then looks up at the teacher for confirmation. Ms. J. looks at the answer, looks back at the problem, and then says, "You're real close." As Raja recounts the cubes, Ms. J. watches her closely. This time Raja counts nine.

Ernestine also connects 18 cubes. Then she counts nine and breaks them off. She counts what she has left. Ernestine exclaims, "I've got it!" Ms. J. looks at Ernestine's answer and says, "No, you're real close." Ernestine does the same procedure over again.

Erik connects nine cubes, and in a separate group he connects 18. He places them next to each other and matches them up, counting across each row to make sure there are nine matches. Then Erik breaks off the unmatched cubes and counts them. "I've got it!" he announces. Erik writes down his answer. He says to Ms. J., "Got it. Want me to tell you?" Ms. J. nods "Yes." Erik goes to Ms. J. and whispers his answer in her ear. Ms. J. nods "Yes" in reply. Turning to the group, she queries, "Okay now, how did you get your answers? Remember, that's what's the important thing: How did you get it? Let's see if we can come up with different ways this time. [Erik has his hand raised.] Erik, what did you do?"

Erik: I had nine cubes, and then I had and then I put 18 cubes and then I put them together. And the 18 cubes . . . I took away some of the 18 cubes.

Ms. J.: Okay, let's see if we can understand what Erik did. Okay, you got—show me 18 cubes.

Erik: Okay. [He puts together two of the three sets of nine he has lined up in front of him.]

Ms. J.: Okay, so you have 18 cubes. Then you had nine.

Erik: [He takes nine cubes in his other hand and puts them side by side.] Yeah.

Ms. J.: Then you compared.

Erik: [Simultaneously with Ms. J.] Then I put them together.

Ms. J.: Then you put them together.

Erik: Then I took . . .

Ms. J.: Nine away.

Erik: Nine away, and I counted them [the ones left], and there were nine.

Ms. J.: Okay. So that's one way to do it. Nice job, Erik. Which way did you do it, Raja?

Ms. J. discusses their solution methods with Raja and Ernestine.

Ms. J.: So we had—how many different ways did we do that problem? Erik, you did it one way, right? Raja, was your way different from Erik's? [Raja nods "Yes."] Was your way different from Ernestine's? [Raja nods "Yes."] So that was two ways. Ernestine, was your way different from Raja?

Ern: Yes.

Ms. J.: Was your way different from Erik?

Ern: Yes.

Ms. J.: So we did the problem in three different ways. Let's read the next problem.

In a CGI [Cognitively Guided Instruction] classroom, the teacher poses problems that each child can solve at his or her level of mathematics knowledge and understanding. The teacher encourages each child to solve mathematical problems using ways that make sense to the child. Ms. J. encourages each child to tell her how he or she solved the problems and uses what the child tells her to make instructional decisions. Children are aware that their thinking is as important as the answer and are not only comfortable, but determined that Ms. J. understand how they have solved each problem.

This excerpt comes from Barbara Means, Carol Chelemer, and Michael S. Knapp, eds., *Teaching Advanced Skills to At-Risk Students* (San Francisco: Jossey-Bass, 1991), pp. 80–83.

critically the content and teaching methods that we bring to the classroom.

The models described here were inspired by research in cognitive psychology, and they focus on teaching the kind of content generally regarded as "conceptual," "higher order," or "advanced." The curricular emphases of these models have long been accepted as appropriate for teaching gifted children, older students, or those from educationally advantaged backgrounds. What has not been adequately appreciated is the value of these models for all learners—young and old, advantaged and disadvantaged alike.

NOTES

1. This article is based on a set of papers commissioned as part of a project sponsored by the U.S. Department of Education. The complete set of papers has been published in Barbara Means, Carol Chelemer, and Michael S. Knapp, eds., *Teaching Advanced Skills to At-Risk Students: Views from Theory and Practice* (San Francisco: Jossey-Bass, 1991).

2. For a description of a nationwide sample of such programs, see Michael S. Knapp et al., *What is Taught, and How, to the Children of Poverty* (Washington, D.C.: Office of Planning, Budget, and Evaluation, U.S. Department of Education, 1991).

3. Richard L. Allington and Anne McGill-Franzen, "School Response to Reading Failure: Chapter 1 and Special Education Students in Grades 2, 4, and 8," *Elementary School Journal*, v. 89, 1989, 529–42; and Jeannie Oakes, "Tracking, Inequality, and the Rhetoric of School Reform: Why Schools Don't Change," *Journal of Education*, v. 168, 1986, 61–80.

4. Jean Anyon, "Social Class and the Hidden Curriculum of Work," *Journal of Education*, v. 162, 1980, 67–92.

5. Beatrice F. Birman et al., *The Current Operation of the Chapter 1 Program: Final Report from the National Assessment of Chapter 1* (Washington, D.C.: U.S. Government Printing Office, 1987).

6. Michael Cole and Peg Griffin, eds., *Contextual Factors in Education: Improving Science and Math Education for Minorities and Women* (Madison: Wisconsin Center for Education Research, University of Wisconsin, 1987).

7. Michael S. Knapp and Patrick M. Shields, "Reconceiving Academic Instruction for the Children of Poverty," *Phi Delta Kappan*, June 1990, 753–58.

8. Ann L. Brown, Bonnie B. Armbruster, and Linda Baker, "The Role of Metacognition in Reading and Studying," in Judith Orasanu, ed., *Reading and Comprehension* (Hillsdale, N.J.: Lawrence Erlbaum, 1986).

9. Annemarie S. Palincsar and Ann L. Brown, "Reciprocal Teaching of Comprehension-Fostering and Comprehension-Monitoring Activities," *Cognition and Instruction*, v. 1, 1984, 117–75.

10. Thomas P. Carpenter, "Learning to Add and Subtract: An Exercise in Problem Solving," in Edward A. Silver, ed., *Teaching and Learning Mathematical Problem Solving: Multiple Research Perspectives* (Hillsdale, N.J.: Lawrence Erlbaum, 1987); and Herbert A. Ginsberg, *The Development of Mathematical Thinking* (New York: Academic Press, 1983).

11. Robert Calfee, "What Schools Can Do to Improve Literacy Instruction," in Means, Chelemer, and Knapp, 178; and Mary Bryson and Marlene Scardamalia, "Teaching Writing to Students at Risk for Academic Failure," in Means, Chelemer, and Knapp, 141–75.

12. Jerie Cobb Scott, "Nonmainstream Groups: Questions and Research Directions," in Jane L. Davidson, ed., *Counterpoint and Beyond* (Urbana, Ill.: National Council of Teachers of English, 1988).

13. Richard Allington, "Teacher Interruption Behavior During Primary-Grade Oral Reading," *Journal of Educational Psychology*, v. 72, 1980, 371–77; and Jere E. Brophy and Thomas L. Good, *Teacher-Student Relationships: Causes and Consequences* (New York: Holt, Rinehart & Winston, 1974).

14. Annemarie S. Palincsar and Laura J. Klenk, "Learning Dialogues to Promote Text Comprehension," in Means, Chelemer, and Knapp, 112–40.

15. Robert D. Sherwood et al., "Macro-contexts for Learning," *Journal of Applied Cognition*, v. 1, 1987, 93–108.

16. Allan Collins, Jan Hawkins, and Sharon M. Carver, "A Cognitive Apprentices for Disadvantaged Students," in Means, Chelemer, and Knapp, 216–54.

17. Nancy Vye et al., "Commentary," in Means, Chelemer, and Knapp, 54–67.

18. Penelope Peterson, Elizabeth Fennema, and Thomas Carpenter, "Using Children's Mathematical Knowledge," in Means, Chelemer, and Knapp, 68–111.

19. Lauren Resnick et al., "Thinking in Arithmetic Class," in Means, Chelemer, and Knapp, 27–67.

20. Luis Moll, "Social and Instructional Issues Educating 'Disadvantaged' Students," in Michael S. Knapp and Patrick M. Shields, eds., *Better Schooling for the Children of Poverty: Alternatives to Conventional Wisdom—Vol. II: Commissioned Paper and Literature Review* (Washington, D.C.: Office of Planning, Budget, and Evaluation, U.S. Department of Education, 1990).

21. Judith J. Richards, "Commentary," in Means, Chelemer, and Knapp, 102–11.

22. Peg Griffin and Michael Cole, "New Technologies, Basic Skills, and the Underside of Education: What's to Be Done?" in Judith A. Langer, ed., *Language, Literacy, and Culture: Issues of Society and Schooling* (Norwood, N.J.: Ablex, 1987), 199–231.

23. Bryson and Scardamalia, 141–75.

24. Palincsar and Brown, 117–75.

25. Collins, Hawkins, and Carver, 216–54.

Shortchanging Girls and Boys

SUSAN McGEE BAILEY

Recently gender equity in education has become a hot, or at least a "reasonably warm," topic in education. Higher education institutions across the country are under renewed pressure to provide equal athletic opportunities for female students. The U.S. Supreme Court is considering cases involving the admission of women to all-male, state-supported military institutions. And the continued under-representation of women in tenured faculty positions is prompting many donors to withhold contributions to Harvard University's fundraising campaign.

But it is at the elementary and secondary school levels that the shortchanging of girls has been most extensively documented (Wellesley College Center for Research on Women 1992, AAUW 1995, Orenstein 1994, Sadker and Sadker 1994, Thorne 1993, Stein et al. 1993). Twenty-four years after the passage of Title IX—which prohibits discrimination on the basis of sex in any educational programs receiving federal funds—girls and boys are still not on equal footing in our nation's classrooms. Reviews of curricular materials, data on achievement and persistence in science, and research on teacher-to-student and student-to-student interaction patterns all point to school experiences that create significant barriers to girls' education. These factors have fostered widespread discussion and action among parents, educators, and policymakers.

Susan McGee Bailey is Director, The Wellesley Center for Research on Women, Wellesley College, 106 Central St., Wellesley, MA 02181.

BARRIERS TO GENDER EQUITABLE EDUCATION

As the principal author of the 1992 study, *How Schools Shortchange Girls*, I have followed the discussion with considerable interest and mounting concern. The central problem posed in the opening pages of this report continues to be ignored in our discussions of public K–12 education

> *[There are] critical aspects of social development that our culture has traditionally assigned to women that are equally important for men. Schools must help girls and boys acquire both the relational and the competitive skills needed for full participation in the workforce, family, and community. (Wellesley College Center for Research on Women 1992, p. 2)*

Too much of the discussion and too many of the proposed remedies rely on simplistic formulations that obscure, rather than address, the complex realities confronting our society.

First among these are the assumptions that (1) gender equity is something "for girls only" and (2) if the situation improves for girls, boys will inevitably lose. These constructions are dangerously narrow and limit boys as well as girls. Gender equity is about enriching classrooms, widening opportunities, and expanding choices for all students.

The notion that helping girls means hurting boys amounts to a defense of a status quo that we all know is serving too few of our students well. Surely it is as important for boys to learn about the contributions of women to our nation as it is for girls to study this information. Surely adolescent pregnancy and parenting are issues for young men as well as young women. And surely boys as well as girls benefit from instructional techniques that encourage cooperation in learning.

A second set of assumptions concern the single-sex versus coed dichotomy. During discussions of gender equity, rarely does anyone stop to consider that coeducation, as the term is generally used, implies more than merely attending the same institution. It is usually assumed to mean a balanced experience as compared to an exclusive, one-sided, single-sex, all-female or all-male one. Thus the term itself undercuts our ability to achieve genuine coeducation by implying that it already exists.

We would do better to describe U.S. public elementary and secondary education as mixed-sex education rather than as coeducation. Girls and boys are mixed together in our schools, but they are not receiving the same quality or quantity of education—nor are they genuinely learning from and about each other. Our task is to find ways to provide the gender equitable education the term coeducation promises, but does not yet deliver.

LESSONS FROM ALL-GIRL SCHOOLS

It may indeed be easier in an all-girl setting both to value skills, career fields, and avocations generally considered feminine *and* to encourage girls in nontraditional pursuits. Pressures on students from peers, from popular culture, and even from many adults around them all define gender stereotypic behavior as normal, expected, and successful. Particularly for young adolescents, the clarity of these stereotypes can be reassuring; questioning them can be uncomfortable and risky. In a world where being labeled a "girl" is the classic insult for boys, single-sex environments for girls can provide a refuge from put-downs and stereotypes.

But these environments may also send messages that can perpetuate rather than eliminate negative gender stereotyping. Removing girls from classes in order to provide better learning opportunities for them can imply that girls and boys are so different that they must be taught in radically different ways. When all-girl classes are set up

specifically in science or math, an underlying, if unintended, message can be that girls are less capable in these subjects. Separating boys from girls in order to better control boys' behavior can indicate that boys are "too wild" to control.

Rather than assuming that we must isolate girls in order to protect them from boys' boisterous, competitive behavior—or that boys will be unduly feminized in settings where girls are valued and comfortable—we must look carefully at why some students and teachers prefer single-sex settings for girls. We must understand the positive aspects of these classrooms in order to begin the difficult task of bringing these positive factors into mixed-sex classes.

In U.S. public schools, this is not only a matter of good sense, but it is a matter of law. Title IX permits single-sex instruction only in very specific situations.* In doing so, we will be moving toward genuinely coeducational environments where the achievements, perspectives, and experiences of both girls and boys, women and men, are equally recognized and rewarded whether or not they fall into traditional categories.

HOW TO ELIMINATE BARRIERS

As long as the measures and models of success presented to students follow traditional gender stereotypes and remain grounded in a hierarchy that says paid work is always and absolutely more important and rewarding than unpaid work, that the higher the pay the more valuable the work *and* the worker who does it, we will be unfairly limiting the development of, and the opportunities available to, all our students. Gender equitable education is about eliminating the barriers and stereotypes that limit the options of *both* sexes. To move in this direction, we need to take three major steps.

1. *We must acknowledge the gendered nature of schooling.* Schools are a part of society. Educators cannot single-handedly change the value structure we ourselves embody, but we can acknowledge

*Under Title IX, portions of elementary and secondary school classes dealing with human sexuality and instruction in sports that involve bodily contact may, but do not have to be, separated by sex. (Title IX Rules and Regulations of the Educational Amendments of 1972, section 86.34)

and begin to question the ways in which gender influences our schooling. *How Schools Shortchange Girls* points out that the emotions and the power dynamics of sex, race, and social class are all present, but evaded, aspects of our classrooms. We can begin to change this by fostering classroom discussions that explicitly include these issues and that value expressions of feelings as well as recitations of facts.

2. *We must take a careful look at our own practices.* Years ago as a first-year teacher, I was proud of my sensitivity to the needs of my sixth graders. I carefully provided opportunities for boys to take part in class discussions and lead group projects in order to channel their energies in positive ways. I was equally careful to ensure that two very shy, soft-spoken girls never had to be embarrassed by giving book reports in front of the class.

Only much later did I realize that rather than helping the boys learn cooperative skills, I may merely have reinforced their sense that boys act while girls observe, and that I may have protected the girls from exactly the experiences they needed in order to overcome their initial uncertainties. Further, in protecting the girls, I also deprived the boys of opportunities to learn that both girls and boys can take the risks and garner the rewards of speaking up in class and speaking out on issues.

One technique that teachers can use to gain a picture of their classes is to develop class projects in which students serve as data collectors. Students are keen observers of the world around them. Having them keep a record of who is taking part in class can serve as a springboard for important discussions. These discussions can raise everyone's awareness of classroom dynamics, dynamics sometimes so ingrained that they have become invisible.

3. *We must learn from all-girl environments about teaching techniques and curricular perspectives that have particular appeal to girls and determine how to use these approaches successfully in mixed-sex classes.* In talking with teachers working in all-girl environments, I hear three frequent suggestions: (1) place less emphasis on competition and speed and more emphasis on working together to ensure that everyone completes and understands the problem or project; (2) place more emphasis on curricular materials that feature girls and women; and (3) increase the focus on practical, real-life applications of mathematics and the sciences.

THREE PRACTICAL SUGGESTIONS

Teachers can apply these three suggestions in mixed-sex settings. The first is the most difficult. What appears to happen naturally in all-girl settings—for example, girls' working together in an environment where they feel empowered to set the pace—must be deliberately fostered in settings where a different style has been the norm. Girls and their teachers speak of all-girl classes as places where fewer students shout out answers and interrupt one another. Teachers indicate that they deliberately work to ensure that all girls take some active part in class activities. If teachers can directly address these factors in an all-girl setting, surely we can begin to address them in mixed-sex settings.

Further, teachers must experiment with instructions and with reward systems that will encourage students to value a thorough understanding of a task as well as a quick answer, and of group success as well as individual performance. In doing so, we will be encouraging strengths many girls have developed and helping boys acquire skills that they need.

The second suggestion is also not without difficulties when transported to mixed-sex settings. As television producers have discovered, girls may watch programs with male characters, but programs featuring girls are less likely to attract or hold boys' interests. But schools are places where students come to learn. Boys *and* girls need to learn to appreciate and value the accomplishments of women and women's groups who have succeeded in traditionally male fields: Shirley Chisholm, Indira Ghandi, Sally Ride, the Women's Campaign Fund, as well as those whose success has been in traditionally female areas of employment and avocation: Jane Addams, Mary McLeod Bethune, the Visiting Nurses Association.

In *Natural Allies, Women's Associations in American History*, Anne Firor Scott notes that "by the 1930s the landscape was covered with libraries, schools, colleges, kindergartens, museums, health clinics, houses of refuge, school lunch programs, parks, playgrounds, all of which owed their existence to one or several women's societies" (1991, p. 3). Our students—male and female—need to learn more of this work if they are to grow into adults who can carry on activities vital to our survival as a viable, humane society.

The third factor is perhaps the least problematic. Although girls may be most enthusiastic about pursuing science when they see it as relevant to daily life, boys will surely not be less interested when presented with more relevance! For teachers to develop new lesson plans and materials in the sciences, however, will require increased support from school administrators and school boards for professional development, new materials and equipment, and perhaps a reorganization of class time.

Operation Smart, an after-school informal science program for girls developed by Girls, Inc., is just one example of new relevant science programs. A unit on water pollution, for example, offers middle school and junior high school girls an opportunity to study the effects of pollution in their own communities and to gain an understanding of the value of scientific knowledge and procedures in improving living conditions (Palmer 1994).

Mixed-sex classes can easily adapt such projects, and many have. Last year my nieces, both middle school students in mixed-sex classes in Mystic, Connecticut, eagerly showed me their science projects. Sarah's, done with her close friend Caitlin, contained several different pieces of cloth, each of which had been put through a series of trials: burned, washed, stretched, and frozen. "We thought the synthetic pieces of cloth would be stronger, but they weren't! Now we know natural material is very tough."

Aidan, a year older, collected samples of river water at points varying in distance from the mouth of the Mystic River where it joins the salt water of Fisher's Island Sound. Expecting that the water would be less salty the farther away it was from the Sound, she was surprised to find that her graph was not a straight line: a very salty sample appeared at a point quite far up river. Trying to figure out what might account for this became the most interesting aspect of the project. For both Sarah and Aidan, science is about their own questions, not out of a book or in a laboratory and it is certainly not a boys-only activity!

MOVING BEYOND STEREOTYPES

As we move into a new century, we must leave behind our boys-only and girls-only assumptions and stereotypes. On any given measure of achievement or skill, we can find greater similarity between the average score of girls as a group and the average score of boys as a group than we can find when comparing among individual girls or among individual boys. We must no longer allow stereotypic assumptions to guide our expectations or obscure the reality that empathy, cooperation, and competition are all important skills—and are important for all our students.

REFERENCES

Orenstein, P. (1994). *SchoolGirls: Young Women, Self-Esteem, and the Confidence Gap.* New York: Doubleday.

Palmer, L. (1994). *The World of Water: Environmental Science for Teens.* New York: Girls Incorporated.

Sadker, D., and M. Sadker. (1994). *Failing at Fairness: How America's Schools Cheat Girls.* New York: C. Scribner's Sons.

Scott, A. F. (1991). *Natural Allies: Women's Associations in American History.* Urbana, Ill.: University of Illinois Press.

Stein, N., N. Marshall, and L. Tropp. (1993). *Secrets in Public: Sexual Harassment in Our Schools.* Wellesley, Mass.: The Wellesley College Center for Research on Women.

Thorne, B. (1993). *Gender Play: Girls and Boys in School.* New Brunswick, N.J.: Rutgers University Press.

Wellesley College Center for Research on Women. (1992). *The AAUW Report: How Schools Shortchange Girls.* Washington, D.C.: American Association of University Women Educational Foundation; reprint ed., (1995), New York: Marlowe and Company.

The Education of Language-Minority Students: Where Are We, and Where Do We Need to Go?

CLAUDE GOLDENBERG

Language-minority children, particularly those who are Spanish-speaking and from low-income backgrounds, generally do not do well in U.S. schools. Unfortunately, our schools' response to the challenge of non-English-speaking students has been uneven, fitful, and laced with political, ideological, and methodological controversies such as those swirling around bilingual education (Carter & Segura, 1979; Crawford, 1991). Despite pockets of success here and there (e.g., Krashen & Biber, 1988), the overall picture for many of these students is troubling. Spanish-speaking students—*even when taught and tested in Spanish*—still score at the thirty-second percentile in relation to a national comparison group (taught and tested in English); in second and third grades, when they are still taught and tested in Spanish, their scores drop to the twenty-seventh percentile (CTB/McGraw-Hill, 1982, 1988). Eighty-five percent of Hispanic fourth and eighth graders read in English at a "basic" level or below. Over half score even below "basic," meaning they cannot demonstrate understanding of a text written at their grade level (Mullis, Campbell, & Farstrup, 1993).

There is little disagreement that a crisis exists. The real question is what should be done about it. Here is where things get difficult because of, first, the difficulty of sorting out the roots of the problem and, second, the scarcity of demonstrably effective

Claude Goldenberg is at California State University, Long Beach.

solutions. I will try to illustrate these difficulties by discussing two of the many topics addressed by the authors of articles in this special issue—(1) low English academic engagement by limited-English-proficient (LEP) students and (2) the challenges of making the transition from native language to mainstream English instruction.

LOW ENGAGEMENT IN ENGLISH: NOT ENOUGH ENGLISH, OR NOT ENOUGH SPANISH?

Consider Arreaga-Mayer and Perdomo-Rivera's findings (1996) that show astonishingly low levels of oral engagement and academic talk among "at-risk" Latino students in regular (English mainstream) and English-as-a-second-language (ESL) middle-elementary classrooms. These findings accord with previous research showing that classrooms with language-minority students fail to provide environments that strongly support linguistic or academic growth (e.g., Ramírez, 1992). Findings such as these have actually been reported regularly in the educational literature for years, and not just for LEP students (Cuban, 1984; Goodlad, 1984). Nonetheless, I was stunned to read that academic talk occurred during only 2% of the day for LEP students in the classrooms Arreaga-Mayer and Perdomo-Rivera studied; total oral engagement was only 4% of the day. The percentages were slightly higher in ESL classes but still lower than anything I have seen reported previously.

Arreaga-Mayer and Perdomo-Rivera argue that "these low levels of oral engagement [in English] illustrate a major reason why LEP students are not learning English in U.S. schools" (p. 251). Their data suggest that teachers' inordinate emphasis on whole-class instruction and individual seatwork severely limits these students' opportunities to talk, ask and answer questions, read aloud, and otherwise actively engage in learning language and content. Arreaga-Mayer and Perdomo-Rivera are undoubtedly correct when they argue that teachers must organize their classrooms differently, making use of individualized instruction and small-group cooperative settings in order to stimulate more active engagement and create an environment for English language and academic development. Certainly, how teachers organize their classrooms has important consequences for students' learning opportunities and their achievement (Slavin, 1989).

Additional considerations are relevant, however, when analyzing the situation Arreaga-Mayer and Perdomo-Rivera depict. The Hispanic students in this study were in a program where they received *no* primary language instruction at any point in their school careers; the only support provided was ESL pull-out. The fact that the academic talk rate was a meager 2% and the general engagement rate was below 50% might not be the result of classroom organizational factors only. These findings could also be a result of these students' not receiving sufficient *primary language instruction* to allow them to participate meaningfully in an English-speaking academic environment—even in ESL classes, which are presumably geared to their English development. True, primary language instruction by itself is not sufficient for high levels of meaningful talk and academic engagement by students (Ramírez, 1992), but it might be necessary for many students who come to school with limited academic backgrounds and opportunities in the home language.

INSTRUCTION IN THE NATIVE LANGUAGE, ACHIEVEMENT IN ENGLISH

The theory that undergirds most bilingual education programs in the United States today (e.g., California State Department of Education, 1981) holds that many non- or limited-English-speaking students re-

quire instruction in their *native language* in order to attain high academic achievement *in English*. This might seem bizarrely counterintuitive to many; however, the idea one could get to the East by sailing West was once also bizarrely counterintuitive. Bilingual education theory, in brief, holds the following:

1. One learns most readily and easily in the language one knows best—the home language. Learning new knowledge and skills in English while at the same time trying to learn to speak the language is very difficult, far more difficult than most people realize. For some learners, it might be academically crippling.
2. One can learn a great deal of academic knowledge and skills in one's first language while simultaneously learning how to speak and understand a second.
3. What one learns in a first language is still known when one learns the second (English in the United States); in fact, what a person learns in a first language might actually help in learning a second, since it will make second language learning more meaningful. Knowledge and skills learned in the first language are available—they transfer—in the second language.

According to this theory, then, language-minority students are generally best served in programs that build academic knowledge *in students' home languages* while helping to build proficiency in English. A body of evidence from both basic (e.g., Fitzgerald, 1995; Hakuta & Snow, 1986) and evaluation (e.g., Ramírez, 1992; Willig, 1985) research supports this theory and many of its tenets.

But both the theory and practice of bilingual education remain enmeshed in controversy. The debates take place on many levels—substantive, political, and ideological (e.g., Crawford, 1991; Porter, 1990) as well as methodological, technical, and statistical (e.g., *Bilingual Research Journal*, 1992; Meyer & Fienberg, 1992). Clearly, bilingual education can claim successes (Krashen & Biber, 1988); better designed and implemented studies are more likely to find positive effects (Willig, 1985); and Spanish-speaking students might start to "catch up" with English-speaking students if they are in effective bilingual programs that use Spanish through much of elementary school (Collier, 1992; Ramírez, 1992; Thomas, 1992).

Nevertheless, evaluations of bilingual programs are mixed, and even when programs appear successful, technical methodological issues cloud conclusions (e.g., Meyer & Fienberg, 1992, on the "Ramírez study"). In addition, even some of the most successful bilingual education models sometimes fail to produce desired effects (e.g., Samaniego & Eubank, 1991). In Massachusetts, the first state to pass a law actually promoting bilingual education, in 1971, Hispanic students in bilingual education programs continue to perform poorly (Commonwealth of Massachusetts, 1994). And many Spanish-speaking students still tend to score below grade-level norms, even in well-established bilingual programs (Gersten & Woodward, 1995). Are these failures of bilingual education theory? Or of how the theory has been operationalized and put into practice? Or is it really a failure of our educational system more generally to address the needs of many culturally and linguistically diverse students, which then limits the effectiveness of an otherwise sound and reasonable theory?

In any case, using the theory as a guide, one could argue that nonparticipation of the students in Arreaga-Mayer and Perdomo-Rivera's study was not due to just classroom structures that discourage English oral academic engagement by LEP students but *also* to a program that fails to provide what many LEP students need most, namely, high-level and challenging instruction in the primary language. (In fairness, I should note that the district where Arreaga-Mayer and Perdomo-Rivera conducted their study served students from 14 different language backgrounds, so it might well be that a primary language program was simply impossible; even when students come from only one or two non-English backgrounds, finding qualified primary language teachers is still a huge problem [Gold, 1992]. These are two major issues that complicate things further.)

If the theory underlying bilingual education is valid, an intervention that fails to include providing language-minority students with adequate primary language instruction is unlikely to be effective. This, of course, remains an empirical question. But it has proven exceptionally difficult to answer with clarity, perhaps because language and language use are never simply empirical matters.

DEALING WITH "TRANSITION"— OR REIFYING THE PROBLEM?

Another thicket of difficulty is transition, the period in their schooling when language-minority students in native language programs make the shift from instruction that relies heavily on the native language to instruction that is exclusively in mainstream English. For many LEP students, issues of transition are not relevant, since they are not in native language programs requiring transition to English at some point. In California, fewer than one-half of LEP students are or have been in programs that make at least some instructional use of their native language (California State Department of Education, 1994b). Nationwide, only 36% of LEP students receive "significant" amounts of instruction in the native language; an additional 21% receive only minimal amounts—greater than 2% of instructional time but less than a "significant" amount. Even in kindergarten through second grade, the years when primary language instruction is most likely to be used, nearly 40% of LEP students receive virtually *none* (less than 2%) of their instruction in the primary language (Development Associates, 1993).

But for those students who do receive native language instruction in their early years, the timing, manner, and dynamics of the transition to English are likely to be important. Depending on a range of factors—the school's and district's program, individual student characteristics and background, when a student happens to begin attending the program—transition can occur anywhere from early elementary to middle school or later. As Russell Gersten (1996, in this issue) notes—and many teachers I know will confirm—the transition years are beset with difficulty and frustration for both students and teachers. During and following transition, students' classroom participation and achievement often go down; uncertainty, confusion, and special education referrals go up.

Transition is, undoubtedly, a crucial period in the education of LEP students, but one about which educators have little solid empirical basis for policy and practice. There is evidence, for example, that it takes students from 5 to 7 years in order to become sufficiently competent in a second language to succeed in mainstream classes (Cummins, 1980); abrupt removal of primary language instruction, moreover, can be detrimental to LEP students' academic progress (Ramírez, 1992).

Many other questions remain, however. For example: When should students make the transition? Is there a threshold of primary language skills (e.g., native language literacy level) or English language skills (e.g., oral proficiency in English) that LEP students should reach before transitioning? How can educators facilitate a successful transition from native language instruction to mainstream English classes? What sort of instruction and learning opportunities are most helpful? What is the appropriate mix of primary language and English—before, during, and after transition? When using English as the instructional medium, are there modifications that can be made so that instruction is both comprehensible *and* presents challenging content? These are questions about which there are strong opinions and many recommendations but little to go on empirically for elementary students and teachers dealing with transition.

It is, on the one hand, gratifying to read the articles in this special issue targeting topics relevant to these critical questions. Many of the ideas contained in this collection—Chamot and O'Malley's Cognitive Academic Language Learning Approach, Anderson and Roit's suggestions for linking reading comprehension and English language development, Klingner and Vaughn's variations on reciprocal teaching, Arreaga-Mayer and Perdomo-Rivera's classroom organizational factors, Rueda and García's insights into the theoretical orientations of teachers, and the many practical examples offered by the teachers profiled in articles by Bos and Reyes and Jiménez, Gersten, and Rivera—offer promising hypotheses for how teachers might help students during this difficult and challenging period. Some of the suggested strategies have been around for a while (e.g., Rodríguez, 1984), but it can only be seen as a good thing that researchers and reflective practitioners are setting their sights more clearly on the transition phase in language-minority students' school careers.

Or is it such a good thing? Perhaps reifying transition—making it into an explicit phase of students' school program—is precisely the wrong thing to do. Some argue that transition is not, or should not be, an issue at all. It is one because schools make it one, and they do this by insisting on cutting off primary language instruction as soon as they think students are able to function in English mainstream classrooms (Wong Fillmore & Valadez, 1986). McLaughlin (1992) points out that many teachers "assume that once children can converse comfortably in English, they are in full control of the language" (p. 6). This is often not the case. Limited-English-speaking students can require up to 7 years before they have mastered the abstract and decontextualized linguistic skills necessary for academic success in regular English classrooms (Cummins, 1980). Further, because of wide variability in the rate and way in which students acquire a second language (McLaughlin, 1992),

there is some question as to whether it makes sense to have a formal transition period, no matter how flexibly it might be applied. Some writers have suggested that students should "self-transition" rather than be "forced into mandatory 'transitional' environments" (García & Colón, 1995, p. 55).

MAINTENANCE INSTEAD OF TRANSITION?

Consider, then, an alternative to having students make the transition from native language programs to all-English programs: Students from non-English-speaking backgrounds, at least until they are redesignated (reclassified) "fluent-English-proficient" (FEP) and ideally, even once they have become FEP, remain in an instructional program that devotes some portion of the day to study in the primary language (e.g., literature or social studies). Students would participate in mainstream English classes, but this would not mean an end to academic study in the primary language. Not only would such an approach be truly *bi*lingual, but, under these circumstances, transition would be less of an issue. Students would still have meaningful opportunities for academic success in the language they have been speaking (and in which they have received instruction) their entire lives. In addition, students might gain other benefits—further primary language development and high-level academic discourse, higher than could be accomplished through the medium of the second language. Both of these benefits can be obtained without sacrificing English language development (McLaughlin, 1992).

Of course, this alternative would generate wild controversy, particularly among those who assume there is a direct, consistent, and positive correlation between time spent in an all-English environment and English language and academic development. The evidence tends to challenge the commonsense notion that language-minority students achieve higher in English as a function of the amount of time they spend in all-English instruction; in fact, there seems to be *no* direct relation between the amount of time spent in English instruction and academic achievement in English (McLaughlin, 1992; Ramírez, 1992), but there is a *positive* relation between time spent in primary language instruction and achievement in English (Collier, 1992). Again, these conclusions run strongly counter to what seems so clearly intuitive.

How should these findings inform transition practices and policies, indeed, the entire conceptualization of transition? One obvious implication is that transition, as a program phase or component, would disappear or at least be absorbed into a more seamless progression in which students develop from monolingual non-English speakers to bilingual fluent English speakers. California's "State Program for Students of Limited-English Proficiency" (California State Department of Education, 1994a) appears to be an example of such a framework. Developmental, or two-way, bilingual programs (Christian, 1994) provide other examples.

Many of the strategies and suggestions contained in the articles in this issue would still be viable, perhaps even more so. The big difference would be that they would be used in strikingly different contexts, ones that seek to use and extend students' home language in order to promote true bilingual competence rather than contexts that use the home language only as much as is necessary to promote competence in English. Bilingual education advocates clearly *value* the former context, and bilingual education theory *predicts* it would produce superior results in terms of student outcomes in English. The question of values is not an empirical one; the question of outcomes surely could be.

PROSPECTS AND POSSIBILITIES— A NEED FOR BALANCE

Given the complexity of the language and instruction issues, what I find most encouraging about the articles in [*Elementary School Journal,* **96**] is the balanced approach to teaching and learning that overall they embody. This perspective—labeled variously throughout the articles as blended, balanced, integrated, nondogmatic, practical—is evident in Jiménez, Gersten, and Rivera's "Conversations with a Chicana Teacher" (1996). In response to the formidable challenge of helping students "build English language ability while teaching grade-level academic content" (Jiménez, 1996, p. 334), the teacher featured here drew from various theoretical perspectives to construct what seemed to be a coherent and comprehensive framework.

This teacher used high-quality children's literature, a great deal of student writing, and student productions and field trips. Because she was from the Latino community, she was knowledgeable about home and community cultural practices, and

she drew from this knowledge in her interactions with students and parents. She saw the students' Spanish language and literacy skills as resources on which to build. She also clearly leaned toward a structured teaching environment, and she explicitly taught students concepts, vocabulary, and skills they would need for success in academic English. The authors note that "she found that her earlier training in [the Hunter model of] explicit/direct instruction enabled her always to conceptualize what her goal or goals were and to focus clearly on helping students achieve that goal" (p. 340).

A complementary case is presented by Bos and Reyes (1996). This special education teacher (Elba Reyes) also used a "blended approach" that "weaves students' first language and culture into instructional conversations and curriculum, yet at the same time she incorporated direct instruction, practice, and transfer" (p. 343). Bos and Reyes's portrait of Elba suggests that this teacher placed less emphasis on structured, directed teaching than the teacher Jiménez et al. portray and more on natural language development, students' sociocultural experiences, and collaborative learning ("Elba came to view learning as an interactive process and the teacher as a facilitator who uses direct instruction only when needed" [p. 345]). Yet, along with the same sort of cultural and linguistic sensitivities demonstrated by the teacher in Jiménez et al., Elba also sees the need for explicit teaching at certain times for specific purposes. But she adds an important caution: "I think that this type of interactive teaching with contextualized, authentic learning yet explicit instruction in skills and strategies is critical for the success of language-minority students with disabilities. However, it is more complex and difficult to orchestrate than using one or the other" (p. 346).

This theme—orchestrating a complex and polyphonous knowledge base—is one that Russell Gersten (1996) addresses in "Literacy Instruction for Language-Minority Students: The Transition Years." Anyone concerned about the educational attainment of language-minority students should take heart from Gersten's ambitious and compelling synthesis of the various literatures that can inform this effort (see also Gersten & Jiménez, 1994). What I found most striking about Gersten's article was precisely what impressed me about the two teacher portraits—a nondoctrinaire, comprehensive view informing a vision of high-level academic achievement for these students. Although I suspect some will regard (or disregard) this synthesis as too eclectic and theoretically impure, I think this is precisely the way to proceed.

At the moment, no one theoretical perspective can claim demonstrable and consistent effects on all aspects of these (or any other) students' academic development. I applaud Gersten and colleagues' willingness and ability to draw from disparate theoretical orientations ranging from effective direct instruction to strategic reading skills training to language- and meaning-intensive literacy experiences for students.

HOW DO YOU DO IT, AND DOES IT WORK?

What is needed now is clear-cut evidence of effects for programs and strategies suggested by these authors. This same need exists for related approaches currently receiving widespread attention. For example, advocates of "sheltered English," sometimes called "specially designed academic instruction in English," say this set of techniques that involves using visual props and a high degree of contextualization and redundancy during instruction can be used to teach intermediate or advanced LEP students challenging content in English, despite their lack of English proficiency (California State Department of Education, 1994b).

As compelling as many of these recommended practices are, there are still many questions about implementation (How do you do it?) and effects (Does it meaningfully influence student learning?). Many of the recommendations (e.g., reciprocal teaching and other strategic reading approaches) were developed with students learning to read in their primary language. It certainly makes sense to try them with students learning in a second language, but educators should not take their efficacy in this different context for granted (see Rosenshine & Meister, 1994).

Other recommendations have considerable intuitive appeal and seem as if they should be fairly straightforward (e.g., promote more natural conversations in the classroom). But engaging students in natural conversations—that also have instructional value—has proven more difficult than one might realize (e.g., Wollman-Bonilla, 1994) and probably requires substantial staff development in contexts that support teachers' making fundamental changes in how they interact with students (Goldenberg & Gallimore, 1991; Saunders & Goldenberg, forthcoming; Saunders, Goldenberg, & Hamann, 1991; Tharp & Gallimore, 1989).

Although all the articles can claim substantial theoretical and/or practical foundation, there is still a significant need for assessment and evaluation data. The authors contributing to this special issue have produced some wonderful leads. The challenges now are, first, to translate this fine work into programs that have demonstrable effects on important student outcomes and, second, to work at making these programs work in schools serving limited-English-speaking students. Researchers and practitioners should not underestimate the challenge of either.

This article was made possible by funds from the Spencer Foundation and the National Center for Research on Cultural Diversity and Second Language Learning, Office of Educational Research and Improvement, U.S. Dept. of Education. My thanks to Russell Gersten and Diane August for their substantive suggestions and comments.

REFERENCES

Arreaga-Mayer, C., & Perdomo-Rivera, C. (1996). Ecobehavioral analysis of instruction for at-risk language-minority students. *Elementary School Journal, 96,* 245–258.

Bilingual Research Journal. (1992). [Entire issue]. **16**(1–2).

Bos, C. S., & Reyes, E. I. (1996). Conversations with a Latina teacher about education for language-minority students with special needs. *Elementary School Journal, 96,* 343–351.

California State Department of Education. (1981). *Schooling and language minority children.* Los Angeles: Evaluation, Dissemination and Assessment Center, California State University, Los Angeles.

California State Department of Education. (1994a). *Building bilingual instruction: Putting the pieces together.* (Available from California State Dept. of Education Bilingual Education Office, [916] 657-2566).

California State Department of Education. (1994b). *Charts and tables based on the Form R30-Language Census, Spring, 1994.* (Available from the California State Department of Education Bilingual Education Office, [916] 657-2566).

Carter, T., & Segura, R. (1979). *Mexican Americans in school: A decade of change.* New York: College Entrance Examination Board.

Christian, D. (1994). *Two-way bilingual education: Students learning through two languages* (EPR #12). Washington, DC: National Center for Research on Cultural Diversity and Second Language Learning.

Collier, V. (1992). A synthesis of studies examining long-term language-minority student data on academic achievement. *Bilingual Research Journal, 16,* 187–212.

Commonwealth of Massachusetts. (1994). *Striving for success: The education of bilingual pupils.* Boston, MA: Bilingual Education Commission.

Crawford, J. (1991). *Bilingual education: History, politics, theory, and practice* (2d ed.). Los Angeles: Bilingual Education Services.

CTB/McGraw-Hill. (1982). *CTBS: Comprehensive Test of Basic Skills (Forms U and V), Norms book, Grades K-3.* Monterey, CA: CTB/McGraw-Hill.

CTB/McGraw-Hill. (1988). *SABE: Spanish Assessment of Basic Education, Technical Report.* Monterey, CA: CTB/McGraw-Hill.

Cuban, L. (1984). *How teachers taught: Constancy and change in American classrooms, 1890–1980.* New York: Longman.

Cummins, J. (1980). The cross-lingual dimensions of language proficiency: Implications for bilingual education and the optimal age issue. *TESOL Quarterly, 14,* 175–187.

Development Associates. (1993). *Number of LEP students receiving instruction in their native language.* Short Turnaround Report No. 5 (No. BE019252). (Available from National Clearinghouse for Bilingual Education, 1118 22d St., NW, Washington, DC 20037).

Fitzgerald, J. (1995). English-as-a-second-language learners' cognitive reading processes: A review of research in the United States. *Review of Educational Research, 65,* 145–190.

García, E., & Colón, M. (1995). Interactive journals in bilingual classrooms: An analysis of language "transition." *Discourse Processes, 19,* 39–56.

Gersten, R. (1996). Literacy instruction for language-minority students: The transition years. *Elementary School Journal, 96,* 227–244.

Gersten, R., & Jiménez, R. (1994). A delicate balance: Enhancing literature instruction for students of English as a second language. *Reading Teacher, 47,* 438–448.

Gersten, R., & Woodward, J. (1995). A longitudinal study of transitional and immersion bilingual education programs in one district. *Elementary School Journal, 95,* 223–239.

Gold, N. (1992, April). *Solving the shortage of bilingual teachers: Policy implications of California's staffing initiative for limited English proficient students.* Paper presented at the annual meeting of the American Educational Research Association, San Francisco.

Goldenberg, C., & Gallimore, R. (1991). Changing teaching takes more than a one-shot workshop. *Educational Leadership, 49*(3), 69–72.

Goodlad, J. (1984). *A place called school.* New York: McGraw-Hill.

Hakuta, K., & Snow, C. (1986). The role of research in policy decisions about bilingual education. *NABE News, 9*(3), 1, 18–20.

Jiménez, R. T., Gersten, R., & Rivera, A. (1996). Conversations with a Chicana teacher: Supporting students' transition from native- to English-language instruction. *Elementary School Journal, 96,* 333–341.

Krashen, S., & Biber, D. (1988). *On course: Bilingual education's success in California.* Sacramento: California Association for Bilingual Education.

McLaughlin, B. (1992). *Myths and misconceptions about second language learning: What every teacher needs to unlearn* (EPR No. 5). Washington, DC: National Center for Research on Cultural Diversity and Second Language Learning.

Meyer, M., & Fienberg, S. (1992). *Assessing evaluation studies: The case of bilingual education.* Washington, DC: National Academy Press.

Mullis, I., Campbell, J., & Farstrup, A. (1993). *NAEP 1992 reading report card for the nation and the states* (Rep. No. 23-ST06). Washington, DC: U.S. Department of Education.

Porter, R. (1990). *Forked tongue: The politics of bilingual education.* New York: Basic.

Ramírez, D. (1992). Executive summary. *Bilingual Research Journal, 16,* 1–62.

Rodríguez, R. (1984). *Teaching reading to minority language students.* Rosslyn, VA: InterAmerica Research Associates, Inc.

Rosenshine, B., & Meister, C. (1994). Reciprocal teaching: A review of the research. *Review of Educational Research, 64,* 479–530.

Samaniego, F., & Eubank, L. (1991). *A statistical analysis of California's case study project in bilingual education* (Tech. Rep. No. 208). Davis: Intercollegiate Division of Statistics, University of California, Davis.

Saunders, W., & Goldenberg, C. (in press). The troublesome dichotomy: Reconciling constructivism and teacher-directed learning. *Elementary School Journal.*

Saunders, W., Goldenberg, C., & Hamann, J. (1992). Instructional conversations beget instructional conversations. *Teaching and Teacher Education, 8,* 199–218.

Slavin, R. (Ed.). (1989). *School and classroom organization.* Hillsdale, NJ: Erlbaum.

Tharp, R., & Gallimore, R. (1989). Rousing schools to life. *American Educator, 13*(2), 20–25.

Thomas, W. (1992). An analysis of the research methodology of the Ramírez study. *Bilingual Research Journal, 16,* 213–245.

Willig, A. (1985). A meta-analysis of selected studies on the effectiveness of bilingual education. *Review of Educational Research, 55,* 269–317.

Wollman-Bonilla, J. (1994). Why don't they "Just Speak?" Attempting literature discussion with more and less able readers. *Research in the Teaching of English, 28,* 231–258.

Wong Fillmore, L., with Valadez, C. (1986). Teaching bilingual learners. In M. Wittrock (Ed.), *Handbook of research on teaching* (3d ed., pp. 648–685). New York: Macmillan.

Chapter 6: Behavioral Views of Learning

Parental Discipline Mistakes

SUSAN G. O'LEARY

The dictionary defines discipline as "training to act in accordance with rules. . . ." We assume that children are not born knowing how to act in accordance with the rules of their families or society. We assume that most children learn (i.e., are taught) to behave appropriately (and inappropriately). Such teaching is one aspect of child rearing, and parents play a key role in disciplining or teaching their children to behave according to a wide range of rules.

Although parental rules vary across families, children's ages, cultures, and historical periods, most people know a rule when they hear one. Common rules for children in American families today include these: Don't hurt other people; do what your parents tell you to do; don't ask loudly in the grocery store, "Why is that man so fat, Mommy?"; don't play with the telephone; don't lie; come home on time; do your homework before you watch television; and don't pester your sister. When children do not behave according to the rules, we say they have misbehaved. When parents use ineffective strategies to manage misbehavior, we say they have made *discipline mistakes*.

Parents are undoubtedly not the only people who significantly influence children's misbehavior. Siblings, day-care providers, teachers, baby-sitters, grandparents, and peers are participants in child rearing. The younger the child, however, the more influential [the] parents are likely to be. Interest in

parental discipline practices has a long history, and scientifically established relations between discipline mistakes and children's behavior disorders have been reported since the early 1950s. Young children's aggressive and oppositional behavior disorders are quite stable; if left untreated, these disorders predict later delinquency, drug and alcohol abuse, family violence, unemployment, and psychiatric disturbance. Understanding what constitutes effective and ineffective parental discipline practice, particularly for young children, should facilitate both the prevention and the treatment of children's behavior problems.

Before I describe what we know about parental discipline, and particularly parental discipline mistakes, four points must be made. First, managing children's misbehavior is certainly not all there is to rearing children; responsive nurturing and the provision of a positive emotional and physical environment are also critical components of responsible child rearing. Second, being a "nice" parent is not equivalent to being a "good" parent. As a matter of fact, one discipline mistake is responding positively to misbehavior. Third, advocating appropriate, effective discipline is not equivalent to advocating stronger punishment; a frequent discipline mistake is being overreactive and harsh. Finally, the focus of this review is parental mistakes in disciplining children's disruptive, oppositional, and aggressive behaviors. We know much less about the relation of parenting to childhood anxiety, fear, and depression. We also do not know whether the discipline mistakes I describe here would still be problematic, ineffective, or both if the child misbehavior were

Susan G. O'Leary is Professor of Psychology and Director of the Doctoral Program in Clinical Psychology at the University at Stony Brook. Address correspondence to Susan O'Leary, Department of Psychology, State University of New York at Stony Brook, Stony Brook, NY 11794-2500; e-mail: soleary@ccmail.sunysb.edu.

construed very differently, as might be the case in another culture.

WHAT ARE PARENTAL DISCIPLINE MISTAKES?

Early, retrospective studies of child rearing indicated that inconsistent, harsh, and excessively lax discipline practices are associated with delinquency and aggression. Similarly, observational studies of preschoolers found that mothers who are harsh in their use of authority tend to have children who are not self-reliant or content and who are aggressive; mothers who are permissive tend to have children who are dependent and not well-behaved.[1] At a more specific level, the degree of parental inconsistency, receptiveness to bargaining, use of indirect commands, lack of enforcement, and demonstration of affection during discipline episodes are associated with the degree of resistance and non-compliance displayed by 1fi- to 3fi-year-olds. Comparisons of normal and clinic samples indicate that parents of aggressive, antisocial, and noncompliant children issue more frequent commands and negative consequences, engage in lengthier and more intense coercive interchanges with their children, are more submissive and ambiguous, and are less consistent in their responses to problem behaviors. These parents also are more likely to reinforce oppositional behavior with attention, softening of commands, or coaxing.

This large number of probable discipline mistakes was identified primarily by time-consuming and expensive observations of parent–child interactions. To increase the efficiency with which we can assess parents' discipline practices, my students and I developed a 30-item self-report Parenting Scale.[2] Factor analyses of the Parenting Scale repeatedly reveal three primary types of mistakes made by mothers of 2- to 4-year-old children: laxness, overreactivity, and verbosity. Laxness includes giving in, not enforcing rules, and providing positive reinforcement for misbehavior. Overreactivity includes anger, meanness, and irritability. Verbosity involves the propensity to engage in lengthy verbal interactions about misbehavior even when the talking is ineffective. These factors are consistent with other theoretical formulations of parental discipline, are reliable, correlate well with observations of maternal behavior, and are comparable across normal and problematic populations. The Parenting Scale appears to be a useful tool for identifying mothers whose discipline strategies may put their children at risk for developing serious behavior problems.

All of the findings just outlined must be viewed with some caution because of the correlational methodologies used in the research; however, recent experiments in my laboratory and elsewhere support a causal link between parental discipline mistakes and young children's misbehavior. Some of this research was conducted in homes, but most took place in laboratory settings. Mothers of both normal and hard-to-manage toddlers and preschoolers were instructed to respond to the relevant misbehaviors in specified ways. We have demonstrated that delayed, long, and gentle (imprudent) reprimands result in higher levels of misbehavior than do immediate, brief, and firm (prudent) reprimands.[3] Another mistake is leaving a two-year-old to his or her own devices for too long. Patterson[4] referred to this mistake as poor monitoring and found it to be one of the best predictors of outcome for older children. We have also learned that mothers are less effective when they try to distract their misbehaving children than when they use clear reprimands. In fact, when distraction does not work and mothers change their tactics to reprimanding, children become upset, as though they are offended by the change. On the other hand, children are not particularly upset when they are consistently and prudently reprimanded.[5] Distraction may be less effective than reprimanding because distraction provides positive attention to misbehavior.

Other examples of lax discipline mistakes can be found. We have all laughed when three-year-olds use unsavory, "adult" language, even though we understand that our laughter reinforces that misbehavior. The same phenomenon occurs when mothers are on the telephone and do not wish to be interrupted, but respond positively to their children's requests for help or a snack. The children are temporarily satisfied but are likely to solicit their mothers' attention again very soon;[6] some mothers even report that picking up the telephone is a signal for their children to pester them.

One last example of a strategy that may inadvertently reinforce misbehavior involves the use of timeout (i.e., removal of the child from sources of reinforcement for a brief period of time). Although time-out can be very effective for reducing noncompliance and aggression, young children often attempt to escape from the commonly used time-out chair. Some parents deal with an escaping child by holding the child in the chair, thus providing attention for the misbehavior. Others give up very quickly and allow the child to determine when time-out is over. Both of these strategies are mistakes and are less effective than ensuring that the child remains in the time-out chair for the assigned period of time, for example, by calmly turning the chair toward the wall.[7]

WHY DO PARENTS MAKE MISTAKES?

In the course of conducting these experimental studies, we have often heard two things from mothers of hard-to-manage toddlers: "I just don't know what to do with him (her)" and "I know I should _____, but I just can't seem to." These comments suggest that parents may need two different kinds of help with discipline: learning what constitutes a discipline mistake and learning why they make such mistakes.

It is not surprising that some parents seem to lack knowledge about effective discipline practices, as most education in how to parent is informal and indirect. We observe our parents and relatives managing child misbehavior, and these people often offer advice about how we should raise our own children. Unfortunately, not all of what we observe or are told is consistent with what the scientific literature tells us. Parents who need to learn what effective discipline is would benefit from more structured educational experiences. The best time for such training might be when parents begin teaching their children to follow rules, that is, when the children begin to crawl. People are probably not particularly motivated to learn before they have children; waiting until the toddler or preschool years means dysfunctional parenting may already be established, and correcting dysfunctional parenting is surely harder than preventing it.

Understanding the parent who knows what is best but who does not or cannot use that knowledge is more complicated. We know that depression, marital discord, social isolation, and economic and employment stresses are related to mothers' dysfunctional discipline practices.[8] Additional factors have emerged from research on abusive mothers and have been substantiated in nonabusive samples as well. First, some mothers are more "upset" than others by children's misbehavior or by the negative affect (i.e., whining and crying) that children display when they are disciplined. A mother's internal reactivity, particularly her own sense of ir-

ritation or anger, is related to the overreactivity or harshness of her discipline. Second, mothers' explanations for why their children misbehave are associated with the type and likelihood of discipline mistakes made by mothers. For example, if a mother views her child as an incorrigible brat, she will be overreactive. If she sees herself as a hopelessly inadequate mother, she will be lax in her discipline. Third, mothers who make discipline mistakes may do so because they tolerate or define child misbehavior differently than effective mothers do. Although both under- and overidentifying misbehaviors should be problematic, more evidence supports overidentification as the problem. A final factor that influences how well a parent disciplines is the child himself or herself. Children with conduct disorders elicit corrective or controlling feedback from all mothers, including mothers of normal children. Having a "difficult" child may compromise a mother's ability to implement appropriate discipline.

Precisely how all of these variables affect mothers' abilities to teach their children to behave according to the rules is not clear. Reasonable hypotheses include interference with the mother's attentional capacities and increases in the mother's motivation to reduce immediately the negative emotions the child elicits in her. Regardless of the mechanisms involved, consideration of these variables would probably enhance the effectiveness of parent training programs and may explain why some parent training efforts are ineffective.

UNCHARTED AREAS

The attentive reader may have realized by now that no specific mention has been made of fathers and their roles in disciplining children. The reason is that relatively little is known about fathers' discipline practices. Traditionally, mothers have spent considerably more time parenting than fathers, but parental roles are changing, making the need to know about fathers' discipline practices especially important. We recently learned that the factor structure of fathers' self-reported discipline practices on the Parenting Scale is virtually identical to the factor structure for mothers. We are currently observing fathers interacting with their toddlers to determine the validity of the Parenting Scale for fathers and to assess whether fathers handle discipline encounters differently than do mothers.

In addition to knowing little about fathers' discipline mistakes, we know little about whether discipline mistakes change over time. Children are, almost by definition, developmental phenomena. Viewing discipline as a developmental phenomenon would probably be equally appropriate. Parents do not discipline their 8- or 12-year-olds in the same ways they discipline their preschoolers. On the one hand, as children's cognitive capacities improve, parents should be able to more effectively use preventive, verbal teaching of rule-governed behavior. Greater delay of consequences should be tolerated by older children. On the other hand, older children have learned about handling conflict by observing their parents and may have learned some bad lessons (e.g., to be argumentative and aggressive, to hold a grudge, and to rely on apologies). Certainly, the concrete consequences implemented by parents change as children grow up. Chair time-outs become weekend groundings. Leaving the park early changes to no television that night. Whether the broad characteristics of what constitutes a discipline mistake remain overreactivity, laxness, and verbosity or whether only the specifics of the teaching techniques (e.g., chair time-out vs. grounding) change as children become young adults is yet to be clarified.

A final "uncharted area" about which I would like to comment is the area of side effects, particularly the side effects of correcting discipline mistakes. The literature contains many examples[9] of positive side effects accompanying the therapeutic use of a variety of punishment procedures. These reports suggest that correcting discipline mistakes might have advantages in addition to reducing the rate of child misbehavior. Let me illustrate this possibility by describing a common clinical experience: Parents and their son are having severe conflicts. If an intervention that is focused almost exclusively on identifying and altering parental discipline mistakes results in the boy behaving more appropriately, other aspects of the parent–child relationship also change even though there has been no specific intervention in these areas. The boy offers to help with a chore; the mother hugs him good-night; the father tells his son for the first time in a long time that he loves him. Such clinical experiences should serve heuristic roles, furthering our understanding of parental discipline mistakes and how to correct them.

NOTES

1. D. Baumrind, Current patterns of parental authority, *Developmental Psychology Monographs, 4* (No. 1, Part 2), 1–103 (1971).

2. D. S. Arnold, S. G. O'Leary, L. S. Wolff, and M. M. Acker, The Parenting Scale: A measure of dysfunctional parenting in discipline situations, *Psychological Assessment, 5,* 137–144 (1993).

3. L. J. Pfiffner and S. G. O'Leary, Effects of maternal discipline and nurturance on toddlers' behavior and affect, *Journal of Abnormal Child Psychology, 17,* 527–540 (1989).

4. G. R. Patterson, *A Social Learning Approach: Vol. 3. Coercive Family Process* (Castalia, Eugene, OR, 1982).

5. L. S. Wolff, *Toddlers' affective and behavioral responses to mothers' reprimands in differing contexts,* unpublished doctoral dissertation, University at Stony Brook, Stony Brook, NY (1993).

6. M. M. Acker, *Effects of consistent and inconsistent maternal feedback on toddlers' behavior,* unpublished doctoral dissertation, University at Stony Brook, Stony Brook, NY (1992).

7. M. W. Roberts and S. W. Powers, Adjusting chair timeout enforcement procedures for oppositional children, *Behavior Therapy, 21,* 257–271 (1990).

8. K. T. Kendziora and S. G. O'Leary, Dysfunctional parenting as a focus for prevention and treatment of child behavior problems, in *Advances in Child Clinical Psychology,* Vol. 15, T. H. Ollendick and R. J. Prinz, Eds. (Plenum Press, New York, 1993).

9. S. Axelrod and J. Apsche, Eds., *The Effects of Punishment on Human Behavior* (Academic Press, New York, 1983).

The Debate about Rewards and Intrinsic Motivation

Protests and Accusations Do Not Alter the Results

JUDY CAMERON and W. DAVID PIERCE

A prevailing view in education and social psychology is that rewards decrease a person's intrinsic motivation. However, our meta-analysis (Cameron & Pierce, 1994) of approximately 100 studies does not support this position. The only negative effect of reward occurs under a highly restricted set of conditions, circumstances that are easily avoided. These results have not been well received by those who argue that rewards produce negative effects under a wide range of conditions. Lepper, Keavney, and Drake (1996), Ryan and Deci (1996), and Kohn (1996) have suggested that the questions asked in our meta-analysis were inappropriate, that critical studies were excluded, that important negative effects were not detected, and that the techniques used in our meta-analysis were unsuitable. In this response, we show that the questions we asked are fundamental and that our meta-analytic techniques are appropriate, robust, and statistically correct. In sum, the results and conclusions of our meta-analysis are not altered by our critics' protests and accusations.

Our research (Cameron & Pierce, 1994) has clearly touched a nerve. The results of our meta-analysis indicate that rewards can be used effectively to enhance or maintain an individual's intrinsic interest in activities. These findings are challenging to those who espouse the view that rewards and reinforcement are generally detrimental to a person's intrinsic motivation. Our article has drawn criticism because the data from approximately 100 experiments show that there is only one small negative effect of reward, an effect that is highly circumscribed and easily avoided. This finding is disconcerting to those who contend that the negative effects of reward are substantial, generalized, and occur across many conditions.

Our analysis of 20 years of research is the most extensive review of the literature on rewards and intrinsic motivation to date. Because of its thoroughness, the data, analysis, and conclusions must be taken seriously. Faced with the evidence, researchers who have argued that rewards produce harmful effects under a wide range of conditions are put in a difficult position. One option they can take is to reanalyze the data in an attempt to show that rewards

Judy Cameron is Assistant Professor, Department of Educational Psychology, University of Alberta, 6–102 Education North, Edmonton, Alberta, Canada T6G 2G5; judy.cameron@ualberta.ca. She specializes in educational psychology.

W. David Pierce is Professor, Centre for Experimental Sociology, 1-48 Tory, University of Alberta, Edmonton, Alberta, Canada T6G 2H4; dpierce@gpu.srv.ualberta.ca. He specializes in social psychology.

have strong negative effects on intrinsic motivation. Our data are readily available for additional analyses, and our procedures are clearly outlined in the original article. Failing this option, a second strategy is to suggest that the findings are invalid due to intentional bias, deliberate misrepresentation, and inept analysis. Our critics have chosen the second strategy.

Lepper, Keavney, and Drake (1996); Ryan and Deci (1996); and Kohn (1996) have responded to the results of our meta-analysis by accusing us of asking inappropriate questions, omitting important moderator variables, excluding critical experiments, and contradicting other reviews on the topic. In addition, they criticize our meta-analytic procedures and decisions as flawed.

In response to these criticisms, we show that all relevant studies were included in our analyses and that the questions and reward conditions we assessed expand on previous reviews to provide a more comprehensive picture of the effects of rewards on intrinsic motivation. We answer the statistical concerns of our critics and show that our analysis is appropriate, accurate, and robust. Most importantly, we show that none of the objections raised by our critics negates our findings.

The results and conclusions of our meta-analysis remain important, especially for those involved in education and other applied settings. An issue of prime concern to educators is how to use rewards effectively to promote learning without disrupting students' intrinsic interest. Contrary to Ryan and Deci's (1996) claim that our "theoretical position acknowledged no conditions under which one should expect negative effects" (p. 33), our results provide important clarifications about the conditions under which rewards produce positive or negative effects on intrinsic motivation. Of primary importance in classroom situations is the finding that rewards can be used to maintain or enhance students' intrinsic interest in schoolwork. Verbal praise and performance feedback increase the value of an activity. When tangible rewards are offered contingent on level of performance or are given unexpectedly, students remain motivated in the subject area. A slight negative effect can be expected when a teacher offers a tangible reward without regard to the students' level of performance. Under this condition, when the rewards are withdrawn, students will continue to like their schoolwork as much as others, but they may spend slightly less time on it in a free per-

iod. This negative effect can be easily prevented by offering students rewards for successful solution of problems, completion of work, or for attaining specified levels of performance on particular tasks. The point is that teachers can reward the level and quality of students' work without disrupting motivation and interest in learning. These conclusions are not altered by the comments of Kohn, Ryan and Deci, and Lepper et al.

In the following commentary we address our critics' concerns. Our response is organized in two sections; the first deals with the general issues that have been raised by our critics, and in the second we focus on specific statistical criticisms.

GENERAL ISSUES

The Overall Question

One issue of contention involves our decision to begin our meta-analysis by investigating the overall effect of reward on intrinsic motivation (overall effect hypothesis). Lepper and his colleagues state that "to ask about the 'overall' or 'in general' effects of rewards or reinforcers is to pose a fundamentally meaningless question" (p. 7). They argue that the question is senseless and misleading, a view echoed by Kohn and by Ryan and Deci.

We maintain that the overall effect hypothesis is central to an understanding of this area of research. One reason is practical. Many educators, parents, and administrators have adopted Kohn's (1993) position that overall, rewards and incentive systems are harmful. In the present context, this stance means that rewards negatively affect students' intrinsic interest, a question of overall effect. Others involved in education are still open to the possibility that rewards may be beneficial. A classroom teacher who wishes to implement an incentive system is first of all interested in whether rewards disrupt intrinsic interest in the subject matter. Of course, it may be advantageous to target particular subgroups or implement additional measures, but the question of the overall effect of reward is crucial to one's teaching strategy.

Another reason to address the main effect hypothesis is that academic journals, introductory textbooks, newspapers, and some of our critics continue to point to the overall negative or harmful effects of reward and reinforcement. In a prominent scientific journal, *Nature,* we learn that "it has been repeatedly shown that if people are rewarded for performing a task they find intrinsically pleasurable, they do it less, not more" (Sutherland, 1993, p. 767). A major introductory psychology textbook informs us that

> *when an extrinsic reward is given, the motivation becomes extrinsic and the task itself is enjoyed less. When the extrinsic rewards are withdrawn, the activity loses its material value. . . . The moral is:* A reward a day makes work out of play. *(Zimbardo, 1992, p. 454, emphasis in the original)*

Even in this issue of *Review of Educational Research,* Kohn asserts that "there is more than adequate justification for avoiding the use of incentives to control people's behavior, particularly in a school setting" (p. 3).

These examples are but a small sample of the claims made about the overall effects of reward. Many university students, educators, and parents have been exposed to this negative main effect assumption and base their own understanding and use of rewards on it. Social policy in our schools and other institutions reflects these beliefs. Because of this, an analysis of the general effects of reward is warranted.

In their critiques of our meta-analysis, Lepper et al. and Ryan and Deci indicate that they and others have long recognized that the negative overall effect hypothesis is incorrect. Nonetheless, numerous writers interpret the research findings as indicative of an overall negative effect and decry the use of rewards in educational and work settings (e.g., see Kohn, 1993). As a result, many parents, teachers, and others are reluctant to use rewards—any rewards—under any circumstances! Lepper and his colleagues suggest that reversing this incorrect conclusion will be harmful. They imply that we are trying to propagate our own myth—that rewards have no negative effects. We do not want to add any more myths to this research area. So let us be clear in stating that our research demonstrates that rewards have either positive or negative effects depending on the way they are administered. Importantly, the only negative effect of reward on intrinsic motivation occurs under a circumscribed set of conditions, namely, when rewards are tangible and promised to individuals without regard to any level of performance.

The Role of Moderator Variables

A major focus of our meta-analysis was to assess the effects of various moderator variables. The moderators we included (type of reward, reward expectancy, and reward contingency) were chosen because of their theoretical and practical importance in the literature on intrinsic motivation as well as replication over a number of experiments. Our results indicate that the detrimental effects of reward are limited and depend on multiple moderators. All of our critics, Lepper et al., Ryan and Deci, and Kohn, are concerned that we failed to assess the impact of additional important moderators. The implication of their comments is that decremental effects of reward occur under numerous conditions and are far more widespread than our analysis suggests. Interestingly, however, as we describe below, an analysis of additional moderators would, in fact, show the opposite.

Lepper et al. point to studies that assessed the impact of initial task interest and reward salience on intrinsic motivation. Other moderator variables hypothesized to influence intrinsic motivation include reward attractiveness, presence or absence of the experimenter, task difficulty, reward magnitude, and so on. It is critical to point out that the few studies designed to investigate the impact of these moderators typically begin with the one condition that produces a negative effect. Furthermore, such moderators have been shown to enhance, mitigate, or reverse the negative effects of expected, tangible, noncontingent reward. For example, Ross (1975) found that salient rewards make the negative effect of tangible, expected, noncontingent reward greater. McLoyd (1979), on the other hand, demonstrated that individuals offered a noncontingent, tangible reward experienced an increase in intrinsic motivation when the task was less interesting, while Williams's (1980) research indicated that the negative effects of tangible, expected, noncontingent reward could be offset by offering attractive rewards. In other words, the variables we have not assessed are moderators that have typically been added to the conditions that produce the single negative effect of reward found in our meta-analysis. Thus, an analysis of studies that included moderators that increase the negative effects of expected, tangible, noncontingent reward would serve to place further restrictions on the circumstances under which rewards undermine intrinsic motivation. That is, the negative effect phenomenon may be even more circumscribed than our data indicate, a finding contrary to the implications hinted at by our critics.

Presently, however, there is no way to assess the theoretical or applied importance of these moderator variables. This is because only one or two studies have replicated the same moderator procedures on a common dependent measure of intrinsic motivation. If the effects of moderators such as reward salience, reward attractiveness, and so on were systematically replicated, a subsequent meta-analysis could be conducted to determine the conditions that moderate the negative effect on intrinsic motivation of tangible, expected, noncontingent rewards when they are removed. Of course, such an analysis would simply extend our findings and show that tangible, expected, noncontingent rewards produce negative effects on intrinsic motivation only when other conditions are present. For example, in terms of reward attractiveness, Williams's (1980) research shows that when tangible, expected, noncontingent, *unattractive* rewards are given, intrinsic motivation decreases; the same reward condition with *attractive* rewards does not produce a decrement. Although present theoretical accounts (e.g., cognitive evaluation theory, the overjustification hypothesis) may be able to organize such circumscribed effects, the theories would become less and less generalizable. In applied settings, negative effects of reward on intrinsic motivation would depend on so many conditions that there would be little need for concern.

Both Kohn (1996) and Ryan and Deci (1996) raise the question of moderators in the context of our finding that verbal praise produces positive effects both on the free time students spend on tasks and on attitude measures of intrinsic motivation. Specifically, they claim that verbal praise directed at controlling student behavior has negative effects on intrinsic motivation, whereas informational praise does not. We did not conduct an analysis on the control-informational dimension of verbal reward because these variables appear in only one or two studies. In addition, most research on this topic has been conducted without adequate no-feedback control groups (e.g., Ryan, 1982). Until a sufficient number of experiments with control groups are conducted, a meta-analysis of conditions that have few replications would not be reliable or beneficial to our understanding of reward and intrinsic motivation. We note, however, that although there are so few studies on this topic, the effects of controlling and informational verbal reward were ana-

lyzed in a recent meta-analysis by Tang & Hall (1995). They found no significant effects on either of these dimensions.

In sum, although our meta-analysis was designed to assess the effects of several moderators on reward and intrinsic motivation, Lepper et al., Ryan and Deci, and Kohn have suggested that many additional important moderators were omitted. As we have shown, an analysis of additional moderators would not alter our conclusions or change any of the results of our meta-analysis. That is, negative effects of reward on intrinsic motivation are highly conditional and occur solely in the presence of multiple moderators. In educational settings, negative effects can be avoided by praising students for their work and making tangible rewards contingent on performance.

Our Findings in Context

Both Ryan and Deci and Lepper et al. argue that our findings contradict previous narrative reviews and other meta-analyses of reward and intrinsic motivation. Lepper et al. are not consistent on this point, and in a later section of their critique they concede that "other recent meta-analyses, . . . as well as numerous previous narrative reviews, have reached exactly [our] conclusion" (p. 7). In this section, we show that our results are in accord with other summaries of reward and intrinsic motivation and that our review advances the knowledge in this area. We briefly comment on three other meta-analyses on this topic (Rummel & Feinberg, 1988; Tang & Hall, 1995; Wiersma, 1992).

The most recent meta-analysis on rewards and intrinsic motivation, conducted by Tang and Hall (1995), was designed to test several theoretical propositions about the overjustification effect. Fifty studies were included, largely a subset of the experiments examined in our review. One analysis concerned assessing the effects of expected, tangible, task-contingent (noncontingent) reward on the free time measure of intrinsic motivation. Tang and Hall found a negative effect, as did we. Also, in accord with our findings, they found no detrimental effect with unexpected, tangible reward. It is difficult to compare our findings on the effects of verbal reward on free time with their study, because their analysis included only two effect sizes (their result was not significant).

Tang and Hall (1995) reported a negative effect on the free time measure for performance-contingent reward, whereas we found no significant effect. This difference in findings is due to Tang and Hall's classification of performance-contingent reward as well as to their omission of several relevant studies. Of the seven studies that Tang and Hall analyzed as performance contingent, six are actually task-contingent reward procedures, as defined by Deci and Ryan (1985). We used Deci and Ryan's definitions and identified 10 studies of performance-contingent reward; overall, there was no evidence of a negative effect. Additional measures of intrinsic motivation (e.g., attitude toward task) that we examined were not reported by Tang and Hall.[1]

The meta-analyses by Wiersma (1992) and Rummel and Feinberg (1988) were discussed in our original article (Cameron & Pierce, 1994). Wiersma analyzed 20 studies, and Rummel and Feinberg analyzed 45 studies. We cannot compare our findings with those of Rummel and Feinberg, because they averaged over different dependent measures of intrinsic motivation. Our meta-analysis shows that this is inappropriate, because the free time and attitude measures do not necessarily covary with the same experimental treatment. In addition, in both Rummel and Feinberg's and Wiersma's analyses, many of the effect sizes reported came from studies where one reward condition was compared to another reward condition. The lack of a no-reward group makes a comparison of findings problematic. Wiersma does, however, report effect size estimates for six experiments on free time that compared a no-reward condition to an expected, tangible, noncontingent reward condition. Though we have not conducted a meta-analysis on his results, we computed the average of the six independent effects sizes and found a negative effect, a finding compatible with our original conclusions.

All in all, our findings for rewards that are tangible, expected, and noncontingent are consistent with other meta-analyses. Our research, however, went beyond an analysis of the one negative reward procedure and assessed the effects of reward under a variety of conditions. In terms of other reward procedures (e.g., verbal reward, performance-contingent reward) and other measures of intrinsic motivation (e.g., attitude toward a task), we failed to find any detrimental effects on intrinsic motivation. That is, our study showed that most reward procedures can be used to maintain or enhance intrinsic motivation; the negative effect other reviews have detected is only a small part of a larger picture. Thus, our meta-analysis provides a more com-

plete account of the effects of rewards on intrinsic motivation.

The Completeness of Our Review

A criticism put forward by Kohn, as well as by Ryan and Deci, is that we failed to include several critical experiments in our meta-analysis. The implication is that had such studies been included, our results would have been different.

Kohn cites a number of studies that he believes we have overlooked. Most of these studies were located in our original search and were not included in our meta-analysis because of the lack of an adequate no-reward control condition. In addition, as we reported in our original article, our meta-analysis included studies published up to and including 1991. The studies from the period 1992–1994 cited by Kohn (Boggiano et al., 1992; Freedman, Cunningham, & Krismer, 1992; Gottfried, Fleming, & Gottfried, 1994) were, of course, not included. Of these, Freedman et al. varied the amount of reward but had no non-reward control group. The article by Boggiano et al. reported past research in order to develop a theory or model of students' achievement patterns. Gottfried et al. examined parental motivational practices; their study did not include any of the reward conditions or dependent measures that we analyzed in our meta-analysis. Earlier studies by Birch, Marlin, and Rotter (1984) and Fabes, Fultz, Eisenberg, May-Plumlee, and Christopher (1989) concerned food preferences and prosocial behavior, respectively. Clearly, all these studies are off topic. Other papers that Kohn cites as missing are, in fact, included in our analyses (a list of all studies is presented in Cameron & Pierce, 1994, pp. 399–403).

In contrast to Kohn, Lepper et al. charge us with including too many "bad" studies. An essential criterion of a reliable meta-analysis, however, is that all the studies done in a field are examined, independently of one's own theoretical position and the degree to which the results of any particular study may be promising. We have met this criterion. In fact, our meta-analysis on the effects of rewards on intrinsic motivation is the most comprehensive review of this literature to date. The results are based on a large number of studies, and, to our knowledge, no relevant published studies were omitted. Due to the large sample of studies included in our analyses, any single study that may have been overlooked would not alter the conclusions. Overall, our results were based on all the available evidence, and the findings are central to an understanding of the effects of rewards on intrinsic motivation.

META-ANALYTIC ISSUES

In addition to the general criticisms discussed above, Lepper and his associates object to our use of meta-analysis for assessing the research on the effects of rewards on intrinsic motivation. In particular, they contend that the distributions of effect sizes in our article indicate that meta-analytic tests should not have been conducted. In accord with Ryan and Deci (1996) and Kohn (1996), they further suggest that the statistical procedures used in our meta-analyses must be flawed. Specifically, they criticize the technique of aggregating effect sizes within a single study when moderator variables are present. In this section, we respond to our critics' meta-analytic and statistical concerns. We show that our analyses are appropriate, that the data are approximately normal and homogeneous, that inclusion or exclusion of outliers does not alter the results, and that our procedures yield correct estimates for the effects of rewards on intrinsic motivation at each level of analysis.

The Appropriateness of Meta-Analysis

There are two main issues that concern Lepper et al. with regard to our use of meta-analytic techniques for assessing the effects of rewards on intrinsic motivation. First, they suggest that the apparent normality of our distributions for the critical measures of intrinsic motivation (free time, attitude) is deceptive. Their second concern is that the data are not homogeneous (equal spread of effect sizes) and that meta-analytic tests should therefore not have been performed.

As Lepper et al. acknowledge (p. 13–14), our distributions of effect sizes approximate a normal shape. However, they attribute the normality of these distributions to the inclusion of "pure zero cases" and random estimates. They argue that our inclusion of "pure zero cases" in our graphic portrayal of effect sizes (Cameron & Pierce, 1994, Figures 1 and 2) guarantees a normal distribution around the value of zero. Pure zero cases refer to studies that did not provide sufficient information to calculate effect sizes or random estimates (4 cases for free time and 17 cases for attitude). The truth is

that we did not include pure zero cases in these figures. This is clearly stated on pages 379 and 384 of our original article. The normality of the distributions centering around zero is not due to pure zero cases. Thus, Lepper and his associates need not be concerned.

In terms of our use of random estimates of effect sizes, our procedure is innovative and may be more appropriate than merely assigning a zero effect to the experiment or omitting the study itself. The procedure depended on the information available in each study. When t or F values were nonsignificant and were reported as less than some value (e.g., < 1), a random number between 0.01 and that value was selected; and an effect size was then calculated. In other cases, t or F values were not available, but means or directions of means were reported. In these situations, a random number between 0.01 and the critical value of t or F at $p = .05$ was drawn, and an effect size was then calculated. (For more information, see Cameron & Pierce, 1994, p. 376).

With regard to the normality of our distributions, it is important to note that the direction of effect for random estimates was always known. If more studies had had negative effects, the distribution would have been pulled in that direction. The actual shape of the distribution shows that positive and negative effect sizes occurred with similar frequency. This is based not on our use of random estimates but on the actual direction of effects reported in such studies. In other words, the use of random estimates in no way biases the results toward an average zero effect size. The normality of the distributions centering around zero is not due to this, and, again, there is no need for concern. The point is that the effect size distributions approximated a normal shape, and meta-analytic tests could be used with confidence.

Although Lepper et al. agree that our distributions are normal, they argue that our data are heterogeneous (lacking equal spread) and therefore inappropriate for meta-analysis. Our decision to use meta-analytic procedures involved a consideration of several issues. Initially, we were concerned with the normality of the distribution of effect sizes. We showed that the distributions were approximately normal and reported the degree of kurtosis and skewness of the free time distribution in the original article (p. 381). Next we considered the results of the Q test for homogeneity. It is well known that this test is liberal in the sense that the null hypothesis (homogeneity) is too often rejected (Hunter, Schmidt, &

Jackson, 1982). Because of this problem, we set the critical value of Q farther out on the chi-square distribution, just below the value at the .01 level (that is, $p > .01$).

Homogeneity was achieved by excluding extreme effect sizes. The exclusion of outliers is not unusual and is recommended by Hedges (1987) as a method for obtaining more equal spread of the effect sizes. To assess any biases due to the removal of outliers, we reported all analyses with extreme values included and excluded. In addition, we identified the studies with extreme values and discussed the conditions that may have led to these atypical results. Inspection of our original article shows that the results do not change to any extent by excluding outliers.

The validity of our meta-analysis is also increased by the use of the CL statistic (McGraw & Won, 1992). CL is another way to express effect size. Importantly, McGraw and Wong conducted 118 tests (simulations) to show that the CL statistic is robust with respect to violations of normality and homogeneity. Because of this, we used CL in all our analyses and reported results identical to those of the other meta-analytic tests.

In sum, the distribution of effect sizes for the critical measures of intrinsic motivation approximated a normal shape. The normality was not due to the inclusion of "pure zero cases" or random estimates as Lepper and his associates have suggested. Homogeneity of effect sizes was achieved by excluding outliers. All results were reported with outliers included and excluded; our findings were not altered to any extent by the exclusion of outliers. In addition, given our use of the CL statistic, we are confident that our analyses are appropriate and that the results are accurate and valid.

Aggregation of Effect Sizes in Meta-Analysis

Lepper et al., Ryan and Deci, and Kohn are critical of the method of aggregating effect sizes within a study to yield a single estimate for each meta-analytic test. They contend that such procedures yield inaccurate estimates of the effects of reward on intrinsic motivation. Underlying this criticism is the supposition that the effects of important moderators and interactions were not detected in our analyses. Again, the implication of these comments is that negative effects of reward are more prevalent than our results communicate.

In response to this concern, we first note that aggregation of effect sizes within a study is a common procedure in meta-analysis that avoids violation of the assumption of independence (Cooper, 1989; Hedges & Olkin, 1985). The procedures for aggregation are clearly described in our original article (pp. 376–377). It is important to point out that a serious statistical violation occurs when more than one effect size from an individual experiment is entered into a single meta-analysis. Typically, in such cases, a control group is compared with more than one experimental treatment within a study, several effect sizes are calculated, and each is entered into a single meta-analytic test. The major problem is that the effect sizes are not independent (errors among observations are correlated). If the dependencies in such data were properly accounted for, the error term would become larger and mean effect sizes would become smaller. Another problem is that a particular study will contribute more weight to the overall meta-analytic outcome than a study yielding only one effect size. Other meta-analyses on reward and intrinsic motivation favored by Lepper et al. (p. 5) have violated the assumption of independence by entering several (sometimes over 10) effect sizes from one study into a single meta-analytic test (e.g., Rummel & Feinberg, 1988; Tang & Hall, 1995). The implication is that conclusions based on these meta-analyses could be incorrect.

The way to achieve independence and at the same time retain effect sizes for an analysis of the impact of various moderators is to (a) aggregate them into a single estimate for an overall analysis of the effects of rewards on intrinsic motivation and (b) conduct further analyses of the effects of various moderator variables. For factorial designs, the main effect of reward is entered into an analysis of the overall effects of reward; interaction effects that have been replicated in a sufficient number of experiments are then analyzed separately. These are the procedures we used in our meta-analyses. As we indicated previously, the moderators we analyzed (reward type, reward expectancy, and reward contingency) were chosen because of their theoretical and applied importance as well as replication.

Lepper et al. are concerned that aggregation of the moderators (rather than separate analyses) yields inaccurate estimates of the effects of reward on intrinsic motivation (p. 11–13). As mentioned earlier, the moderators not assessed in our analyses (e.g., presence of experimenter, reward attractiveness, salience, distraction, etc.) have appeared in only one or two studies, and in these studies they have been added to the tangible, expected, noncontingent reward condition to decrease, mitigate, or increase the negative effect. In terms of such studies, it is possible to obtain an unbiased estimate of the effect size of tangible, expected, noncontingent reward. When the results are pooled across all studies, the effects of any additional moderators are averaged out. That is, although any one of these manipulations may push intrinsic interest up (e.g., reward attractiveness) or down (e.g., surveillance, reward salience) in a given study, their effects are expected to cancel out across many studies. In other words, the best estimate of the effect size of tangible, expected, noncontingent reward when additional moderators are present is the average of all the comparisons of the rewarded conditions with nonrewarded control groups.

Of course, additional meta-analyses could be conducted on the effects of these moderators if they were sufficiently replicated. As we pointed out, however, because they are added to the one reward procedure that produces a reliable negative effect, the results would show that decremental effects of reward on intrinsic motivation depend on even stricter conditions than our analysis indicates. This is demonstrated in Lepper et al.'s analysis of three factorial experiments (Calder & Staw, 1975; Loveland & Olley, 1979; McLoyd, 1979) that crossed initial task interest (high, low) with reward (reward, no reward). Lepper et al. (p. 10) show that in these three studies, rewarding activities with high intrinsic interest yields a large negative effect size. In contrast, rewarding a task with low initial interest produces a positive effect size. In each of these studies, the reward procedure involved tangible, expected, noncontingent (or task-contingent) rewards—the one procedure that produces a negative effect on the free time measure of intrinsic motivation.

Thus, if Lepper et al.'s analysis is reliable, the results indicate that tangible, expected, noncontingent rewards are harmful only when delivered for more interesting tasks. It is worth mentioning here, however, that a study excluded in Lepper et al.'s analysis (Mynatt et al., 1978) also crossed task interest with tangible, expected, noncontingent reward but found positive effects of reward for both low- and high-interest tasks. Given that there are so few studies of the interest variable, the results from this one study could substantially alter Lepper et al.'s conclusions about the importance of level of task inter-

est when rewards are tangible, expected, and noncontingent.

In summary, the procedures used in our meta-analysis yield correct estimates for the effects of reward on intrinsic motivation at each level of analysis. Our critics have implied that analyses of additional moderators and interactions would yield more general negative effects of reward on intrinsic motivation. However, as we have shown, further analyses would actually reveal that positive effects of reward are more general and that decremental effects of reward occur under even more restricted circumstances than our results indicate.

CONCLUSION

A prominent view in education and social psychology is that rewards decrease a person's intrinsic motivation. Our meta-analysis of 20 years of research suggests that this view is incorrect. The findings from approximately 100 studies indicate that rewards can be used effectively to enhance or maintain intrinsic interest in activities. The only negative effect of reward occurs under a highly specific set of conditions, circumstances that are easily avoided. Not surprisingly, these results have not been well received by those who argue that rewards produce negative effects on intrinsic motivation under a wide range of conditions.

In response to the findings, Lepper, Keavney, and Drake (1996), Ryan and Deci (1996), and Kohn (1996) have suggested that the questions asked in our meta-analysis were inappropriate, that critical studies were excluded, that important negative effects were not detected, and that the techniques used in our meta-analysis were unsuitable. In this response, we have shown that the questions asked are fundamental to an understanding of the relationship between rewards and intrinsic motivation and that our meta-analytic techniques are appropriate, robust, and statistically correct. Our meta-analysis includes all relevant studies on the topic, and the results clearly show that negative effects of rewards occur under limited conditions. All told, the results and conclusions of our meta-analysis are not altered by our critics' protests and accusations.

Our findings have important practical implications. In applied settings, the results indicate that verbal rewards (praise and positive feedback) can be used to enhance intrinsic motivation. When tangible rewards (e.g., gold stars, money) are offered contingent on performance on a task or are delivered unexpectedly, intrinsic motivation is maintained. A slight negative effect of reward can be expected when tangible rewards are offered without regard to level of performance. Under this condition, when the rewards are withdrawn, individuals report as much interest in the activity as those in a nonrewarded group, but they may spend slightly less time on it in a free period.[2] This negative effect can be prevented by rewarding people for completing work, solving problems successfully, or attaining a specified level of performance. In other words, rewards can be used effectively in educational and other applied settings without undermining intrinsic motivation.

NOTES

1. Tang and Hall (1995) reported effect sizes for questionnaire measures of intrinsic motivation. The studies they analyzed used questionnaire items to index attributions of causality; moral obligation; attitude toward the task; perceptions of luck, ability, effort, and difficulty; feelings of competence; negative affect; self-esteem; and so on. Tang and Hall combined the effect sizes of all these measures and reported meta-analyses based on this composite index. They did not examine attitude toward the task separately, as we did. Thus, we cannot compare our findings on the attitude measure of intrinsic motivation.

2. It may be informative to consider how serious the negative effect of expected, tangible, noncontingent reward on free time really is. How much less time would students spend on academic subjects if a teacher implemented this reward procedure and then removed it? Results from our meta-analysis indicate that the average effect size for a comparison between people who receive an expected, tangible, noncontingent reward and nonrewarded individuals on time on task following withdrawal of reward is -0.26.

In the original experiments, time on task was typically measured over an 8-minute period. In order to convert the effect size of -0.26 to real time, one needs to know the pooled standard deviation of rewarded and nonrewarded groups. Because many researchers reported only t or F statistics, we will use a well-designed study by Pretty and Seligman (1984) to estimate a pooled standard deviation. Their study reported two experiments with large sample sizes and readily available statistical information. Both experiments compared a condition of expected, tangible, noncontingent reward ($N = 30$) with a nonrewarded control group ($N = 30$) on 8 minutes of free time. The pooled standard deviation was 2.6 minutes.

Using this estimate of error, we are able to convert the negative effect size from the meta-analysis into real time.

An effect size of -0.26 would mean that in an 8-minute period, the average individual who is promised a noncontingent, tangible reward will spend about 41 seconds less time on the task when the reward procedure is withdrawn than the average nonrewarded individual. Given this result, what would happen if a teacher implemented this incentive procedure in a reading program and then removed it? According to the estimate, students who are offered gold stars for reading would spend about 3 minutes, 25 seconds less time reading in a 40-minute free-choice period than students not given the incentive. Of course, this is a hypothetical example, but it does illustrate the magnitude of this negative effect size in terms of real time.

REFERENCES

Birch, L. L., Marlin, D. W., & Rotter, J. (1984). Eating as the "means" activity in a contingency: Effects on young children's food preference. *Child Development, 55,* 431–439.

Boggiano, A. K., Shields, A., Barrett, M., Kellam, T., Thompson, E., Simons, J., & Katz, P. (1992). Helplessness deficits in students: The role of motivational orientation. *Motivation and Emotion, 16,* 271–296.

Calder, B. J., & Staw, B. M. (1975). Self-perception of intrinsic and extrinsic motivation. *Journal of Personality and Social Psychology, 31,* 599–605.

Cameron, J., & Pierce, W. D. (1994). Reinforcement, reward, and intrinsic motivation: A meta-analysis. *Review of Educational Research, 64,* 363–423.

Cooper, H. M. (1989). *Integrating research: A guide for literature reviews* (2nd ed.). Beverly Hills, CA: Sage.

Deci, E. L., & Ryan, R. M. (1985). *Intrinsic motivation and self-determination in human behavior.* New York: Plenum.

Fabes, R. A., Fultz, J., Eisenberg, N., May-Plumlee, T., & Christopher, F. S. (1989). Effects of rewards on children's prosocial motivation: A socialization study. *Developmental Psychology, 25,* 509–515.

Freedman, J. L., Cunningham, J. A., & Krismer, K. (1992). Inferred values and the reverse-incentive effect in induced compliance. *Journal of Personality and Social Psychology, 62,* 357–368.

Gottfried, A. E., Fleming, J. S., & Gottfried, A. W. (1994). Role of parental motivation practices in children's academic intrinsic motivation and achievement. *Journal of Educational Psychology, 86,* 104–113.

Hedges, L. (1987). How hard is hard science, how soft is soft science? The empirical cumulativeness of research. *American Psychologist, 42,* 443–455.

Hedges, L., & Olkin, I. (1985). *Statistical methods for meta-analysis.* Orlando, FL: Academic.

Hunter, J. E., Schmidt, F. L., & Jackson, G. B. (1982). *Meta-analysis: Cumulating research findings across studies.* Beverly Hills, CA: Sage.

Kohn, A. (1993). *Punished by rewards.* Boston: Houghton Mifflin.

Kohn, A. (1996). By all available means: Cameron and Pierce's defense of extrinsic motivators. *Review of Educational Research, 66,* 1–4.

Lepper, M. R., Keavney, M., & Drake, M. (1996). Intrinsic motivation and extrinsic rewards: A commentary on Cameron and Pierce's meta-analysis. *Review of Educational Research, 66,* 5–32.

Loveland, K. K., & Olley, J. G. (1979). The effect of external reward on interest and quality of task performance in children of high and low intrinsic motivation. *Child Development, 50,* 1207–1210.

McGraw, K. O., & Wong, S. P. (1992). A common language effect size statistic. *Psychological Bulletin, 111,* 361–365.

McLoyd, V. C. (1979). The effects of extrinsic rewards of differential value on high and low intrinsic interest. *Child Development, 50,* 1010–1019.

Mynatt, C., Oakley, D., Arkkelin, D., Piccione, A., Margolis, R., & Arkkelin, J. (1978). An examination of overjustification under conditions of extended observation and multiple reinforcement: Overjustification or boredom? *Cognitive Therapy and Research, 2,* 171–177.

Pretty, G. H., & Seligman, C. (1984). Affect and the overjustification effect. *Journal of Personality and Social Psychology, 46,* 1241–1253.

Ross, M. (1975). Salience of reward and intrinsic motivation. *Journal of Personality and Social Psychology, 32,* 245–254.

Rummel, A., & Feinberg, R. (1988). Cognitive evaluation theory: A meta-analytic review of the literature. *Social Behavior and Personality, 16,* 147–164.

Ryan, R. M. (1982). Control and information in the intrapersonal sphere: An extension of cognitive evaluation theory. *Journal of Personality and Social Psychology, 43,* 450–461.

Ryan, R. M., & Deci, E. L. (1996). When paradigms clash: Comments on Cameron and Pierce's claim that rewards do not undermine intrinsic motivation. *Review of Educational Research, 66,* 33–38.

Sutherland, S. (1993). Impoverished minds. *Nature, 364,* 767.

Tang, S., & Hall, V. (1995). The overjustification effect: A meta-analysis. *Applied Cognitive Psychology, 9,* 365–404.

Wiersma, U. J. (1992). The effects of extrinsic rewards in intrinsic motivation: A meta-analysis. *Journal of Occupational and Organizational Psychology, 65,* 101–114.

Williams, B. W. (1980). Reinforcement, behavior constraint, and the overjustification effect. *Journal of Personality and Social Psychology, 39,* 599–614.

Zimbardo, P. G. (1992). *Psychology and life* (13th ed.). New York: Harper Collins.

► Chapter 7: Cognitive Views of Learning

Putting Learning Strategies to Work

SHARON J. DERRY

Recent research in cognitive and educational psychology has led to substantial improvements in our knowledge about learning. Researchers have identified certain mental processing techniques—learning strategies—that can be taught by teachers and used by students to improve the quality of school learning. Let me illustrate.

As a professor of educational and cognitive psychology, I often begin the semester with a simulation exercise designed to illustrate major principles about the role of learning strategies in classroom instruction. For example, recently I presented my students with the following scenario:

> You are a high school student who has arrived at school 20 minutes early. You discover that your first-period teacher is planning to give a test covering Chapter 5. Unfortunately, you have prepared the wrong chapter, and there is no one around to help you out. Skipping class is not the solution, since this results in an automatic "F," and you would never dream of cheating. So you open your book and use the next 15 minutes as wisely as you can.

I gave my students 15 minutes to study. They then took a quiz with eight main idea questions and two application questions. At the end of the quiz, I

Sharon J. Derry is Associate Professor and Chair, Cognitive and Behavioral Sciences, Department of Psychology, Florida State University, Tallahassee, FL 32306-1051.

asked them to write in detail exactly what they did when they studied. Quizzes (without names) were collected and then distributed randomly to the class for scoring and for analyzing the study strategies reported in them.

Few people performed well on this test. A student who did wrote the following:

> There wasn't enough time for details. So I looked at the chapter summary first. Then I skimmed through the chapter and tried to understand the topic paragraphs and the summary paragraphs for each section. I also noticed what the headings said, to get the organization, and I noticed certain names that went with each heading, figuring they did something related to each topic, a study or something. I started to do some memory work on the headings, but time was up before I finished.

By comparison, most students answered only two or three of the main idea questions, reporting a study strategy something like the following.

> Panic. There was not enough time! I started going over the chapter and got as far as I could, but it was hopeless. I assume you do not plan to grade this quiz, because that would be unfair!

As illustrated in these two examples, the differences between successful and unsuccessful learning strategies often are clear and striking. Whereas the successful learners assessed the learning situation and calmly developed a workable plan for dealing with it, the less successful learners were occupied with fruitless worries and vague strategies but little planning effort.

Such an exercise serves to introduce the following important principles about self-directed learning:

1. The plan that one uses for accomplishing a learning goal is a person's learning strategy. Learning strategies may be simple or complex, specific or vague, intelligent or unwise. Obviously, some learning strategies work better than others.

2. Learning strategies require knowledge of specific learning skills, or "tactics" (e.g., Dern, and Murphy 1986), such as skimming, attending to chapter structure, and memorization techniques. The ability to devise appropriate learning strategies also requires knowledge about when and when not to use particular types of learning tactics.

3. Learning is a form of problem solving that involves analyzing a learning task and devising a strategy appropriate for that particular situation. Different learning situations may call for different strategies.

Further, I asked my students to determine whether any reported learning strategy had produced useful knowledge. Alas, no participant had applied the knowledge acquired in the 15-minute study session to the two application questions on the quiz. Even when learning strategies are apparently successful according to one form of measurement, the resultant learning is not necessarily usable later in problem solving. Thus, we added a fourth principle to our list:

4. In most school learning situations, strategies should be devised with the aim of creating usable, rather than inert, knowledge. Clearly, not all learning strategies will lead to the formation of usable knowledge structures.

Next I will elaborate these principles in greater detail, suggesting how they can influence classroom practice.

STRATEGIES AS LEARNING PLANS

There is much confusion about the term *learning strategy*. The term is used to refer to (1) specific learning tactics such as rehearsal, imaging, and outlining (e.g., Cook and Mayer 1983, Levin 1986); (2) more general types of self-management activities such as planning and comprehension monitoring (e.g., Pressley et al. in press a); and (3) complex plans that combine several specific techniques (e.g., Derry and Murphy 1986, Snowman and McCown 1984).

To clarify the uses of the term, I distinguish between the specific tactics and the learning strategies that combine them. Thus, a learning strategy is a complete plan one formulates for accomplishing a learning goal; and a learning tactic is any individual processing technique one uses in service of the plan (Derry and Murphy 1986, Snowman and McCown 1984). That is, a learning strategy is the application of one or more specific learning tactics to a learning problem. Within this definition, the plethora of learning techniques (popularly called "strategies") being promoted by various researchers and practitioners can be viewed as potentially useful learning tactics that can be applied in various combinations to accomplish different learning jobs.

This definition points to the need for two distinct types of strategies instruction: specific tactics training and training in methods for selecting and combining tactics into workable learning plans. Teachers can incorporate both types of training into regular classroom instruction by thoughtfully combining different study tactics—outlining plus positive self-talk, for example—and assigning them along with regular homework.

LEARNING STRATEGIES EMPLOY SPECIFIC LEARNING TACTICS

In this section I discuss tactics in three major categories: (1) tactics for acquiring verbal knowledge, that is, ideas and facts fundamental to disciplines such as science, literature, and history; (2) tactics for acquiring procedural skills such as reading, using language, and solving problems that underlie various curriculum disciplines; and (3) support tactics for self-motivation, which are applicable to all types of learning situations. (For a more thorough treatment of these topics, see the reviews by Derry and Murphy 1986, Weinstein and Mayer 1985, Levin 1986, and Pressley et al. in press b.)

Verbal Learning Tactics

Strategies aimed at improving comprehension and retention of verbal information should build upon

Category	Examples	Some Conditions of Use	Strengths or Weaknesses
Attentional Focusing			
Simple focusing	Highlighting. Underlining.	Structured, easy materials. Good readers.	No emphasis on importance or conceptual relations of ideas.
Structured focusing	Looking for headings, topic sentences. Teacher-directed signaling.	Poor readers. Difficult but considerate materials.	Efficient, but may not promote active elaboration, deep thinking.
Schema Building	Use of story grammars, theory schemas. Networking.	Poor text structure. Goal is to encourage active comprehension.	Inefficient, but develops higher-order thinking skills.
Idea Elaboration	Some types of self-questioning. Imagery.	Goal is to comprehend and remember specific ideas.	Powerful, easy to combine. Difficult for some students unassisted. Will not ensure focus on what is important.

FIGURE 1 **Tactics for Learning Verbal Information**

tactics that enhance these mental processes: (1) focusing attention on important ideas, (2) schema building, and (3) idea elaboration (see Figure 1).

Attentional Focusing

Two types of attention-focusing tactics are simple focusing and structured focusing. In the simple focusing category, highlighting and underlining are common examples. Unfortunately, the use of simple focusing procedures does not necessarily ensure identification of important information. I have often confirmed this point by requesting to see the textbooks of students who are having academic problems. Frequently I find almost every word in their texts highlighted.

Students, weaker ones in particular, should be taught to combine simple focusing with structured focusing, whereby the learner directs primary attention to headings, topic sentences, or other signals provided by the instructional presentation. The teaching of structured focusing is a well-established practice in English classes, and it can profitably be reinforced in other courses to help students identify information they need to learn. However, the success of structured focusing depends heavily on well-structured, considerate instructional presentations (as well as on considerate teachers who test for the main ideas). And the use of these tactics does not ensure that the ideas identified will actually be remembered.

Schema Building

A more powerful type of verbal-learning tactic is schema building, which encourages active analysis of an instructional presentation and formation of a synthesizing framework. One well-known form of schema building is networking (Dansereau 1985, Dansereau et al. 1979), whereby a student draws a node-link map representing the important ideas in a text and the interrelationships among them. This technique is powerful, but it is difficult to teach and time-consuming to apply (McKeachie 1984). Simpler forms of schema building include the use of teacher-suggested schemas, such as the well-known tactic of requiring students to analyze stories in English literature by identifying the theme, setting, plot, resolution, and so on. Similar assignments can facilitate verbal learning in other courses of study. For example, Dansereau (1985) improved students' performance on science tests by teaching them to use a theory schema as a study aid for scientific text.

Schema building encourages in-depth analysis and is particularly useful if instruction is inconsiderate or unclear. Schema-building strategies are generally employed as comprehension aids; however, they also aid memory through the organization and elaboration of ideas.

Idea Elaboration

Idea elaboration is a memory-enhancing process whereby students link each important new idea with prior knowledge so as to connect them. These linkages can be based on an image, a logical inference, or on anything else that serves to connect new ideas to prior knowledge (Gagne 1985).

Many elaboration tactics capitalize on imagery, a powerful memory-enhancing technique. For example, the key-word method for acquiring foreign vocabulary involves creating a mental image (prior knowledge) representing the sound of a foreign word (new information), and relating that image to another image (prior knowledge) representing the meaning of the word's English equivalent. Many types of elaboration tactics facilitate memorization (e.g., Bransford and Stein 1984), and these can be employed to great advantage in many courses.

Procedural Learning Tactics

Most learning strategies research has examined tactics for acquiring verbal information. However, some strategy researchers are developing techniques for acquiring procedural skills. Procedural learning has three aspects (Anderson 1983, Gagne 1985): (1) learning how to carry out basic actions such as performing long division or executing a tennis lob; (2) learning to recognize the conceptual patterns that indicate when it is appropriate to perform particular actions (such as recognizing that a word problem is a division situation or that a tennis lob is required); and (3) learning to combine many pattern-action pairs into a smooth overall system of response. Consider, for example, the complex combining of subskills that underlies the actual playing of a tennis match.

Based on this view, Figure 2 presents three categories of mental tactics for procedural learning: (1) tactics for learning conceptual patterns that cue applicability of associated actions; (2) tactics for acquiring the component actions (performance subskills) themselves; and (3) tactics for perfecting and tuning complex overall performance.

Pattern-Recognition Tactics

Pattern recognition plays an important role in the development of procedural performance; however,

Category	Examples	Some Conditions of Use	Strengths or Weaknesses
Pattern Learning			
Hypothesizing	Student reasons and guesses why particular pattern is or isn't example of concept.	Goal is to learn attributes of concepts and patterns.	Inefficient unless feedback given. Encourages independent thinking.
Seeking reasons for actions	Student seeks explanations why particular actions are or are not appropriate.	Goal is to determine which procedures are required in which situations.	Develops meta-cognitive knowledge. Inefficient if not guided. If too guided, might not promote thinking skills.
Reflective Self-Instruction	Student compares reification of own performance to expert model.	Goal is to tune, improve complex skill.	Develops understanding of quality performance. May increase self-consciousness, reduce automaticity.
Practice			
Part practice	Student drills on one specific aspect of performance.	A few specific aspects of a performance need attention.	Develops subskill automaticity. Doesn't encourage subskill integration.
Whole practice	Student practices full performance without attention to subskills.	Goal is to maintain or improve skill already acquired or to integrate subskills.	May consolidate poorly executed subskills. Helps develop smooth whole performance.

FIGURE 2   **Tactics for Learning Procedural Knowledge**

students are probably not aware of this. Thus, developing students' procedural learning abilities includes both conveying the important function of pattern recognition and helping students develop tactics for acquiring performance-related patterns.

Examples of tactics in the patterns-acquisition category include hypothesizing and seeking reasons for actions. In applying these tactics, the learner attempts to discover the identifying features of a pattern or concept through guesswork, reasoning, and investigation. For example, while watching a tennis pro at work, the student might hypothesize about the features of play that cause the pro to execute a lob or a groundstroke. Hypotheses are confirmed or altered through continued observation, until the pattern features are known. Alternatively, the student might seek reasons by consulting the tennis pro directly. Seeking information overcomes the major weakness of the hypothesizing tactic, inefficiency. However, the virtue of hypothesizing is that it can be used in situations where expert advice is not available.

Practice Tactics
Other aspects of procedural learning include the acquisition of basic component actions (subskills) and, ultimately, the development of smooth complex performances that combine those subskills. There are learning tactics that can help students derive maximum benefit from their practice sessions. One example is part practice, whereby the student attempts to improve a complex performance by perfecting and automating an important subcomponent of that performance. For example, a student might greatly improve performance on mathematics tests by memorizing and practicing square-root tables. Or performance in tennis might be improved by concentrating practice on service and smashes. Part practice should be alternated with whole practice (Schneider 1985), whereby the student practices the full complex performance with little attention to individual subskills.

Reflective Self-Instruction
Another class of procedural learning tactics is reflective self-instruction, whereby the student attempts to improve personal performance by studying an expert model. For example, a student might videotape her tennis swing and compare that to a tape of an expert's swing. Or the student might critically compare her homework solution for a geometry proof to the teacher's expert solution presented on the board. Reflective self-instruction can concentrate either on specific component subskills or on whole complex performances. One key to successful self-instruction is the availability of adequate performance models. By providing models of expert performance and guiding students in how to benefit from those models while learning, teachers can provide training in the valuable technique of reflective self-instruction.

Mental Support Tactics

Acquiring useful knowledge in school is a lengthy and difficult process demanding a great investment of time and effort on the part of the student. Thus, tactics are needed for helping learners maintain a positive attitude and a high state of motivation during learning and practice. Researchers (e.g., Dansereau et al. 1979, 1985; Meichenbaum 1980; McCombs 1981–82) recommend several types of support tactics: (1) behavioral self-management, (2) mood management, and (3) self-monitoring (see Figure 3).

The behavioral self-management category includes such tactics as breaking a complex learning chore into subgoals, developing a schedule for meeting subgoals, devising a reporting procedure for charting progress, and devising a self-reward system for completing major subgoals. Mood management tactics include concentration and relaxation techniques (useful for combating test anxiety); and positive self-talk, used to establish and maintain a positive frame of mind before and during learning and performance (e.g., Meichenbaum 1980). Finally, an example of self-monitoring is the technique of stopping periodically during learning and practice to check and, if necessary, readjust strategy, concentration, and mood.

Frequently used by professional athletes, mental support tactics can also be used by students to increase academic performance and motivation and to decrease tension associated with evaluation. They are applicable to all types of learning situations and can be combined with both verbal and procedural learning tactics in study assignments. For example, to study for a history test, a student might devise a learning strategy that orchestrates several specific tactics, such as positive self-talk with self-checking (to maintain motivation), networking (to help organize facts in a meaningful way), and use of imagery or mnemonics (to help with memorization).

Category	Examples	Some Conditions of Use	Strengths or Weaknesses
Behavioral Self-Management	Student breaks task into sub-goals, creates goal-attainment plan, rewards.	Complex, lengthy task; low motivated students.	Promotes extrinsic, rather than intrinsic, motivation. Very powerful.
Mood Management			
Positive self-talk	Student analyzes, avoids negative self-statements, creates positive self-statements.	Preparation for competitive or difficult performance; presence of negative ideas.	Good intrinsic motivator; requires conscious attention during performance.
Relaxation techniques	Student uses deep breathing, counting, other clinical relaxation methods.	Text anxiety; highly anxious students.	Techniques controversial in some districts.
Self-Monitoring	Student stops self during performance to consciously check mood, progress, etc.	Goal is to increase conscious awareness and control of thinking process.	May interrupt concentration.

FIGURE 3 **Tactics for Developing Motivation**

STRATEGY-BUILDING AS PROBLEM SOLVING

The ultimate aim of tactics training is to provide students with tools that will enable them, as autonomous learners, to devise their own strategies. Unfortunately, a persistent problem in strategy training has been students' failure to apply tactics in situations outside the class in which they were learned originally.

However, several training techniques can alleviate these problems. A large number of researchers (e.g., Baron 1981, Bransford and Stein 1984) suggest teaching students to respond to all learning tasks using a general problem-solving model. For example, Derry, Jacobs, and Murphy (1987) taught soldiers to use the "4Cs" to develop plans for study reading. The 4Cs stood for: clarify learning situation, construct a learning strategy, carry out the strategy, and check results.

One presumed advantage of such plans is that they remind students to stop and think reflectively about each learning situation prior to proceeding with the task (Baron 1981). Also, such plans may serve as mnemonic devices that help students recall previously learned tactics associated with each step. There is some empirical support for the idea that problem-solving models enhance tactics transfer (Belmont et al. 1982).

Another procedure for inducing tactics transfer is informed training (Campione et al. 1982, Pressley et al. 1984). This procedure enhances direct tactics instruction with explicit information regarding the effectiveness of various tactics, including how and when they should be used. As Levin (1986) points out, there are different learning tools for different learning jobs. With informed training, students learn that tactics selection is always influenced by the nature of the instructional material as well as the nature of the learning goal. For example, if a text is not highly structured and the primary aim of study is to comprehend and remember important ideas, a strategy that combines networking with idea elaboration would be appropriate. However, if the aim is primarily comprehension rather than retention, a schema-building technique alone would suffice. Informed training is superior to "blind training" in producing transfer and sustained use of specific learning tactics (Pressley et al. 1984, Campione et al. 1982).

Previously I suggested that teachers can help develop students' learning skills by devising, assigning, and explaining learning strategies and by providing feedback on strategy use. Such established classroom practices are excellent vehicles for informed training.

LEARNING STRATEGIES SHOULD PRODUCE USEFUL KNOWLEDGE

Cognitive psychology has taught us much about the nature and structure of usable knowledge. Verbal information is likely to be called into service only if it is understood when learned and only if it is stored in memory within well-structured, well-elaborated networks of meaningfully related ideas. Procedural skills, on the other hand, are likely to be accessed and accurately executed only if they have been developed through extensive practice and only if the environmental patterns that indicate their applicability are well learned. If the primary aim of schooling is the creation of useful knowledge, then strategy application should result in the deliberate creation of a well-structured knowledge base, whether verbal, procedural, or both.

It is unlikely that reliance on any single learning tactic alone will ensure the creation of well-constructed knowledge. Rather, multiple tactics are usually required. For example, if an elaboration technique is applied for the purpose of enhancing individual ideas, another schema-building tactic may be needed to tie related ideas together. Or if practice is used to perfect a specific aspect of procedural performance, a pattern-learning tactic may still be needed to ensure that the skill is executed only when appropriate. Thus, useful knowledge is most likely to evolve through a dynamic process requiring, first, an informed analysis of each learning problem, then selection and combining of all the learning tactics needed to produce a well-formed mental structure.

Not every learning strategy produces useful knowledge. Some strategies lead to isolated, unstructured bits of learning that will remain forever inert. For this reason, both teachers and students should be aware of the nature and form of useful knowledge and of learning strategies that are likely to facilitate its creation.

STRATEGY TRAINING FOR LIFELONG LEARNING

Students who receive good strategy training during their years in school can acquire a form of knowledge especially useful in coping with the wide variety of learning situations they will encounter throughout their lives. Given the amount of time that people spend in school, in job-related training, and in acquiring knowledge associated with their interests and hobbies, the ability to find good solutions to learning problems may be the most important thinking skill of all.

REFERENCES

Anderson, J. R. (1983). *The Architecture of Cognition.* Cambridge, Mass.: Harvard University Press.

Baron, J. (1981). "Reflective Thinking as a Goal of Education." *Intelligence* 5: 291–309.

Belmont, J. M., E. C. Butterfield, and R. P. Ferretti. (1982). "To Secure Transfer of Training Instruct Self-Management Skills." In *How and How Much Can Intelligence Be Increased,* edited by D. K. Detterman and R. J. Sternberg, pp. 147–154. Norwood, N.J.: ABLEX.

Bransford, J. D., and B. S. Stein. (1984). *The Ideal Problem Solver: A Guide For Improving Thinking, Learning, and Creativity.* New York: Freeman.

Campione, J. C., A. L. Brown, and R.A. Ferrara. (1982). "Mental Retardation and Intelligence." In *Cognitive Strategy Research: Educational Applications,* edited by P. J. Sternberg, pp. 87–126. New York: Springer-Verlag.

Cook, L. K., and R. E. Mayer. (1983). "Reading Strategies Training for Meaningful Learning from Prose." In *Cognitive Strategy Research: Educational Applications,* edited by M. Pressley and J. R. Levin, pp. 87–126. New York: Springer-Verlag.

Dansereau, D. F. (1985). "Learning Strategy Research." in *Thinking and Learning Skills,* edited by J. W. Segal, S. F. Chipman, and R. Glaser, vol. 1, pp. 209–240. Hillsdale, N.J.: Erlbaum.

Dansereau, D. F., K. W. Collins, B. A. McDonald, C. D. Holley, J. C. Garland, G. M. Diekhoff, and S. H. Evans. (1979). "Development and Evaluation of an Effective Learning Strategy Program." *Journal of Educational Psychology* 79: 64–73.

Derry, S. J., J. Jacobs, and D. A. Murphy. (1987). "The JSEP Learning Skills Training System." *Journal of Educational Technology Systems* 15, 4: 273–284.

Derry, S. J. and D. A. Murphy. (1986). "Designing Systems That Train Learning Ability: From Theory to Practice." *Review of Educational Research* 56, 1: 1–39.

Gagne, E. D. (1985). *The Cognitive Psychology of School Learning.* Boston: Little, Brown and Company.

Levin, J. R. (1986). "Four Cognitive Principles of Learning-Strategy Instruction." *Educational Psychologist* 21, 1 and 2: 3–17.

McCombs, B. L. (1981–82). "Transitioning Learning Strategies Research in Practice: Focus on the Student in

Technical Training." *Journal of Instructional Development* 5: 10–17.

McKeachie, W. J. (1984). "Spatial Strategies: Critique and Educational Implications." *In Spatial Learning Strategies: Techniques, Applications, and Related Issues,* edited by C. D. Holley and D. F. Dansereau, pp. 301–312. Orlando, Fla.: Academic Press.

Meichenbaum, D. H. (1980). "A Cognitive-Behavioral Perspective on Intelligence." *Intelligence* 4: 271–283.

Pressley, M., J. G. Borkowski, and J. T. O'Sullivan. (1984). "Memory Strategy Instruction Is Made of This: Metamemory and Durable Strategy Use." *Educational Psychologist* 19: 94–107.

Pressley, M., J. G. Borkowski, and W. Schneider. (In press a). "Cognitive Strategies: Good Strategy Users Coordinate Metacognition and Knowledge." In *Annals of Child Development,* edited by R. Vasta and G. Whitehurst, vol. 4. Greenwich, Conn.: JAI Press.

Pressley, M., F. Goodchild, J. Fleet, R. Zajchowski, and E. D. Evans. (in press b). "The Challenges of Classroom Strategy Instruction." In *The Elementary School Journal.*

Schneider, W. (1985). "Training High-Performance Skills: Fallacies and Guidelines." *Human Factors* 27: 285–300.

Snowman, J., and R. McCown. (April 1984). "Cognitive Processes In Learning: A Model for Investigating Strategies and Tactics." Paper presented at the annual meeting of the American Educational Research Association, New Orleans.

Weinstein, C. E., and F. E. Mayer. (1985). "The Teaching of Learning Strategies." *In Handbook of Research on Teaching,* 3rd ed., edited by M. C. Wittrock. New York: Macmillan.

Practicing Representation

Learning with and about Representational Forms

JAMES G. GREENO and ROGERS P. HALL

Our title is deliberately ambiguous. In one interpretation, "practicing representation" refers to a kind of exercise that is required of students, especially in mathematics and science. They have to practice using the standard forms of representation, such as arithmetic expressions, tables, graphs, and equations. In another interpretation, "practicing representation" must always be part of a social practice. Viewed in this way, learning to construct and interpret representations involves learning to participate in the complex practices of communication and reasoning in which the representations are used. This learning involves much more than simply learning to read and write symbols in arrangements corresponding to the accepted forms.

A theoretical perspective—sometimes called the *situative* perspective—that is currently developing in research emphasizes those practices in which students participate as they learn. Teachers know the importance of student participation in the activities of learning, and they commit much effort to designing activities that will engage the participation of students. What is often overlooked is that, in their participation, students learn the prevailing practices of learning and knowing that occur in their school setting.

For example, if students' learning activities include formulating questions and proposing and explaining alternative solutions, they can learn how to participate in those activities of inquiry. However, if they learn to give only the answers and explanations that are specified by teachers and textbooks, they are likely to learn the practices of memorizing.

To be still more specific, if students need to construct tables and graphs to complete a project report in mathematics or science, they can learn how to consider whether and how these forms are effective in communicating the information that they think is important. Or if students draw graphs corresponding to equations for, say, linear versus exponential growth in order to explore the effects of changes in their parameters, they can learn how to use graphs to consider differences in meaning between the concepts of additive and multiplicative change. But if

James G. Greeno is Margaret Jacks Professor of Education in the School of Education, Stanford University, Stanford, CA, and a research fellow at the Institute for Research on Learning, Menlo Park, CA. Rogers P. Hall is an assistant professor in the Graduate School of Education, University of California, Berkeley, and a research affiliate at the Institute for Research on Learning. The research reported here was supported by grants from the National Science Foundation and the Spencer Foundation.

students simply complete assignments of constructing representations in forms that are already specified, they do not have opportunities to learn how to weigh the advantages and disadvantages of different forms of representation or how to use those representations as tools with which to build their conceptual understanding.

We discuss here the process of learning to construct and interpret representations from the perspective of social practice. We and others have been conducting research on practices of representation in schools and in other work settings, and we believe that this research has implications for curriculum and instruction in school mathematics and science. Our discussion makes three main points.

- Forms of representation need not be taught as though they are ends in themselves. Instead, they can be considered as useful tools for constructing understanding and for communicating information and understanding.
- When representations are used as tools for understanding and communicating, they are constructed and adapted for the purposes at hand. Often a nonstandard representation serves these purposes better than a standard form, and students should learn how to generate representations flexibly for their use.
- For something to function as a representation, people must interpret it to give it meaning. Of course, standard forms of representation are valuable; a sizable community shares their conventions of interpretation, and it is important for students to learn how to use these standard forms of representation. However, students can also become more actively involved in learning to construct and interpret representations by participating in discussions of the properties of representations, including their advantages and limitations.

REPRESENTATIONS ARE IMPORTANT FOR THEIR USES

Many forms of representation are taught explicitly in schools, especially in mathematics and science. Students learn how to construct and interpret tables, graphs, equations, and other forms of technical representation because they are essential tools for communicating and reasoning about concepts and information in mathematics, science, and other domains.

Unfortunately, technical representations are often taught as though they were ends in themselves. Learning to make graphs and to write equations and interpret them correctly becomes important not for understanding and communicating concepts but for getting high scores on tests. Under the pressure to cover the prescribed curriculum, teachers often feel that there is not enough time to teach students what representations are for and why the forms are useful and effective.

The changes that many reformers are advocating in mathematics and science education include more emphasis on students' learning to apply what they learn to their activities of working, thinking, and socializing, both within and outside of school.[1] In this way of thinking, forms of representation are *tools* that students can learn to use as resources in thinking and communicating.[2]

A classroom example. New mathematics curricula provide experiences in which students learn to use forms of representation for purposes other than encoding information in correct form. In one example, groups of middle school students work on a project in which they build models of a biological system with two populations, wolves and caribou. Their job is to develop recommendations that could be sent to the state of Alaska about alterative policies for controlling the populations of wolves on public lands. The students are to develop one or more simulation models that support their recommendations.

We have observed middle school students working on such projects in classes where their teachers use a curriculum unit called "LifeLines," developed at the Institute for Research on Learning.[3] This design-based unit includes a computer modeling environment called "HabiTech." LifeLines is one of several curriculum units that have been developed recently in line with the standards issued by the National Council of Teachers of Mathematics. We discuss it here as an example of a general trend in mathematics and science education.

In their activity with the LifeLines unit, students use and construct representations involving tables, graphs, and equations. Students read information contained in a database. The different forms of representation in the database illustrate the different ways in which representations are useful. For example, the database includes tables of census data and text that present quantitative information about animal populations in different locales. These provide estimates of the sizes of wolf and caribou populations in different years. The tables and accompanying text are particularly useful if students want to find out the size of a population in any given year. But it is not easy for students to use the tables to see general trends in the population sizes. It is easier to judge from a graph of the data whether a population grew or declined in a regular way or stayed relatively the same over a period of years, whether the rate of increase or decrease was more or less constant over the period, whether there was a more rapid change during the early or later years, or whether there was a sudden change that occurred at one particular time.

One student attempted to build an explicit link between the number of wolf packs that hunt caribou and the number of caribou that die every year. The form of this representation provided by the computer program was a network, with quantities in the model represented by boxes and with relations between the quantities shown by arrows between the boxes. (The arrows indicated that changes in one quantity depended on the values of other quantities in the model.) This network allowed the student to integrate two quantities: the number of wolf packs in Alaska and the number of caribou eaten over the course of a year. As the student put it, the model should show that, as more wolves are killed, fewer caribou will be eaten. He used this model to explore a policy recommendation by his group, advising the state to allow hunters to kill wolves in order to stabilize the caribou population.

While working with the model, the student could move between modifying the functions in the network, changing the equations typed into the boxes, and evaluating the results in tabular and graphical form. For example, after running this model and watching a graph of the caribou population plummet below zero, the student completely revised the function that linked wolf and caribou population sizes and produced a model in which caribou and wolf populations both grew slowly over a five-year period.

Teachers who engage their students in these project-based activities usually have groups of students present their work to the rest of the class. In some projects, presentations by students are videotaped and submitted to a panel of reviewers, as well as being seen by students in other classes who are working on projects involving the same problems.[4] These presentations are a major source of information for

assessment and a valuable learning activity. Teachers in the Middle-School Mathematics Through Applications Project have found it essential to have presentations midway through students' work. The presentations are reviewed by teachers and by other groups of students. The students preparing presentations learn to evaluate alterative ways of representing their ideas and findings. Those reviewing other students' presentations learn ways of judging the effectiveness of representations for communicating understanding.

An important educational goal is for students to learn to use multiple forms of representation in communicating with one another. In classrooms that use the LifeLines curriculum, students use a variety of representational forms to communicate their understanding in several ways: (1) presentations using networks, tables, and graphs in complex narrative descriptions of the models they have constructed; (2) qualitative expectations about relations between quantities in their models, usually described with reference to the node/link representation of the network and the resulting graph; and (3) explicit descriptions of the relation between the model results and the group's policy recommendations.

As in any classroom setting, the extent to which students give fully articulated versions of their work varies, but the practices found in these classrooms often involve extensive use of interrelated representational forms to communicate understanding. A heterogeneous mix of representational forms becomes a valuable resource for students when they communicate the sense of their work to teammates, to other students in the class, and to their teachers.

An example of professional work. When students learn to use representations as tools, they are preparing for the kinds of activities that are common among mathematicians, scientists, engineers, and others who use mathematics in their professional work. Research examining these work practices has shown that people working on a problem use diagrams, equations, and other notations to keep track of partial results and to derive implications of results they have already developed. They also choose representations to communicate their conclusions effectively to other people.

In one example, Rogers Hall and Reed Stevens studied the activity of civil engineers working on design projects and compared it with that of middle-schoolers working on projects in their mathematics class.[5] In a case drawn from the adult workplace, two civil engineers were reviewing the design of a "collector" roadway that would cut through a hilly region in a large housing development. Their physical design documents consisted of "plan," "profile," and "section" views of the proposed development and associated roadways. These representations were printed out separately on large sheets of paper by using CAD (computer-aided design) software. Each view provided a different perspective on the design, but they all used a conventional set of measures and labels (e.g., feet of elevation above sea level, numbered surveying stations, and linear offsets from these stations).

The use of standard representational forms in this roadway design provides an illustration of two points about representations as "boundary objects"—that is, representations that can be interpreted by people from different communities in ways that allow them to share information.[6] Our first point is that standard representational forms help communicate the results of analytical work to other people. This is one function of the representations that students can learn in such classroom activities as the LifeLines curriculum when they present their results to an audience.

In the engineering firm studied, plan, profile, and section views were expected by clients and, in some cases (e.g., in the design of a clinic for a large health maintenance organization), were even mandated by law. The representations were constructed in working design sessions within the firm and were used in other settings, including project reviews with clients and senior management of the firm, design reviews by municipal boards, and eventual work with the developer's construction crews. For example, just before the design meetings that Hall and Stevens observed, preliminary design documents had been sent out for review by the city, a new soils report had been completed by a different group of engineers (using a plan view of the housing site with topographic contour lines), and an environmental impact report had been requested.

Our second point about this example is that standard representational forms, when effectively combined, allow people to think about situations that they are not in or that may not yet exist. In a curriculum such as LifeLines, representations provide students with information about populations of animals in Alaska, and the students construct hypothetical models about those populations. In the engineering task, representations let many people (the civil engineers, their clients, municipal review boards, or construction workers) think about the complex system of roadways and residential sites being proposed. In a design meeting that Hall and Stevens analyzed closely, engineers focused on the various "paper views" of their design in progress. For example, when the grade (or slope) of a proposed collector roadway was found to exceed the city guideline maximum of 15%, the engineers began searching through a sizable collection of paper views, putting some views aside and shifting or rolling back others to construct a layered, coordinated display. With this display in hand, they could talk about the design tradeoff that was "driving" the unusually steep roadway.

When the junior engineer in this pair cautioned that they would need a "brutal" amount of fill dirt under the proposed roadway, the more senior engineer (also the project manager) used a pencil to sketch a less desirable design. The alterative he sketched would save fill dirt in a relatively steep canyon, but it would rip down an entire forested hillside at the top of the proposed roadway. Given standardized forms and a shared understanding of how to assemble them to make a design proposal, these engineers were able to make present many objects and activities that could never literally have been brought into the office: the topography of a hilly development site, the existing distribution of trees and other foliage on the site, alternative roadways that construction crews would need to "snake through" the site, cubic yards of dirt they would "cut" and "fill" in the process, and the nonoverlapping concerns of both their client and a host of regulatory agencies.[7]

When we observe students working with Life-Lines and other design-based curricula, we see that they, too, use representations to reason about situations that they are unable to experience directly. They rely on a kind of "hypothetical reality" that anchors their mathematical reasoning. As they watch a graph of increasing population, someone may say, "They're growing fast—too fast." Or as they watch a graph decreasing to zero, someone might say, "They're dead—goodbye." This kind of involvement with the meanings of representations is often missing when students work on traditional word problems.

CONSTRUCTING UNDERSTANDING

People use representations to aid understanding when they are reflecting on an activity or working on a problem. As individuals or groups work on problems, they may make drawings, write notes, or construct tables or equations. These representations help them keep track of ideas and inferences they have made and also serve to organize their continuing work. Sometimes people construct an analysis to be sure that a conclusion is valid or correct, and then the representation can also be used as an argument that supports the conclusion.

The representational work that people do often uses nonstandard forms, which are constructed for the immediate purpose of developing their understanding. In most practices, people generate representational forms in ways that serve immediate local purposes. In addition to being representations *of* something, they are *for* something.[8] This contrasts with a common practice in school, wherein students learn to construct representations of information without having a real purpose.[9]

Recent research on problem solving in mathematics and design provides examples of this distinction that suggest ways of rethinking how we teach mathematics in school. It might be thought that flexible construction of understanding using representations occurs only with problems that arise in such complex practices as engineering. But people working on school-like tasks also construct understanding in flexible, adaptive ways.

Several findings in this line of research are important for our argument about how representational forms might be made and used in new kinds of classroom practices.

- Representations are *constructed for specific purposes* during attempts to solve problems and communicate with others about these attempts. In addition, the meanings of representations can shift as problem-solving purposes and difficulties change. Under these circumstances, representations often *match the processes of solving the problem*, providing a kind of model of the students' thinking as they work.[10] This contrasts with common methods of teaching and assessment, in which students are instructed to represent problems with standard forms that depend on a classification of problem types, rather than on the processes of solution.[11]

- Students often construct representations in forms that help them see patterns and perform calculations, taking advantage of the fact that *different forms* provide *different supports* for inference and calculation. Thus solving a problem involves an interactive process in which students construct representations based on partial understanding and then can use the representations to improve their understanding, which leads to a more refined representation, and so on.

- Students often use *multiple forms of representation* in working on a problem, some of which are invented by the students and differ from forms that are explicitly taught in the curriculum. These hybrid combinations often show that students have significant partial understanding of difficult mathematical concepts.[12] The invention of novel forms by students shows that they can use representational material constructively as they build their understanding.[13]

Rogers Hall conducted a study comparing the practices of students, teachers, and advanced engineering undergraduates in solving algebra "story" problems.[14] The standard representational forms that students are taught to use for these problems are algebraic equations. Hall found that approximately half of the representational forms produced during the participants' solution attempts involved systems of representation other than algebraic expressions. Diverse representational forms were used by all three groups of participants in the study. Figure 1 shows two of these nonstandard forms: a drawing of successive "states" in motion and a table that organizes intermediate quantities during these states. Problem solvers also gave brief oral narratives that coordinated time and distance across related rates. For example, an algebra teacher, trying to explain an inference about times while working on a motion problem, produced the following narrative: "If you put two people on the trains and started their watches at the same time the train left, then their watches would say the same thing when you took the measurement between the trains."[15]

These nonstandard representational forms were frequently combined to construct models of a problem's structure. When problem solvers introduced correct inferences about the problem, they were more likely to use nonstandard forms (e.g., narratives or drawings) than their standard counterparts (e.g., algebraic expressions or formula "charts"). Nonstandard forms were also used to repair errors made while participants were using more standard forms. Hall characterized the use of such multiple representations as the construction of "material designs," arguing that their written features were im-

Problem: Two trains leave the same station at the same time. They travel in opposite directions. One train travels 60 km/h and the other 100 km/h. In how many hours will they be 880 km apart?

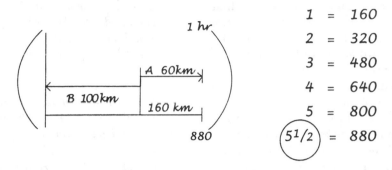

FIGURE 1   **Multiple Representational Forms**

portant for inference and calculation and that combined representations were actively designed for specific purposes.

The results of this study and others[16] show that people do not use only the forms of representation that they have been taught to use, but they also construct novel forms. These constructions help them to identify or repair inferences about problem structure, as well as providing resources that help to manage calculation. We miss many of these nonstandard competencies when we restrict our attention (or that of our students) exclusively to standard representational forms.

USING AND CONSTRUCTING CONVENTIONS OF INTERPRETATION

There is a common (and unfortunate) assumption that physical notations (texts, numerals, pictures, equations, and so on) *by themselves* constitute representations—that is, that information is somehow contained in the physical patterns that are written or drawn on paper or stored in computer files. This notion neglects the very basic principle, stated many decades ago by Charles Sanders Peirce, that for a notation to function as a representation, someone has to *interpret* it and thereby give it meaning.[17] (In Peirce's view, with which we agree, there are three things involved whenever there is a representation: something that is represented, the referent; the referring expression that represents the referent; and the interpretation that links the referring expression to the referent.) According to this principle, such

physical notations as tables, equations, and graphs are *potential* representations. They can become representations when someone gives them meaning by interpreting them. Of course, the person who produced a representation in the first place had an interpretation in mind, and therefore the notation was a representation for that person. But if it is to be a representation for other people, they have to do the interpreting.

Standard forms—such as equations, Cartesian graphs, and tables—have widely shared *conventions of interpretation*, and it is important for students to learn these so that they can understand these forms when they encounter them and construct them to communicate their ideas. Standard instructional practices in mathematics provide students with opportunities to learn the conventions of interpretation of standard representational forms at an operational level. Teachers explain how to construct and interpret tables, graphs, and equations, and students are asked to construct representations of given information in these forms and to interpret representations that they are given. In these activities students can learn to follow the standard conventions of interpretation for the forms, and with this learning the forms function as representations for the students.

These school practices are valuable, as far as they go, but they have an unfortunate limitations. They often treat written and drawn notations as though they *are* representations, rather than *potential* representations that depend on interpretation.

School practice is now moving toward better recognition that interpretation is an essential part of representations in mathematics and science. In these practices, students not only learn to follow standard conventions of interpretation, but they also can come to understand how representations work. Understanding representations includes knowing that there can be different interpretations of the same notation. It is important to know the conventional interpretations of standard forms, but it is often productive to construct nonstandard representations with special interpretations in working on problems and communicating about ideas.

Increasingly, classroom discussions are organized so that students participate in the construction and understanding of representations using mathematical and scientific notations.[18] One example is the Algebra Project, led by Robert Moses, in which there is strong emphasis on involving students in processes of developing symbolic representations that express their understandings of mathematical concepts and principles in relation to their experience.[19] The practices of learning in these classrooms include *participation by students* in discussions about conventions of interpretation used in their community. This participation establishes the role of students as contributing agents in the construction of the meanings of representations. It also can help students appreciate the fact that forms of representation are significant in the construction and communication of understanding.

An example from records of teaching by Magdalene Lampert has been analyzed by Rogers Hall and Andee Rubin. Lampert's fifth-grade mathematics class spent part of a class period working in groups on the problem: "A car is traveling 40 miles per hour. How far will it go in 3fi hours? How long will it take to go 70 miles?" At the end of the class period, Lampert led a discussion of the answer to the first part of the problem, and the students agreed that it should be 140 miles. Lampert then continued:

Now one of the things that I saw as I was walking around was something that I'd like to see a lot more of. I gave Karim a very special challenge. One member of his group said, "I really don't understand these kinds of problems at all." And I went over there and I said, "Karim, can you help this person explain? Can you explain? Help this person understand?" And he said, "Oh yeah, it's just three times, you know, three times, ah, 40, that's all." I said, "But what if the person doesn't know why you're supposed to times? How could you explain that?" And do you know what he did? He said, "I know how I can explain that." And he drew a line in his notebook [Lampert drew a line at the board], and he explained it, using that line. Karim, do you think you could come up here and show the whole class what you did?

Karim went to the board and drew on Lampert's line the representation shown in Figure 2, which both he and Ellie, another student, used in constructing explanations of the multiplicative relation between the time and distance of a trip taken at a constant speed. Karim said, "Well, like, every hour, you're going, every hour you're going 40 miles, and so I just added, um, I got three hours and then I added 40, three times, and then it gave me 120, then I had to, um, take a . . . I had to divide 40 in two, in half, and that gave me 20, so I added 20 'cause a half an hour is half of, like, an hour."

Ellie gave her version using the same drawing. "Um, it's a good strategy because . . . it says miles per hour and [*pointing to labels of "1 hr" and "40" below and above the line*] one hour for each one and it's really, it's . . . when you get up to 120, which is four, which is three, fours, you, uh, put a [*indicating the vertical mark after the "3 hr" mark on the line*] half in there because it says three and a half hours, so

FIGURE 2   **Karim's Representation of "Why You Multiply"**

you put a half right in there. And, uh, since half of 40 is 20, you add another 20 on and it's 140."

By engaging students in these conversations, Lampert arranged for them to participate in the construction of representations that they used to construct and communicate the meanings of mathematical symbols and operations. They reached understandings of basic concepts and had opportunities to learn how to communicate their understandings through representations that they and their classmates had constructed.

We have discussed research that emphasizes the expressive or inventive properties of representations in mathematics and science. Technical forms of representation, such as tables, graphs, and equations, are often contrasted with representations in fields such as painting, sculpture, and literature, which are adapted to particular uses of expression and communication, are flexibly constructed, and are open to multiple interpretations. But we argue that representations in mathematics and science *also have these properties*. We believe that educational purposes are better served if students are involved in activities in which they learn to construct versions of representations flexibly and to participate in discussions in which conventions of interpretation are developed. Such an approach enables them to understand and appreciate that mathematical and scientific representations, like those in other domains, are adapted for particular uses.

Of course, there are fundamental differences in the forms and uses of representations in different domains. Numerical tables and algebraic equations are not literary texts, and Cartesian graphs are not abstract paintings. Different forms of representation are developed by different communities and focus on different aspects of experience. Forms of representation in science and mathematics are designed to represent highly selected properties of systems, often involving quanitative properties. Important differences exist between the kinds of learning afforded to students as they make and use representations in different disciplinary domains. Thus every student's educational activities should include the rich variety of experience and learning made possible through participation in multiple practices of representation. Across domains, these practices share important features of use, adaptability, and interpretation that should be included in classroom learning.

NOTES

1. *Curriculum and Evaluation Standards for School Mathematics* (Reston, Va.: National Council of Teachers of Mathematics, 1989); and National Research Council, *National Science Education Standards* (Washington, D.C.: National Academy Press, 1996).

2. Richard Lesh and Susan J. Lamon, "Assessing Authentic Mathematical Performance," in idem, eds., *Assessment of Authentic Performance in School Mathematics* (Washington, D.C.: AAAS Press, 1992), pp. 17–62.

3. Shelley Goldman, James G. Greeno, Raymond McDermott, and George Pake, *Middle-School Mathematics Through Applications Project: Final Report to the National Science Foundation* (Menlo Park, Calif.: Institute for Research on Learning and Stanford University, 1996).

4. See, for example, Brigid J. Barron et al., "A SMART Model of New Standards and Assessments in Mathematics," Learning Technology Center, Vanderbilt University, Nashville, Tenn., n.d.

5. Rogers Hall and Reed Stevens, "Making Space: A Comparison of Mathematical Work in School and Professional Design Practices," in Susan Leigh Star, ed., *The Cultures of Computing* (London: Basil Blackwell, 1995), pp. 118–45.

6. Susan Leigh Star and James R. Griesemer, "Institutional Ecology, 'Translations,' and Boundary Objects: Amateurs and Professionals in Berkeley's Museum of Vertebrate Zoology," *Social Studies of Science*, vol. 19, 1989, pp. 387–420.

7. Rogers Hall, "Representation as Shared Activity: Situated Cognition and Dewey's Cartography of Experience," *Journal of the Learning Sciences*, vol. 5, 1996, pp. 209–38; and Steven Monk, Rogers Hall, Ricardo Nemirovsky, and Reed Stevens, "Conversations and Representational Media: Accomplishing Shared Meaning," presentation to a symposium at the annual meeting of the American Educational Research Association, New York, 1996.

8. Bruno Latour, "Visualization and Cognition: Thinking with Eyes and Hands," *Knowledge and Society: Studies in the Sociology of Culture Past and Present*, vol. 6, 1986, pp. 1–40; Jean Lave, *Cognition in Practice* (Cambridge: Cambridge University Press, 1988); and Lucy A. Suchman, "Making Work Visible," *Communications of the ACM*, vol. 38, 1995, pp. 56–65.

9. Koeno Gravemeijer, "Educational Development and Developmental Research in Mathematics Education," *Journal for Research in Mathematics Education*, vol. 25, 1994, pp. 443–71.

10. Rogers Hall et al., "Exploring the Episodic Structure of Algebra Story Problem Solving," *Cognition and Instruction*, vol. 6, 1989, pp. 223–83.

11. Richard E. Mayer, Jill H. Larkin, and Joseph B. Kaldane, "A Cognitive Analysis of Mathematical Problem-Solving Ability," in Robert Sternberg, ed., *Advances in*

the Psychology of Human Intelligence, vol. 2 (Hillsdale, N.J.: Erlbaum, 1984), pp. 231–73.

12. John P. Smith, Andrea A. diSessa, and Jeremy Roschelle, "Misconceptions Reconceived: A Constructivist Analysis of Knowledge in Transition," *Journal of the Learning Sciences,* vol. 3, 1993, pp. 115–63.

13. Andrea A. diSessa et al., "Inventing Graphing: Meta-Representational Expertise in Children," *Journal of Mathematical Behavior,* vol. 10, 1991, pp. 117–60.

14. Rogers Hall, "Making Mathematics on Paper: Constructing Representations of Stories About Related Linear Functions" (Doctoral dissertation, University of California, Irvine, 1990); and Hall et al., op. cit.

15. Hall, "Making Mathematics on Paper," p. 126.

16. See, for example, Luciano Meira, "The Micro-evolution of Mathematical Representations in Children's Activity," *Cognition and Instruction,* vol. 13, 1995, pp. 269–313.

17. C. S. Peirce, "Logic as Semiotic: The Theory of Signs," in Justus Buchler, ed., *Philosophical Writings of Peirce* (1893–1910; reprint, New York: Dover, 1955), pp. 98–119.

18. Magdalene Lampert, "Connecting Inventions with Conventions," in Leslie P. Steffe and Terry Wood, eds., *Transforming Children's Mathematics Education* (Hillsdale, N.J.: Erlbaum, 1990), pp. 253–65.

19. Robert Moses et al., "The Algebra Project: Organizing in the Spirit of Ella," *Harvard Educational Review,* vol. 59, 1989, pp. 423–43.

Chapter 8: Complex Cognitive Processes

The Language of Thinking

SHARI TISHMAN and DAVID PERKINS

What comes first, a word or a thought? The relationship between thinking and language has intrigued scholars and artists for centuries. Anticipating Lev Vygotsky's view that thought is not only expressed in words but comes into existence through them, Emily Dickinson took this stand:

> A word is dead
> When it is said,
> Some say.
>
> I say it just
> Begins to live
> That day.[1]

Words and thoughts live through each other. One interesting realm in which to examine how this happens is that of the special class of words we have for talking *about* thought—words for talking about the thinking processes that lead to products of thought such as ideas and theories. What is this "language of thinking"—what is its lexicon, what is it for, how does it work, and what role does it play in human development and education? We hope to shed some light on these questions by exploring the various ways we talk about thought and by looking at how, to borrow Emily Dickinson's phrase, the language of thinking makes thinking "begin to live" by shaping and regulating conceptual development.

WHAT IS THE LANGUAGE OF THINKING?

The language of thinking embraces the many ways we describe our own and others' mental states and mental processes. For example, we use the language of thinking when we talk about the thinking processes involved in developing a theory, examining a claim, making a decision, or creating a work of art. We use the language of thinking when we characterize others' mental states by saying things like: *Julia believes that everyone should vote; Juan thinks that it will snow; Martin concluded that he doesn't like papayas; I suspect that you're telling the truth.*

The English language has a remarkable number of finely nuanced terms for describing thinking. For example, consider the words *guess, suppose, surmise, assume,* and *speculate.* All of them concern forming an opinion based on inconclusive evidence. At the same time, each term suggests a subtle but important difference in the relationship of evidence to opinion. For another example, consider the words *contemplate, ruminate, reflect,* and *ponder.* Each of these terms describes a form of slow and deep cerebration, yet each carries its own distinct meaning.

Shari Tishman is a research associate at Project Zero, Harvard Graduate School of Education, Cambridge, Mass., where David Perkins is co-director. This article was written as part of a project funded by the John D. and Catherine T. MacArthur Foundation. Correspondence may be sent to Shari Tishman, Project Zero, Harvard Graduate School of Education, 313 Longfellow Hall, Appian Way, Cambridge, MA 02138. Ph. 617/495-4376 (e-mail: shari_tishman@pz.harvard.edu).

The vocabulary of thinking can be roughly divided into terms that fill three different functions: terms that mark an epistemic stance,[2] terms that describe an intellectual process, and terms that describe an intellectual product.

Epistemic-stance terms indicate a stance or attitude toward a claim to knowledge. Examples include such terms as *conjecture, conclude, believe, confirm, doubt, know, suggest, speculate, suspect,* and *theorize.* To see how these terms function as stance indicators, consider the claim "Grasshoppers dream in color" and the following sentences.

- *I believe that grasshoppers dream in color.*
- *I have confirmed that grasshoppers dream in color.*
- *I suspect that grasshoppers dream in color.*
- *I am certain that grasshoppers dream in color.*

Each of these sentences takes a quite different stance toward the truth of the claim. And it is the stance markers that provide essential information about how the claim should be taken.

Epistemic-stance terms function by characterizing the relationship of thought to fact. Intellectual-process terms characterize the *process* of thinking and express its flow, structure, and feel. Intellectual-process terms include such words as *analyze, contemplate, discern, interpret, investigate, ponder, examine,* and *recollect,* to name but a few. What is distinctive about intellectual-process terms is that they discriminate among *ways* of thinking. To say that one is pondering something is to characterize one's thinking in quite a different way than to say that one is analyzing, reviewing, considering, or investigating something. As is the case with epistemic-stance terms, the nuances of meaning of intellectual-process terms are subtle (*ponder* versus *ruminate,* for example).

Intellectual-product terms are nouns that name and mark differences among kinds of ideas—ideas that are typically the outcome of a thinking process or that play a particular role in a thinking process. The word *idea* is itself a loosely defined intellectual-product term that is frequently used to cover a range of mental outcomes, from solutions to insights to suggestions to intuitions. But the word *idea* tends toward the generic, and, when specificity is desirable, we have plenty of intellectual-product terms at our disposal that differentiate among kinds of ideas or outcomes—terms such as *conclusion, hypothesis, option, solution, reason, claim,* and *theory.*

Naturally, the functions of these three groups of terms are related: intellectual processes tend to yield epistemic stances, which in turn yield intellectual products. For example, by musing or speculating, one is often led to assert, dispute, or assume things, and eventually led to make a claim, propose a theory, or draw a conclusion. Because these three categories name different linguistic functions rather than different groups of words, the terms in each category often overlap, and the same word can play different roles, depending on whether it functions as a noun or a verb and whether, as a verb, it is used to indicate an epistemic stance or an intellectual process. For example, the sentence *I doubt that x* indicates a stance toward a proposition. But the word *doubt* could also be referring to a mental process, for example if the speaker's intended meaning is actually *I am in the process of doubting x.* And of course the term *doubt* can also be used as a noun to describe a particular sort of intellectual product, as in *I have my doubts* or *she raises an important doubt.*

Complicated as it is to analytically disentangle the linguistic functions of language-of-thinking terminology, it is testimony to the efficacy and elegance of the language of thinking that we very easily understand these different functions when we experience them in context. For example, consider the sentence: *Claire doubted whether Michael's claim was true, but she recognized the need to investigate it further.* We have no trouble at all understanding that Claire's epistemic stance is one of doubt, that the intellectual product she is referring to is Michael's claim, and that the intellectual activity she plans to undertake is to investigate Michael's claim.

As the foregoing example suggests, the language of thinking is rich with terms that specifically and often technically describe mental states and processes—terms such as *analyze, doubt, claim, investigate,* and so on. But the language of thinking also expresses the affective side of cognition—the passions, emotions, motivations, and attitudes that are an integral part of the experience of thinking.

Does thinking really involve feeling? All the time. Consider William James' description of an instance of thinking in which "the transition from a state of puzzle and perplexity to rational comprehension is full of lively relief and pleasure."[3] Puzzlement, confusion, concern, and consternation are all feelings that accompany thinking, as are feelings of joy, delight, relief, thrill, and aesthetic appreciation. Although psychologists and philosophers sometimes dichotomize cognition and affect, the language of feeling is abundantly present in our everyday language of thinking. Mathematicians talk about the pleasure of an elegant proof. Poets talk about the beauty of an image. Scientists talk about the thrill of discovery and the joy of verification. Indeed, the feelings of joy and surprise that often accompany intellectual work play such a distinctive role in thinking that the philosopher Israel Scheffler has described them as "cognitive emotions." Not only do they characterize thinking, he argues, but also they are epistemologically relevant to the practice of reasoning because they provide important information about the thinker's beliefs, predictions, and expectations.[4]

Negative emotions abound in thinking, too. For example, it is said that one of the greatest pains of the human experience is the pain of a new idea. And learning difficult material, as any schoolchild will tell you, can be a torturous task. Thinking well can be tough, and we often feel frustrated and even angry at the difficulties of coming to the right conclusion or decision or belief. Of course, it is possible to avoid the negative emotions associated with thinking. "Abandon learning," says the Chinese philosopher Lao-Tse, "and you will be free from trouble and distress."

Besides expressing emotions, the language of thinking also expresses attitudes toward our own and others' thinking. For example, the critical distance associated with rigorous reasoning is often described attitudinally: we speak of an attitude of objectivity, of detachment, of fair-mindedness. But there are other possible attitudes toward thinking, too. For instance, we talk about adopting an attitude of sympathy or skepticism toward an argument, of receptivity or resistance to a point of view, and so on.

THE COMMUNICATIVE FUNCTION OF THE LANGUAGE OF THINKING

What is the language of thinking *for?* Why have we developed such extensive and nuanced ways of talking about the life of the mind? One obvious and important purpose is communication. We use the language of thinking to communicate information about the character and intent of our mental states and processes in all sorts of everyday contexts. When we explain to a friend the thinking process that led us to choose one candidate over another in a local election, we are using the language of think-

ing. We do likewise when we explain how we came to hold or reject a particular belief, how we developed an idea, how we made a decision, or how we solved a problem.

Most of the time, the everyday use of the language of thinking is quite informal. But there are more formal venues too, where its terms take on a more technical aspect. For example, scholarly papers that report scientific findings and develop or critique theories use the language of thinking very carefully. In these contexts, it is quite important for the writer to indicate exactly which lines of thought are inferential, which are speculative, what statements are meant to be taken as conclusions, what counts as evidence, and so on. Words such as *assume, conclude, suggest, hypothesize, infer, assert,* and so on alert readers to the "epistemic game" being played by the author and indicate the standards by which the ideas put forth should be evaluated.

In a dialect less technical but no less evocative, the language of thinking also communicates the thinking behind creativity. For example, painters, writers, dancers, and other artists often talk about the thinking involved in the creative process. They discuss such things as the genesis of an idea, the source of an inspiration, and the struggle to realize a vision. If their lexicon is not as technical as that of the scholar or scientist, it is because their products of thought—paintings, poems, novels, dances—are not meant to be evaluated primarily as products of reasoning. It makes no more sense to reject a sculpture because its conclusion isn't supported by verifiable evidence than it does to reject a report of a scientific experiment because it isn't aesthetically compelling.

That said, it is important to recognize that inspiration, intuition, and aesthetic considerations can play a large and legitimate role in critical scholarship and that critical reasoning often plays a large and legitimate role in the production of art. The language of thinking duly reports these intertwinings. Thus we sometimes hear scientists discussing the intuitions and aesthetic yearnings that gave rise to a theory and artists talking about the critical reasoning that led them to a particular artistic approach.

THE REGULATIVE FUNCTION OF THE LANGUAGE OF THINKING

The language of thinking does more than help us communicate. It shapes and regulates thought by providing concepts to guide our thinking. Although this view has received special attention in recent decades, the notion that language shapes thought is nothing new. Most people have heard the saying "I can't know what I think until I hear what I say." Vygotsky emphasized the social context of language and its role in shaping conceptual development.[5] Even the ancient Greeks stressed the role of language in thought. Socrates, in the *Theatetus*, described thinking as "a discourse the mind carries on with itself" and judgment as "a statement pronounced . . . silently to oneself."[6]

Just as the colors on an artist's palette influence the painting that emerges, the words we have available to us influence the way we think about the world, including the inner world of our own mental life. In recent years, cognitive psychologists have used the term *metacognition* to refer to the mental processes involved in thinking about one's own thinking. Widely recognized as a key component of high-level thinking and effective learning, metacognition involves stepping back from the flow of one's thought to better understand it, assess it, and guide it.[7] The connection between metacognition and the language of thinking is straightforward: the language of thinking provides the words and concepts with which thought evaluates and regulates itself.

This is both an everyday reality and an educational opportunity. For a touch of the latter, imagine that students in two fifth-grade classrooms are studying the life of Amelia Earhart, and both teachers are conducting a discussion about her mysterious disappearance somewhere in the South Pacific. The first teacher ask his class, "What do you think happened?" One student ventures a guess: "Maybe she wanted to disappear because she didn't like so much publicity." "That's an interesting idea," the teacher responds, then asks another student for her opinion, and then a third student for his.

In the second classroom, the teacher says to his students, "There are several theories about what happened to Amelia Earhart. Do any of you have a theory?" As in the first class, one student suggests that Amelia Earhart deliberately disappeared in order to avoid publicity. "What are your reasons?" the teacher asks. "What evidence do you have to support your view?" The student ponders for a moment, then says, "Well, I guess some evidence is that no one ever found a trace of her or her plane. That's pretty unusual, in plane crashes."

"Are you sure that's supporting evidence?" the teacher asks. And so the discussion continues. This second teacher is using the language of thinking with his students. By introducing them to the terms and concepts involved in theory building, he draws them into a culture of concepts they can use to reflect on their own thinking in what Socrates called "the discourse the mind carries on with itself."

Reasoning is only one of the cognitive processes that invites metacognitive regulation through the language of thinking. For another kind of example, consider the word *brainstorming*. The general notion of generating multiple ideas is nothing new. But for those of us in the last couple of decades who have come to associate the term with a specific set of procedures, the word *brainstorming* invokes certain patterns of ideation—e.g., thinking broadly about possibilities, piggybacking on the ideas-so-far, deferring criticism and critical selection until later, and so on. The term *brainstorming* functions metacognitively when it invokes standards with which we shape and evaluate the thinking that ensues.

Where does metacognitive language come from? Words like *brainstorming* tend to draw their expressiveness from metaphor and analogy. This is true of many of the words and phrases we use to describe creative thought. Consider, for example, the familiar analogies that compare insight to a light bulb going off or describe it as a flash of brilliance. The story line for the metacognitive language involved in critical thinking—the language of reasoning, analysis, and theory building—may be somewhat different. In an interesting and persuasive line of thought, David Olson and Janet Wilde Astington argue that the language for reflecting on critical thinking connects closely to literacy.[8]

Literacy, they propose, affects how we reflect on our own thinking by introducing terms for talking about text (terms that also apply to thinking and talking about one's own cognition). Written language, stabilized on paper, invites kinds of reflection not so natural to oral exchanges. The written statement is more easily examined, checked, contradicted, doubted, challenged, or affirmed. Such processes give rise to a specialized terminology for characterizing text-based thinking. So it is not surprising that much of the terminology of the language of thinking, in English at any rate, comes from Latin, which was introduced into English in the 16th and 17th centuries primarily as a text-based language—the language of legal and official documents. For example, terms such as *assert, assume, criticize, discover, explain, hypothesize,* and *interpret* all have Latinate roots. They represent concepts involved in thinking about and analyzing the thinking in texts, and they can also be applied to thinking about one's own and others' mental states and processes.

Does this mean that only people who read and write well can think metacognitively? Absolutely not. Once such literacy-based concepts become prominent in a language, they are as available for oral as for written exchanges. Witness the critical debates in many classrooms and colloquia. In such contexts, literacy is defined not by scribal competence but by the ability to use literacy-based concepts in thinking and talking. "To be literate," argue Olson and Astington, "is to be competent to participate in a certain form of discourse, *whether one can read or write or not.*"[9]

DISPOSITIONS AND THE REGULATIVE FUNCTION

As we emphasized earlier, thinking and learning involve emotions and attitudes in addition to cognitive skill, and good thinking involves being disposed toward certain sorts of affects. In recent years, several researchers have been investigating the dispositional side of thinking and have proposed that teaching high-level thinking involves cultivating students' "thinking dispositions" in addition to teaching thinking skills.[10] *Thinking dispositions* are tendencies or leanings toward particular patterns of intellectual behavior, such as the tendencies to be reflective, to seek reasons, to be intellectually strategic, or to be intellectually adventurous. Thinking skills alone may show up well on exercises and tests, but, without dispositions to spur them into actions, they are likely to remain inactive in real-life situations.

Language in general is a cultural force with the power to shape dispositional behavior, and the situation with the language of thinking is no different. The language of thinking supports the development of thinking dispositions in several ways. To begin with, the language of thinking encourages thinking-dispositional behavior by inspiring it in context. To make an analogy, a coach inspires her team's best performance with language that invokes the spirit of competition and excellence, and athletes often psych themselves up for an event by using this same language in talking to themselves. Although most of the time thinking is not a competitive event, the language of thinking has a similar effect. Simply hearing and using certain language in certain contexts invokes thinking-dispositional behavior. For example, the language of planning and strategizing tends to encourage goal-setting; the language of self-reflection tends to inspire introspection.

Beyond episodes of a minute or an hour, we can expect long-term developmental effects from the use of the language of thinking. When thinking-rich language pervades a learning environment—when it sees regular use by teachers and learners, as in the Amelia Earhart example—it provides not only information but also an invitation to embrace and cultivate certain habits of mind. For example, frequent exposure to the language of argumentation, with such terms as *premise, reason, conclusion, evidence, theory,* and *hypothesis,* draws learners into the values and commitments of critical analysis. The language of creative problem solving, with expressions such as *wild idea, pushing the edge of the envelope, new point of view,* and *breaking set,* fosters the mindset of creative ideation.

Dispositional behavior depends not only on wanting to do the right thing but also on noticing when to do it. Here, too, using the language of thinking in the classroom helps develop learners' sensitivity to occasions for engaging in high-level thinking. Terms like *claim, option, opinion, guess,* and *doubt* alert learners to opportunities to do such things as probe an assumption, seek evidence, identify reasons, or look at a problem from a new point of view.

THE DIALECTS OF THINKING

Lawyers speak of precedents, but physicists do not. Physicists do experiments to read the book of nature carefully, while mathematicians rarely mention the word *experiment* and instead seek deductive proof from axioms. Literary reviewers freely report how a work impressed or distressed or inspired or exasperated them as evidence of its meaning and worth, something a lawyer or mathematician would rarely do, or at least rarely admit to doing. We have written of the language of thinking, but plainly there is more than one. Or better, the one has many dialects that vary with the intellectual territory. How can we get a clearer view of these dialects and their significance?

A helpful concept here is the notion of epistemic games.[11] Inquiry of whatever sort tends to involve three broad epistemic pursuits: characterization, explanation, and justification. Any area of inquiry, from literary criticism to quantum physics, includes efforts to characterize something (the favorite theme of an author or the properties of a proposed elementary particle), explain something (What does the theme mean and imply? How does the particle fit with fundamental theory?), and justify something (What is the evidence for the presence of the theme in the author's work? What empirical evidence do we have that the particle exists?). However, the way the epistemic game is played varies from field to field in its typical forms, moves, goals, and rules. Literary criticism, for example, involves the form of one interpretation among others, moves such as advancing and critiquing interpretations, goals such as illumination and soundness, and rules of thumb about attention to the context, awareness of the authors' likely intentions based on other works and biographical information, and so on—all very different from the forms, moves, goals, and rules of the quantum physicist.

There is a natural connection to dialects of thinking. In everyday thinking, we play a kind of generic epistemic game of characterization, explanation, and justification, communicating and metacognizing about it in plain words like *idea, reason, brainstorm, doubt,* and so on. But the epistemic games of particular fields add more specialized concepts and dialects. For instance, psychologists add to the everyday lexicon phrases such as *null hypothesis, control of variables, fair samples,* and *statistical significance*—concepts that are part of a technical dialect about justification that is especially pertinent to empirical psychology.

The notion of dialects of thinking illuminates two important issues: the generality of thinking and the complexity of learning to think better. As to the first, some scholars have argued that good thinking is profoundly situated.[12] Whatever supports good thinking in quantum mechanics or auto mechanics has little that is general in it. Thinking at its best, and cognition more generally, is an inherently specialized enterprise, contend the proponents of this view. The idea of general, powerful thinking skills and dispositions is misguided. Teaching thinking in any general sense is a waste of time.

While this is a complex issue that we cannot fully examine here, the notion of dialects of thinking suggests a more balanced stance. Plainly, effective thinking in many fields involves being conversant with the dialects of thinking that are important to those fields, both for communication and for metacognitive self-regulation. At the same time, thinking in particular fields and thinking about everyday matters commonly fall prey to hastiness, narrowness, and other hazards.[13] Here the generic language of thinking provides a regulative resource. Such common-coin terms as *argument, evidence, counterexample, other side of the case, point of view,* and so on help to expand and redirect thinking in ways that cannot be taken for granted in either ordinary or technical situations. Effective thinking, in other words, has both general and situated aspects, corresponding to the general language of thinking and its dialects.

The second theme is the complexity of learning to think better. Many school-based approaches to the teaching of thinking foreground a few strategies for problem solving and decision making and leave it at that. Such efforts often do some good in our view. But they certainly underestimate the scope of the enterprise. Even the everyday language of thinking has many sides to it—and then there are the dialects that serve different specialized styles of inquiry. While only professionals need be deeply versed in those styles, general competence calls for a nodding acquaintance with them. People who have no feel for the control of variables in science, or the "beyond reasonable doubt" principle in legal argument, or the importance of sample size and lack of bias in social research do not understand the rich world of ideas they inevitably live in.

If we are to lead students to an enlightened world of creative and critical thinking, we must do so in recognition that this world is rich in the variety of its challenges and the conceptual and linguistic skills and dispositions needed to meet them. While point-blank instruction in concepts, strategies, and even terminology is helpful, deep and lasting impact calls for an enculturative approach.[14] Only when students spend hours a day in classrooms where the culture and language of thinking are commonplace are they likely to become fully awake to their intellectual potentials.

Unfortunately, such a vision of the commonplace goes well beyond business as usual. Although classrooms and texts seem likely places for a rich language of thinking, the language in these places can be surprisingly sparse. For example, science texts at all grade levels, including college, tend to leave out terms that precisely identify intellectual processes—terms such as *explain, hypothesize, conclude*, and so on.[15] Further, as a result of a well-meaning but sometimes misguided effort to make learning easier and more palatable, teachers' talk can also be lean in language-of-thinking terminology. As Olson and Astington have pointed out, teachers will often ask students to construct explanations, make hypotheses, draw inferences, and so on without referring to these processes by name.[16] What happens instead? They use generic terms like *think* and *feel* and *opinion* to cover a vast range of more nuanced cognitive states and activities, as illustrated by the first teacher in our Amelia Earhart example.

SO MUCH MORE THAN WE CAN SAY

The language of thinking can tell a remarkably expressive story about the character of mental life. But even so, thinking is so much more than we can say in words. Imagine Picasso sketching studies for *Guérnica*. Or imagine Mozart composing a symphony in his head during a bumpy coach ride. Or imagine Einstein imagining himself riding along beside a light wave. How much of this is a matter of language at all, in any reasonable sense? How can the language of thinking do justice to the rich, multimodal character of thinking? Perhaps the language of thinking masks the true enterprise of thinking.

Certainly there is a risk here, so let us take its measure. First, it's important to clarify the issue. The language of thinking as used here means the language we use to talk *about* thinking—terms like *hypothesis, reason, option, imagination*, and so on. Language *about* thinking is mostly language in the familiar sense of words and sentences. But certainly people think *in* many other languages as vehicles—the languages of mathematics, or music, or visual images, if one can call these languages in a metaphorically extended sense. More properly, people think *in* many symbolic vehicles.

If anything, this point only sharpens the dilemma. It seems all the more true that the thinking we do involves so much more than we can say in words about that thinking. The language of thinking concerns only a part of the thinking: roughly its structural organization. Moreover, the language of thinking does not *do* the thinking. It simply offers a high-level, somewhat removed description of what is or could be or should be done.

In fairness though, the language of thinking is not special in this way. Language in general is in the business of "aboutness." The language of auto mechanics, politics, or dance is about a rich physical and experiential realm. Language never comes close to being a surrogate for the thing itself. Even language about language does not: it is a standard point of aesthetics that the language a critic uses to comment on the shortest poem does not provide anything like an adequate experience of the poem, nor is it meant to. Sometimes critics seek to evoke something of the experience of a fine concert through the expressive use of language, but without any expectation that readers should feel happy about staying at home and reading the newspaper instead of going to the concert. There is no reason that we should expect the language of thinking to provide any more of a surrogate for thinking than the language of anything else does for its referent.

Does it follow that the language of thinking cannot illuminate or guide? No such conclusion holds in other cases. Even though the language of auto mechanics stands at considerable remove from fixing a car, it is patently useful in instruction, in collaboration among mechanics, and in talking oneself through problems—reminding oneself what one knows, what might be going on, and what one might try to do about it. Likewise, the language of thinking can say things that are useful to a scientist or artist or auto mechanic, as well as to students in any of those domains. Questions from oneself, a partner, or coach—such as *Is there a not-so-conventional, more creative option here?* or *Are you making any risky assumptions here, and can you get away with them?* or *What reason do you have to believe that?*—make sense and do good service for all three (or for most anyone engaged in thinking).

Although thinking involves much more than we can say, we would have far less access to that "more" without the language of thinking. Another idea from aesthetics emphasizes that language commonly has a pointing function. The use of language in the presence of a work of art does not substitute for the work but cues us to see or hear things we would otherwise miss. In classrooms or offices, seminars or senates, far from standing between us and our thinking, the language of thinking helps us discern more clearly and deeply what we are doing, where we are going, and where we might better go when we think.

NOTES

1. Emily Dickinson, "A Word Is Dead," in T. H. Johnson, ed., *The Complete Poems of Emily Dickinson* (Boston: Little, Brown, 1960), p. 534. Used with permission.

2. David R. Olson, "Languages of Thinking: Internal Conference Memo," Project Zero, Harvard Graduate School of Education, 1990.

3. William James, *The Will to Believe and Other Essays in Popular Philosophy* (1896; reprint, New York: Dover, 1956), p. 63.

4. Israel Scheffler, "In Praise of the Cognitive Emotions," *Teachers College Record,* vol. 79, 1977, pp. 171–86.

5. Lev S. Vygotsky, *Thought and Language* (Cambridge, Mass.: MIT Press, 1962).

6. Plato, *Theatetus,* in Edith Hamilton and Huntington Cairns, eds., *The Collected Dialogues of Plato* (Princeton, N.J.: Princeton University Press, 1961), p. 190a.

7. See, for example, David N. Perkins, *Outsmarting IQ: The Emerging Science of Learnable Intelligence* (New York: Free Press, 1995); Robert J. Sternberg, *Beyond IQ: A Triarchic Theory of Human Intelligence* (New York: Cambridge University Press, 1985); and Marlene Scardamalia and Carl Bereiter, "Fostering the Development of Self-Regulation in Children's Knowledge Processing," in Susan F. Chapman, Judith W. Segal, and Robert Glaser, eds., *Thinking and Learning Skills, Vol. 2: Research and Open Questions* (Hillsdale, N.J.: Erlbaum, 1985), pp. 563–77.

8. David R. Olson, *The World on Paper* (Cambridge: Cambridge University Press, 1994); and David R. Olson and Janet Wilde Astington, "Talking About Text: How Literacy Contributes to Thought," *Journal of Pragmatics,* vol. 14, 1991, pp. 705–21.

9. Olson and Astington, p. 711, italics in original.

10. Jonathan Baron, *Rationality and Intelligence* (New York: Cambridge University Press, 1985); Robert H. Ennis, "A Taxonomy of Critical Thinking Dispositions and Abilities," in Joan B. Baron and Robert J. Sternberg, eds., *Teaching Thinking Skills: Theory and Practice* (New York: W. H. Freeman, 1987), pp. 9–26; Perkins, *Outsmarting IQ;* and Shari Tishman, David N. Perkins, and Eileen Jay, *The Thinking Classroom: Learning and Teaching in a Culture of Thinking* (Needham, Mass.: Allyn and Bacon, 1995).

11. Allan Collins and William Ferguson, "Epistemic Forms and Epistemic Games: Structures and Strategies to Guide Inquiry," *Educational Psychologist,* vol. 28, pp. 25–42; David N. Perkins, "The Hidden Order of Open-Ended Thinking," in John Edwards, ed., *Thinking: Interdisciplinary Perspectives* (Victoria, Australia: Hawker Brownlow Education, 1994); and idem, "Epistemic Games," *International Journal of Educational Research,* in press.

12. John S. Brown, Allan Collins, and Paul Duguid, "Situated Cognition and the Culture of Learning," *Educational Researcher,* January/February 1989, pp. 32–42; Jean Lave, *Cognition in Practice: Mind, Mathematics, and Culture in Everyday Life* (Cambridge: Cambridge University Press, 1988); and Jean Lave and Etienne Wenger, *Situated Learning: Legitimate Peripheral Participation* (New York: Cambridge University Press, 1991).

13. Baron, op. cit.; Raymond S. Nickerson, David N. Perkins, and Edward E. Smith, *The Teaching of Thinking* (Hillsdale, N.J.: Erlbaum, 1985); and Perkins, *Outsmarting IQ.*

14. Shari Tishman, Eileen Jay, and David N. Perkins, "Thinking Dispositions: From Transmission to Enculturation," *Theory Into Practice,* vol. 32, 1993, pp. 147–53; and Tishman, Perkins, and Jay, op. cit.

15. Janet Wilde Astington and David R. Olson, "Metacognitive and Metalinguistic Language: Learning to Talk About Thought," *Applied Psychology: An International Review,* vol. 39, 1990, pp. 77–87; and Jack Lochhead, "Languages of Thinking: Internal Conference Memo," Project Zero, Harvard Graduate School of Education, 1991.

16. Olson and Astington, op. cit.; and B. Othanel Smith and Milton O. Meux, *A Study of the Logic of Teaching* (Urbana: University of Illinois Press, 1970).

Teaching for Understanding— Within and Across the Disciplines

HOWARD GARDNER and VERONICA BOIX-MANSILLA

As they enter middle and high school, students are expected to understand central concepts in several disciplines. While students may succeed in "parroting back" phrases from lectures and texts, they often falter when asked to apply their understanding to new situations. What does it take to demonstrate understanding within and across disciplines? Consider the many different ways to approach the following hypothetical but plausible situations:

- *The New York Times* announced that the Queen of England has stepped down from her throne and at the same time has disestablished the House of Windsor. The English monarchy is at an end.
- *The New England Journal of Medicine* has published a study in which two groups of elementary school students were randomly assigned to two after-school programs: indoor gymnasium sports and personal computer work. Twice as many students in the first group contracted colds. The speculation is that after-school athletics may be injurious to one's health.

Howard Gardner is Professor of Education and Co-Director of Project Zero at the Harvard Graduate School of Education; Veronica Boix-Mansilla is a doctoral student and Researcher at Project Zero and the Harvard Graduate School of Education. Both may be reached at 323 Longfellow Hall, Appian Way, Cambridge, MA 02138.

Wearing the hat of the disciplinarian, we can consider our first example as drawn from history or social studies and the second from biology or general science. Either account could serve as the point of departure of a set of lessons in appropriate high school classes. If reworded, they could be used with students at virtually any grade level. The first account—which could also refer to the death of a president or the deposing of any kind of leader—raises questions such as "What makes a boss a boss?" or "Why do all civilizations have hierarchies of authority?" The second account could be reformulated to describe any source of disease and to encourage reflections about what keeps us healthy, what is illness, and how to prevent it.

Here we attempt to place current efforts at teaching for understanding into a sharper perspective by considering the way in which this performance view plays out in different disciplines.

UNDERSTANDING WITHIN THE DISCIPLINES

The four-part framework developed by our Teaching for Understanding group is deliberately broad enough to cover the range of disciplines. (See "Putting Understanding Up Front," [*Educational Leadership*, February 1994] p. 4.) At the same time, however, all disciplines are not equal. In fact, distinct disciplines have developed over the ages precisely because they allow scholars and students to take different kinds of perspectives and actions in order to elucidate specific kinds of phenomena.

Consider our opening examples. In each case, we are dealing with a central concept: (1) injury to the body politic, and (2) injury to the physical body. Analysis and evaluation of concepts are legitimate tacks in both examples.

In other respects, however, the disciplinary terrains prove quite different. For instance, to gain relevant expertise in our abdication situation, students might draw on knowledge about British history and its current form of government, as well as the legal and symbolic implications of the abolition of monarchy. Students can "perform" their understandings in any number of ways—ranging from a comparison of the situation at the time of the beheading of King Charles I or the abdication of Edward VIII, to a hypothetical argument in a local pub about the abolition, to the creation of a diagram of the new governmental organization.

By their very nature, historical phenomena are unique. One can compare abdications and beheadings, but they are never the same. When dealing with individual personalities, varying contexts, and dynamic events, the complexity of the events can never be mastered nor the consequences predicted. Finally, events in this sphere take on symbolic as well as literal/legal importance. While in practice the British monarchy has little authority, in actuality it assumes significant symbolic power. A disciplinary understanding of the possible impacts of disestablishment on British public life is grounded in these specific features of historical events.

In contrast to the historical example, the realm of health and illness, at least in principle, should be open to explanation and prediction. This realm lends itself to the development of models of what causes illness and the testing of the models through experimentation. A well-founded model is able to predict results across diverse populations. Moreover, explicit methodologies exist for mounting experiments and for analyzing data, ones that can be used by anyone schooled in science. Consequently, in the case of colds among athletes, students might gain relevant expertise by drawing on knowledge about health and illness, including bacterial and viral theories of infection, as well as understandings of the nature of scientific hypotheses, experimental designs, and inferences from data. To demonstrate

their understanding, students might conduct similar experiments, perform retrospective examinations of the incidence and plausible causes of their own recent colds, or construct rival models of disease.

FROM COMMON SENSE TO INTERDISCIPLINARY STUDY

So far, we have dealt with might be called "normal" disciplinary work at the secondary level. We have assumed that there are classes that deal with historical-political studies, those that deal with scientific inquiry, and a set of roles and performances appropriate to students in those respective classes.

But we have also argued that younger students could approach the questions raised in appropriate ways. To illustrate, we single out four stages, corresponding roughly to different points in the growth patterns of students (Gardner and Boix-Mansilla 1993).

1. *Common sense.* Novices fruitfully consider generative questions by relying on their intuitive theories of the world—their natural theories of mind, matter, and life (Gardner 1991). Students as young as 5 or 6 can consider what it means to be a leader and then voluntarily or involuntarily to renounce one's position as boss. They can consider what would happen if the teacher or the boss stepped down and no one took his or her place. Adults can ask young students to draw on their own theories of power—the person who is strongest, loudest, bossiest, or the person chosen by someone even more powerful—to debate these issues.

These same students can also be guided into discussions of health. All youngsters are interested in their bodies—what makes them strong, weak, sick, or healthy. They can apply their own naive theories—you are sick because you were bad, because you sat near someone who was sick, because you did not wash your hands—to new events, including the appearance of a new sickness or a new cure. Note that in these cases, it is not important that students espouse the "right theories," but that they draw fully on their own ideas in an effort to make sense—to perform their understandings—of intriguing phenomena.

2. *Protodisciplinary knowledge.* Even in the absence of formal disciplinary study, students in our culture pick up certain moves that are made by systematic thinkers—through, for example, the media, debates among peers, and partial understanding of texts. Long before they have heard of college catalogues, and despite the movie *JFK*, students in the late primary or early middle grades begin to appreciate the difference between a historical account (what actually happened) and a literary account (a description invented for aesthetic purposes). By the same token, they begin to distinguish claims that are based on conviction or prejudice from claims based on empirical evidence, which itself can be confirmed or questioned.

At this stage, youngsters can proceed in a more sophisticated way. They can read historical or scientific accounts, summarize them, conduct further research, and debate the validity of various claims. And they can engage in projects—such as holding a mock trial or conducting a survey—that introduce them naturally to the tools of the disciplines.

3. *Disciplinary knowledge.* By late middle school and thereafter, students do most work under the rubric of classical disciplines, such as history, literature, and the sciences. Because it is fashionable to look askance at the disciplines, we feel it is important to make two points. First, disciplines are not the same as subjects. Disciplines constitute the most sophisticated ways yet developed for thinking about and investigating issues that have long fascinated and perplexed thoughtful individuals; subject matters are devices for organizing schedules and catalogues. Second, disciplines represent the principal ways in which individuals transcend ignorance. While disciplines can blind or sway, they become, when used relevantly, our keenest lenses on the world.

When well taught, students are introduced to the disciplines in several ways. First, they observe teachers or experts who embody the practices of the disciplines. Second, students behold and create exhibitions that capture the accumulated wisdom of the discipline. Third, students encounter the concepts, theories, and methods that disciplinarians have evolved over the years, and receive ample opportunities to put them into practice. Only through such sustained work—work that is "disciplined" in both senses of the term—may students acquire the expertise that we have described.

4. *Beyond disciplinary knowledge.* Even as it is now fashionable to critique the disciplines, it is trendy to advocate "interdisciplinary" work. At its best, interdisciplinary work is indeed vital and impressive. However, such work can only be legitimately attempted if one has already mastered at least portions of the specific disciplines. Unfortunately, much of what is termed "interdisciplinary" work is actually predisciplinary work—that is, work based on common sense, not on the mastery and integration of a number of component disciplines.

Those who have slogged through a number of specific disciplines are in a privileged position. They can conduct *multidisciplinary* work in which, for example, they look at the abdication of King Edward VIII as portrayed in art, literature, history, and philosophy. They can undertake *interdisciplinary* work, in which they consider the concept of health in terms of both medicine and individual psychology, and then synthesize these perspectives in coming up with a more general account. They can carry on *metadisciplinary* work, in which they compare the practices of particular disciplines, as we have done earlier in this article. And they can engage in *transdisciplinary* work, where they examine a concept, like "body," as it appears in political and in physical discourse.

DISCIPLINARY POWERS AND LIMITATIONS

In our view, the disciplines are the most useful means for illuminating those generative issues that have perennially engaged the curiosity of thoughtful human beings. What in the past was approached first through common sense, and later through art, mythology, and religion, can now be approached as well through systematic studies, such as political science or medical experimentation.

While we should be respectful of disciplines, we should remain aware of at least three limitations:

1. *Far from being ends in themselves, the disciplines are means for answering generative "essential" questions.* Indeed, armed with the disciplines and with the possibility of interdisciplinary work, individuals are in the best position to revisit these essential questions and to arrive at their own, often deeply personal answers.

2. *Disciplines are differently transfigured, depending on purpose and developmental levels.* For elementary education, it may be enough to separate out the arts and humanities, on the one hand, and the experimental sciences on the other. At the high school level, a distinction into three or four disciplinary terrains probably suffices (Sizer 1992). And at the university level, a quite fine differentiation and articulation among disciplines is appropriate.

3. *All disciplinary boundaries are tentative.* Disciplines have not been, and probably never will be, marked in stone. Rather, they develop out of specific conditions, and as these conditions change, boundaries are redrawn. Moreover, even within the most established disciplines, serious disagreements exist with respect to content, methods, and scope. The dynamism of disciplines reflects the always growing, ever-changing nature of knowledge.

ASSESSMENT WITHIN AND ACROSS THE DISCIPLINES

Some aspects of assessment are appropriate for all disciplines, while others turn out to be far more specific to particular disciplinary practices. At the generic level, each discipline features certain characteristic roles—the historical analyst, the designer of experiments—and certain characteristic performances or exhibitions—a historical account, an experimental write-up. Students need to be immersed in instances of these roles and performances of understanding, particularly as they are practiced by proficient individuals.

But even the best instances do not suffice. It does not benefit the rookie pianist to hear Arthur Rubinstein or the novice tennis player only to witness Martina Navratilova. Rather, students must encounter individual benchmarks on the trail from novice to expert, as well as road maps of how to get from one milestone to the next. Given these landmarks, along with ample opportunity to perform their understanding with appropriate feedback, most individuals should be able to steadily enhance their competence in any discipline.

Of course, disciplines lend themselves to different kinds of roles and performances. To read texts critically, in the manner of a historian, is a quite different matter than to design a crucial experiment and analyze data relevant to competing models of an infectious process. Different disciplines call on different analytic styles, approaches to problem solving and findings, temperaments, and intelligences. Therefore, a keen assessment must be alert to these disciplinary differences. By the same token, an effective teacher should help youngsters to appreciate that what counts as cause and effect, data and explanation, use of language and argument, varies across the disciplines.

FROM DISCIPLINARY TO PERSONAL KNOWLEDGE

All individuals the world over, not just knowledgeable people, ask generative questions. Children do not ask about the meaning of life and death or good and bad merely because others talk about these issues. Rather, these questions arise spontaneously, prompting children to pose them in their own way and to come up with imaginative answers. The disciplines, individually and jointly, offer the best current efforts to approach, and to supply, provisional answers for these enduring questions. As we saw in our two simple examples (about abdication and illness), just as questions come from different points and lead to different kinds of answers, the disciplines themselves have disparate roots and lead, by varying routes, to different kinds of accounts.

Drawing on the disciplines, we should find it possible to mount increasingly comprehensive approaches to generative questions—approaches that are appropriate to particular contexts and populations. In the end, however, we need to keep in mind that the disciplines remain but the means for tackling these questions. The most important answers are those that individuals ultimately craft for themselves, based on their disciplinary understandings, their personal experiences, and their own feelings and values.

REFERENCES

Gardner, H. (1991). *The Unschooled Mind.* Basic Books: New York.

Gardner, H., and V. Boix-Mansilla. (1993). "Teaching for Understanding in the Disciplines . . . and Beyond." Paper prepared for the conference Teachers' Conceptions of Knowledge, Tel Aviv, Israel, June 1993. To be published in the Proceedings.

Sizer, T. (1992). *Horace's School.* Boston: Houghton Mifflin.

Chapter 9: Learning and Instruction

The Use of Scaffolds for Teaching Higher-Level Cognitive Strategies

BARAK ROSENSHINE and CARLA MEISTER

The teaching of higher-level thinking operations is a topic that interests many of today's educators. These operations include comprehension and interpretation of text, scientific processes, and mathematical problem solving. While much has been written on the need for students to perform higher-level thinking operations in all subject areas, the teaching of these operations often fails, not because the idea is poor, but because the instruction is inadequate.

How does one help students perform higher-level operations? One solution that researchers have developed is to teach students cognitive strategies (Pressley et al. 1990; Perkins et al. 1989; Weinstein 1979). A strategy is not a direct procedure; it is not an algorithm. Rather a strategy is a heuristic that supports or facilitates the learner as he or she learns to perform the higher-level operations.

For example, to facilitate reading comprehension, students may be taught to use cognition strategies such as generating questions about their reading. To generate questions, students need to search the text and combine information, which in turn helps them comprehend what they read. To

help students in the writing process, they may be taught how to organize their writing and how to use self-talk prompts to facilitate the revision process. These cognitive strategies are more like supports or suggestions than actual step-by-step directives.

But how does one teach cognitive strategies? Our review of about 50 studies in which students ranging from 3rd grade through college were taught cognitive strategies showed that successful teachers of such strategies frequently used instructional procedures called *scaffolds* (Palincsar and Brown 1984; Paris et al. 1986, Wood et al. 1976). Scaffolds are forms of support provided by the teacher (or another student) to help students bridge the gap between their current abilities and the intended goal. Scaffolds may be tools, such as cue cards, or techniques, such as teacher modeling. Although scaffolds can be applied to the teaching of all skills, they are particularly useful, and often indispensable, for teaching higher-level cognitive strategies, where many of the steps or procedures necessary to carry out these strategies cannot be specified. Instead of providing explicit steps, one supports, or scaffolds, the students as they learn the skill. (See box, page 139, for steps in teaching cognitive strategies.)

The support that scaffolds provide is both temporary (Tobias 1982) and adjustable, allowing learners "to participate at an ever-increasing level of competence" (Palincsar and Brown 1984, p. 122). Scaffolding gradually decreases as the learning process unfolds and students become proficient.

Barak Rosenshine is Professor of Educational Psychology and Carla Meister is a Teacher in School District #129, Aurora, Illinois, and a doctoral student in educational psychology at the University of Illinois. They can be reached at the University of Illinois, Bureau of Educational Research, 230 Education Building, 1310 S. Sixth St., Champaign, IL 61820-699.

This research was supported by the Bureau of Educational Research, College of Education, University of Illinois.

Before using scaffolds, it is important to determine whether students have sufficient background ability to learn a new cognitive strategy. Researchers (particularly Palincsar and Brown 1984) note that scaffolds are only useful within the student's "zone of proximal development" (Vygotsky 1978), that is, the area where the student cannot proceed alone, but can proceed when guided by a teacher using scaffolds. When Palincsar and Brown (1984) taught strategies designed to foster reading comprehension, they selected students whose decoding skills were near grade level, but whose comprehension was below grade level. They did not select students with poor decoding skills, because such students did not have sufficient background skills to profit from this instruction. Similarly, scaffolds cannot help students read a physics text or history text for which they do not have the necessary background knowledge.

PRESENTING A NEW COGNITIVE STRATEGY

In the studies we reviewed, teachers typically began teaching a cognitive strategy by introducing and explaining a concrete prompt. Concrete prompts, also called procedural facilitators (Scardamalia et al. 1984), are scaffolds specific to the strategy being taught, yet general enough to allow application to a variety of different contexts. For example, to help students learn the strategy of generating questions, some teachers first gave students "question words" —*who, what, when, where, why, how*—and taught them to use these words as prompts. These six simple question words were the concrete prompts. In the study by King (1989), students used a list of general question stems that could be used to form questions about a particular passage:

How are _____ and _____ alike?
What is the main idea of _____?
What do you think would happen if _____?
What are the strengths and weaknesses of _____?
In what way is _____ related to _____?
How does _____ affect _____?
Compare _____ and _____ with regard to _____.
What do you think causes _____?
How does _____ tie in with what we have learned before?

Which one is the best _____ and why?
What are some possible solutions for the problem of _____?
Do you agree or disagree with this statement: _____? Support your answer.
What do I (you) still not understand about _____?

Several different concrete prompts have also been developed for teaching the strategy of summarizing. Baumann (1984) and Taylor (1985) used the following prompt:

Identify the topic.
Write two or three words that reflect the topic.
Use these words as a prompt to help figure out the main idea of the paragraph.
Select two details that elaborate on the main idea and are important to remember.
Write two or three sentences that best incorporate these important ideas.

Palincsar (1987) used a different prompt for teaching summarizing:

Step 1: Identify the topic sentence.
Step 2: If there is not a topic sentence, identify the topic and the most important information about that topic.
Rule 1: Leave out unimportant information.
Rule 2: Give steps or lists a title.
Rule 3: Cross out information that is redundant/repeated.

To assist students during the writing process, Scardamalia, Bereiter, and Steinbach (1984) offered students cues to stimulate their thinking about the planning of compositions. These cues took the form of introductory phrases and were grouped according to the function they served: planning a new idea, improving, elaborating, goal setting, and putting it all together. Students first determined the type of cue needed, then chose a particular cue to incorporate into a silent planning monologue (see box page 140, for cues for opinion essays). Other investigators developed specific prompts to help students improve their writing. For example, Englert, Raphael, Anderson, Anthony, and Stevens (1991) provided Plan Think-Sheets that cued students to consider their audience ("Who am I writing for?" "Why am I writing this?"), and Organize Think-Sheets to help students sort their ideas

---

How to Teach Higher-Order Cognitive Strategies

1. Present the new cognitive strategies.
    (a) Introduce the concrete prompt.
    (b) Model the skill.
    (c) Think aloud as choices are made.

2. Regulate difficulty during guided practice.
    (a) Start with simplified material and gradually increase the complexity of the task.
    (b) Complete part of the task for the student.
    (c) Provide cue cards.
    (d) Present the material in small steps.
    (e) Anticipate student errors and difficult areas.

3. Provide varying contexts for student practice.
    (a) Provide teacher-led practice.
    (b) Engage in reciprocal teaching.
    (c) Have students work in small groups.

4. Provide feedback.
    (a) Offer teacher-led feedback.
    (b) Provide checklists.
    (c) Provide models of expert work.

5. Increase student responsibility.
    (a) Diminish prompts and models.
    (b) Gradually increase complexity and difficulty of the material.
    (c) Diminish student support.
    (d) Practice putting all the steps together (consolidation).
    (e) Check for student mastery.

6. Provide independent practice.
    (a) Provide extensive practice.
    (b) Facilitate application to new examples.

---

into categories ("What is being explained?" "What are the steps?").

After presenting the concrete prompt, the teacher modeled its application as the students observed. Thus, when teaching students to generate questions, the teacher modeled how to use the cues to think of questions related to a particular passage. When teaching students to write a summary, the teacher identified the details of a paragraph or passage, used the details to form a main idea, and stated the details in the summary. In writing an explanation paper, the teacher used the planning cues in a self-talk (monologue) style. The teacher modeled how to use the Plan Think-Sheet to record ideas and thoughts about the topic.

Modeling of the process by the teacher gradually diminished as students began to take on more of the responsibility for completing the task. The teacher continued to model only the part(s) of the process that students were unable to complete at a particular time. Often during the transitional stage, when the students were ready to take on another part of the task, the teacher continued to model, but requested hints or suggestions from the students on how to complete the next step in the task. Several studies also relied on more capable students to provide the modeling.

Another scaffold, similar to modeling, is "thinking aloud." For example, when teaching students to generate questions, the teacher describes the thought processes that occur as a question word is

selected and integrated with text information to form a question.

Anderson (1991) provides illustrations of think-alouds for several cognitive strategies in reading:

> For clarifying difficult statements or concepts: *I don't get this. It says that things that are dark look smaller. I know that a white dog looks smaller than a black elephant, so this rule must only work for things that are about the same size. Maybe black shoes would make your feet look smaller than white ones would.*

> For summarizing important information: *I'll summarize this part of the article. So far, it tells where the Spanish started in North America and what parts they explored. Since the title is "The Spanish in California," the part about California must be important. I'd sum up by saying that Spanish explorers from Mexico discovered California. They didn't stay in California, but lived in other parts of America. These are the most important ideas so far.*

> For thinking ahead: *So far this has told me that Columbus is poor, the trip will be expensive, and everyone's laughing at his plan. I'd predict that Columbus will have trouble getting the money he needs for his exploration.*

In a mathematics study by Schoenfeld (1985), the teacher thought aloud as he went through the steps

---

Planning Cues Used for Opinion Essays

New Idea

An even better idea is . . .
An important point I haven't considered yet is . . .
A better argument would be . . .
A whole new way to think of this topic is . . .
No one will have thought of . . .

Improve

I'm not being very clear about what I just said so . . .
A criticism I should deal with in my paper is . . .
I really think this isn't necessary because . . .

Putting It Together

If I want to start off with my strongest idea, I'll . . .
I can tie this together by . . .
My main point is . . .

Elaborate

An example of this . . .
This is true, but it's not sufficient so . . .
My own feelings about this are . . .
I'll change this a little by . . .
The reason I think so . . .
Another reason that's good . . .
I could develop this idea by adding . . .
Another way to put it would be . . .
A good point on the other side of the argument is . . .

Goals

A goal I think I could write is . . .
My purpose is . . .

---

in solving mathematical problems. He also identified and labeled the problem-solving procedures he was using (for example, making diagrams, breaking the problem into parts). Thus, as Schoenfeld points out, thinking aloud may also provide labels that students can use to call up the same processes in their own thinking.

When teaching mathematical problem solving, Schoenfeld (1985) asked the college students in his class to provide him with particularly difficult problems. Each class began with his attempt to solve one of the problems. Through modeling and thinking aloud, he applied problem-solving procedures and revealed his reasoning about the problems he encountered. Students saw the flexibility of the strategies as they were applied to a range of problems and observed that the use of a strategy did not guarantee success.

The following excerpt is an example of Schoenfeld modeling his thinking process as he gets a feel for a problem:

> *What do you do when you face a problem like this? I have no general procedure for finding the roots of a polynomial, much less for comparing the roots of two of them. Probably the best thing to do for the time being is to look at some simple examples and hope I can develop some intuition from them. Instead of looking at a pair of arbitrary polynomials, maybe I should look at a pair of quadratics: at least I can solve those. Now, what happens if . . .*

As individual students accepted more responsibility in the completion of a task, they often modeled and thought aloud for their less capable classmates. Not only did student modeling and think-alouds involve the students actively in the process, but it allowed the teacher to better assess student progress in the use of the strategy. Thinking aloud by the teacher and more capable students provided novice learners with a way to observe "expert thinking" usually hidden from the student.

REGULATING DIFFICULTY DURING GUIDED PRACTICE

In order to help the learner, many teachers began with simpler exercises and then gradually increased the difficulty of the task. This allowed the learner to begin participating very early in the process. For example, in a study by Palincsar (1987), an early task consisted of generating questions about a *single sentence*. The teacher first modeled how to generate questions, and this was followed by student practice. Then the complexity was increased to generating questions after reading a *paragraph*, followed by more student practice. Finally, the teacher modeled and the class practiced generating questions after reading an entire *passage*.

When learning the strategy of summarizing, students in the study by Dermody (1988) first learned how to write summary statements on single paragraphs. After students received guided practice on this task, teachers showed them how to combine several summary statements to produce a single summary for a longer passage and had them practice this more difficult task.

In many of the studies, instruction on the cognitive strategy began with the teacher completing most or all of the task through modeling and thinking aloud. The teacher continued to carry out the parts of the task not yet introduced to the students or those parts students were unable to complete at the time. Additional components were added to the students' responsibilities as they became more skillful. Sometimes, their participation began at a very simple level. For example, as the teacher modeled the strategy, the students were asked to provide the label. Or students were requested to state the next step in the process the teacher needed to model. As student involvement increased, teacher involvement was withdrawn. Teachers provided hints, prompts, suggestions, and feedback when students encountered difficulty in their attempts to complete part of the task. Sometimes these difficulties required the temporary increase of teacher involvement until students were able to overcome the difficulty.

In some studies, students received cue cards containing the concrete prompts they had been taught. Having a cue card allows the student to put more effort into *applying* the prompt, rather than *remembering* it. For example, in the study by Billingsley and Wildman (1984), the students were provided with a card containing the list of question words (*who, what, why*) they could use to generate questions. Singer and Donlon (1982) taught students to use the elements of story grammar (for example, leading character, goal, obstacles, outcomes, and theme) as a prompt to generate questions and gave them lists of these story elements for reference. Wong and Jones (1982) provided students with cue cards printed with a concrete prompt to use as they generated questions on the main idea of a passage. Eventually the cue cards were removed, and students were asked to formulate questions or write summaries without them. Below is a Self-Questioning Cue Card:

(a) *Why are you studying this passage? (So you can answer some questions you will be given later.)*

(b) *Find the main idea/ideas in the paragraph and underline it/them.*

(c) *Think of a question about the main idea you have underlined. Remember what a good question should be like.*

(d) *Learn the answer to your question.*

(e) *Always look back at the questions and answers to see how each successive question and answer provides you with more information.*

When presenting a prompt that has several steps, the difficulty can be regulated by "teaching in small steps," that is, first teaching one step and providing for student practice before teaching the next step. In this way, students deal with manageable, yet meaningful, bits. In a study (Blaha 1979) in which students were taught a strategy for summarizing paragraphs, the teacher explained and modeled the first step, identifying the topic of a paragraph, and provided for student practice on new paragraphs. Then she taught the concept of main idea, and students practiced both finding the topic and locating the main idea. Following this, she taught students to identify the supporting details, and the students practiced that part of the task. Finally, the students practiced doing all three steps of the strategy.

Another way to regulate the difficulty of learning a new cognitive strategy is to anticipate and discuss potential student errors. For example, in one study the teacher anticipated errors in summarizing by presenting a summary with a poorly written topic sentence and asking students to identify the problem. In a questioning study, the teacher showed questions that were inappropriate because they were about a minor detail and then asked students to state why they were inappropriate. The students then used these hints and suggestions as they generated their questions.

Another example of anticipating errors occurs in the study conducted by Brady (1990). The investigator noticed that students had a tendency to produce summary statements that were too broad, often providing only the general topic of the passage (for example, "This paragraph was about toads.") To help students avoid this error, Brady developed a simple yet successful concrete prompt; he suggested students begin their summary statements with the phrase "This paragraph tells us that _____." This prompt significantly improved the quality of summary statements.

VARYING THE CONTEXT FOR PRACTICE

Students in most studies practiced the application of cognitive strategies in one or more of three different contexts: teacher-guided practice, reciprocal teaching, and work in small groups. When teaching cognitive strategies, the teachers guided students by providing hints, reminders of the concrete prompts, reminders of what was overlooked, and suggestions on how something could be improved. Students participated by giving answers and deciding upon the correctness of other students' answers. Where appropriate, students were asked to justify their procedures by explaining their thinking. Through this process, students' "oversimplified and naive conceptions are revealed" (Brown and Campione 1986). Such dialogue may also aid in understanding. As Brown and Campione (1986) write, "Understanding is more likely to occur when a student is required to explain, elaborate, or defend his or her position to others; the burden of explanation is often the push needed to make him or her evaluate, integrate, and elaborate knowledge in new ways."

In some studies, guided practice took place in the context of a dialogue among teacher and students—reciprocal teaching (Palincsar and Brown 1984)—with students and teacher rotating the role of teacher. This allowed for shifting of responsibility to the students and gradual internalization of the cognitive strategies. As the student took on the role of the teacher in the process of applying the strategies to a text, the teacher was able to evaluate the student's progress and provide feedback or assistance.

Collaborative social dialogue was also emphasized in Englert and colleagues' (1991) Cognitive Strategy Instruction in Writing. During guided practice, students were invited to participate in a dialogue about a class writing project. Students and teacher worked collaboratively to generate self-questions, apply the new cognitive strategies, and carry on the dialogue to complete a class paper. The students progressively took on more responsibility for completing the writing task. The investigators contend that as students accept more responsibility in the exchange that takes place during the instructional dialogues, they begin to internalize the dialogue. The investigators suggest that this inner dialogue allows students to (1) talk to themselves about their own writing, (2) hear what their own writing has to say, and (3) talk to others about their writing.

In some studies, notably those conducted with high school and college students, the students practiced the task in small groups without the teacher.

For example, King (1989) reported that after hearing a lecture, students met in small groups and practiced generating questions about the lecture. Students in Schoenfeld's (1985) study had opportunities to participate in small group mathematical problem solving. Schoenfeld suggests small group work facilitates the learning process in four ways. First, it provides an opportunity for the teacher to assess students, to provide support and assistance as students actively engage in problem solving. Second, group decision making facilitates the articulation of knowledge and reasoning as students justify to group members their reasons for choosing alternative solutions. Third, students receive practice in collaboration, a skill required in real-life problem solving. Fourth, students who are insecure about their abilities to solve problems have the opportunity to see more capable peers struggle over difficult problems.

PROVIDING FEEDBACK

Feedback is important in teaching cognitive strategies as it is for all forms of learning. Traditional feedback from teachers and other students on the correctness of response took place throughout the lessons on cognitive strategies.

In several studies the teacher provided self-checking procedures to increase student independence. For example, as part of their instruction in teaching students to summarize a passage, Rinehart, Stahl, and Erickson (1986) had students use the following list of questions to check their summaries:

> *Have I found the overall idea that the passage is about?*
> *Have I found the most important information that tells me more about the overall idea?*
> *Have I used any information that is not directly about the main idea?*
> *Have I used any information more than once?*

Checklists for writing programs ranged from checklists on punctuation ("Does every sentence start with a capital letter?") to checklists on style elements. For example, students being taught to write explanations were taught to ask, "Did I tell what materials you need?" "Did I make the steps clear?" (Englert et al. 1991). Teachers usually presented these checklists at the end of guided practice. The teacher modeled the use of the checklist and provided students with guidance as they began to use the checklists.

In some studies, students were provided with expert models to compare their work to. For example, where students were taught to generate questions, they could compare their questions with those generated by the teacher. Similarly, when learning to write summaries, students could compare their summaries on a passage with those generated by an expert.

INCREASING STUDENT RESPONSIBILITY

Just as it is important to simplify material and provide support for students in the initial stages of learning a cognitive strategy, it is also important to reduce the number of prompts and provide students with practice using more complex material. Thus, the responsibility for learning shifts from the teacher to the student. This gradual decrease in supports and gradual increase in student responsibility has been described as a shift in the teacher's role from that of coach to that of supportive and sympathetic audience (Palincsar and Brown 1984).

After the students in the study by Wong and Jones (1982) had used cue cards to develop fluency in writing a summary, the cue cards were removed and students wrote summaries without these prompts. In the studies by King (1989), in which students used half-completed sentences as references when generating questions, the teacher withdrew the supports after the guided practice, and students were left to generate questions on their own.

Increasing the complexity of material was evident in the study by Palincsar (1987), in which students learning to generate questions began by working on a single sentence, then a paragraph, and finally, an entire passage. Schoenfeld (1985) sequenced the problems he presented to his students when teaching mathematical problem solving. He first gave students problems they were incapable of solving on their own; this provided the motivation for learning the strategy he planned to introduce. After presenting the strategy, he provided problems that were easily solved when the strategy was applied. As students became skilled at applying the strategy, he introduced a new strategy. Interspersed among these new problems were several problems requiring the application of previously taught problem-solving strategies, forcing students to discriminately apply the strategies learned to the type of problems encountered. As the course progressed, students were expected to combine strategies to solve complex problems.

In some studies, the support that students received from other students was also diminished as work progressed. For example, in the study by Nolte and Singer (1985), the students first spent three days working in groups of five or six and then three days working in pairs before working alone on the task.

In the study by Englert and colleagues (1991), in which students were taught cognitive strategies in writing, students first participated in a collaborative dialogue that centered on the application of the newly learned strategies to a whole-class writing project. Students then chose their own topic, applying the same strategies used in the group writing. Students were encouraged to collaborate with a peer or peers by sharing ideas, discussing each other's writing, asking questions, getting feedback, reporting progress, or asking advice. The teacher provided additional support by finding examples of strategy use or problems found in the students' writing, displaying them on the overhead. The teacher initiated a class dialogue on the student examples, focusing the discussion on the strategies used, the problems encountered by the students, and possible solutions. After the students completed this piece of writing, the teacher asked them to independently write another paper for publication in a class book.

When series of steps have been taught and practiced separately, as in some summarizing and writing strategies, one of the final tasks during guided practice is having the students practice putting the component parts of the strategy together. A teacher can then assess student implementation of the complete strategy, correct errors, and determine whether additional teaching or practice is necessary. Such assessment is important before students begin independent practice.

PROVIDING INDEPENDENT PRACTICE

The goal of independent practice is to develop *unitization* of the strategy, that is, the blending of elements of the strategy into a single, unified whole. The extensive practice, and practice with a *variety* of material—alone, in groups, or in pairs—also *decontextualizes* the learning. That is, the strategies become free of their original "bindings" and can now be applied, easily and unconsciously, to various situations (Collins et al. 1990). Cognitive Strategy Instruction in Writing (the program implemented in the Englert et al. 1991 study) provided students with several opportunities to apply the strategies they had been taught, first in a whole-group setting, then individually with peer and teacher assistance, and then a third time independently.

TOWARD A BROADER APPLICATION?

Scaffolds and the procedures for using them provide us with many ways to think about how to help students learn cognitive strategies. Such concepts as modeling, thinking aloud, using cue cards, anticipating errors, and providing expert models can also be applied to the teaching of well-structured skills. This suggests that instead of a dichotomy, there is a continuum from well-structured explicit skills to cognitive strategies. At all points in the continuum, some instructional processes, such as presenting information in small steps and providing guided practice, are important. Yet, as one moves from well-structured skills to cognitive strategies, the value of providing students with scaffolds—models, concrete prompts, think-alouds, simplified problems, suggestions, and hints—increases.

The tools and techniques we refer to as scaffolds are at a middle level of specificity. That is, they provide support for the student, but they do not specify each and every step to be taken. There is something appealing about this middle level. It lies somewhere between the specificity of behavioral objectives that seemed overly demanding to some, and the lack of instruction that many criticized in discovery learning settings. Perhaps it is the beginning of a synthesis.

Authors' note: We hope that the ideas presented here can serve as a heuristic for teachers to support their classroom instruction in cognitive strategies. The teaching of cognitive strategies is a higher-level operation itself; there is no specific, predetermined, or guaranteed path of instructional procedures to follow. Rather, there are sets of procedures, suggestions and scaffolds that a teacher selects, develops, presents, attempts, modifies, and even abandons in order to help students learn the cognitive strategy.

REFERENCES

Anderson, V. (April 1991). "Training Teachers to Foster Active Reading Strategies in Reading-Disabled Adolescents." Paper presented at the annual meeting of the American Educational Research Association, Chicago.

Baumann, J. F. (1984). "The Effectiveness of a Direct Instruction Paradigm for Teaching Main Idea Comprehension." *Reading Research Quarterly* 20: 93–115.

Billingsley, B. S., and T. M. Wildman. (1984). "Question Generation and Reading Comprehension." *Learning Disability Research* 4: 36–44.

Blaha, B. A. (1979). "The Effects of Answering Self-Generated Questions on Reading." Unpublished doctoral diss., Boston University School of Education.

Brady, P. L. (1990). "Improving the Reading Comprehension of Middle School Students Through Reciprocal Teaching and Semantic Mapping Strategies." Unpublished doctoral diss., University of Oregon.

Brown, A. L., and J. C. Campione. (1986). "Psychological Theory and the Study of Learning Disabilities." *American Psychologist* 41: 1059–1068.

Collins, A., J. S. Brown, and S. E. Newman. (1990). "Cognitive Apprenticeship: Teaching the Crafts of Reading, Writing, and Mathematics." In *Knowing, Learning, and Instruction: Essays in Honor of Robert Glaser*, edited by L. Resnick. Hillsdale, N.J.: Erlbaum Associates.

Dermody, M. M. (1988). "Effects of Metacognitive Strategy Training on Fourth Graders' Reading Comprehension." Unpublished doctoral diss., University of New Orleans.

Englert, C. S., T. E. Raphael, L. M. Anderson, H. Anthony, and D. D. Stevens. (1991). "Making Strategies and Self-Talk Visible: Writing, Instruction in Regular and Special Education Classrooms." *American Educational Research Journal* 28: 337–372.

King, A. (April 1989). "Improving Lecture Comprehension: Effects of a Metacognitive Strategy." Paper presented at the annual meeting of the American Educational Research Association, San Francisco.

Nolte, R. Y., and H. Singer. (1985). "Active Comprehension: Teaching a Process of Reading Comprehension and Its Effects on Reading Achievement." *The Reading Teacher* 39: 24–31.

Palincsar, A. S. (April 1987). "Collaborating for Collaborative Learning of Text Comprehension." Paper presented at the annual meeting of the American Educational Research Association, Washington, D.C.

Palincsar, A. M., and A. L. Brown. (1984). "Reciprocal Teaching of Comprehension-Fostering and Comprehension-Monitoring Activities." *Cognition and Instruction* 2: 117–175.

Palincsar, A. S. (1986). "The Role of Dialogue in Providing Scaffolded Instruction." *Educational Psychologist* 21: 73–98.

Paris, S. G., K. K. Wixson, and A. S. Palincsar. (1986). "Instructional Approaches to Reading Comprehension." In *Review of Research in Education*, edited by E. Z. Rothkof. Washington, D.C.: American Educational Research Association.

Perkins, D. N., R. Simmons, and S. Tishman. (March 1989). "Teaching Cognitive and Metacognitive Strategies." Paper presented at the annual meeting of the American Educational Research Association, San Francisco.

Pressley, M., J. Burkell, T. Cariglia-Bull, L. Lysynchuk, J. A. McGoldrick, B. Schneider, S. Symons, and V. E. Woloshyn. (1990). *Cognitive Strategy Instruction*. Cambridge, Mass.: Brookline Books.

Rinehart, S. D., S. A. Stahl, and L. G. Erickson. (1986). "Some Effects of Summarization Training on Reading and Studying." *Reading Research Quarterly* 21: 422–437.

Scardamalia, M., C. Bereiter, and R. Steinbach. (1984). "Teachability of Reflective Processes in Written Composition." *Cognitive Science* 8: 173–190.

Schoenfeld, A. H. (1985). *Mathematical Problem Solving*. New York: Academic Press.

Singer, H., and D. Donlan. (1982). "Active Comprehension: Problem-Solving Schema with Question Generation of Complex Short Stories." *Reading Research Quarterly* 17: 166–186.

Taylor, B. M. (1985). "Improving Middle-Grade Students' Reading and Writing of Expository Text." *Journal of Educational Research* 79: 119–125.

Tobias, S. (1982). "When Do Instructional Methods Make a Difference?" *Educational Researcher* 11: 4–10.

Vygotsky, L. S. (1978). *Mind in Society: The Development of Higher Psychological Processes*, edited and translated by M. Cole, V. John Steiner, S. Schribner and E. Souberman. Cambridge, Mass.: Harvard University Press.

Wong, Y. L., and W. Jones. (1982). "Increasing Metacomprehension in Learning Disabled and Normally Achieving Students Through Self-Questioning Training." *Learning Disability Quarterly* 5: 228–239.

Wood, D. J., J. S. Bruner, and G. Ross. (1976). "The Role of Tutoring in Problem Solving." *Journal of Child Psychology and Psychiatry* 17: 89–100.

Reading Comprehension: What Works

LINDA G. FIELDING and P. DAVID PEARSON

Perhaps the most sweeping changes in reading instruction in the last 15 years are in the area of comprehension. Once thought of as the natural result of decoding plus oral language, comprehension is now viewed as a much more complex process involving knowledge, experience, thinking, and teaching. It depends heavily on knowledge—both about the world at large and the worlds of language and print. Comprehension inherently involves inferential and evaluative thinking, not just literal reproduction of the author's words. Most important, it can be taught directly.

Two years ago we reviewed the most recent research about comprehension instruction (Pearson and Fielding 1991). Here, we revisit that research, supplementing it with current thinking about reading instruction, and transform the most consistent findings into practical guidelines for teachers.

We contend that a successful program of comprehension instruction should include four components:

- large amounts of time for actual text reading,
- teacher-directed instruction in comprehension strategies,
- opportunities for peer and collaborative learning, and
- occasions for students to talk to a teacher and one another about their responses to reading.

Linda G. Fielding is Assistant Professor of Curriculum and Instruction, The University of Iowa, N275 Lindquist Center, Iowa City, IA 52242. P. David Pearson is Professor and Dean, College of Education, University of Illinois at Urbana-Champaign, 38 Education Bldg., 1310 S. Sixth St., Champaign, IL 61820.

A program with these components will set the stage for students to be interested in and to succeed at reading—providing them the intrinsic motivation for continual learning.

AMPLE TIME FOR TEXT READING

One of the most surprising findings of classroom research of the 1970s and '80s was the small amount of time that children spent actually reading texts. Estimates ranged from 7 to 15 minutes per day from the primary to the intermediate grades (Anderson et al. 1985). Children typically spent more time working on reading skills via workbook-type assignments than putting these skills to work in reading connected texts. The skill time/reading time ratio was typically the highest for children of the lowest reading ability (Allington 1983b). Allocating ample time for actual text reading and ensuring that students are actually engaged in text reading during that time are among teachers' most important tasks in comprehension instruction.

Why is time for text reading important? The first benefit of time for reading is the sheer opportunity to orchestrate the skills and strategies that are important to proficient reading—including comprehension. As in sports and music, *practice makes perfect* in reading, too.

Second, reading results in *the acquisition of new knowledge*, which, in turn, fuels the comprehension process. Research of the late 1970s and early '80s consistently revealed a strong reciprocal relationship between prior knowledge and reading comprehension ability. The more one already knows, the more one comprehends; and the more one comprehends, the more one learns new knowledge to enable comprehension of an even greater and broader array of topics and texts.

The first part of this reciprocal relationship was the focus of much research of the last 15 years—developing methods for activating and adding to readers' knowledge base before reading to increase text understanding (Beck et al. 1982, Hansen and Pearson 1983). More recently, researchers have emphasized the second part of the relationship: the role that actual text reading plays in building knowledge. For example, increases in vocabulary and concept knowledge from reading silently (Nagy et al. 1987, Stallman 1991) and from being read to (Elley 1989) have been documented. Further, the positive statistical relationship between amount of time spent reading and reading comprehension (Anderson et al. 1988) may be largely attributable to the knowledge base that grows through text reading.

Recent research has debunked the misconception that only already-able readers can benefit from time spent in actual text reading, while less able readers should spend time on isolated skills instruction and workbook practice (Anderson et al. 1988, Leinhardt et al. 1981). A newer, more compelling argument is that the differing amounts of time teachers give students to read texts accounts for the widening gaps between more able and less able readers throughout the school grades (Allington 1983b, Stanovich 1986).

How much time should be devoted to actual text reading? At present research offers no answers, but we recommend that, of the time set aside for reading instruction, students should have more time to read than the combined total allocated for *learning* about reading and *talking or writing* about what has been read.

GETTING THE MOST OUT OF READING TIME

The equivocal results of sustained silent reading programs throughout the years (Manning and Manning 1984) suggest, though, that simply allocating time is not enough. Teachers can increase the likelihood that more time for contextual reading will translate into improved comprehension skills in the following ways.

1. *Choice.* Teachers can give children opportunities and guidance in making text selections. Although we know of no research that directly links choice to reading comprehension growth, we speculate that choice is related to interest and motivation, both of which are related directly to learning (Anderson et al. 1987).

2. *Optimal difficulty.* Teachers can monitor students' and their own selections to ensure that all students spend most of their time reading books that are appropriate in difficulty—not so hard that a student's cognitive resources are occupied with just figuring out how to pronounce the words and not so easy that nothing new is likely to be learned.

3. *Multiple readings.* Teachers can honor and encourage rereading of texts, which research suggests leads to greater fluency and comprehension (Allington 1983a). Although most research about repeated reading of passages has focused on improvements in reading speed, accuracy, phrasing, and intonation, a growing number of studies have documented improved comprehension as well (Dowhower 1987).

4. *Negotiating meaning socially.* "Silent" reading time shouldn't be entirely silent. Teachers can (a) allow part of the time for reading in pairs, including pairs of different abilities and ages (Koskinen and Blum 1986, Labbo and Teale 1990); and (b) provide regular opportunities for readers to discuss their reading with the teacher and with one another. We view reading comprehension as a social as well as a cognitive process. Conversation not only raises the status of independent silent reading from a time filler to an important part of the reading program; it also gives students another opportunity to practice and build comprehension skills collaboratively, a topic to which we return below. Atwell (1987) and Hansen (1987) further argue that these conversations help to build the all-important community of readers that is the essence of literature-based programs.

TEACHER-DIRECTED INSTRUCTION

Research from the 1980s indicated that in traditional reading classrooms, time for comprehension instruction was as rare as time for actual text reading.

After extensive observations in intermediate-grade classrooms, Durkin (1978–1979) concluded that teachers were spending very little time on actual comprehension instruction. Although they gave many workbook assignments and asked many questions about text content, Durkin judged that these exercises mostly tested students' understanding instead of teaching them how to comprehend.

In response to Durkin's findings, much research in the 1980s was devoted to discovering how to teach comprehension strategies directly. In the typical study of this type, readers were directly taught how to perform a strategy that skilled readers used during reading. Then, their abilities both in strategy use and text comprehension were compared either to their own performance before instruction or to the performance of similar readers who were not taught the strategy directly. *Explicit instruction,* the name given to one such widely researched model, involves four phases: teacher modeling and explanation of a strategy, guided practice during which teachers gradually give students more responsibility for task completion, independent practice accompanied by feedback, and application of the strategy in real reading situations (Pearson and Dole 1987).

In one of the biggest success stories of the time period, research showed repeatedly that comprehension can in fact be taught. Many strategies have been taught successfully:

- using background knowledge to make inferences (Hansen and Pearson 1983) or set purposes (Ogle 1986);
- getting the main idea (Baumann 1984);
- identifying the sources of information needed to answer a question (Raphael and Pearson 1985); and
- using the typical structure of stories (Fitzgerald and Spiegel 1983) or expository texts (Armbruster et al. 1987) to help students understand what they are reading.

One of the most exciting results of this body of research was that comprehension strategy instruction is especially effective for students who began the study as poor comprehenders—probably because they are less likely to invent effective strategies on their own. In some studies, less able readers who had been taught a comprehension strategy were indistinguishable from more able readers who had not been taught the strategy directly.

After more than a decade of research and criticism from both sides of the controversy about com-

prehension strategy instruction, we have a much clearer understanding of what quality instruction looks like and how to make it part of a larger comprehension instructional program.

Authenticity of strategies. First, the strategies students are taught should be as much as possible like the ones actual readers use when they comprehend successfully. To meet this criterion of authentic use, instruction should focus on the flexible application of the strategy rather than a rigid sequence of steps. It should also externalize the thinking processes of skilled readers—not create artificial processes that apply only to contrived instructional or assessment situations.

Demonstration. Teachers should also demonstrate how to apply each strategy successfully—what it is, how it is carried out, and when and why it should be used (Duffy et al. 1988, Paris et al. 1991). Instead of just talking about a strategy, teachers need to illustrate the processes they use by thinking aloud, or modeling mental processes, while they read.

Guided practice. A phase in which teachers and students practice the strategy together is critical to strategy learning, especially for less-successful comprehenders. During this time teachers can give feedback about students' attempts and gradually give students more and more responsibility for performing the strategy and evaluating their own performance (Pearson and Dole 1987). This is also the time when students can hear about one another's reasoning processes—another activity especially important for less strategic readers.

Authenticity of texts. Finally, students must be taught, reminded, and given time to practice comprehension strategies while reading everyday texts—not just specially constructed materials or short workbook passages. We would like to see real texts used more and earlier in comprehension strategy instruction. Using real texts, we believe, will increase the likelihood that students will transfer the use of taught strategies to their independent reading—and that, after all, is the ultimate goal of instruction.

OPPORTUNITIES FOR PEER AND COLLABORATIVE LEARNING

We are becoming more and more aware of the social aspects of instruction and their influence on cognitive outcomes. In addition to equity and the sense of community fostered through peer and collaborative learning, students gain access to one another's thinking processes.

Perhaps the most widely researched peer learning model is *cooperative learning.* This approach has been examined in a variety of academic disciplines (Johnson and Johnson 1985, Slavin 1987)—with the focus in a few cases on literacy learning, including comprehension (Meloth 1991, Stevens et al. 1987). A synthesis of this research suggests that cooperative learning is most effective when students clearly understand the teacher's goals, when goals are group-oriented and the criterion of success is satisfactory learning by each group member, when students are expected and taught to explain things to one another instead of just providing answers, and when group activities supplement rather than supplant teacher-directed instruction. At its best, cooperative learning has positive social and cognitive benefits for students of all abilities.

Other models of peer teaching also have been investigated—for example, *reciprocal teaching.* In this model, students take turns leading dialogues that involve summarizing, asking an important question about what was read, predicting information, and attempting to clarify confusions. Reciprocal teaching is effective when students, not just teachers, teach their peers to engage in these dialogues (Palincsar et al. 1987).

TIME TO TALK ABOUT READING

Some form of discussion or explication of a text has been a feature of reading classrooms for years, but traditional teacher-student discussions have been consistently criticized because they emphasize teacher control and learning a single interpretation. Critics have tended to advocate student-centered discussions that honor multiple interpretations. Cazden (1986) and many others noted a universal format of traditional teacher-student discussions, called the IRE format. The teacher *initiates* a question, a student *responds,* and the teacher *evaluates* the response before moving to another question.

Recently, various forms of teacher-student discussions have been geared toward achieving the following three goals.

1. *Changing teacher-student interaction patterns.* In the traditional recitation format, teachers choose the topics and, through feedback to students, control which student answers are viewed as correct and incorrect. One outcome of the recitation format is that teachers talk a lot! Typically, teachers talk as much as or more than all students combined, because their questions and feedback focus on transmitting the text interpretation they have in mind and because of the monitoring function that teachers naturally perform when they are in charge of a discussion.

Tharp and Gallimore (1989) use the terms *responsive teaching* and *instructional conversations* to contrast effective teacher-student dialogues with such recitations. In responsive teaching, teachers plan instruction by anticipating a range of student responses in addition to thinking about their own interpretations. They then use student input into discussions and student text interpretations to move the discussion to higher levels. Teachers might still nominate topics and opinions for group consideration, but student input drives the discussion forward.

Changing the pattern of classroom discussions to allow more student input and control is no easy task. Alvermann and Hayes (1989), for example, found that it was much easier for teachers to change the *level* of questions they asked (for example, move to more inferential, evaluative, and critical thinking questions) than it was for them to change the basic *structure* or pattern of interactions in classroom discussions. Teachers suggested two main reasons for the persistence of the recitation format in their classrooms: maintaining control and ensuring coverage of important information and canonical interpretations.

2. *Accepting personal interpretations and reactions.* A broader definition of comprehension, one that includes the possibility of multiple interpretations and the importance of readers' responses to their reading, is behind many of the changes proposed for discussions in recent years. This respect for individual response and interpretation has been nurtured by the growth in popularity of the response to literature tradition (Beach and Hynds 1991). In particular, Rosenblatt's (1978) distinction between *efferent reading*—that from which a reader gets information or basic meaning—and *aesthetic reading*—the actual lived-through experience of reading and responding personally to a text—has allowed us to treat reading experiences differentially. Recently, the process of allowing students to build, express, and defend their own interpretations has become a *revalued* goal of text discussions.

Eeds and her colleagues use the term *grand conversations* to describe literature discussions in which the teacher's role is to be a coequal in the discussion, instead of the leader of a *gentle inquisition* (Eeds and Wells 1989, Peterson and Eeds 1990). In this role, the teacher can capitalize on teachable moments, help clarify confusions, keep track of students' ideas, and suggest ideas for consideration without insisting on a unitary interpretation of the text.

A typical concern about such discussions is that students might spend a lot of time talking about personal reactions but come away from the discussion not really "understanding" what they have read or not having taken the opportunity to discuss important text features. In analyses of such discussions of literary texts, however, Eeds and Wells (1989) and others (Raphael et al. 1992, Rogers 1991) have found that students engage in a variety of activities important to understanding:

- using the whole range of responses, from literal to critical and evaluative;
- clarifying the basic meaning of the text when there are confusions or disagreements; and
- using the opinions of others—including classmates, teacher, and published critics—to help clarify their thinking about a text.

In some of these studies, writing also has been an important avenue for students to understand text: (a) by documenting their independent thinking before group discussion and, (b) by synthesizing information and figuring out how their thinking has changed after discussion.

3. *Embedding strategy instruction in text reading.* Even in teacher-student discussions focused around a shared understanding of important text information, new ideas are emerging about how to build this shared understanding in a way that will teach students something about comprehension as well as text information. For example, in *situated cognition* (Brown et al. 1989), learning about comprehension strategies is embedded in discussions about texts. The cognitive activities students engage in are much like the ones that have been the focus of research about explicit instruction in comprehension strategies, such as summarizing and getting the main idea. The difference is that the focus is on learning authentic information in the texts—for example, discovering how photosynthesis works by reading a chapter about it—with comprehension strategy learning as a secondary

outcome of repeated engagement in such discussions about many different texts. The belief is that students will internalize effective comprehension strategies through repeated situations in which they read and discuss whole texts with a teacher and peers.

A CALL FOR MULTIPLE APPROACHES

When we teach courses about reading instruction for preservice and inservice teachers, we sometimes hear the complaint that researchers seem to pit approaches against one another instead of exploring how a particular innovation might operate as part of a total program. This is a legitimate concern, because if innovations are viewed as dichotomous, children may end up with instruction that is deficient in some areas.

Anything less than a well-rounded instructional program is a form of discrimination against children who have difficulty with reading. Delpit (1988), for example, asserts that children from nonmainstream backgrounds deserve to be taught directly what their mainstream teachers want them to do in order to read and comprehend texts. Slavin (1987) contends that an important outcome of cooperative learning is that it eliminates the segregation along racial and socioeconomic lines that often accompanies ability grouping. And Stanovich (1986) argues that if less able readers continually are denied opportunities to read actual texts, they will inevitably fall further and further behind—the rich will get richer and the poor will get poorer. Clearly, then, multiple approaches to comprehension improvement are in order. To use the recent language of the standards debate, a full portfolio of teacher strategies designed to promote a full portfolio of student strategies could be construed as essential in meeting opportunity-to-learn standards.

We see no reason why all four of the components described here—ample time for actual text reading, teacher-directed comprehension strategy instruction, opportunities for peer and collaborative learning, and time to talk about what has been read—should not complement one another in the same classroom. Nor do we see why the appropriateness of any component would depend on whether the primary reading material is children's literature or basal readers. We do believe, however, that if our ultimate goal is to develop independent, motivated comprehenders who choose to read, then a substantial part of children's reading instructional time each day must be devoted to self-selected materials that are within the students' reach. It is through such reading that children can experience the successful comprehension, learning, independence, and interest that will motivate future reading.

REFERENCES

Allington, R. L. (1983a). "Fluency: The Neglected Reading Goal." *The Reading Teacher* 36: 556–561.

Allington, R. L. (1983b). "The Reading Instruction Provided Readers of Differing Reading Abilities." *Elementary School Journal* 83: 548–559.

Alvermann, D. E., and D. A. Hayes. (1989). "Classroom Discussion of Content Area Reading Assignments: An Intervention Study." *Reading Research Quarterly* 24: 305–335.

Anderson, R. C., E. H. Hiebert, J. A. Scott, and I. A. G. Wilkinson. (1985). *Becoming a Nation of Readers.* Washington, D. C.: National Institute of Education.

Anderson, R. C., L. Shirey, P. T. Wilson, and L. G. Fielding. (1987). "Interestingness of Children's Reading Material." In *Aptitude, Learning, and Instruction. Vol. 3: Conative and Affective Process Analyses,* edited by R. Snow and M. Farr. Hillsdale, N. J.: Erlbaum.

Anderson, R. C., P. T. Wilson, and L. G. Fielding. (1988). "Growth in Reading and How Children Spend Their Time Outside of School." *Reading Research Quarterly* 23: 285–303.

Armbruster, B. B., T. H. Anderson, and J. Ostertag. (1987). "Does Text Structure/Summarization Instruction Facilitate Learning From Expository Text?" *Reading Research Quarterly* 22: 331–346.

Atwell, N. (1987). *In the Middle.* Montclair, N. J.: Boynton/Cook.

Baumann, J. F. (1984). "Effectiveness of a Direct Instruction Paradigm for Teaching Main Idea Comprehension." *Reading Research Quarterly* 20: 93–108.

Beach, R., and S. Hynds. (1991). "Research on Response to Literature." In *Handbook of Reading Research: Vol. II,* edited by R. Barr, M. Kamil, P. Mosenthal, and P. D. Pearson. New York: Longman.

Beck, I. L., R. C. Omanson, and M. G. McKeown. (1982). "An Instructional Redesign of Reading Lessons: Effects on Comprehension." *Reading Research Quarterly* 17: 462–481.

Brown, J. S., A. Collins, and P. Duguid. (1989). "Situated Cognition and the Culture of Learning." *Educational Researcher* 18, 1: 32–42.

Cazden, C. (1986). "Classroom Discourse." In *Handbook of Research on Teaching,* 3rd ed., edited by M. C. Wittrock. New York: Macmillan.

Delpit, L. (1988). "The Silenced Dialogue: Power and Pedagogy in Educating Other People's Children." *Harvard Educational Review* 58, 3: 280–298.

Dowhower, S. L. (1987). "Effects of Repeated Reading on Second-Grade Transitional Readers' Fluency and Comprehension." *Reading Research Quarterly* 22: 389–406.

Duffy, G., L. Roehler, and B. Hermann. (1988). "Modeling Mental Processes Helps Poor Readers Become Strategic Readers." *The Reading Teacher* 41: 762–767.

Durkin, D. (1978–1979). "What Classroom Observations Reveal About Reading Comprehension Instruction." *Reading Research Quarterly* 15: 481–533.

Eeds, M., and D. Wells. (1989). "Grand Conversations: An Exploration of Meaning Construction in Literature Study Groups." *Research in the Teaching of English* 23: 4–29.

Elley, W. B. (1989). "Vocabulary Acquisition from Listening to Stories." *Reading Research Quarterly* 24: 174–187.

Fitzgerald, J., and D. L. Spiegel. (1983). "Enhancing Children's Reading Comprehension Through Instruction in Narrative Structure." *Journal of Reading Behavior* 15, 2: 1–17.

Hansen, J. (1987). *When Writers Read.* Portsmouth, N. H.: Heinemann.

Hansen, J., and P. D. Pearson. (1983). "An Instructional Study: Improving Inferential Comprehension of Good and Poor Fourth-Grade Readers." *Journal of Educational Psychology* 75: 821–829.

Johnson, D., and R. Johnson. (1985). "The Internal Dynamics of Cooperative Learning Groups." In *Learning to Cooperate, Cooperating to Learn,* edited by R. Slavin, S. Sharon, S. Kagan, R. Hertz-Lazarowitz, C. Webb, and R. Schmuck. New York: Plenum Press.

Koskinen, P., and I. Blum. (1986). "Paired Repeated Reading: A Classroom Strategy for Developing Fluent Reading." *The Reading Teacher* 40: 70–75.

Labbo, L., and W. Teale. (1990). "Cross-Age Reading: A Strategy for Helping Poor Readers." *The Reading Teacher* 43: 362–369.

Leinhardt, G., N. Zigmond, and W. Cooley. (1981). "Reading Instruction and Its Effects." *American Educational Research Journal* 18: 343–361.

Manning, G. L., and M. Manning. (1984). "What Models of Recreational Reading Make a Difference?" *Reading World* 23: 375–380.

Meloth, M. (1991). "Enhancing Literacy Through Cooperative Learning." In *Literacy for a Diverse Society: Perspectives, Practices, and Policies,* edited by E. Hiebert. New York: Teachers College Press.

Nagy, W. E., R. C. Anderson, and P. A. Herman. (1987). "Learning Word Meanings from Context During Normal Reading." *American Educational Research Journal* 24: 237–270.

Ogle, D. (1986). "K-W-L: A Teaching Model That Develops Active Reading of Expository Text." *The Reading Teacher* 39: 564–570.

Palincsar, A. S., A. L. Brown, and S. M. Martin. (1987). "Peer Interaction in Reading Comprehension Instruction." *Educational Psychologist* 22: 231–253.

Paris, S. G., B. A. Wasik, and J. C. Turner. (1991). "The Development of Strategic Readers." In *Handbook of Reading Research: Vol. II,* edited by R. Barr, M. Kamil, P. Mosenthal, and P. D. Pearson New York: Longman.

Pearson, P. D., and J. A. Dole. (1987). "Explicit Comprehension Instruction: A Review of Research and a New Conceptualization of Instruction." *Elementary School Journal* 88, 2: 151–165.

Pearson, P. D., and L. G. Fielding. (1991). "Comprehension Instruction." In *Handbook of Reading Research: Vol. II,* edited by R. Barr, M. Kamil, P. Mosenthal, and P. D. Pearson. New York: Longman.

Peterson, R., and M. Eeds. (1990). *Grand Conversations: Literature Groups in Action.* New York: Scholastic.

Raphael, T., S. McMahon, V. Goatley, J. Bentley, F. Boyd, L. Pardo, and D. Woodman. (1992). "Research Directions: Literature and Discussion in the Reading Program." *Language Arts* 69: 54–61.

Raphael, T. E., and P. D. Pearson. (1985). "Increasing Students' Awareness of Sources of Information for Answering Questions." *American Educational Research Journal* 22: 217–236.

Rogers, T. (1991). "Students as Literary Critics: The Interpretive Experiences, Beliefs, and Processes of Ninth-Grade Students." *Journal of Reading Behavior* 23: 391–423.

Rosenblatt, L. (1978). *The Reader, the Text, the Poem: The Transactional Theory of a Literary Work.* Carbondale, Ill.: Southern Illinois University Press.

Slavin, R. E. (1987). "Cooperative Learning and the Cooperative School." *Educational Leadership* 45, 3: 7–13.

Stallman, A. (1991). "Learning Vocabulary from Context: Effects of Focusing Attention on Individual Words During Reading." Doctoral diss., University of Illinois, Urbana-Champaign.

Stanovich, K. (1986). "Matthew Effects in Reading: Some Consequences of Individual Differences in the Acquisition of Literacy." *Reading Research Quarterly* 21: 360–407.

Stevens, R., N. Madden, R. Slavin, and A. Farnish. (1987). "Cooperative Integrated Reading and Composition: Two Field Experiments." *Reading Research Quarterly* 22: 433–454.

Tharp, R. G., and R. Gallimore. (1989). *Rousing Minds to Life: Teaching, Learning and Schooling in Social Context.* New York: Cambridge University Press.

Constructivist Cautions

PETER W. AIRASIAN and MARY E. WALSH

Recently, the concept of "constructivism" has been receiving a great deal of attention. At the conceptual level, constructivists debate such questions as, What is knowledge? What is teaching? What is learning? And is objectivity possible?[1] At the practical level, these complex issues have, in many cases, been reduced to catch phrases such as "Students construct their own knowledge" or the slightly narrower "Students construct their own knowledge based on their existing schemata and beliefs." Many efforts are under way to translate constructivist epistemology into classroom practices that will enable students to become "constructors of their own knowledge." While readily acknowledging that constructivism has made and will continue to make a significant contribution to educational theory and practice, we wish to sound a cautionary note about the euphoria surrounding constructivism.

WHAT IS CONSTRUCTIVISM?

Constructivism is an epistemology, a philosophical explanation about the nature of knowledge. Although constructivism might provide a model of knowing and learning that could be useful for educational purposes, at present the constructivist model is descriptive, not prescriptive. It describes in the broadest of strokes the human activity of knowing and nowhere specifies the detailed craft of teaching. It is important to understand at the outset that constructivism is not an instructional ap-

Peter W. Airasian and Mary E. Walsh are professors in the School of Education, Boston College, Chestnut Hill, MA.

proach; it is a theory about how learners come to know. Although instructional approaches are typically derived from such epistemologies, they are distinct from them. One of the concerns that prompted us to undertake this discussion is the rush to turn the constructivist epistemology into instructional practice with little concern for the pitfalls that are likely to ensue.

Constructivism describes how one attains, develops, and uses cognitive processes. Multiple theories, such as those of Piaget and Vygotsky, have been proposed to explain the cognitive processes that are involved in constructing knowledge. While constructivism provides the epistemological framework for many of these theories, it is not itself an explanation for the psychological factors involved in knowing.

In general, constructivists compare an "old" view of knowledge to a "new," constructivist view. In the old view, knowledge is considered to be fixed and independent of the knower. There are "truths" that reside outside the knower. Knowledge is the accumulation of the "truths" in a subject area. The more "truths" one acquires, the more knowledge one possesses. In sharp contrast, the constructivist view rejects the notion that knowledge is independent of the knower and consists of accumulating "truths." Rather, knowledge is produced by the knower from existing beliefs and experiences. All knowledge is constructed and consists of what individuals create and express. Since individuals make their own meaning from their beliefs and experiences, all knowledge is tentative, subjective, and personal. Knowledge is viewed not as a set of universal "truths," but as a set of "working hypotheses." Thus constructivists believe that knowledge can never be justified as "true" in an absolute sense.

Constructivism is based on the fundamental assumption that people create knowledge from the interaction between their existing knowledge or beliefs and the new ideas or situations they encounter. In this sense, most constructivists support the need to foster interactions between students' existing knowledge and new experiences. This emphasis is perceived to be different from the more traditional "transmission" model, in which teachers try to convey knowledge to students directly.

These fundamental agreements among constructivists are tempered by some important areas of difference about the process of constructing knowledge. These differences are reflected in two versions of constructivist theories of cognition: developmental and sociocultural. Developmental theories, such as Piaget's, represent a more traditional constructivist framework. Their major emphasis is on describing the universal forms or structures of knowledge (e.g., prelogical, concrete, and abstract operations) that guide the making of meaning. These universal cognitive structures are assumed to be developmentally organized, so that prelogical thinking occurs prior to concrete logical thinking in a developmental sequence. Within this framework, the individual student is considered to be the meaning maker, with the development of the individual's personal knowledge being the main goal of learning.

Critics of developmental theories of cognition point out that this perspective does not take into account "how issues such as the cultural and political nature of schooling and the race, class, and gender backgrounds of teachers and students, as well as their prior learning histories, influence the kinds of meaning that are made in the classroom."[2] Cognitive-developmental theories, it is claimed, divorce meaning making from affect by focusing on isolating universal forms of knowledge and thus limiting consideration of the sociocultural and contextual influences on the construction of knowledge.[3]

A second version of constructivism is reflected in the social constructivist or situated social constructivist perspective. As its name suggests, this type of constructivism puts its major emphasis on the social construction of knowledge and rejects the individualistic orientation of Piagetian theory. Within the sociocultural perspective, knowledge is seen as constructed by an individual's interaction with a social milieu in which he or she is situated, resulting in a change in both the individual and the milieu. Of course, it is possible for an individual to "reside" in many milieus, from a classroom milieu through a much more general cultural milieu. The point, however, is that social constructivists believe that knowledge has a social component and cannot be considered to be generated by an individual acting independently of his or her social context.[4] Consequently, recognition of the social and cultural influences on constructed knowledge is a primary emphasis. Because individual social and cultural contexts differ, the meanings people make may be unique to themselves or their cultures, potentially resulting in as many meanings as there are meaning makers. Universal meanings across individuals are not emphasized.

Critics of this perspective have pointed to the chaos that might be inherent in a multiplicity of potential meanings. While the social constructivists' concern with particular contextual or cultural factors that shape meaning enhances their recognition of differences across meanings, it limits their recognition of the universal forms that bring order to an infinite variety of meanings. Arguably, the critics of each version of constructivism exaggerate the positions espoused by these theories; however, they do set into relief the relative emphasis of each theory on the individual or the context.

This brief overview of constructivism omits many of the nuances and issues that characterize the debate over constructivist theory. However, our purpose is not to provide an in-depth portrait of constructivism, but rather to identify fundamental tenets that most constructivists would endorse and to point out that constructivism is not a unitary viewpoint. This latter fact is often overlooked in practice-oriented activities that derive from the slogan "Students are constructors of their own knowledge." The conflict between the two versions of constructivism is not merely "a matter of theoretical contemplation. Instead, it finds expression in tensions endemic to the act of teaching."[5] The particular version of constructivism one adopts—developmental or social constructivist—has important implications for classroom practices,[6] for the definition of knowledge,[7] for the relative emphasis on individual versus social learning,[8] for the role of the teacher,[9] and for the definition of successful instruction.[10]

WHY IS CONSTRUCTIVISM SO READILY ACCEPTED?

In the broad sense, constructivism represents a shift in the perspective of the social sciences and humanities from a view in which truth is a given to a view in which it is constructed by individuals and groups. There has been an inevitable spillover of this view from the social sciences and the humanities to education.

However, most educational theories and innovations are adopted with high levels of uncertainty. The wisdom of their adoption and the range of their impact are rarely known in advance of their implementation. Thus the justification for adopting a theory or innovation must come from outside the theory or innovation per se.[11] Typically, the justification is supplied by the existence of a pressing need or problem that requires quick amelioration or by the moral symbolism inherent in the theory or innovation. This is as true for constructivism as it has been for all educational theories and innovations that have sought to make their way into practice. However, it is very important to emphasize that there is a crucial difference between evidence that documents the need for change and evidence that documents the efficacy of a particular strategy of change. The specific strategy selected to produce change must seek its own validation, independent of the evidence of the need for change of some kind.

To understand its rapid acceptance, we must examine both present educational needs and the symbolic aspects of constructivism. The pressing educational need that fuels interest in constructivism is the perception that what we have been doing in schools has failed to meet the intellectual and occupational needs of the majority of our students; schools seem not to be promoting a sufficiently broad range of student outcomes. In particular, "thinking" or "higher-order" skills are not receiving sufficient instructional emphasis. A large part of the explanation for the perceived deficiency in pupil learning is thought to be an emphasis on "reductionist" or rote outcomes and forms of instruction. Reorienting instruction to nonrote outcomes makes such skills as generalizing, analyzing, synthesizing, and evaluating very important. From an instructional point of view, it puts much more of the onus on the student to construct personal meanings and interpretations. There is a link, then, between an epistemology that focuses on students' constructing their own knowledge and an education system that seeks to promote higher-level learning outcomes.

Also linking constructivism and educational need is the current emphasis on bottom-up as opposed to top-down approaches to reform. Thus recent reforms have increasingly allocated discretion for reforming the educational process to individual schools, teachers, students, and parents. In particular, teachers are given more discretion to construct their own meanings and interpretations of what will improve classroom teaching and learning. Moreover, because constructivism is an epistemology of how people learn, its focus is logically on classroom practice. The increased teacher discretion over teaching and learning, combined with the classroom orientation and higher-level focus of constructivism, has sparked teachers' interest in the potential of constructivism for classroom practice.

Of course, it is not just increased teacher discretion and the classroom focus of constructivism that prompt interest. Constructivism is also appealing for other, more symbolic reasons. First, the rhetoric that surrounds constructivism is seductive. It plays off the metaphor of "lighting the flame" of student motivation (constructivism) against that of "filling the bucket" of students' heads with facts (present methods).[12] Constructivists claim that they emphasize autonomy as opposed to obedience, construction as opposed to instruction, and interest as opposed to reinforcement.[13] The implication is that, if one is opposed to constructivism, one is opposed to student autonomy, construction of meaning, and interest. Thus opponents are viewed as being against lighting the flame of student motivation. Such rhetoric plays a potent role in the reception of all innovations, including constructivism.

Second, since knowledge consists of what is constructed by the learner and since attainment of absolute truth is viewed as impossible, constructivism makes the implicit assumption that all students can and will learn—that is, construct knowledge. The vision of the constructivist student is one of activity, involvement, creativity, and the building of personal knowledge and understanding. This is an appealing symbol in an education system that is perceived to be inadequate for meeting the learning needs of many students. However, our consideration of constructivism should extend beyond process to an examination of the nature of the knowledge actually constructed.

Third, in a variety of ways and with a variety of potential consequences, constructivism symbolizes emancipation. From one perspective, constructivism can be interpreted as a symbol of the emancipation of teachers from the primary responsibility for student learning, since constructivism passes the onus of creating or acquiring knowledge from the teacher to the student. This notion is mistaken. The teacher will no longer be a supplier of information, but he or she will remain very much involved in the learning process, coordinating and critiquing student constructions, building his or her own knowledge of constructivism in the classroom, and learning new methods of instruction. Constructivism can also be interpreted as a symbol of the emancipation of teachers from the burden of dealing with the difficult issue of motivation, since many constructivists view the student's sense of ownership of and empowerment over the learning process as providing its own intrinsic motivation.[14]

Constructivism certainly is emancipatory and dovetails well with the agendas of many interest groups through its social constructivist emphasis on context as a critical feature of knowledge construction. When context becomes an important aspect of knowledge construction, it is logical to conclude that involvement in different contexts will lead to the construction of different knowledge, even if the same set of "data" is presented in the different contexts. Given a problem or an issue, a context—which is often designated in social, economic, racial, and gender terms—will influence the interpretations, conclusions, motives, and attitudes of individuals in that context. When confronted with the same problem or issue, individuals in different milieus may construct different interpretations and conclusions. In this case, "truth" becomes what those in a given milieu construct. And since different milieus vary in their constructions and since there is no absolute truth to search for, knowledge becomes relative to the milieu one inhabits.

This view is certainly symbolically emancipatory for many disempowered groups, but with what effect on the classroom? It would be naive to ignore the sociopolitical agendas and potential consequences for education that constructivism can evoke, particularly those emanating from the social constructivist version of constructivism.

Thus there are strong forces that underlie the growing interest in and acceptance of the constructivist epistemology. These forces stem from the perceived need to alter educational practice from an associational approach to one that emphasizes the higher-level knowledge construction needed to cope with the rapid expansion of information. They also stem from symbolic features of constructivism, particularly the symbols associated with the rhetoric of constructivism.

CAUTIONS

Despite the persuasiveness of the above forces, it is important to be aware that the application of constructivism in classrooms is neither widespread nor systemic. This is not to suggest that there are no successful applications of constructivism. In fact, a number of writers have described approaches to constructivist teaching in special education classrooms, in largely African American classrooms, and in afterschool programs.[15] With the exception of Ann Brown's Community of Learning schools, however, most applications of constructivism have tended to be recent, narrowly focused pilot studies. In discussing her ongoing work, even Brown indicates that, "for the past 10 years or so, my colleagues and I have been gradually evolving learning environments [to foster grade school pupils' interpretive communities]."[16] Accentuating the need for gradual development is important, because in simultaneously mounting constructivist teaching and endeavoring to remain faithful to constructivist tenets, teachers and administrators will be confronted with a number of obstacles and issues.

We turn now to some cautions that need to be kept in mind as teachers attempt to implement constructivism in their classrooms. Some of these cautions are pertinent to any classroom innovation. Others are specific to constructivism.

Do not fail to recognize the difference between an epistemology of learning and a well-thought-out and manageable instructional approach for implementing it. We do not have an "instruction of constructivism" that can be readily applied in classrooms. There are suggestions for methods that are likely to foster student construction of knowledge, primarily those that emphasize nonrote tasks and active student participation in the learning process (e.g., cooperative learning, performance assessments, product-oriented activities, and "hands-on" learning, as well as reciprocal teaching and initiation-reply-evaluation methods). However, it is not clear how such methods relate to learning in different content areas or whether these methods will be equally successful across all subject areas.[17]

It is even more important to recognize that the selection of a particular instructional strategy represents only part of what is necessary in the constructivist approach. Selection of a strategy does not necessarily lead to appropriate implementation or to the provision of individual feedback to students regarding their constructions. Implementing constructivism calls for a "learn as you go" approach for both students and teachers; it involves many decisions and much trial and error. Commenting on the relevance of this theory for contemporary practices and procedures in education, Kenneth Gergen writes:

> There is no means by which practical derivatives can simply be squeezed from a theory of knowledge. As has been seen, theories can specify neither the particulars to which they must be applied nor the contexts in which they may be rendered intelligible. There are no actions that follow necessarily from a given theory. . . . Thus, rather than seeking clear and compelling derivatives of constructionist theory, we should explore the kinds of practices that would be favored by the perspective within current conventions of understanding.[18]

Do not fall into the trap of believing that constructivist instructional techniques provide the sole means by which students construct meanings. This is not the case. Students construct their own knowledge and interpretations no matter what instructional approach is implemented and no matter what name is given to it. What teacher has not taught a didactic, rote-oriented topic or concept only to find that the students constructed a variety of very different meanings from those anticipated by the teacher? Thus no single teaching method ought to be used exclusively. One of the leading advocates of constructivism in education has compellingly argued that, from a constructivist point of view, it is a misunderstanding to consider teaching methods such as memorization and rote learning useless. "There are, indeed, matters that can and perhaps must be learned in a purely mechanical way."[19] One's task is to find the right balance between the activities of constructing and receiving knowledge, given that not all aspects of a subject can or should be taught in the same way or be acquired solely through "hands-on" or student-centered means.

Because students always make their own meaning from instruction, the important curricular and instructional choice is not a choice between making and not making personal meaning from instructional activities, but a choice among the ideas, concepts, and issues that we want our students to construct meaning about. It is in this area that states such as Kentucky, California, and Vermont, among others, are redefining the expectations for student learning and reinforcing those expectations through statewide assessments. Similarly, it is in this area that such organizations as the National Council of Teachers of Mathematics are promulgating and advocating newer, more performance-oriented goals in their subject areas. The issues addressed by states and professional organizations are much more focused on the outcomes than on the means of instruction.

Do not assume that a constructivist orientation will make the same demands on teaching time as a nonconstructivist orientation. Time is an extremely important consideration in implementing constructivist education in two regards.

1. *Time is needed for teachers and pupils to learn and practice how to perform in a constructivist classroom.* If criticisms of "reductionist" education are valid, then substituting another approach, whether in part or in toto, will call for a redefinition of both teachers' and students' roles. In a constructivist approach, teachers will have to learn to guide, not tell; to create environments in which students can make their own meanings, not be handed them by the teacher; to accept diversity in constructions, not search for the one "right" answer; to modify prior notions of "right" and "wrong," not stick to rigid standards and criteria; to create a safe, free, responsive environment that encourages disclosure of student constructions, not a closed, judgmental system.

Students will also have to learn new ways to perform. They will have to learn to think for themselves, not wait for the teacher to tell them what to think; to proceed with less focus and direction from the teacher, not to wait for explicit teacher directions; to express their own ideas clearly in their own words, not to answer restricted-response questions; to revisit and revise constructions, not to move immediately on to the next concept or idea.

It is easy to *say* that constructivist teachers must create an open, nonjudgmental environment that permits students to construct, disclose, and expose their constructions to scrutiny. But listening and responding to student constructions will be difficult and time-consuming.[20] Teachers will have to become accustomed to working with quite different and more general goals, since the instructional emphasis will be on the viability of varied, idiosyncratic student constructions. Teachers will need to serve as initiators of activities that will evoke students' interest and lead to new constructions and as critics of the constructions that students produce. In a sense, much of the responsibility for learning will be turned over to the students through "hands-on" experiences and activities designed to spur their constructions of meaning. The more teachers become engaged in this process, the more the resulting constructions will be theirs, not the students'.

Finding a balance between teacher involvement or noninvolvement in the process of learning will be a challenge. It is legitimate to ask how well—and how soon—teachers will be able to create such an environment and reorient their practice. In this regard it is noteworthy that, with few exceptions,[21] there is considerably less discussion about the role and activities of the *teacher* in constructivist education than there is about the role and activities of the *students*. But changes in orientation for both teacher and students will not occur immediately, especially for those who have had a long time to become accustomed to the current norms of classroom practice. New ways of thinking, acting, organizing, and judging will always take time to develop.

2. *In the shift to constructivist teaching, considerable time will be required for responding to the individual constructions of students.* Student constructions have two important properties: (1) they are complex in form, and (2) they differ from student to student. Because constructions represent understandings and connections between prior and new knowledge, they cannot be conveyed in a word or a phrase. To convey one's construction of meaning will require an in-depth presentation about one's knowledge and how one arrived at or justifies that knowledge. If constructions are reduced to multiple-choice items or to some other truncated representational form, the richness and meaning of constructivism will be lost. Hence, to review, understand, and respond to student constructions will require substantial teacher time and perhaps the involvement of parents and community members as well.

Moreover, different students are likely to produce quite different constructions, making it difficult to apply the same frame of reference to the review of their constructions. Each construction and its underlying logic will need to be examined, understood, and reviewed. Hence, the amount of time needed to respond to these constructions will be further increased. Responding to student constructions will be more like reading essays or viewing oral reports than like scoring multiple-choice or short-answer tests.

Implicit in the need for increased time are other important time-related issues, such as the tradeoff between coverage and depth. It is likely that the quality of students' knowledge constructions will depend in part on the time they are given to construct. More time will mean richer and deeper constructions. Teachers and schools will have to face the question of whether it is better to cover a large amount of content at a rather shallow level or to cover a smaller amount of content in great depth. The constructivist approach fits much better with the latter choice, since it aims for personal meaning and understanding, not rote associations.

Do not believe that the opposite of "one-right-answer" reductionism is "anything-goes" constructivism. Implicit in any form of classroom instruction guided by any theory of learning is the need for standards and criteria of judgment. This matter is both important and challenging in constructivist thought and application. Among the questions that constructivist teachers will have to confront regarding standards and criteria are: On what basis should students have to justify their constructions? Can the teacher who facilitates the constructions also be an objective evaluator of them? What constitutes a "reasonable" or "acceptable" student construction? Should the teacher try to avoid transmitting standards and criteria that end up influencing or controlling the nature of student constructions? If so, how? Are evaluation standards and criteria independent of context or are they contextually bound?

A teacher who accepts the constructivist tenet that knowledge is constructed by individuals and that knowledge and experience are subjective must inevitably face the relationship between truth and meaning. In practical terms, the teacher must decide how much emphasis will be placed on the relative "truthfulness" of students' constructions or on their "meaningfulness" to the student. Since there is no one best construction and since people must construct their own meanings from personal experiences and understandings, there are many viable constructions.[22] Further, if it is assumed that knowledge is ego- and context-specific, the likelihood of agreeing on common standards of evaluation is diminished greatly. This perspective could create many problems when applied in classrooms.

A rejoinder to this view argues that the lack of one best construction does not mean that some constructions cannot be deemed better than others. Moreover, sole reliance on personal meaning to justify constructions leads to rampant relativism and potentially biased, self-serving, and dishonest constructions.[23] In this view, the role of the teacher is to challenge students to justify and refine their constructions in order to strengthen them.

At the opposite end of the spectrum from meaningfulness is truthfulness. Absolute certainty is alien to the tenets of constructivism. However, there can be intermediate positions between absolute and relative truthfulness. Thus it is possible to evaluate some constructions as being more truthful (i.e., reasonable) than others. If a position of modified or relative truthfulness is adopted, as it inevitably will be in real classrooms, the teacher is directly confronted by the need to establish standards and criteria for evaluating the merits of students' constructions.

However, in facing this need, the teacher also faces an issue that should be approached with awareness and caution. In evaluating some constructions as being better than others, the teacher will find that the more explicit the evaluation standards and criteria, the greater the likelihood that they will be transmitted to and adopted by the students. When standards and criteria are constructed jointly by teachers, students, and parents, transmission and adoption become desirable. However, if the teacher is the sole determiner of standards and criteria, he or she is likely to have the primary influence on the nature of classroom constructions. Students may not construct meaning on their own, for they know that high grades derive from meeting the teacher's standards and criteria. Constructivism is thus compromised. The problem of guiding and evaluating students without undermining their constructivist activities is a thorny one. The development of standards and criteria that are clear but that allow variance in evaluation is paramount, and each teacher will have to find his or her appropriate balance, given that few external guidelines for defining such standards and criteria exist.

In the preceding discussion we have pointed out the difference between the theory of constructivism and its practical application. In particular, we have argued that the consequences of implementing constructivism in the classroom will be considerably more challenging than might be anticipated from the simple slogans that advocates repeat. But our comments and cautions should not be taken as criticisms of the constructivist viewpoint. Indeed, we recognize and appreciate the positive role that this orientation can play in changing educational practice. Rather, our comments are meant to illuminate and anticipate important issues that will inevitably arise in attempts to implement constructivism in practical, classroom settings. These are not reasons to avoid trying to implement constructivism; they are efforts to help readers know something about what they are adopting at a more substantive level. Knowing some of the nuances and problems of a theory or innovation makes one better able to move beyond rhetoric to consider the implications for one's own practice.

NOTES

1. Richard S. Prawat, "Teachers' Beliefs About Teaching and Learning: A Constructivist Perspective," *American Journal of Education*, vol. 100, 1992, pp. 354–95; Carl Bereiter, "Constructivism, Socioculturalism, and Popper's World 3," *Educational Researcher*, October 1994, pp. 21–23; Rosalind Driver et al., "Constructing Scientific Knowledge in the Classroom," *Educational Researcher*, October 1994, pp. 5–12; and Neil M. Agnew and John L. Brown, "Foundations for a Model of Knowing: II. Fallible but Functional Knowledge," *Canadian Psychology*, vol. 30, 1989, pp. 168–83.

2. Michael O'Loughlin, "Rethinking Science Education: Beyond Piagetian Constructivism Toward a Sociocultural Model of Teaching and Learning," *Journal of Research in Science Teaching*, vol. 29, 1992, p.792.

3. Martin L. Hoffman, "Development of Moral Thought, Feeling, and Behavior," *American Psychologist*, vol. 34, 1979, pp. 958–66.

4. Kenneth J. Gergen, "Exploring the Postmodern: Perils or Potentials," *American Psychologist*, vol. 49, 1994, pp. 412–16; and James V. Wertsch and Chikako Toma, "Discourse and Learning in the Classroom: A Sociocultural Approach," in Leslie P. Steffe and Jerry Gale, eds., *Constructivism in Education* (Hillsdale, N.J.: Erlbaum, 1995), pp. 159–74.

5. Paul Cobb, "Where Is the Mind? Constructivist and Sociocultural Perspectives on Mathematical Development," *Educational Researcher*, October 1994, p. 13.

6. Deborah L. Ball, "With an Eye on the Mathematical Horizon: Dilemmas of Teaching Elementary School Mathematics," *Elementary School Journal*, vol. 93, 1993, pp. 373–97.

7. Virginia Richardson, "Constructivist Teaching: Theory and Practice," paper presented at the annual meeting of the American Educational Research Association, New Orleans, 1994; and Bereiter, op. cit.

8. Driver et al., op. cit.

9. Ibid.

10. Ginnette Delandshire and Anthony J. Petrosky, "Capturing Teachers' Knowledge: Performance Assessment," *Educational Researcher*, June/July 1994, pp. 11–18.

11. Peter W. Airasian, "Symbolic Validation: The Case of State-Mandated, High-Stakes Testing," *Educational Evaluation and Policy Analysis*, vol. 4, 1988, pp. 301–13.

12. David Elkind, "Spirituality in Education," *Holistic Education Review*, vol. 5, no. 1, 1992, pp. 12–16.

13. Rhete DeVries and Lawrence Kohlberg, *Constructivist Early Education* (Washington, D.C.: National Association for the Education of Young Children, 1987).

14. Aire W. Kruglanski, *Lay Epistemics and Human Knowledge* (New York: Plenum Press, 1989); Penny Oldfather, "Sharing the Ownership of Knowing: A Constructivist Concept of Motivation for Literacy Learning," paper presented at the annual meeting of the National Reading Conference, San Antonio, 1992; and O'Loughlin, op. cit.

15. Ann Brown, "The Advancement of Learning," *Educational Researcher*, November 1994, pp. 4–12; Richardson, op. cit.; Gloria Ladson-Billing, *The Dreamkeepers: Successful Teaching of African-American Children* (San Francisco: Jossey-Bass, 1994); and Wertsch and Toma, op. cit.

16. Brown, "Advancement of Learning," p. 7.

17. Susan S. Stodolsky, *The Subject Matters* (Chicago: University of Chicago Press, 1988); and Cobb, op. cit.

18. Kenneth Gergen, "Social Construction and the Educational Process," in Steffe and Gale, pp. 17–39.

19. Ernst von Glasersfeld, "A Constructivist Approach to Teaching," in Steffe and Gale, p. 5.

20. Peter W. Airasian, "Critical Pedagogy and the Realities of Teaching," in Henry Perkinson, *Teachers Without Goals, Students Without Purposes* (New York: McGraw-Hill, 1993), pp. 81–93.

21. See, for example, Brown, "The Advancement of Learning"; and Ladson-Billing, op. cit.

22. Geraldine Gilliss, "Schön's Reflective Practitioner: A Model for Teachers?" in Peter Grimmett and Gaalen Erickson, eds., *Reflection in Teacher Education* (New York: Teachers College Press, 1988), pp. 47–54.

23. Bereiter, op. cit.; and Karl Popper, *Objective Knowledge: An Evolutionary Approach* (Oxford: Clarendon, 1972).

Chapter 10: Motivation—Issues and Explanations

Sorting Out the Self-Esteem Controversy

JAMES A. BEANE

The idea of enhancing self-esteem seems innocent enough to most people. Common sense suggests that those who have positive self-esteem are likely to lead satisfying lives while those who do not are just as likely to find life dissatisfying and unhappy. Yet, like so many other seemingly common-sensical things, the idea of self-esteem has become a source of considerable controversy and contention in the school context. So it is that, as we enter the 1990s, another "great debate" is emerging. This one is about whether schools ought to try to enhance self-esteem and, if so, how, on what grounds, and to what extent?

That the school might play a role in the development of self-esteem is not a recent idea. It has been part of educational thinking for most of this century, particularly since the 1960s, when many educators came to realize that affect in general and self-esteem specifically loom large in school life.[1] But it was in the 1980s that self-esteem was catapulted into educational policy thinking. It became linked not only to academic achievement but also to substance abuse, antisocial acts, adolescent pregnancy, suicide, and other self-destructive behaviors. The theory was this: people, including the young, will not hurt themselves if they like themselves. Moreover, if they have self-confidence, they are more likely to do well at whatever they might try to do.

James A. Beane is a Professor in the National College of Education at National-Louis University, Evanston, Ill. He can be reached at 928 West Shore Dr., Madison, WI 53715.

This theory has driven many states and school districts to add development of self-esteem to their list of goals. It also served as the underlying theme of the notorious California self-esteem project that simultaneously appealed to the most humane impulses of some while offending the Puritan streak of self-denial that still runs deep in the values of others.[2] Meanwhile, in the schools, the terrain is cluttered with conflicting and contradictory theories about self-esteem and ways to enhance it. The purpose of this article is to sort out this "mess" and to make some sense out of the idea of enhancing self-esteem in schools.

WHY ENHANCE SELF-ESTEEM?

The argument for enhancing self-esteem in schools follows three lines of reasoning. The first speaks to the school's role as a social agency that is meant to contribute to the general health and well-being of young people. We are living in very complex times. This is the age of discontinuity and disbelief, of ambiguity and ambivalence. As difficult as it is for so many adults to find anything to hang on to, we can only imagine what this age looks like through the eyes of young people who typically lack the resources that are available to most adults. The litany of statistics about self-destructive tendencies such as substance abuse, crime, and suicide must surely be seen as a signal from young people that many do not find much about themselves to like. The idea of

161

enhancing self-esteem becomes a moral imperative for schools, especially in a time when other social institutions and agencies seem unwilling or unable to provide support and encouragement in the process of growing up.

The second line of reasoning is found within the school itself. When we look at the growing collection of studies on self-esteem, we find a persistent correlation between it and such school concerns as participation, completion, self-direction, and various types of achievement.[3] This last correlation, between self-esteem and achievement, is a driving force in the growing interest in self-esteem. Nonetheless, it is widely misunderstood. The correlation is relatively weak when global self-esteem is involved but strong when self-esteem is situation-specific, as in the case, for example, of self-esteem in mathematics, reading, physical education, or some other area.[4] This link between self-esteem and school concerns ought to persuade those who have trouble with the moral argument that they, too, have a vested interest in enhancing self-esteem.

The third line of reasoning is less often used, yet more powerful. It extends the idea of personal development beyond coping with problems and into personal efficacy or power, which, in turn, may lead toward action.[5] Only the most ignorant or arrogant could fail to see that we face increasing problems with inequitable distribution of wealth, power, and justice. Conditions like racism, sexism, poverty, and homelessness detract from human dignity and for that reason debilitate one of its central features, self-esteem. The resolution of these issues will depend less on rhetoric and more on action, but action is not likely unless people believe they can make a difference.

When looked at this way, enhancing self-esteem helps build the personal and collective efficacy that helps us out of the morass of inequity that plagues us. Needless to say, the hint of social reconstructionism in this line of reasoning may account for its absence in most of the rhetoric of the self-esteem movement. Nevertheless it is a powerful argument for the schools, which have a responsibility to extend democracy, human dignity, and cultural diversity throughout the larger society.

VERSIONS OF SELF-ESTEEM IN SCHOOL

Over the past few decades, the idea of enhancing self-esteem in schools has become increasingly pop-

ular. True, many school officials have questioned the idea by contending they have enough on their hands, with the deluge of mandates coming down from state legislatures, without having to take on issues that ought to be addressed by the home and other "socializing" agencies. Certainly not all of these people are uncaring toward young people; often they speak out of frustration over multiplying demands placed upon the school and taking the flack for any lack of progress on these demands. Even so, such protests have diminished as the evidence linking self-esteem and school success has grown.

Now the issue is not *whether* the schools should try to enhance the self-esteem of young people, but *how*. It is here that we encounter the cluttered terrain of conflicting and contradictory methods for enhancing self-esteem. There are three main approaches that account for most efforts in this area.

The first approach follows from personal development activities, such as sensitivity training, that enjoyed some popularity in the late 1960s and early 1970s. To envision how this approach is practiced, we might picture a teacher and a group of students sitting in a circle talking about how much they like themselves and everyone else for 20 minutes on a Wednesday afternoon. Such activities are like parlor games of pop psychology and, no doubt, have about the same momentary effects in real life. Saying "I like myself and others" in front of a group is not necessarily the same as actually feeling that way, especially if I am only doing it because I am supposed to. Being nice has a place in enhancing self-esteem, but it is not enough.

The second approach involves putting young people through a self-esteem program or course offered in a set-aside time slot during the school day. Here the teacher comes armed with more than good feelings, namely a self-esteem "curriculum," locally prepared or commercially purchased, assuring that students who go through the program will have better self-esteem and thus be immune to self-destructive behaviors and school failure. In 1970 Weinstein and Fantini estimated that there were at least 350 such programs with about 3,000 "affective exercises and techniques."[6] The number may be greater now, although I estimate that about 30 are widely known and used.[7] That schools would buy a package to enhance self-esteem is not surprising when we remember that the commodification of the self was an idea promoted in the 1980s. If "we are what we buy," then perhaps we can also buy our way into self-esteem.

The "self-esteem program" approach suffers from two problems, one practical and the other conceptual. Hartshorne and May, in the late 1920s, showed that direct instruction in courselike settings does not produce lasting or strong effects in the affective domain.[8] While their research focused on character education, similar conclusions were drawn more recently by Lockwood and others in reviewing studies on values clarification and moral development.[9] Aside from glowing testimonials by participants (which cannot be completely disregarded) after self-esteem programs, there is scant evidence to warrant claims made by program developers.

Current research suggests that one area in which packaged programs evidence little short-term gain is "self in school."[10] This may seem hard to believe when we remember that such programs are sponsored and taught in schools by school personnel. Yet why would we expect otherwise if there is no guarantee that anyone in any other place in the school will care much about newfound self-esteem, personal goals, or decision-making skills?

Beyond that, self-esteem programs suffer from a conceptual problem that they share with most personal development programs. Their underlying theory is that to enhance self-esteem we must go inside individuals and encourage them to push ahead with confidence, even in the face of difficult odds. Such an inside-out approach ignores the fact that in the balance of interactions between the individual and the environment out of which self-esteem grows, the environment is almost inevitably more powerful. If we want to enhance self-esteem, we must first check to see whether the social environment is safe for the individual. A debilitating environment is likely to squash fledgling self-confidence no matter how much we exhort the individual to persist. We may all know individuals who have defied this rule, but the fact that we can name them suggests they are the exception rather than the rule.

Since the environment powerfully informs their self-perceptions, insisting that young people are responsible for their own self-esteem is blatantly unjust. Moreover, suggesting that self-esteem can be preserved by developing "coping skills" endorses the status quo and, in so doing, ignores the fact that having positive self-esteem is almost impossible for many young people, given the deplorable conditions under which they are forced to live by the inequities in our society.

The third approach to enhancing self-esteem in school recognizes the power of the environment and searches for possibilities across the whole institution.[11] Every nook and cranny in the school has the potential to enhance or debilitate self-esteem.

For example, a school that enhances self-esteem could be characterized by a humanistic and democratic climate, student participation in governance, heterogeneous grouping, and positive expectations. In the areas of curriculum and teaching, a premium would be placed upon collaborative teacher-student planning, cooperative learning, thematic units that emphasize personal and social meanings, student self-evaluation, multicultural content, community service projects, and activities that involve making, creating, and "doing." This approach also emphasizes the need to enhance adults' self-esteem, particularly teachers', since it is unlikely they can contribute to positive self-esteem in young people if their own is negative.

Proponents of this third approach recognize that even our most salutary efforts in the area of self-esteem are threatened by poor conditions outside the school. To what extent can we expect progress within the school to stand up in the face of poverty, homelessness, racism, sexism, and ageism? Hence, we must place the larger community and society under the same scrutiny as the school, so that we may see what work is needed there.

THE GREAT SELF-ESTEEM DEBATE

Recently the argument over which approach to use in enhancing self-esteem has been overshadowed by a much larger debate concerning the assumption that positive self-esteem is necessary for school achievement. Three factors fuel this debate. First, it seems that while young people in South Korea and Japan score higher than those in the United States on international comparison tests in mathematics, the U.S. students come out on top in measures of self-esteem.[12] Second, there has been considerable backlash against the California task force report on self-esteem, which is seen by many people as an unsupported statement of New Age, pop psychology "fluff."[13] Third, the present Conservative Restoration in education and elsewhere rings with the rhetoric of self-denial that those of the New Right believe is necessary for "repairing" the "frayed" moral fabric of society.[14] Put together, these factors make a superficially convincing argument against the usual view of enhancing self-esteem, yet one that can be packaged in neat slogans like the title of a *Time* magazine commentary, "Education: Doing Bad and Feeling Good."[15]

However, when this rhetoric is examined, its transparency is revealed. For example, I asked some South Korean, Japanese, and Chinese educators to explain how they might account for the inverse correlation between self-esteem and mathematics scores reported from the international comparisons of achievement. Their uncomplicated answer was this: "In our cultures it is impolite to say one can do well, even if one thinks so." While this is not evidence to end the argument, it at least raises the question of whether United States' students are arrogant incompetents or victims of criticism based upon culturally embedded differences in educational findings.[16]

As for the other two factors, we might easily write off the first as an interpretation of a report (that of the California Task Force) that represents a sometimes unclear vision of enhancing self-esteem[17] and the second as another piece of the belt-tightening rhetoric of 1980s educational "reform." We might further ask when and how young people were excluded from the right to be happy. And one might facetiously suggest that the international tests indicate that we who value self-esteem are doing a good job with it while those enamored with academic achievement are not pulling their weight. These criticisms should not be taken so lightly, however, because they have deeper implications.

First, by focusing only on the pop psychology school of enhancing self-esteem, these criticisms ignore other versions which are quite different from it. In so doing, the very idea of self-esteem enhancement is threatened by the same red-flag mentality that fails to differentiate between the cross-curriculum values clarification theory and the collections of cute activities, like the venerable "lifeboat" simulation, that ruined its reputation.

Even more dangerous is the kind of statement made by critic Mike Schmoker: "Self-esteem, as it is now used, isn't something earned, but given."[18] "The fact is that it is neither. In its practical form, self-esteem is personally constructed out of interactions with the environment; in other words, it is learned. At a conceptual level self-esteem is a central feature in human dignity and thus an inalienable human entitlement."[19] As such, schools and other agencies have a moral obligation to help build it and avoid debilitating it. The "no pain, no gain" metaphor may be justified in the weight room, but it is dangerous in human development, especially when pain is already inequitably distributed and gain so inequitably accessible. The failure to recognize the obligation to enhance self-esteem works harshly against all young people, but particularly so against those in our society who are least privileged.

So that I do not seem to be imagining this last point, another illustration from the self-esteem critics might be helpful. One of the more obvious ways to contribute to clear self-concept and positive self-esteem is to expand curriculum content in ways that include the stories of diverse cultures so that more young people can see themselves as part of what is valued in the school's curriculum. Yet Krauthammer, for example, extends his concern about self-esteem enhancement into an attack on multicultural inclusion in the curriculum. Among other things, he claims "there is little to be said . . . about the contribution of women to the Bill of Rights."[20] Perhaps so, but there is much to be said about why; and young people, especially women, should not be denied the opportunity to find out. Nor should all young people, especially Native Americans, be left ignorant of the influence of the "Great Law of the Iroquois" on early documents of white, United States democracy like the Articles of Confederation and the Bill of Rights.[21] Criticism of multicultural education and its connection to self-esteem is a thinly veiled version of the Eurocentric arrogance that has marred schools and is unbecoming in a culturally diverse society.

I believe that the "Great Debate" over self-esteem at this level should be seen for exactly what it is: a part of the tug-of-war between the long line of progressive efforts to create humane schools and the new Conservative Restoration that grew up in the 1980s. The latter is not a unidimensional movement. It is a package that involves interrelated interests of economic utilitarianism, classical Eurocentric humanism, and old-line "get tough" pedagogy. There is little room for the idea of enhancing self-esteem beyond its relation to individual achievement, especially as it is broadly defined in the context of personal efficacy and the resolution of large social inequities. This package marginalizes the same nonprivileged young people upon whom the schools have always worked most harshly and continues the unjust status they have historically been assigned.

In saying this, I do not mean to glorify or over-romanticize the self-esteem "movement." Many of those involved in it still fail to differentiate between self-concept (the description of self) and self-esteem (the evaluation of self) or to understand the intricate role played by values in self-esteem judgments.[22] Efforts to improve self-perceptions must contribute to the quality of all three dimensions. For example, multicultural education and cooperative learning have as much to do with expanding the concept of self and promoting the value of interdependence as they do with self-esteem. Critics such as those cited above apparently do not understand this, but their analyses seem all the more accurate when people inside the schools also do not.

Moreover, as I have pointed out, the self-esteem movement is still full of the kind of fluff and radical individualism that is as threatening to authentic progressivism as the conservative restoration. In fact, the overly individualistic tendencies of many self-esteem programs and projects play right into the hands of that restoration by focusing on self-protection mechanisms rather than the environment that creates their need. This is, of course, "privatizing" at its extreme. It is a theory of alienation that pits the individual against the world.

BEYOND THE "MESS"

In retrospect, it may seem ironic that the idea of enhancing self-esteem would become a buzzword amidst the hardening of academic categories in the 1980s. As we have seen, however, this should not be surprising since that idea has many different meanings, some of which fit rather well with the Horatio Alger reform notions in the last decade. The important question now focuses on what we will do to find our way out of the confusion and contradiction that has arisen.

I suggest that we stop seeing self-esteem only in individualistic terms and move instead toward an integrated view of self and social relations. This transition would involve at least three main parts. First, the construction of personal meanings should be understood as emerging from interactions with the environment. Self-perceptions are a central feature of human personality from which flow many social manifestations, but environment powerfully informs self-perceptions. Moreover, it is clear that people do not learn about themselves either apart from or prior to learning about their world. Rather, they learn about both simultaneously and in light of their interdependence.

Second, self-esteem is properly seen as one dimension of the larger concept of affect that also involves values, morals, ethics, character, and the like, and is connected to cognition. By itself, self-esteem addresses only part of what Dewey called the "affective-ideational" connection that underlies social relations.[23] When we make self-esteem decisions, we do so on the basis of our values.[24] Moreover, such decisions involve thinking; they may be more or less thoughtful, but they are not empty of thought.[25] Thus, if schooling for self-esteem does

not simultaneously address other aspects of affect as well as cognition, it is incomplete and artificial.

Third, self-esteem alone is an incomplete definition of the concept of human dignity upon which work on self-esteem is partly justified. It is not enough that young people like themselves. They must also have a sense that what they say, and think, and do counts for something. In other words, self-esteem must be accompanied by a sense of personal efficacy. But even that is not enough. Individuals do not live in isolation, and to imply such is dangerous. Personal efficacy must be connected to collective efficacy so that individuals see themselves as part of groups that can and do have meaning and power. In making this point, I am connecting the idea of enhancing self-esteem to the broader themes of democracy, human dignity, and cultural diversity—themes that ostensibly permeate the lives of those in our society.[26]

What does this mean for schools' role in enhancing self-esteem? It means they must place a premium on authentic participation, collaborative action, a problem-centered curriculum, and interdependent diversity. Likewise, they should work to remove policies and practices that can debilitate self-esteem like tracking, autocratic procedures, unicultural curriculum, and competition.

This kind of effort is not without controversy. After all, it suggests that people not only feel good about themselves, but also come to believe they can change things. Perhaps it is here that the gatekeepers of the school as well as the advocates of the conservative restoration sense the real problem with self-esteem. Perhaps it is here, too, that we may understand the individualistic "coping strategies" of packaged programs as something of a failure of nerve. Work with self-esteem that promotes integration of self and social interests and personal and social efficacy offers the possibility that young people will challenge the status quo, not simply accept it. Besides, the very idea of packaged programs seems largely inappropriate for any genuine work with self-esteem.

In the end we are faced with some very serious challenges. Finding our way out of the self-esteem "mess" must begin with several understandings. First, being nice is surely a part of this effort, but it is not enough. Second, there is a place for some direct instruction regarding affective matters, but this is not enough either. Self-esteem and affect are not simply another school subject to be placed in set-aside time slots. Third, the negative affect of "get tough" policies is not a promising route to self-esteem and efficacy. This simply blames young people for problems that are largely not of their own making. Fourth, since self-perceptions are powerfully informed by culture, comparing self-esteem across cultures without clarifying cultural differences is distracting and unproductive.

Authentic work in the area of self-esteem is more complex than most people, including participants in the great debate, have been willing to admit. It involves broadening our understanding of the reasons behind such work, extending the definition of self-esteem into a larger concept of affect that integrates self and social interests, extending self-enhancement efforts across the entire school, and relating the work of the school with the larger world of conditions that detract from human dignity. Self-esteem is not just a psychological construct. It also has meaning for creating and understanding the philosophical and sociological themes that permeate our lives. Clearly, enhancing self-esteem is not the soft or simple work that so many people believe it to be.

NOTES

1. See, for example, A. W. Combs, ed., (1962), *Perceiving, Behaving Becoming: A New Focus for Education*, (Washington, D.C.: Association for Supervision and Curriculum Development).

2. California Task Force to Promote Self-Esteem and Personal and Social Responsibility, (1990), *Toward a State of Esteem*, (Sacramento: State of California). The report was supplemented by a larger volume: A. M. Mecca, N. S. Smelser, and J. Vasconellos, (1989), *The Social Importance of Self-Esteem*, (Berkeley: University of California Press).

3. See, for example, W. W. Purkey, (1970), *Self-Concept and School Achievement*, (Englewood Cliffs, N.J.: Prentice-Hall); M. Rosenberg, (1979), *Conceiving the Self* (New York: Basic Books); and J. A. Beane and R. P. Lipka, (1986), *Self-Concept, Self-Esteem and the Curriculum*, (New York: Teachers College Press).

4. B. M. Byrne, (1984), "The General/Academic Self-Concept Nomological Network: A Review of Construct Validation Research," *Review of Educational Research* 54: 427–456.

5. J. A. Beane, (1990), *Affect in the Curriculum: Toward Democracy, Dignity and Diversity* (New York: Teachers College Press).

6. G. Weinstein and M. D. Fantini, (1970), *Toward Humanistic Education: A Curriculum of Affect*, (New York: Praeger).

7. A content analysis of many of these is included in A. M. Kaiser-Carlso, (1986), *A Program Description and Analysis of Self-Esteem Programs for the Junior High School*, (Santa Clara, Calif: Educational Development Center).

8. H. Hartshorne and M. A. May, (1928, 1929, 1930, respectively), *Studies in the Nature of Character: Volume I: Studies in Deceit, Volume II: Studies in Service and Self-Control, Volume III* (with F. K. Shuttleworth): *Studies in the Organization of Character*, (New York: Macmillan.)

9. See, for example, A. L. Lockwood, (1978), "The Effects of Values Clarification and Moral Development Curricula on School-Age Subjects: A Critical Review of Research," *Review of Educational Research* 48: 325–64; J. S. Leming, (1981), "Curricular Effectiveness in Value/Moral Education," *Journal of Moral Education* 10: 147–64.

10. See, for example, P. E. Crisci, (1986). "The Quest National Center: A Focus on Prevention of Alienation," *Phi Delta Kappan* 67: 440–42.

11. See, for example, Beane and Lipka, op. cit.

12. C. Krauthammer, (February 5, 1990), "Education: Doing Bad and Feeling Good," *Time*, p. 78.

13. See, for example, J. Leo, (April 2, 1990), "The Trouble With Self-Esteem," U.S. *News and World Report*, p. 16. The California report was also a target, on these same grounds, of *Doonesbury* cartoonist Gary Trudeau.

14. See B. Ehrenreich, (1989), *Fear of Falling: The Inner Life of the Middle Class*, (New York: Random House). Ehrenreich argues that self-denial is a persistent theme in the rhetoric, if not the real lives, of the professional/managerial middle class.

15. Krauthammer, op. cit.

16. This same critique might be aimed at most of the reactive instruments typically used to "measure" self-esteem since the statements that make up the instruments reflect the values of their developer(s) and not necessarily those of the young people who are subjected to them.

17. In what may have been anticipation of this criticism, the California Task Force expanded its work to include the connection of self-esteem to personal and social responsibility.

18. M. Schmoker, (January-February 1990). "Self-Esteem Is Earned, Not Learned," newsletter of the Thomas Jefferson Center, pp. 1 ff.

19. Beane, op. cit.

20. Krauthammer, op. cit.

21. D. Grinde, (1988), "It Is Time to Take Away the Veil," *Northeast Indian Quarterly* 4 and 5: 28–34. Two Iroquois ideas that the framers of the white documents of democracy "forgot" were equality of women and the prohibition of slavery.

22. J. A. Beane and R. P. Lipka, "Self-Concept and Self-Esteem: A Construct Differentiation," *Child Study Journal* 10: 1–6.

23. J. Dewey, (1939), *Theory of Valuation*, (Chicago: University of Chicago Press).

24. Beane and Lipka, op. cit.

25. Beane, op. cit.

26. For further discussion of these ideas, see Beane, op. cit.

Students Need Challenge, Not Easy Success

MARGARET M. CLIFFORD

Hundreds of thousands of apathetic students abandon their schools each year to begin lives of unemployment, poverty, crime, and psychological distress. According to Hahn (1987), "Dropout rates ranging from 40 to 60 percent in Boston, Chicago, Los Angeles, Detroit, and other major cities point to a situation of crisis proportions." The term *dropout* may not be adequate to convey the disastrous consequences of the abandonment of school by children and adolescents; *educational suicide* may be a far more appropriate label.

School abandonment is not confined to a small percentage of minority students, or low ability children, or mentally lazy kids. It is a systemic failure affecting the most gifted and knowledgeable as well as the disadvantaged, and it is threatening the social, economical, intellectual, industrial, cultural, moral, and psychological well-being of our country. Equally disturbing are students who sever themselves from the flow of knowledge while they occupy desks, like mummies.

Student apathy, indifference, and underachievement are typical precursors of school abandonment. But what causes these symptoms? Is there a remedy? What will it take to stop the waste of our intellectual and creative resources?

To address these questions, we must acknowledge that educational suicide is primarily a motivational problem—not a physical, intellectual, financial, technological, cultural, or staffing prob-

Margaret M. Clifford is Professor of Educational Psychology, University of Iowa, College of Education, Iowa City, IA 52242.

lem. Thus, we must turn to motivational theories and research as a foundation for examining this problem and for identifying solutions.

Curiously enough, modern theoretical principles of motivation do not support certain widespread practices in education. I will discuss four such discrepancies and offer suggestions for resolving them.

MODERATE SUCCESS PROBABILITY IS ESSENTIAL TO MOTIVATION

The maxim, "Nothing succeeds like success," has driven educational practice for several decades. Absolute success for students has become the means *and* the end of education: It has been given higher priority than learning, and it has obstructed learning.

A major principle of current motivation theory is that tasks associated with a moderate probability of success (50 percent) provide maximum satisfaction (Atkinson 1964). Moderate probability of success is also an essential ingredient of intrinsic motivation (Lepper and Greene 1978, Csikszentmihalyi 1975, 1978). We attribute the success we experience on easy tasks task ease; we attribute the success we experience on extremely difficult tasks to luck. Neither type of success does much to enhance self-image. It is only success at moderately difficult or truly challenging tasks that we explain in terms of personal effort, well-chosen strategies, and ability; and these explanations give rise to feelings of pride, competence, determination, satisfaction, persistence, and personal control. Even very young children show a preference for tasks that are just a bit beyond their ability (Danner and Lonky 1981).

Consistent with these motivational findings, learning theorists have repeatedly demonstrated that moderately difficult tasks are a prerequisite for maximizing intellectual development (Fischer 1980). But despite the fact that moderate challenge (implying considerable error-making) is essential for maximizing learning and optimizing motivation, many educators attempt to create error-proof learning environments. They set minimum criteria and standards in hopes of ensuring success for all students. They often reduce task difficulty, overlook errors, de-emphasize failed attempts, ignore faulty performances, display "perfect papers," minimize testing, and reward error-free performance.

It is time for educators to replace easy success with challenge. We must encourage students to reach beyond their intellectual grasp and allow them the privilege of learning from mistakes. There must be a tolerance for error-making in every classroom, and gradual success rather than continual success must become the yardstick by which learning is judged. Such transformations in educational practices will not guarantee the elimination of educational suicide, but they are sure to be one giant step in that direction.

EXTERNAL CONSTRAINTS ERODE MOTIVATION AND PERFORMANCE

Intrinsic motivation and performance determine when external constraints such as surveillance, evaluation by others, deadlines, threats, bribes, and rewards are accentuated. Yes, even rewards are a form of constraint! The reward giver is the General who dictates rules and issues orders; rewards are used to keep the troops in line.

Means-end contingencies, as exemplified in the statement, "If you complete your homework, you may watch TV" (with homework being the means and TV the end), are another form of external constraint. Such contingencies decrease interest in the first task (homework, the means) and increase interest in the second task (TV, the end) (Boggiano and Main 1986).

Externally imposed constraints, including material rewards, decrease task interest, reduce creativity, hinder performance, and encourage passivity on the part of students—even preschoolers (Lepper and Hodell 1989)! Imposed constraints also prompt individuals to use the "minimax strategy"—to exert the minimum amount of effort needed to obtain the maximum amount of reward (Kruglanski et al. 1977). Supportive of these findings are studies showing that autonomous behavior—that which is self-determined, freely chosen, and personally controlled—elicits high risk interest, creativity, cognitive flexibility, positive emotion, and persistence (Deci and Ryan 1987).

Unfortunately, constraint and lack of student autonomy are trademarks of most schools. Federal and local governments, as well as teachers, legislate academic requirements; impose guidelines, create rewards systems; mandate behavioral contracts; serve warnings of expulsion, and use rules, threats, and punishments as routine problem-solving strategies. We can legislate school attendance and the conditions for obtaining a diploma, but we cannot legislate the development of intelligence, talent, creativity, and intrinsic motivation—resources this country desperately needs.

It is time for educators to replace coercive, constraint-laden techniques with autonomy-supportive techniques. We must redesign instructional and evaluation materials and procedures so that every assignment, quiz, test, project, and discussion activity not only allows for, but routinely *requires*, carefully calculated decision making on the part of students. Instead of minimum criteria, we must define multiple criteria (levels of minimum, marginal, average, good, superior, and excellent achievement), and we must free students to choose criteria that provide optimum challenge. Constraint gives a person the desire to escape; freedom gives a person the desire to explore, expand, and create.

PROMPT, SPECIFIC FEEDBACK ENHANCES LEARNING

A third psychological principle is that specific and prompt feedback enhances learning, performance, and motivation (Ilgen et al. 1979, Larson 1984). Informational feedback (that which reveals correct responses) increases learning (Ilgen and Moore 1987) and also promotes a feeling of increased competency (Sansone 1986). Feedback that can be used to improve future performance has powerful motivational value.

Sadly, however, the proportion of student assignments or activities that are promptly returned with informational feedback tends to be low. Students typically complete an assignment and then wait one, two, or three days (sometimes weeks) for its return. The feedback they do get often consists of a number or letter grade accompanied by ambiguous comments such as "Is this your best?" or "Keep up the good work." Precisely what is good or what needs improving is seldom communicated.

But, even if we could convince teachers of the value of giving students immediate, specific, informational feedback, our feedback problem would still be far from solved. How can one teacher provide 25 or more students immediate feedback on their tasks? Some educators argue that the solution to the feedback problem lies in having a tutor or teacher aide for every couple of students. Others argue that adequate student feedback will require an increased use of computer technology. However, there are less expensive alternatives. First, answer keys for students should be more plentiful. Resource books containing review and study activities should be available in every subject area, and each should be accompanied by a key that is available to students.

Second, quizzes and other instructional activities, especially those that supplement basic textbooks, should be prepared with "latent image" processing. With latent image paper and pens, a student who marks a response to an item can watch a hidden symbol emerge. The symbol signals either a correct or incorrect response, and in some instances a clue or explanation for the response is revealed. Trivia and puzzle books equipped with this latent image, immediate feedback process are currently being marketed at the price of comic books.

Of course, immediate informational feedback is more difficult to provide for composition work, long-term projects, and field assignments. But this does not justify the absence of immediate feedback on the learning activities and practice exercises that are aimed at teaching concepts, relationships, and basic skills. The mere availability of answer keys and latent image materials would probably elicit an amazing amount of self-regulated learning on the part of many students.

MODERATE RISK TAKING IS A TONIC FOR ACHIEVEMENT

A fourth motivational research finding is that moderate risk taking increases performance, persistence, perceived competence, self-knowledge, pride, and satisfaction (Deci and Porac 1978, Harter 1978, Trope 1979). Moderate risk taking implies a well-considered choice of an optimally challenging task, willingness to accept a moderate probability of success, and the anticipation of an outcome. It is this combination of events (which includes moderate success, self-regulated learning, and feedback) that captivates the attention, interest, and energy of card players, athletes, financial investors, lottery players, and even juvenile video arcade addicts.

Risk takers continually and freely face the probability of failing to attain the pleasure of succeeding under specified odds. From every risk-taking endeavor—whether it ends in failure or success—risk takers learn something about their skill and choice of strategy, and what they learn usually prompts them to seek another risk-taking opportunity. Risk taking—especially moderate risk taking—is a mind-engaging activity that simultaneously consumes and generates energy. It is a habit that feeds itself and thus requires an unlimited supply of risk-taking opportunities.

Moderate risk taking is likely to occur under the following conditions.

- The success probability for each alternative is clear and unambiguous.
- Imposed external constraints are minimized.
- Variable payoff (the value of success increases as risk increases) in contrast to fixed payoff is available.
- The benefits of risk taking can be anticipated.

My own recent research on academic risk taking with grade school, high school, and college students generally supports these conclusions. Students do, in fact, freely choose more difficult problems (a) when the number of points offered increases with the difficulty level of problems, (b) when the risk-taking task is presented within a game or practice situation (i.e., imposed constraint or threat is minimized), and (c) when additional opportunities for risk taking are anticipated (relatively high risk taking will occur on a practice exercise when students know they will be able to apply the information learned to an upcoming test). In the absence of these conditions we have seen students choose tasks that are as much as one-and-a-half years below their achievement level (Clifford, 1988). Finally, students who take moderately high risks express high task interest even though they experience considerable error making.

In summary, risk-taking opportunities for students should be (a) plentiful, (b) readily available, (c) accompanied by explicit information about success probabilities, (d) accompanied by immediate feedback that communicates competency and error information, (e) associated with payoffs that vary with task difficulty, (f) relatively free from externally imposed evaluation, and (g) presented in relaxing and nonthreatening environments.

In today's educational world, however, there are few opportunities for students to engage in academic risk taking and no incentives to do so. Choices are seldom provided within tests or assignments, and rarely are variable payoffs made available. Once again, motivational theory, which identifies risk taking as a powerful source of knowledge, motivation, and skill development, conflicts with educational practice, which seeks to minimize academic risk at all costs.

We must restructure materials and procedures to encourage moderate academic risk taking on the part of students. I predict that if we fill our classrooms with optional academic risk-taking materials and opportunities so that all students have access to moderate risks, we will not only lower our educational suicide rate, but we will raise our level of academic achievement. If we give students the license to take risks and make errors, they will likely experience genuine success and the satisfaction that accompanies it.

USING RISK CAN ENSURE SUCCESS

Both theory and research evidence lead to the prediction that academic risk-taking activities are a powerful means of increasing the success of our educational efforts. But how do we get students to take risks on school-related activities? Students will choose risk over certainty when the consequences of the former are more satisfying and informative. Three basic conditions are needed to ensure such outcomes.

- First, students must be allowed to freely select from materials and activities that vary in difficulty and probability of success.
- Second, as task difficulty increases, so too must the payoffs for success.
- Third, an environment tolerant of error making and supportive of error correction must be guaranteed.

The first two conditions can be met rather easily. For example, on a 10-point quiz, composed of six 1-point items and four 2-point items, students might be asked to select and work only 6 items. The highest possible score for such quizzes is 10 and can be obtained only by correctly answering the four 2-point items and any two 1-point items. Choice and variable payoff are easily built into quizzes and many instructional and evaluation activities.

The third condition, creating an environment tolerant of error making and supportive of error correction, is more difficult to ensure. But here are six specific suggestions.

First, teachers must make a clear distinction between formative evaluation activities (tasks, that guide instruction during the learning process) and summative evaluation activities (tasks used to judge one's level of achievement and to determine one's grade at the completion of the learning activity). Practice exercises, quizzes, and skill-building activities aimed at acquiring and strengthening knowledge and skills exemplify formative evaluation. These activities promote learning and skill development. They should be scored in a manner that excludes ability judgments, emphasizes error detection and correction, and encourages a search for better learning strategies. Formative evaluation activities should generally provide immediate feedback and be scored by students. It is on these activities that moderate risk taking is to be encouraged and is likely to prove beneficial.

Major examinations (unit exams and comprehensive final exams) exemplify summative evaluation; these activities are used to determine course grades. Relatively low risk taking is to be expected on such tasks, and immediate feedback may or may not be desirable.

Secondly, formative evaluation activities should be far more plentiful than summative. If, in fact, learning rather than grading is the primary objective of the school, the percentage of time spent on summative evaluation should be small in comparison to that spent on formative evaluation (perhaps about 1:4). There should be enough formative evaluation activities presented as risk-taking opportunities to satisfy the most enthusiastic and adventuresome learner. The more plentiful these activities are, the less anxiety-producing and aversive summative activities are likely to be.

Third, formative evaluation activities should be presented as optional; students should be enticed, not mandated, to complete these activities. Enticement might be achieved by (a) ensuring that these activities are course-relevant and varied (e.g., scrambled outlines, incomplete matrices and graphs, exercises that require error detection and correction, quizzes); (b) giving students the option of working together; (c) presenting risk-taking activities in the context of games to be played individually, with competitors, or with partners; (d) providing immediate, informational, nonthreatening feedback; and (e) defining success primarily in terms of improvement over previous performance or the amount of learning that occurs during the risk-taking activity.

Fourth, for every instructional and evaluation activity there should be at least a modest percentage of content (10 percent to 20 percent) that poses a challenge to even the best students completing the activity. Maximum development of a country's talent requires that all individuals (a) find challenge in tasks they attempt, (b) develop tolerance for error making, and (c) learn to adjust strategies when faced with failure. To deprive the most talented students of these opportunities is perhaps the greatest resource-development crime a country can commit.

Fifth, summative evaluation procedures should include "retake exams." Second chances will not only encourage risk taking but will provide good reasons for students to study their incorrect responses made on previous risk-taking tasks. Every error made on an initial exam and subsequently corrected on a second chance represents real learning.

Sixth, we must reinforce moderate academic risk taking instead of error-free performance or excessively high or low risk taking. Improvement scores, voluntary correction of errors, completion of optional risk-taking activities—these are behaviors that teachers should recognize and encourage.

TOWARD A NEW DEFINITION OF SUCCESS

We face the grim reality that our extraordinary efforts to produce "schools without failure" have not yielded the well-adjusted, enthusiastic, self-confident scholars we anticipated. Our efforts to mass-produce success for every individual in every educational situation have left us with cheap reproductions of success that do not even faintly represent the real thing. This overdose of synthetic success is a primary cause of the student apathy and school abandonment plaguing our country.

To turn the trend around, we must emphasize error tolerance, not error-free learning; reward error condition, not error avoidance; ensure challenge, not easy success. Eventual success on challenging tasks, tolerance for error making, and constructive responses to failure are motivational fare that school systems should be serving up to all students. I suggest that we engage the skills of researchers, textbook authors, publishers, and educators across the country to ensure the development and marketing of attractive and effective academic risk-taking materials and procedures. If we convince these experts of the need to employ their creative efforts toward this end, we will not only stem the tide of educational suicide, but we will enhance the quality of educational success. We will witness self-regulated student success and satisfaction that will ensure the intellectual, creative, and motivational well-being of our country.

REFERENCES

Atkinson, J. W. (1964). *An Introduction to Motivation*, Princeton, N.J.: Van Nostrand.

Boggiano, A. K. and D. S. Main. (1986). "Enhancing Children's Interest in Activities Used as Rewards: The Bonus Effect." *Journal of Personality and Social Psychology* 51: 1116–1126.

Clifford, M. M. (1988). "Failure Tolerance and Academic Risk Taking in Ten- to Twelve-Year-Old Students." *British Journal of Educational Psychology* 58. 15–27.

Csikszentmihalyi, M. (1975). *Beyond Boredom and Anxiety.* San Francisco: Jossey-Bass.

Csikszentmihalyi, M. (1978). "Intrinsic Rewards and Emergent Motivation." In *The Hidden Costs of Reward*, edited by M. R. Lepper and D. Greene. N.J.: Lawrence Erlbaum Associates.

Danner, F. W., and D. Lonky. (1981). "A Cognitive-Developmental Approach to the Effects of Rewards on Intrinsic Motivation." *Child Development* 52: 1043–1052.

Deci, E. L., and J. Porac. (1978). "Cognitive Evaluation Theory and the Study of Human Motivation." In *The Hidden Costs of Reward*, edited by M. R. Lepper and D. Greene. Hillsdale, N.J.: Lawrence Erlbaum Associates.

Deci, E. L., and R. M. Ryan. (1987). "The Support of Autonomy and the Control of Behavior." *Journal of Personality and Social Psychology* 53: 1024–1037.

Fischer, K. W. (1980). "Learning as the Development of Organized Behavior." *Journal of Structural Learning* 3: 253–267.

Hahn, A. (1987). "Reaching Out to America's Dropouts: What to Do?" *Phi Delta Kappan* 69: 256–263.

Harter, S. (1978). "Effectance Motivation Reconsidered; Toward a Developmental Model." *Human Development* 1: 34–64.

Ilgen, D. P., and C. F. Moore. (1987). "Types and Choices of Performance Feedback." *Journal of Applied Psychology* 72: 401–406.

Ilgen, D. P., C. D. Fischer, and M. S. Taylor. (1979). "Consequences of Individual Feedback on Behavior in Organizations." *Journal of Applied Psychology* 64: 349–371.

Kruglanski, A., C. Stein, and A. Riter. (1977). "Contingencies of Exogenous Reward and Task Performance: On the 'Minimax' Strategy in Instrumental Behavior." *Journal of Applied Social Psychology*, 2: 141–148.

Larson, J. P., Jr. (1984). "The Performance Feedback Process: A Preliminary Model." *Organizational Behavior and Human Performance* 33: 42–76.

Lepper, M. R., and D. Greene. (1978). *The Human Costs of Reward*. Hillsdale, N.J.: Lawrence Erlbaum Associates.

Lepper, M. R., and M. Hodell. (1989). "Intrinsic Motivation in the Classroom." In *Motivation in Education, Vol. 3*, edited by C. Ames and R. Ames. N. Y.: Academic Press.

Sansone, C. (1986). "A Question of Competence: The Effects of Competence and Task Feedback on Intrinsic Motivation." *Journal of Personality and Social Psychology* 51: 918–931.

Trope, Y. (1979). "Uncertainty Reducing Properties of Achievement Tasks:" *Journal of Personality and Social Psychology* 37: 1505–1518.

History of Motivational Research in Education

BERNARD WEINER

The 10th anniversary of the founding of the Motivation in Education Special Interest Group of the American Educational Research Association provided the occasion for me to look back on the field of motivation and ask where we have been and where we are going. There are many possible strategies to take in reaching a retrospective summary. One might count and catalog past articles, solicit and synthesize opinions of the major figures in the field, and so forth. The material for my analysis of the state of motivational psychology is provided by the *Encyclopedia of Educational Research,* which is perhaps a compromise between personal cataloging and soliciting the opinions of others. This volume has been published each decade starting in 1941; thus five articles exist and a sixth is forthcoming which summarize the research conducted between 1930 and 1990. I have been asked to write the chapter for the 1990 edition. This will be my second review, for I also wrote the chapter 20 years earlier for the 1970 publication. Hence, not only am I able to examine the contents of the field over a 60-year time span, but I also can overcome the confounding

involved in comparing the writings and biases of different authors by considering differences within the same author (myself) over a 20-year time span (making the questionable assumption that my own biases remained constant over this period).

In this article, I will use the contents of the *Encyclopedia of Educational Research* articles as a scaffold for discussing the history of our field, the emergence and disappearance of central issues in motivation, the progress that has and has not been made, the problems that exist, current directions, and a potpourri of related topics.

I view this field with a schizophrenic reaction. On the one hand, I feel some despair. The question that teachers and parents ask of us is how to motivate their students and children, and we are not very adept at providing answers. The lofty place that motivation once occupied in the research enterprise of psychology is no longer held. At one time, motivation was the dominant field of study; certainly this is no longer true. During the decades between 1950 and 1970, the *Nebraska Symposium on Motivation* was one of the most prestigious publications and commanded a great deal of attention; that is no longer the case. In one year, Clark Hull, the pivotal figure in the growth of drive theory and the experimental approach to motivation, was cited in almost 70% of the published experimental articles; we have no contemporary figure of such dominance.

At the other pole of my schizophrenic reaction, I feel optimistic. There are now well more than 150

This article was an invited address given to the Motivation in Education Special Interest Group at the convention of the American Educational Research Association, April 1990, Boston, Massachusetts.

Thanks are extended to Russell Ames and Jaana Juvonen for their roles in initiating this project. Correspondence concerning this article should be addressed to Bernard Weiner, Department of Psychology, University of California, 405 Hilgard Avenue, Los Angeles, California 90024-1563.

active members of the Motivation in Education Special Interest Group, many with their own students and research groups. Interest in and articles about motivation are increasing in a number of journals (see Ball, 1984); there is a recent three-volume set edited by R. Ames and C. Ames (1984) and C. Ames and R. Ames (1985, 1989) on motivation in education; and for the first time in nearly 20 years, there is going to be a *Nebraska Symposium* volume that is actually devoted to motivation (Dienstbier, 1990). The future therefore looks promising for the general field of motivation and for motivational research related to education.

Having shared my deeply mixed emotions, let me turn my thoughts to history. This will allow further opportunity for expression of these conflicting personal opinions.

MOTIVATION AS REPRESENTED 1940–1960

The first two motivation chapters in the *Encyclopedia of Educational Research* were written by Paul Thomas Young (1941, 1950). Young, who was at the University of Illinois, was known for his hedonic theory of motivation and his examination of the intrinsic emotional and motivational properties of substances such as saccharin. He was a prolific writer, producing some of the very early books that outlined an experimental approach to the study of motivation. Young wrote both the 1941 and 1950 chapters, following the same outline in each publication.

The contents of his chapters are shown in Table 1. It can be seen in Table 1 that the major research topics in the field were activity level, appetites and aversions, homeostasis, chemical controls, and neural structures, as well as incentives, defense mechanisms, and the degree of motivation (the Yerkes-Dodson law of optimal motivational level). Some specific concerns for educators were discussed, including praise and reproof, success and failure, knowledge of results (feedback), cooperation and competition, and reward and punishment. The educational topics not only overlap but also appear more contemporary and familiar than his outline of general motivational research.

These fields of study, popular just 40 years ago between 1930 and 1950, are readily understandable, given the roots of motivational psychology. Initially, the experimental study of motivation (the Latin root of *motive* means to move) was linked with the search

for the motors of behavior and was associated with concepts such as instinct, drive, arousal, need, and energization. Motivational psychologists were concerned with what moved a resting organism to a state of activity. Accordingly, hungry rats were deprived of food, and even curious monkeys were placed in rooms without visual stimulation. It was believed that a discrepancy between an ideal "off" state and a less-than-ideal "on" state (i.e., the presence of a need) would be detected by the organism and would initiate activity until this disequilibrium was reduced to zero. Hence, the effects of a variety of need states on a variety of indexes of motivation, including speed of learning and choice behavior, were examined. Borrowing concepts such as energy systems from the physical sciences and using machine-based metaphors such as overflowing energy and drainage from a container of fixed capacity constituted one strategy used to gain scientific respectability for this uncertain field.

The concept of a deprived organism living in an environment of limited resources gave a functionalistic, Darwinian flavor to the field of motivation, which in the decades between 1930 and 1950 was dominated by the tribal leaders of Hull and Spence and by the less expansionistic Tolman. It also gave rise to taxonomies of instincts and basic need states, as exemplified in the writings of William McDougall (1923) and Henry Murray (1938), and to other issues related to the dynamics of behavior and the instrumental value of action. For example, motivational psychologists examined conflict resolution under circumstances in which a positive goal is located in a shocked region, what behavior follows when an anticipated goal is not attained, and whether psychological equilibrium requires reduction in need state to a zero level of internal stimulation (as opposed to an optimal level greater than zero). The reader is directed to Atkinson (1964), Brown (1961), Mook (1987), Petri (1986), and Weiner (1972, 1980) for historical overviews of earlier research activities. It is evident, then, that Young captured the mainstream preoccupations in motivation through his coverage of need and activity, approach and avoidance tendencies, homeostasis, and underlying motivational mechanisms.

The topics linked with educational psychologists were quite divorced from the mainstream of the study of motivation. Basic research in motivation was associated with subhuman behavior, for example, the maze or straight-alley actions of hungry or thirsty rats. Human behavior was considered too complex to study directly and not subject to experimental

TABLE 1   Contents of the Chapters on Motivation in the *Encyclopedia of Educational Research, 1941–1990*

Descriptor	1941 and 1950	1960	1969	1982	1990
Author	P. T. Young	M. Marx	B. Weiner	S. Ball	B. Weiner
Contents	Need and activity level	Theories	Theories	Attribution theory	Cognitions
	Appetite and aversion	Techniques	Associative	Achievement	Causal attributions
	Equilibrium and	Drive and learning	Drive	motivation	Self-efficacy
	homeostasis	Drive and frustration	Cognitive	Anxiety	Learned helplessness
	Chemical controls	Activation of drives	Psychoanalytic	Self-esteem	Individual differences
	Neural structures	and motives	Topics	Curiosity	Need for achievement
	Incentives	Reward	Curiosity (exploratory	Minor areas	Anxiety about failure
	Defense mechanisms	Knowledge of results	behavior)	Level of aspiration	Locus of control
	Degree of motivation	Fear and anxiety	Affiliation	Affiliation	Attributional style
	Education Applications	Arousal	Imbalance	Biochemical correlates	Environmental
	Praise and reproof		(dissonance)	Reinforcement theory	determinants
	Success and failure		Frustration		Cooperation versus
	Knowledge of results		Aggression		competition
	Cooperation and		Relation to Processes		(goal structure)
	competition		Learning		Intrinsic versus
	Reward and		Perception		extrinsic rewards
	punishment		Memory		Praise

manipulation, which meant deprivation because the basic motivational model embraced viscerogenic needs and homeostasis.

Forty years after 1950, the problem of being out of the mainstream no longer applies to educational psychologists, as is discussed in the following paragraphs. However, another problem that in 1941 was considered to have been solved has remained a serious burr in our saddles. The dilemma involves the motivation-learning or performance-acquisition distinction. A key juncture in the field of motivation occurred in the 1930s when it separated from the field of learning. Hullians had argued that in order for learning to occur, there must be response reinforcement and drive reduction. That is, a response must be followed by an incentive for there to be a change in habit strength and a subsequent increase in strength of motivation. But Tolman (1932), in his acclaimed research on latent learning, demonstrated that there can be learning without reward and drive reduction; incentives, which were introduced into the goal box after an animal had an opportunity to explore the maze, were shown to affect performance, or the utilization of structure, rather than learning, or the change in structure. Motivational psychologists at that time argued that the study of motivation is therefore separable from the study of learning; motivation examines the use, but not the development, of knowledge.

However, for the educational psychologist, the prime issue always has been how to motivate people to engage in new learning, not how to get people to use what they already know, which is a more appropriate issue for industrial psychologists. The study of motivation for the educational researcher thus has been confounded with the field of learning; indeed, motivation often is inferred from learning, and learning usually is the indicator of motivation for the educational psychologist. This lack of separation, or confounding, between motivation and learning has vexed those interested in motivational processed in education, in part because learning is influenced by a multiplicity of factors including native intelligence. This confounding problem can even be seen in the outline of Young, because he included knowledge of results, for example, among the determinants of motivation, yet it surely influences the degree of learning.

I will mention only briefly the ensuing *Encyclopedia of Educational Research* article because it contin-

ued in the tradition set forth by Young. The chapter was written by Melvin Marx (1960) of the University of Missouri (see Table 1). Marx also linked motivation with energy and drive level. The main topics he examined (after a lengthy discussion of types of drive theories and methods of study) were drive and learning, drive and frustration, activation of drive, rewards, knowledge of results, fear and anxiety (which were considered learned drives) and arousal. Hence, Marx remained in the tradition of Hull, Spence, Mowrer, N. Miller, and others of the Yale and Iowa schools who were guided by the machine metaphor of motivation. The center of motivational research still had little connection with or relevance for educational psychologists.

MOTIVATION AS REPRESENTED IN 1969

I was responsible for the next *Encyclopedia of Educational Research* chapter, which summarized the research in the 1960s (Weiner, 1969). The topics covered are in Table 1. First, I reviewed the four most dominant theoretical approaches: associationistic theory (John Watson), drive theory (Hull and Spence), cognitive theory (Kurt Kewin and John Atkinson), and psychoanalytic theory (Freud). In addition, the specific research areas reviewed included exploratory behavior, affiliation, balance (dissonance), frustration, and aggression. Furthermore, motivation was related to other process areas including learning, perception, and memory. It is quite evident that although Hull and Spence were represented, there was relatively little discussion of drive, energy, arousal, homeostasis, and other mainstays of drive theory.

One can attribute this rather dramatic shift to the writer, but as a chronicler (i.e., a historian without a philosophy) I deserve neither the credit nor the blame. Major changes had occurred, some starting before Marx (1960) wrote his chapter on motivation and others flowering in the 1960s. First, there was the more general shift in psychology away from mechanism and toward cognition. For example, in the psychology of Edward Thorndike, which was entirely incorporated by Hull, proponents believed that a reward would automatically increase the probability of the immediately prior response, thus augmenting later motivation when in that environment. However, it was gradually learned that if reward is perceived as controlling, then it undermines future effort, whereas reward perceived as positive feedback is motivating (Deci, 1975). Furthermore, reward for successful completion of an easy task is a cue to the receiver of this feedback that he or she is low in ability, a belief that inhibits activity, whereas reward for successful completion of a difficult task indicates that hard work was expended in conjunction with high ability, a belief that augments motivation. In addition, reward in a competitive setting is based on social comparison information, signaling that one has high ability and is better than others, whereas reward in a cooperative context signals that one has bettered oneself and has tried hard. Hence, it became recognized that reward has quite a variety of meanings and that each connotation can have different motivational implications. For the field of motivation, this ultimately signaled that the "winner" of the Hull-Tolman debate was Tolman, the cognitivist, rather than Hull, the mechanist. The broader Tolman cognitive camp included, or was preceded by, Lewin, who at times teamed with Tolman at Berkeley, and John Atkinson, as well as Julian Rotter, who was unfortunately and unfairly overlooked in my 1969 chapter.

The cognitivists had, in general, a different research agenda than did the mechanists. For example, one of Lewin's main research interests was level of aspiration, or the goal for which one is striving. In a similar manner, Atkinson devoted his attention to the choice between achievement-related tasks differing in level of difficulty. Thus, when cognitive approaches to motivation carried the day, this resulted not only in a different theoretical orientation but also in a new empirical outlook. That is, it was not "business as usual" with Tolman's cognitive maps merely replacing Hull's habit strengths. Rather, researchers began to concentrate on human rather than on infrahuman behavior. It became just as respectable to generalize from human to nonhuman behavior as vice versa. So, just as Hull speculated about human motivation from studies of rats, Lewin speculated about the behavior of rats from the study of humans! Furthermore, of the many possible topics for human research, issues associated with success and failure and achievement strivings formed the heart of the empirical study of motivation. This was in part because of the manifest importance of achievement strivings in our lives. In addition, success and failure could be readily manipulated in the laboratory and their effects on subsequent performance determined.

This was perhaps no more difficult than depriving or not depriving lower organisms of food and testing the effects of deprivation on performance. Finally, there were many naturally occurring instances of achievement outcomes that could be subject to field research, including the classroom. There was an open door for educational research.

In sum, motivational research became almost synonymous with achievement motivation research. Educational psychology thus shifted into the spotlight, away from the periphery where it was, properly, first identified in the reviews of Young (1941, 1950) and Marx (1960) shown in Table 1. Of course, other uniquely human concerns were captured in the 1960s, including affiliative behavior and cognitive balance. But these pale in comparison to the attention given to achievement strivings.

However, in the 1960s motivational psychologists were not totally transformed by the general shift from mechanism to cognition. For example, research concerned with cognitive balance and dissonance made use of drive theory concepts, particularly drive reduction and homeostasis (e.g., cognitive dissonance, or an imbalance among cognitive beliefs, was considered to be a drive, and humans were believed to be driven to bring themselves back to a state of equilibrium, or cognitive consonance, in which all beliefs "fit"). In addition, theorists in the 1960s primarily (but not quite exclusively) embraced the concept of subjective expectancy of success, albeit little else from the vast array of relevant motivational thoughts. Thus, there was some contentment merely in eliminating the term *drive* and replacing the notion of *habit* with that of *expectancy*.

In addition, the cognitive motivational theorists remained wedded to the "grand formal theory" approach of Hull and Tolman, setting as their task the isolation of the determinants of behavior and the specification of the mathematical relation among these factors. This is illustrated in the very dominant Motive ˘ Probability ˘ Incentive formula of Atkinson (1957, 1964) and the very closely related (and prior) theories of Lewin (1935) and Rotter (1954). All of these were known as expectancy–value theories—motivation was determined by what one expected to get and the likelihood of getting it. The cognitive approach also embraced the "slice in time" construal advocated by Lewin. An ahistorical construal of motivation lent itself to analysis of variance as the appropriate statistical methodology, so that variables typically were manipulated in 2 ˘ 2 designs (or what might be called "Noah's Arc" experiments). Finally, it became accepted that organisms always are active, and as a result, the key dependent variables in motivation became choice and persistence, indicators of the direction of behavior.

With the waning of "mechanism," of machine metaphors, drive and homeostasis as motivational constructs, and research with lower organisms, along with the advent of cognitivism, rational person metaphors, human motivational research, and achievement strivings as the center of motivational thought, there also came another important research direction. Attention began to be focused on individual differences, with persons characterized as high or low in achievement needs, high or low in anxiety, high or low in internal control, and so forth (following the Noah's Arc paradigm). For the educational psychologist, so interested in those individuals not performing well in the classroom, this was an important and a compatible shift that could not have come about with a psychology based on nonhumans.

The main individual differences that were studied were not derived from broad concerns about personality structure. Rather, an individual difference variable was selected on the basis of motivational theory; a measure of that variable was created; and then this measure was added to other factors within a more encompassing research design that included individual differences as one variable. How this structure related to or fit with other personality structures was not of concern, and researchers often paid little attention to the measure in comparison with the measures developed by assessment psychologists. When Spence was asked what he would do if a measure of anxiety did not result in the predictions made by drive theorists, he quickly said that he would throw out the assessment instrument!

The dominant individual differences that were studied and their linked assessment instruments—need for achievement and the Thematic Apperception Test, anxiety about failure and the Test Anxiety Questionnaire or the Manifest Anxiety Scale, and locus of control and the Internal-External Scale—share a common process of development. First it was demonstrated within a well-articulated theoretical framework that a particular situational manipulation had a motivational effect. Then it was documented that individuals could be selected who differed in ways that mirrored the environmental effect. For example, achievement theory specified

that when achievement concerns are aroused by means of test instructions or failure, achievement strivings are augmented as compared with a neutral or nonarousing manipulation (see Atkinson, 1964). It was then contended that some individuals act as if they are more aroused than others when both groups are in the identical environment. That is, some individuals are more sensitized to achievement cues than are others and thus exhibit augmented achievement strivings, as though the two groups actually were in differentially arousing environments. In sum, the creation of the individual difference measure followed the successful manipulation of a situational variable that captured a particular motivational phenomenon.

In a similar manner, drive theorists had demonstrated that conditioning is more rapid when individuals are exposed to a large aversive stimulus, such as an intense shock, than when subject to a less severe shock. It was then reasoned that some individuals might be more emotionally aroused in the same aversive environment than are others, and thus would condition faster. Such people were labeled as high in drive or high in anxiety (Spence, 1958). Subsequent demonstrations showing that individuals who scored high on the Manifest Anxiety Scale did condition faster than those who scored low not only validated the individual difference measure but also lent supporting evidence to drive theory.

Finally, social learning theorists had documented that expectancy shifts are more typical (increments after success, decrements after failure) when individuals' perform on skill rather than chance tasks. Social learning theorists then reasoned that some individuals would perceive events in the world as skill determined and therefore subject to personal control, whereas others would construe events as chance determined and therefore not amenable to personal control. Thus, in the identical neutral context, individuals in the former group would exhibit more typical expectancy shifts than luck-oriented individuals (Rotter, 1966).

To summarize, individual difference measures for achievement needs, anxiety, and locus of control were devised to identify persons thought to differ in motivationally significant ways. In their early stages of development, these measures and their corresponding predictions were closely tied to the theories that spawned them and generated a vast amount of research, which I touched upon in the 1969 *Encyclopedia of Educational Research* article.

MOTIVATION AS DEPICTED IN 1982

The next motivation chapter in the *Encyclopedia of Educational Research* appeared in 1982 and was written by Samuel Ball. Ball is in part known to us because of his service as editor of the *Journal of Educational Psychology*. In that capacity, he very much encouraged the submission of motivation articles, and publications in motivation flourished under his editorship.

The topics covered by Ball (1982) included attribution theory, achievement motivation, anxiety, self-esteem, curiosity and, to a much lesser extent, level of aspiration, affiliation, biochemical correlates of motivation, and reinforcement (see Table 1). Thus, there clearly is a continuation of the trends observed in the 1960s. That is, there is even greater focus on human behavior, particularly achievement strivings; there is an increasing range of cognitions documented as having motivational significance, such as causal ascriptions; and there is enduring interest in individual differences in achievement needs, anxiety about failure, and perceptions of control. In addition, we see the beginnings of attention paid to the self, as illustrated in self versus other causal ascriptions for success and failure, strategies that maintain personal beliefs in high ability, self-efficacy (Bandura, 1977), and so forth. During the 1970s, the study of infrahuman motivation (excluding the physiological mechanisms) and the associated drive concept had virtually vanished, indeed not that many years after the heyday of Hull and Spence.

MOTIVATION TODAY

Finally, we come to the 1990 motivation chapter (Weiner, in press). The outline is shown in Table 1. The topics include the cognitions of causal attributions, self-efficacy, and learned helplessness; the individual differences of need for achievement, anxiety about failure, locus of control, and attributional style; and the environmental variables of competitive versus cooperative contexts, intrinsic versus extrinsic rewards, and praise. It is of interest to note that the category of environmental determinants includes topics similar to those contained in the outlines of Young (1941, 1950). The remaining topics, however, were not existent in his earlier articles.

This indicates not only the emergence of new areas of research but also the ascendance of issues relevant to educational psychologists.

Let me expand somewhat on the chapter contents and link this material with the larger historical framework that has been outlined.

1. The grand formal theories that composed the first part of my 1969 chapter—drive, psychoanalytic, cognitive, and associationistic conceptions—have for the most part faded away. After all, Freud's emphasis on the unconscious, sexual motivation, and conflict and Hull's emphasis on drive and drive reduction, seem to have little relevance in classroom contexts. What remain are varieties of cognitive approaches to motivation; the main theories today are based on the interrelated cognitions of causal ascriptions, efficacy and control beliefs, helplessness, and thoughts about the goals for which one is striving.

There is some loss with the fading of larger theories, because this is exactly what a number of central ideas and concepts in motivational psychology need. For example, the differentiation of intrinsic and extrinsic motivation, which was of central importance in the history of the cognitive emergence, is not developed in the sense of being included within a system of interrelated concepts. Thus, its relation to other concepts such as origin-pawn, internal-external control, the flow of experience, and so forth, is unclear. The lack of theoretical elaboration reduces both the generality and the precision of these intertwined approaches.

2. Achievement strivings remain at the center of the study of motivation. There are major pockets of research on power motivation, affiliation, exploratory behavior and curiosity, altruism, aggression, and so on. But these are circumscribed areas in which researchers focus on domain-specific content rather than on the development of general theory. I regard this narrowing as a major shortcoming of the field, one that greatly limits the generality of our laws as well as the likelihood of discovering new regularities. On the other hand, for those solely interested in classroom achievement strivings, the lack of theoretical generality may not be of great concern.

Within the achievement field, a somewhat new approach is vying for a dominant role with the need for achievement and causal ascriptions. This approach, sometimes called "goal theory," embraces the linked concepts of ego-involvement, competitive reward structure, social comparison as the indicator of success and ability attributions (as contrasted with task-involvement, cooperative structure, self-comparison as the indicator of success and effort attributions; Ames, 1984; Covington, 1984; Nicholls, 1984). I regard this as a major new direction, one pulling together different aspects of achievement research.

3. As intimated previously, there is increasing incorporation of a variety of cognitive variables, as exemplified in the triad of causal cognitions, efficacy beliefs, and helplessness, as well as in the source of information (self or others) that is used to determine subjective success or failure. However, the main new cognitive direction is the inclusion of the self. Indeed, even the aforementioned cognitions all concern perceptions about the self as a determinant of prior or future success and failure. Add to these the constructs of self-actualization, self-concept, self-determination, self-esteem, self-focus, self-handicapping, and the remainder of the self-alphabet, and it is evident that the self is on the verge of dominating motivation.

4. The review of the individual difference variables conveyed that this direction of motivational research is rapidly diminishing, if it has not already been abandoned. The difficulty with motivational (as opposed to cognitive) trait concepts, which was pointed out by Mischel (1968), is the lack of cross-situational generality. This has created a tremendous barrier for the motivational psychologist. For example, if an individual has high achievement strivings in sports but not academics, and this individual is classified as high in achievement needs, then predictions will be upheld in one situation but disconfirmed in the other. A second major problem is that the individual difference variables took on lives of their own and became more popular and focal than their founding theories; these monsters consumed their masters so that, for example, locus of control was related to a huge number of variables but not to expectancy of success, which was the one variable that it was linked with theoretically.

I do not mourn the passing of this stage, but I do mourn the loss of activity that the motivational trait approach spawned. One reason for the current void in research on individual differences is the lack of

larger theoretical frameworks that provide the context for the identification and growth of pertinent individual difference variables. The importance of theory for individual difference research has been recently documented in the creation of attributional style questionnaires, which developed from learned helplessness and attribution theory (Seligman, 1975; Weiner, 1986).

5. There is growing interest in emotion, which is touched upon in the forthcoming *Encyclopedia of Educational Research* motivation chapter (see Clark & Fiske, 1982). When Hull argued for the centrality of drive and Tolman argued for the centrality of cognition, they both neglected emotion (save for the acceptance of the very general pleasure-pain principle). In addition, other investigators considered only in a cursory manner affects such as pride (Atkinson, 1964) or frustration (Lewin, 1935). However, the neglect of emotion is now being redressed. The central cognitions of causal ascriptions and helplessness perceptions are linked with emotional reactions. In a similar manner, focus on the self has promoted interest in self-directed emotions including pride, shame, and guilt. I feel quite certain that emotions will be examined at great length in the *Encyclopedia of Educational Research* motivation article written for the year 2000. At that time, there will be some mapping between the structure of thought, discrete emotional experiences, and the motivational messages of these experiences.

MOTIVATION IN THE FUTURE

In addition to the research agendas implied in the prior paragraphs, there are two others that I believe or hope will become manifest. First, there should be a greater number of motivational investigations that are not linked with learning. There is an abundance of evidence that motivation influences a vast array of other variables, including affective experience, self-esteem, and so forth. Educational psychologists must broaden their nets to capture the richness of motivational impact.

My second hoped-for agenda stems from the current dominance of issues related to the self, self-directed emotions, and what may be called a psychology of the individual. I view this narrow focus with mixed emotions and some trepidation. To explain this reaction, let me return to some basics about motivation and what this concept means to teachers and parents. When teachers and parents say that a child is "not motivated," they may refer to a behavioral observation (e.g., the child is not working with intensity or persistence at homework), to inferences about intrinsic interest (e.g., the child is studying only because of extrinsic bribes), or to engagement in activities that are antithetical to the goals of teachers and parents (e.g., the child is engaged in sports). Thus, for example, if someone is playing baseball whenever possible and spending time thinking about baseball rather than school-related concerns, then that person is considered by teachers and parents as "not motivated." However, if this same behavior characterized a professional baseball player, then that person would be described as highly motivated. He or she would be admired and praised. Motivation therefore is a work-related rather than a play-related concept and must be considered within the context of social values and the goals of the superordinate culture.

When the study of motivation shifted from animal to human research, there indeed was an increase in the accepted importance of cognitions as determinants of behavior and in the centrality of achievement strivings as opposed to deprivation-related activity. But there is another overlooked aspect of this research shift, namely, achievement behavior influences and affects others, who have behavioral expectations. Rats are engaged in a zero-sum game; if they do not strive to get food, the other rats are not necessarily unhappy about this and Darwinian principles are likely to prevail. However, learning need not be divided and shared and school motivation requires the development and the incorporation of the values of others. Hence, we have to consider frameworks larger than the self, and older motivational constructs, such as "belongingness," must be brought into play when examining school motivation. This has been implicitly part of the trend toward cooperative learning, but it must be explicitly recognized and studied. In sum, school motivation cannot be divorced from the social fabric in which it is embedded, which is one reason that claims made upon motivational psychologists to produce achievement change must be modest. There will be no "person-in-space" for the field of classroom motivation unless there is corresponding social change.

A CONCLUDING NOTE

Tracing the history of our field through the motivation chapters of the *Encyclopedia of Educational Research* reveals great vigor and movement. In just 60 years there have been major upheavals in the field, metaphors replaced, important new areas uncovered, and essential new concepts introduced. We now have a broad array of cognitions and emotions to work with, the self to consider, thoughts about goals, and so forth. In addition, we still have many uncharted areas to incorporate. In sum, we are in a fine position.

REFERENCES

Ames, C. (1984). Competitive, cooperative, and individualistic goal structures: A cognitive-motivational analysis. In R. Ames & C. Ames (Eds.), *Research on motivation in education: Vol. 1. Student motivation.* (pp. 177–207). San Diego, CA: Academic Press.

Ames, C., & Ames, R. (Eds.). (1985). *Research on motivation in education: Vol. 2. The classroom milieu.* San Diego, CA: Academic Press.

Ames, C., & Ames, R. (Eds.). (1989). *Research on motivation in education: Vol. 3. Goals and cognitions.* San Diego, CA: Academic Press.

Ames, R., & Ames, C. (Eds.). (1984). *Research on motivation in education: Vol. 1. Student motivation.* San Diego, CA: Academic Press.

Atkinson, J. W. (1957). Motivational determinants of risk-taking behavior. *Psychological Review, 64,* 359–372.

Atkinson, J. W. (1964). *An introduction to motivation.* Princeton, NJ: Van Nostrand.

Ball, S. (1982). Motivation. In H. E. Mitzel (Ed.), *Encyclopedia of educational research,* (5th ed., pp. 1256–1263). New York: Macmillan.

Ball, S. (1984). Educational psychology as an academic chameleon: An editorial assessment. *Journal of Educational Psychology, 76,* 993–999.

Bandura, A. (1977). Self-efficacy: Toward a unifying theory of behavioral change. *Psychological Review, 84,* 191–215.

Brown, J. S. (1961). *The motivation of behavior.* New York: McGraw-Hill.

Clark, M. S., & Fiske, S. T. (Eds.). (1982). *Affect and cognition: The 17th annual Carnegie symposium on cognition.* Hillsdale, NJ:

Covington, M. (1984). The motive for self-worth. In R. Ames & C. Ames (Eds.), *Research on motivation in education: Vol. 1. Student motivation.* (pp. 77–112). San Diego, CA: Academic Press.

Deci, E. L. (1975). *Intrinsic motivation.* New York: Plenum Press.

Dienstbier, R. A. (Ed.). (1990). *Nebraska Symposium on Motivation: Vol. 38. Perspectives on motivation.* Lincoln, NE: University of Nebraska Press.

Lewin, K. (1935). *A dynamic theory of personality.* New York: McGraw-Hill.

Marx, M. (1960). Motivation. In L. W. Harris (Ed.), *Encyclopedia of educational research,* (3rd ed., pp. 888–901). New York: Macmillan.

McDougall, W. (1923). *Outline of psychology.* New York: Scribner.

Mischel, W. (1968). *Personality and assessment.* New York: Wiley.

Mook, D. G. (1987). *Motivation.* New York: Norton.

Murray, H. A. (1938). *Explorations in personality.* New York: Oxford University Press.

Nicholls, J. G. (1984). Conceptions of ability and achievement motivation. In R. Ames & C. Ames (Eds.), *Research on motivation in education: Vol. 1. Student motivation* (pp. 39–73). San Diego, CA: Academic Press.

Petri, H. L. (1986). *Motivation.* Belmont, CA: Wadsworth.

Rotter, J. B. (1954). *Social learning and clinical psychology.* Englewood Cliffs, NJ: Prentice-Hall.

Rotter, J. B. (1966). Generalized expectancies for internal versus external control of reinforcements. *Psychological monographs, 80,* 1–28.

Seligman, M. E. P. (1975). *Helplessness: On depression, development, and death.* San Francisco: Freeman.

Spence, K. W. (1958). A theory of emotionally based drive (D) and its relation to performance in simple learning situations. *American Psychologist, 13,* 131–141.

Tolman, E. C. (1932). *Purposive behavior in animals and man.* New York: Appleton-Century-Crofts.

Weiner, B. (1969). Motivation. In R. L. Ebel (Ed.) *Encyclopedia of educational research,* (4th ed., pp. 878–888). New York: Macmillan.

Weiner, B. (1972). *Theories of motivation.* Chicago: Rand McNally.

Weiner, B. (1980). *Human motivation.* New York: Holt, Rinehart, & Winston.

Weiner, B. (1986). *An attributional theory of motivation and emotion.* New York: Springer-Verlag.

Weiner, B. (in press). Motivation. In M. C. Alkin (Ed.), *Encyclopedia of educational research, 6th ed.* New York: Macmillan.

Young, P. T. (1941). Motivation. In W. S. Monroe (Ed.), *Encyclopedia of educational research* (pp. 735–742). New York: Macmillan.

Young, P. T. (1950). Motivation. In W. S. Monroe (Ed.), *Encyclopedia of educational research,* (Rev. ed., pp. 755–761). New York: Macmillan.

▶ Chapter 11: Motivation, Teaching, and Learning

Learning with Peers

From Small Group Cooperation to Collaborative Communities

PHYLLIS C. BLUMENFELD, RONALD W. MARX,
ELLIOT SOLOWAY, and JOSEPH KRAJCIK

Peer learning has been suggested by many as an educational innovation that can transform students' learning experiences. Policymakers and researchers see small group work as a way to improve attitudes toward school, foster achievement, develop thinking skills, and promote interpersonal and intergroup relations. Yet, like most other simple suggestions such as lengthening the school year or assigning more homework, learning from peers in cooperative or collaborative groups is complex and difficult to achieve. When practiced in an uninformed manner, it can stigmatize low achievers, exacerbate status differences and create dysfunctional interactions among students. There are ways to overcome these problems, but none assure unqualified success and

Phyllis C. Blumenfeld is a professor in the School of Education, University of Michigan, 610 E. University Avenue, Ann Arbor, MI 48109-1259. Her specialties are motivation, classroom processes, and instruction.

Ronald W. Marx is a professor of education, University of Michigan, 610 E. University Avenue, 1225 SEB, Ann Arbor, MI 48109-1259. He specializes in cognition and motivation in classrooms and research on teaching.

Elliot Soloway is a professor of electrical engineering and computer science and professor of education, University of Michigan, 1101 Beal, 146 ATL, Ann Arbor, MI 48109-2122. His areas of specialization are human-computer interaction and learner-centered design.

Joseph S. Krajcik is an associate professor of science education, University of Michigan, 610 E. University Avenue, 1323 SEB, Ann Arbor, MI 48109-0597. He specializes in science education and technology.

none can be applied as a recipe. Rather, the ways to overcome these problems must be adapted to the unique circumstances of students, curriculum, and context. Creating successful group work is not simply a matter of putting students together. Students do not automatically become more involved, thoughtful, tolerant, or responsible when working with others.

The effects of group work depend on how the group is organized, what the tasks are, who participates, and how the group is held accountable. Teachers must consider the purposes in designing group work and address potential problems of process if group work is to be successful. In this article, we illustrate variations in purposes and types of group work and then detail factors that influence the process. Finally, we describe new developments in peer learning, collaborative communities, highlighting potential contributions of technology.

FORMS OF GROUP WORK

Teachers are often advised through policy statements that they should have their students work in small groups. The reasoning behind this advice can come from disparate sources. One major source comes from recent successes in American business that are often claimed to be the result, in part, of changes in the way workers and management interact. Small-group problem-solving has replaced topdown, rigid management. To some, it follows that if small groups are going to be the problem-solving units in businesses, schools should have the same arrangement so that students can learn early in their lives how to work in small groups. Regardless of the validity or wisdom of this advice, it is not so easy to transform the culture of schools to incorporate extensive use of small-group learning. One major reason is that there is an enormous variety in the ways in which small groups can be organized. Teachers have to be selective in their choices depending on their goals, the work that is to be accomplished in the group, and how performance will be evaluated.

Several widely used types of research-based group work are available to teachers. All conceive of this approach as part of a larger set of instructional methods, not as a panacea to change classroom teaching and learning completely. These approaches differ; there is no one way to do group work. Although developers have comprehensive goals, they tend to emphasize academics (e.g., Johnson & Johnson, 1986; Sharan, 1980; Slavin, 1990) or improved group relations (Aronson, Blaney, Stephan, Sikes, & Snapp, 1978; Cohen, 1986). The tasks vary from highly structured worksheets where students practice skills or learn definitions to more open-ended activities where students identify and solve problems. Cooperation is established in some by prescribing student roles. In Aronson's "jigsaw," the learning material is divided into small portions, and each group member works with members of other groups to study and become expert in one segment of the material. These "experts" return to their original groups to explain their portion. The group is held accountable for learning all the material. In other programs, such as Sharan's "group investigation," ways to ensure cooperation are not prescribed. Products can be created by individuals or developed by the whole group. Students may be rewarded for their own work, or rewards may be interdependent and determined by group performance. Some programs do not specify how to determine rewards. Slavin's programs combine individual accountability and group interdependence through quizzes and by basing team rewards on aggregate individual performance. In some, competition among groups is included; in others, rewards are not conditional on how other groups performed.

Obviously, adding small-group work to classroom instruction is not simple. Teachers need to have clear purposes when using group work, and they need to be aware of some of the many limitations and considerations to successful use. It is to these that we now turn.

HOW GROUPS WORK

Even if teachers decide that they want to use small-group learning, what problems might they confront? Will students actually learn more information and learn to think more deeply if they work in groups? Will they cooperate with each other, sharing in the labor and contributing to the thinking? Will they help each other and seek guidance from peers when they need it? Will they be happy with lowered grades if one of the group members does not understand a concept? Will they be willing to work with students who look different from themselves, speak English with a different accent, or have different attitudes about the world? These are very real questions for which teachers need to have answers if they are going to change.

Research has shown that successful groups promote (a) student exchanges that enhance reasoning and higher-order thinking; (b) cognitive processing such as rehearsing, organizing, and integrating information; (c) perspective-taking and accommodation to others' ideas; and (d) acceptance and encouragement among those involved with work (Bossert, 1988–1989). Recent reviews note that research focused on outcomes reports different findings than research focused on processes. The latter report potentially serious problems and factors that influence their occurrence (Good, Mulryan, and McCaslin, 1992; Webb & Palincsar, 1996). For group work to succeed, educators must consider norms, tasks, help giving and seeking, and group composition.

Group Norms

Effective group work requires students to share ideas, take risks, disagree with and listen to others, and generate and reconcile points of view. These norms do not necessarily pervade classrooms. Students are used to working individually, being rewarded for right answers, and competing with each other for grades. Placing students in groups does not mean they will actually cooperate. There is considerable and disturbing evidence that students often do not behave prosocially. One problem is failure to contribute. When groups create a single product and receive one grade, students sometimes do not do their fair share. They try to get a free ride or engage in social loafing. Moreover, students who do most of the work feel exploited and reduce their efforts or work on their own. Forceful students may also dominate discussions, pressure others to accept their perspective, or force conclusions on the group. Others may ridicule and exclude group members or discount their contributions. Rejected members are likely to be humiliated and withdraw. Managing interpersonal relations often detracts from learning content, as well. Attempts to promote positive norms include pretraining for cooperation, including listening and resolving conflicts, teaching students to appreciate the skills and abilities of others, and using rewards that promote interdependency.

Tasks

Tasks influence student interchanges and the opportunities for learning that result. Students can benefit when they share ideas, accommodate others' perspectives, and give and receive help. This is likely to occur when tasks entail problem-solving and involve more than one right answer, not when students complete worksheets aimed at improving low level skills or recall. When students connect their ideas and explain them to others or when students generate problem solutions based on information they have gathered, more discussion and elaborated responses will be needed to help peers understand their perspective. Such desirable interchanges are uncommon. Palinscar, Anderson, and David (1993) have shown that students need considerable assistance in the process of argumentation and have developed a program to help students systematically consider alternative explanations for phenomena and offer justifications for their reasoning. Moreover, negotiating such complex tasks requires considerable skill to plan, monitor, and evaluate progress.

Giving and Seeking Help

Giving and seeking help are central to learning in groups. Help-giving can benefit even high achievers, but only when they give elaborated explanations that require clarified and organized thinking. Help-seekers do not always benefit from the help they get. The help must be timely, elaborated, comprehensible, cogent, and must be correct to avoid reinforcing misconceptions. Effective help is automatic. Stu-

dents may not know how to help effectively and may require special training to learn how to elaborate their thinking. Suggestions for helping students craft good explanations include giving examples, creating analogies, and using multiple representations. Moreover, students may not be aware that they need help nor seek it when needed. They may not know how to ask questions that identify their problem, or they may be unable to make use of help they receive. More troubling though are students who remain silent or withdraw because they believe that needing help indicates incompetence (Nelson-LeGall, 1985).

Accountability

Rewards influence group interactions and whether students are willing to give help. Evaluation can be based on individual performance regardless of how the group does. Alternatively, groups can be assessed on a single product with all students earning the same grade. Some argue that interpersonal relations suffer when there is a single group grade; failing groups have lower self-perceptions, less satisfaction, and blame low achievers for the group's performance (Ames, 1981). Slavin (1990) asserts that individual accountability and group rewards are essential to ensure cooperation. Individual accountability ensures that one student does not do the group's work. Unless group rewards are interdependent, students view interaction as wasteful. Slavin's programs also stress intergroup competition and prizes. However, critics claim that such rewards are actually detrimental because they focus students on grades more than learning. When rewards are based on competition between groups, the results can be detrimental for relations with other classmates.

Group Composition

The mix of achievement levels, race and ethnicity, and gender influences how students interact, who benefits, and whether students actually engage in serious thought. Low achievers and special education students are sometimes stigmatized in heterogeneous groups. High-ability students may dominate group discussion; low-ability students may lack necessary skills and misinterpret tasks. When speed is important, more able students may take over if they resent students who slow down work. When group rewards are interdependent, high achievers are more likely to offer help. Generally, groups are more successful when members are drawn from high and middle or middle and low achievement levels or where students are all in the middle. When three levels are included, middle students benefit less because they are less likely to give explanations. The mix of student backgrounds also affects peer acceptance, encouragement, and interaction. Cohen (1986) suggests that status differences become even more salient during group work; minority students generally are presumed by majority students to be less competent and may be rejected or excluded. To address these problems, she has developed approaches to help teachers and majority students view minority students as competent. These include having low-status students teach a task on which they received prior training to high-status students and using tasks that require multiple abilities so all students can contribute.

The factors discussed in this section show that teachers need to make many decisions about how to promote group norms, help students develop skills and habits to learn with peers, design and select tasks and group students in a way that promotes learning, and determine ways to hold students accountable.

COLLABORATION

Newer models of group work are available to help promote some of the benefits that are presumed to accrue from small-group learning. Recent research portrays collaboration as a key to help students construct knowledge and to introduce them to disciplinary language, values, and ways of knowing. The disciplines represented in school subjects have special vocabularies, bodies of knowledge, and methods for gathering evidence and evaluating findings that novices need to learn. Collaborative learning that engages students in the construction of shared meaning will help advance the learning of disciplinary knowledge and understanding (Brown, 1995).

In Webb and Palincsar's (1996) view, collaboration subsumes cooperation but extends it in several important ways. The aim is to build communal knowledge through conversation. Collaboration can occur within a whole class, among groups in a class, and with people and groups outside the classroom. As students converse, they are exposed to and draw on the expertise of others and learn from them (Bruer, 1995). In collaboration of this sort, groups are not highly structured nor are specialized roles assigned. Collaborative tasks tend to be open ended

and answers are not predetermined. Knowledge generation is emphasized as students pose questions or define problems. They gather information and data, interpret findings, and use evidence to draw conclusions. Individuals, groups, or the whole class may create unique artifacts to represent understanding. Because the aim is to share ideas with the whole class or community, interdependence is highlighted; there is little emphasis on group rewards to ensure cooperation or group competitions to motivate students. These newer approaches to peer learning entail some of the same difficulties described above regarding small-group learning. To address them, emerging computing and communications technologies (e.g., powerful, low-cost computers; the Internet; and the World Wide Web) are being used to support collaboration.

Technological Support for Collaboration

Technologies such as E-mail increase opportunities for conversations by enabling large groups of students to exchange data and share observations in asynchronous conversations (i.e., conversations that do not require all parties to be involved at the same time). Programs also support synchronous conversations in which students converse by typing. Technology also helps to support and keep track of dialogue among students and serves as a public archive of conversations. Software (e.g., CSILE, Scardamalia & Bereiter, 1991) specifies and organizes elements of conversations such as generating hypotheses or predictions and commenting on others' work. Unlike E-mail systems then, these collaborative software applications are expressly designed to support the creation of shared understanding. In addition, conversations can be stored, reflected on, and reacted to, creating a common knowledge base that is open to review, comment, and manipulation (i.e., searching conversations by date, subject, or author) by many—not just the conversants. Experience indicates that students who do not typically engage in classroom discussion participate in these computer-based, classroom-wide conversations. The newest generation of collaborative environments supports conversations but goes substantially further by providing a "place" to which students can go. This new generation of environments (such as those under development by Soloway and Krajcik, 1995) provides tools to accumulate and integrate a range of communications functions. Such software will constitute a suite of virtual Internet rooms where students can go to collaborate. Conversations can take place in the context of digital artifacts. Students can view the same drawing, text document, or interactive program in one window as their conversations go on in another window, or students can drop output from their simulation program into a collaborator's visualization program, all the while chatting synchronously.

A number of technological challenges need to be addressed for these new tools to have an impact (e.g., adequate computer availability, easily mastered programs suited to learners' needs). More importantly, effective instructional strategies are needed to help students use such systems productively. While considerable research has examined small-group collaboration, there is no comparable body of experience for the use of technology-supported small groups.

CONCLUSIONS

Peer learning can be a powerful tool. However, it is not a guaranteed solution to educational problems. Small-group instruction can be used in appropriate as well as inappropriate ways. Results can be positive when close attention is paid to norms, tasks, the mix of participants and their skills, and methods to ensure accountability.

This article was prepared in part with support from the National Science Foundation (Grant Nos. TPE-9153759, RED-9554205, RED-9353481, and REC-9555719).

REFERENCES

Ames, C. (1981). Competitive versus cooperative reward structures: The influence of individual and group performance factors on achievement attributions and affect. *American Educational Research Journal, 18*, 273–287.

Aronson, E., Blaney, N., Stephan, C., Sikes, J., & Snapp, M. (1978). *The jigsaw classroom.* Beverly Hills, CA: Sage.

Bossert, S. T. (1988–1989). Cooperative activities in the classroom. In E. Z. Rothkopf (Ed.), *Review of research in education* (Vol. 15, pp. 225–252). Washington, DC: American Educational Research Association.

Brown, A. L. (1995). The advancement of learning. *Educational Researcher, 23*(8), 4–12.

Bruer, J. (1995). Classroom problems, school culture, and cognitive research. In K. McGilly (Ed.), *Classroom lessons: Integrating cognitive theory and classroom practice* (pp. 273–290). Cambridge, MA: MIT Press.

Cohen, E. G. (1986). *Designing group work: Strategies for the heterogeneous classroom.* New York: Teachers College Press.

Good, T., Mulryan, C., & McCaslin, M. (1992). Grouping for instruction in mathematics: A call for programmatic research on small-group processes. In D. Grouws (Ed.), *Handbook of research on mathematics teaching and learning* (pp. 165–196). New York: Macmillan.

Johnson, D. W., & Johnson, R. T. (1986). *Learning together and alone* (2nd ed.). Englewood Cliffs, NJ: Prentice Hall.

Nelson-LeGall, S. (1985). Help-seeking behavior in learning. In E. V. Gordon (Ed.), *Review of research in education* (Vol. 12, pp. 55–90). Washington, DC: American Educational Research Association.

Palincsar, A. S., Anderson, C., & David, Y. M. (1993). Pursuing scientific literacy in the middle grades through collaborative problem solving. *The Elementary School Journal, 93*, 643–658.

Scardamalia, M., & Bereiter, C. (1991). Higher levels of agency for children in knowledge building: A challenge for the design of new knowledge media. *The Journal of the Learning Sciences, 1*, 37–68.

Sharan, S. (1980). Cooperative learning in small groups: Recent methods and effects on achievement, attitudes, and ethnic relations. *Review of Educational Research, 50*, 241–272.

Slavin, R. E. (1990). *Cooperative learning: Theory, research, and practice.* Englewood Cliffs, NJ: Prentice Hall.

Soloway, E., & Krajcik, J. S. (1995). *Computational support for authentic science inquiry* (National Science Foundation Grant No. REC-9555719). University of Michigan, Ann Arbor.

Webb, N. M., & Palincsar, A. S. (1996). Group processes in the classroom. In D. C. Berliner & R. Calfee (Eds.), *Handbook of educational psychology* (pp. 841–873). New York: Macmillan.

What Do Students Want (and What Really Motivates Them)?

RICHARD STRONG, HARVEY F. SILVER, and AMY ROBINSON

Ten years ago, we began a research project by asking both teachers and students two simple questions: What kind of work do you find totally engaging? and What kind of work do you hate to do? Almost immediately, we noticed distinct patterns in their responses.

Engaging work, respondents said, was work that stimulated their curiosity, permitted them to express their creativity, and fostered positive relationships with others. It was also work at which they were *good*. As for activities they hated, both teachers and students cited work that was repetitive, that required little or no thought, and that was forced on them by others.

How, then, would we define engagement? Perhaps the best definition comes from the work of Phil Schlecty (1994), who says students who are engaged exhibit three characteristics: (1) they are attracted to their work, (2) they persist in their work despite challenges and obstacles, and (3) they take visible delight in accomplishing their work.

Most teachers have seen these signs of engagement during a project, presentation, or lively class discussion. They have caught glimpses of the inspired inner world of a child, and hoped to sustain this wonder, enthusiasm, and perseverance every day. At the same time, they may have felt stymied by traditions of reward and punishment. Our challenge is to transcend these very real difficulties and provide a practical model for understanding what our students want and need.

GOALS AND NEEDS: THE *SCORE*

As the responses to our questions showed, people who are engaged in their work are driven by four essential goals, each of which satisfies a particular human need:

- *Success* (the need for mastery),
- *Curiosity* (the need for understanding),
- *Originality* (the need for self-expression),
- *Relationships* (the need for involvement with others).

These four goals form the acronym for our model of student engagement—*SCORE*. Under the right classroom conditions and at the right level for each student, they can build the motivation and *Energy* (to complete our acronym) that is essential for a complete and productive life. These goals can provide students with the energy to deal constructively with the complexity, confusion, repetition, and ambiguities of life (the drive toward *completion*).

Richard Strong is Vice President and Director of Curriculum Development, Harvey F. Silver is Vice President and Director of Program Development, Amy Robinson is Director of Research and Publishing, Hanson Silver Strong and Associates Inc., 34 Washington Rd., Princeton Junction, NJ 08550.

RETHINKING MOTIVATION

The concept of "score" is a metaphor about performance, but one that also suggests a work of art, as in a musical score. By aiming to combine achievement and artistry, the SCORE model can reach beyond strict dichotomies of right/wrong and pass/fail, and even bypass the controversy about intrinsic and extrinsic motivation, on which theories of educational motivation have long been based.

Extrinsic motivation—a motivator that is external to the student or the task at hand—has long been perceived as the bad boy of motivational theory. In *Punished by Rewards,* Alfie Kohn (1995) lays out the prevailing arguments against extrinsic rewards, such as grades and gold stars. He maintains that reliance on factors external to the task and to the individual consistently fails to produce any deep and long-lasting commitment to learning.

Intrinsic motivation, on the other hand, comes from within, and is generally considered more durable and self-enhancing (Kohn 1993). Still, although intrinsic motivation gets much better press, it, too, has its weaknesses. As Kohn argues, because intrinsic motivation "is a concept that exists only in the context of the individual," the prescriptions its proponents offer teachers, are often too radically individualized, or too bland and abstract, to be applied in classroom settings (See "Punished by Rewards? A Conversation with Alfie Kohn," p. 13).

Perhaps it is the tradition of separating extrinsic and intrinsic motivation that is flawed. Robert Sternberg and Todd Lubart recently addressed this possibility in *Defying the Crowd* (1995). They assert that any in-depth examination of the work of highly creative people reveals a blend of both types of motivation.

KNOWING THE SCORE

After taking into consideration the needs and drives we've mentioned, our model poses four important questions that teachers must ask themselves in order to score the level of engagement in their classrooms.

1. Under what conditions are students most likely to feel that they can be successful?
2. When are students most likely to become curious?
3. How can we help students satisfy their natural drive toward self-expression?
4. How can we motivate students to learn by using their natural desire to create and foster good peer relationships?

Much of what we will discuss is already taking place in classrooms across the country. The point of our SCORE model of engagement is first to help teachers discover what they are already doing right and then to encourage the cultivation of everyday classroom conditions that foster student motivation and success.

CONVINCING KIDS THEY CAN *Succeed*

Students want and need work that enables them to demonstrate and improve their sense of themselves as competent and successful human beings. This is the drive toward mastery. But success, while highly valued in our society, can be more or less motivational. People who are highly creative, for example, actually experience failure far more often than success.

Before we can use success to motivate our students to produce high-quality work, we must meet three conditions:

1. We must clearly articulate the criteria for success and provide clear, immediate, and constructive feedback.
2. We must show students that the skills they need to be successful are within their grasp by clearly and systematically modeling these skills.
3. We must help them see success as a valuable aspect of their personalities.

All this seems obvious enough, but it is remarkable how often we fail to meet these conditions for our students. Take skills. Can you remember any crucial skills that you felt you did not successfully master because they were not clearly taught? Was it finding themes in literature? Reading and interpreting primary texts? Thinking through nonroutine math problems? Typically, skills like these are routinely assigned or assumed, rather than systematically modeled or practiced by teachers.

So how can we help students master such skills? When teaching your students to find themes, for example, deliberately model interpretation. Ask your students to give you a poem you have never seen, and then interpret it both for and with them. If they are reading primary texts, use what we call the "main idea" strategy. Teach them how to find the topic (usually a noun or noun phrase), the main idea (a sentence that states the text's position on the topic), and reasons or evidence to support the main idea. If students are concerned about writer's block, remember that perhaps the most difficult task of a teacher is to teach how to think creatively. Model the process of brainstorming, demonstrating that no idea is unworthy of consideration.

These are not revolutionary ideas. They simply illustrate how easily classroom practices can be improved, thus increasing the chance that your students will succeed.

But what of the *criteria* for success? Teachers define success in many ways. We must not only broaden our definition, but also make sure the definition is clear to everyone. In this way, students will *know* when they have done a good job, and they will *know* how to improve their work.

To achieve this clarity, we can present examples of work that illustrate high, average, and low levels of achievement. Such exemplars can significantly motivate students, as well as increase their understanding of their own ability to achieve.

AROUSING *Curiosity*

Students want and need work that stimulates their curiosity and awakens their desire for deep understanding. People are naturally curious about a variety of things. Einstein wondered his whole life about the relationships among gravity, space, and electromagnetic radiation. Deborah Tannen, the prominent linguistic psychologist, has spent years pondering the obstacles that prevent men and women from conversing meaningfully.

How can we ensure that our curriculum arouses intense curiosity? By making sure it features two defining characteristics: the information about a topic is fragmentary or contradictory, and the topic relates to students' personal lives.

It is precisely the *lack* of organization of a body of information that compels us to understand it further. This may explain why textbooks, which are highly organized, rarely arouse student interest. We have stimulated students' curiosity by using a strategy called "mystery." We confront the class with a problem—for example, "What killed off the dino-

saurs?"—and with the actual clues that scientists or historians have used to try to answer that question and others. Clues might include:

- Mammals survived the changes that killed the dinosaurs.
- Chickens under stress lay eggs with thinner shells than do chickens not under stress.
- While flowering plants evolved, dinosaurs increased in population and in number of species.
- Some flowering plants contain alkaloids.

Students then work together in groups, retracing the steps scientists took in weighing the available evidence to arrive at an explanation. We have seen students work diligently for several days dealing with false hypotheses and red herrings, taking great delight when the solutions begin to emerge.

As for topics that relate to students' lives, the connection here cannot be superficial; it must involve an issue or idea that is both manageable and unresolved. We must ask, With what issues are adolescents wrestling? How can we connect them to our curriculum? Figure 1 illustrates some possibilities for adolescents.

ENCOURAGING *Originality*

Students want and need work that permits them to express their autonomy and originality, enabling them to discover who they are and who they want to be. Unfortunately, the ways schools traditionally focus on creativity actually thwart the drive toward self-expression. There are several reasons for this.

First, schools frequently design whole programs (art, for example) around projects that teach technique rather than self-expression. Second, very often only students who display the most talent have access to audiences, thus cutting off all other students from feedback and a sense of purpose. Finally, and perhaps most destructive, schools frequently view creativity as a form of play, and thus fail to maintain the high standards and sense of seriousness that make creative work meaningful.

How, then, should self-expression be encouraged? There are several ways.

- *Connect creative projects to students' personal ideas and concerns.* One of our favorite teachers begins her study of ceramics by having students exam-

Adolescent Issue	Topic	Connection
Independence: How can I separate myself from parents and other adults?	American Revolution	When is rebellion justified?
The search for identity: Who do I want to be? What do I want to become?	Percentages	To determine your likes and dislikes, compute the percentage of your life spent in various activities.
Relationships and stature: How important are my opinions of my peers, my family?	Jane Austen's *Emma*	Discuss how stature and reputation affect Emma's decisions and your own.
Responsibility: For what do I want to take responsibility? What is expected of me?	Ecology	Investigate social organizations working to improve the environment.

FIGURE 1   **The Curiosity Connection: Relating Content to Student's Lives**

Adapted from Beane, J. A., and R. P. Lipka. (1986). *Self-Concept, Self-Esteem, and the Curriculum.* New York: Teachers College Press.

ine objects found in the homes of a variety of ancient civilizations. She then asks the class to design a ceramic object that expresses their feeling about their home.

- *Expand what counts as an audience.* One of the most successful creative projects we have seen involved an audience of one. Each student in a middle school class was linked to an older member of the community and asked to write that person's "autobiography."

- *Consider giving students more choice.* The medium of expression, for example, is often as important to an artist as the expression itself. What would have happened to the great tradition of American blues if the early musicians were forced to adhere to traditions of European music? This is one more argument for instructional methods that emphasize learning styles, multiple intelligences, and cultural diversity.

- *Use the "abstracting" strategy to help students fully understand a genre and to maintain high standards* (Marzano et al. 1992). Too often, students prefer video art to a book because they perceive it as less demanding or requiring less commitment. Teaching students to abstract the essence of a genre will change their perceptions.

Begin by studying examples of high-quality work within a genre (the science-fiction story, poster art, sonnets, frontier diaries, television news programs, and so on). Examine the structure of the works and the standards by which they are judged.

Then, ask students to produce their own work in that genre that expresses their own concerns, attempting to meet the high standards embodied in the original work. Finally, have the students ask themselves four questions about their work: How good is my technique? Does my work truly express my own concerns? Does it demonstrate my understanding of the genre in which I am working? Does it successfully relate to its audience?

Some people worry that the stringency of this model might actually block self-expression, but our experience is precisely the opposite. Students' drive toward self-expression is ultimately a drive to produce work that is of value to others. Lower standards work to repress, not to enhance, the creation of high-quality work.

FOSTERING PEER *Relations*

Students want and need work that will enhance their relationships with people they care about. This drive toward interpersonal involvement is pervasive in all our lives. Further, most of us work hardest on those relationships that are reciprocal—what you have to offer is of value to me, and what I have to offer is of some value to you. In general, unbalanced, nonreciprocal relationships prove transient and fail to generate much energy or interest.

How does this insight apply to life in the classroom? Consider a student's perception of homework. The only relationship that can be advanced through the typical homework assignment is the one between student and teacher. And this relationship is essentially unbalanced. Students do not feel that the teacher needs their knowledge, and the teacher, with possibly 145 students a day, probably isn't seeking a deep relationship either.

But suppose student work is complementary: one student's job is to learn about tortoises, another's is to learn about snakes, and a third student is boning up on lizards. After they do their research, they jointly develop a poster comparing and contrasting these three reptile types. The students actually need one another's knowledge.

Annemarie Palincsar Brown has applied this "jigsaw" strategy to inner-city students using in-classroom computer networks (Brown et al. 1993). She found that it significantly improved their motivation, reading, and writing. Elizabeth Cohen (1994) builds reciprocal groups by asking students with different talents and abilities to work on one project that requires all of their gifts.

ORCHESTRATING CLASSROOM PERFORMANCE

As teachers, the first thing we should try to "score" is our *own* performance. Different people value the four goals we have discussed to different degrees in different situations. Which ones are particularly important to you? How does this preference affect the way you run your classroom? By observing and understanding how classroom conditions can create or repress student engagement, we can gradually move toward a more successful, curious, creative, and reciprocal school system.

All students, to some extent, seek mastery, understanding, self-expression, and positive interpersonal relationships. But they are all different as well. Imagine what could happen if we engaged our stu-

dents in a discussion of these four types of motivation. What might they tell us about themselves and their classrooms? Could we actually teach them to design their own work in ways that match their own unique potential for engagement?

Last, we can score the change process itself. What professional conditions block teachers' motivation? We can redesign staff development to promote understanding and respect among school staff members.

By seeking to break down boundaries between teacher and teacher, teacher and student, student and the learning process, we will learn what students want and need. As a result, more and more teachers may go to bed at night remembering the images of wonder, enthusiasm, and perseverance on the faces of their students.

REFERENCES

Brown, A., D. Ash, M. Rutherford, K. Nakagawa, A. Gordon, and J. Campione. (1993). "Distributed Expertise in the Classroom." In *Distributed Cognitions: Psychological and Educational Considerations*, edited by G. Salomon. New York: Cambridge University Press.

Cohen, E. G. (1994). *Designing Groupwork: Strategies for the Heterogeneous Classroom*. 2nd Edition. New York: Teachers College Press.

Kohn, A. (1993). *Punished by Rewards: The Trouble with Gold Stars, Incentive Plans, A's, Praise, and Other Bribes*. Boston: Houghton Mifflin.

Marzano, R., D. Pickering, D. Arredondo, G. Blackburn, R. Brandt, and C. Moffett. (1992). *Dimensions of Learning*. Alexandria, Va.: Association for Supervision and Curriculum Development.

Schlecty, P. (January 1994). "Increasing Student Engagement." Missouri Leadership Academy.

Sternberg, R. J., and T. I. Lubart. (1995). *Defying the Crowd: Cultivating Creativity in a Culture of Conformity*. New York: The Free Press.

Chapter 12: Creating Learning Environments

What Research Really Shows about Assertive Discipline

GARY F. RENDER, JE NELL M. PADILLA, and H. MARK KRANK

In the October 1988 issue of *Educational Leadership*, Lee Canter ("Let the Educator Beware: A Response to Curwin and Mendler") cited studies that he believes provide strong support for the effectiveness of Assertive Discipline. He has also stated that Assertive Discipline is based on research and will produce an 80 percent reduction in student misbehavior (Canter and Associates 1987). Canter has made this statement repeatedly (Canter 1979a, 1979b, 1983) but has provided no evidence to support it.

A SMALL DATABASE

We believed that a program in existence for 12 years and so widely used (reports suggest that 500,000 people have been trained in Assertive Discipline) would have generated an extensive database (Canter and Associates 1987). We therefore reviewed the literature (Render et al. in press, Render et al. 1987) and reported only studies in which information was gathered in some systematic way and in which results were presented. We found only 16 studies (10 dissertations, 3 journal articles, and 3 other reports)

Gary F. Render is Professor of Educational Psychology, University of Wyoming, College of Education, Department of Educational Foundations and Instructional Technology, Box 3374, Laramie, WY 82071. Je Nell M. Padilla and H. Mark Krank both are Ph.D. candidates in Educational Psychology, Department of Educational Foundations and Instructional Technology, University of Wyoming.

meeting our criteria. Equally surprising is the nature of the studies. Not one study systematically investigated the program's effectiveness compared with any other specific approach. The studies of Assertive Discipline have been generated primarily by beginning researchers, and no strongly generalizable data have resulted. The research is sparse and unsophisticated.

Figure 1 [on pages 194–195] presents a brief description of the existing studies of Assertive Discipline. We have presented the information as it was reported without any interpretations of the data.

LIMITED EVIDENCE

The claims made by Canter (1988) and also made in Barrett's (1987) review are simply not supported by the existing and available literature. We would agree that Assertive Discipline could be helpful in severe cases where students are behaving inappropriately more than 96 percent of the time, as in the study of Mandelbaum and colleagues (1983). We would also argue that teachers such as the one in that study would benefit from *any* intervention. However, we can find no evidence that Assertive Discipline is an effective approach deserving schoolwide and districtwide adoption.

Canter has also stated that teachers have no need for educational literature; they need "answers" (1988, p. 73). We believe teachers deserve answers based on more than limited studies that

FIGURE 1 Studies of Assertive Discipline (AD)

Authors	Subjects	Variables	Findings
1. Ersavas (1981)	Teachers, administrators, and 5th grade students.	Perceptions of AD implementation.	The school with the highest California assessment program achievement results experienced the least growth from AD. Students who perceived themselves as reading better than their peers experienced the least growth from AD.
2. Bauer (1982)	Grade 9 students drawn from high school using AD. Comparison from high school not using AD (no N reported).	Reduction of discipline problems. Increasing student satisfaction. Improving student attitude.	AD effective in discipline areas related to social skills. Problems related to learning not affected. Teachers reported greater satisfaction. No increase in student morale or attitudes (no data reported).
3. Henderson (1982)	Elementary teachers (no N reported).	Locus of control, pupil control ideology, self-concept, assertive teacher characteristics.	Teachers trained in AD were significantly different from controls on all measures. No study was made of behavior of these teachers' students.
4. Moffett, Jerenka, and Kovan (1982)	67% of district teachers (N = 94)	Teachers' perceptions of AD.	21% perceived student behavior as somewhat improved; 48% as improved in an observable degree; 30% as totally improved. Authors claim that AD "virtually eliminated classroom disruptions."
5. Crawley (1983)	Teachers (N = 52) and students (N = 580)	Perceptions of teachers trained or not trained in AD. Perceptions of students of teachers trained or not trained in AD.	" . . . There are no benefits measured by this study derived from Assertive Discipline training."
6. Mandelbaum, Russell, Krouse, and Gonter (1983)	One 3rd grade classroom (N = 31) and the teacher.	Student out-of-seat behavior (OB). Student inappropriate talking (IT) measured in percent of time.	(see table below)
7. Fereira (1983)	Elementary students in one school of 356 students (1979–80) and 365 students (1982–83).	Number of students referred to office for disciplinary reasons.	During 1979–80 school year 350 students referred to office. During 1982–83 school year 247 students referred. Referrals changed from interpersonal problems to on-task behavior problems. No indication of what actually happened in classrooms.
8. Ward (1984)	Not reported.	Classroom disruptions.	Before AD—17.09 disruptions/100 students/day. After AD—10.44 disruptions/100 students/day. Seven other variables were significantly related to the results.
9. Allen (1984)	7th, 8th, and 9th grade students (N = 353).	Disciplinary referrals.	There was a 31.8% ($p < .05$) decrease in referrals from 3,646/year to 2,492/year. A survey of the staff indicated that AD was effective. The number of referrals after AD suggests the school still had a severe discipline problem.

Findings for study 6 (Mandelbaum et al.):

	Before AD	After AD	Remove AD	Reinstate AD
OB	96%	45%	87%	42%
IT	99%	54%	91%	65%

Never did out-of-seat behavior occur less than 35% of the time.

FIGURE 1   *(Continued)*

Authors	Subjects	Variables	Findings
10. Smith (1984)	Student teachers trained in AD (no N reported).	Student teachers' assertiveness.	Student teachers trained in AD rated themselves more assertive than controls. Supervising teachers agreed. No report on student behavior in these student teachers' classrooms.
11. Webb (1984)	Teachers K–12 (N = 129), principals (N = 12).	Perceptions of teachers and principals regarding effectiveness of AD.	86% liked AD; 82% perceived improved student behavior; 77% perceived improved control of student behavior; 43% perceived improvement in student behavior to be lasting.
12. Braun, Render, and Moon (1984)	Elementary and junior high students (N = 1,087), teachers (N = 86), and parents (N = 446).	Involvement of students in the establishment of classroom rules and consequences of misbehavior.	71% of students said they rarely or never were given an opportunity for input in establishing classroom rules or consequences for misbehavior.
13. McCormack (1985)	36 3rd grade classes; 18 using AD, 18 not (N = 687).	Off-task behavior during reading instruction.	Students in classes without AD off-task 13% of time. Students with AD were off-task 5% less. AD was said to account for 9% of the variance in off-task behavior.
14. Parker (1985)	Administrators, secondary teachers, students, and parents (no N reported).	Perceptions of AD.	AD favored by administrators. Teachers preferred their own discipline styles. Parents generally approved but did not expect or desire to see AD used with their own children.
15. Barrett and Curtis (1986)	Student teachers trained in AD (N – 248) 1981–82; student teachers not trained in AD (N = 288) 1982–83; supervisors (N = 396) rated student teachers not trained in AD in 1981–82. Supervisors (N = 307) rated student teachers trained in AD in 1982–83.	Perceptions of student teachers regarding their ability to use appropriate discipline techniques. Perceptions of supervisors regarding student teachers' use of techniques.	Student teachers trained in AD perceived significantly ($p < .05$) better preparation in use of techniques. Supervisors rated student teachers trained in AD significantly ($p < .05$) better at using appropriate techniques. Appropriate techniques were not defined. The use of assertive discipline techniques was not a focus of the study. The study does not support or fail to support the use of AD. The *use* of AD techniques was not studied.
16. Barrett (1987)	A review of literature on AD, all of which is included here.	The same variables listed above. Findings are drawn from several of the studies listed here—no others than listed here.	"Based upon research conducted at this early stage [AD] has proven to be effective." "It [AD] has been proven beneficial in both decreasing the number of referrals and as an effective means to increase on-task behavior of students." "[AD] also has proven significantly effective in reducing student disruptions."

suffer from a lack of generalizability to various settings, teachers, subject areas, and grade levels. (We suggest that readers form their conclusions regarding Assertive Discipline by evaluating the existing literature.)

WHERE ARE THE FACTS?

Canter and Assertive Discipline advocates suggest that the program is "proven" effective. Even after years of investigation and numerous studies and replications, no reputable scholar would state that "the research *proves*" any particular educational approach. Ten dissertations, three journal articles, and three other reports is certainly limited evidence to support *any* educational strategy. We agree with Canter that "facts are hard to dispute" (1988, p. 71); however, facts result from systematic, scientific investigations, replications, and evaluations by scholars, not from hopeful claims and promotions.

REFERENCES

Allen, R. D. (1984). "The Effect of Assertive Discipline on the Number of Junior High School Disciplinary Referrals." *Dissertation Abstracts International* 44: 2299A–2300A.

Barrett, E. R. (1987). "Assertive Discipline and Research." Unpublished manuscript available from Canter and Associates, P. O. Box 2113, Santa Monica, CA 90406.

Barrett, E. R., and K. F. Curtis. (Spring/Summer 1986). "The Effect of Assertive Discipline Training on Student Teachers." *Teacher Education and Practice*: 53–56.

Bauer, R. L. (1982). "A Quasi-Experimental Study of the Effects of Assertive Discipline." *Dissertation Abstracts International* 43: 25A.

Braun, J. A., G. F. Render, and C. E. Moon. (1984). "Assertive Discipline: A Report of Student, Teacher, and Parent Perceptions." *Journal of the Association for the Study of Perception* 19, 1: 18–25.

Canter and Associates. (1987). "Abstracts of Research Validating Effectiveness of Assertive Discipline." Unpublished manuscript available from Canter and Associates, P. O. Box 2113, Santa Monica, CA 90406.

Canter, L. (1979a). "Competency-Based Approach to Discipline—It's Assertive." *Thrust for Educational Leadership* 8:11–13.

Canter, L. (1979b). "Taking Charge of Student Behavior." *National Elementary Principal* 58, 4:33–36, 41.

Canter, L. (October 1983). "Assertive Discipline: A Proven Approach." *Today's Catholic Teacher*: 36–37.

Canter, L. (October 1988). "Let the Education Beware: A Response to Curwin and Mendler." *Educational Leadership* 46, 2: 71–73.

Crawley, K. E. (1983). "Teacher and Student Perceptions with Regard to Classroom Behavior Conditions, Procedures, and Student Behavior in Classes of Teachers Trained in Assertive Discipline Methods." *Dissertation Abstracts International* 43: 2840A.

Ersavas, C. M. (1981). "A Study of the Effect of Assertive Discipline at Four Elementary Schools." *Dissertation Abstracts International* 42: 473A.

Fereira, C. L. (1983). *A Positive Approach to Assertive Discipline.* Martinez, Calif.: Martinez Unified School District. (ERIC Document Reproduction Service No. ED 240 058).

Henderson, C. B. (1982). "An Analysis of Assertive Discipline Training and Implementation on Inservice Elementary Teachers' Self-Concept. Locus of Control, Pupil Control Ideology, and Assertive Personality Characteristics." *Dissertation Abstracts International* 42: 4797A.

Mandelbaum, L. H., S. C. Russell, J. Krouse, and M. Gonter. (1983). "Assertive Discipline: An Effective Classwide Behavior Management Program." *Behavior Disorders* 8, 4: 258–264.

McCormack, S. L. (1985). "Students' Off-Task Behavior and Assertive Discipline." (Doctoral diss., University of Oregon.) *Dissertation Abstracts International* 46: 1880A.

Moffett, K. L., D. J. Jurenka, and J. Kovan. (June/July/August 1982). "Assertive Discipline." *California School Boards*: 24–27.

Parker, P. R. (1985). "Effects of Secondary-Level Assertive Discipline in a Central Texas School District and Guidelines to Successful Assertion and Reward Strategies." *Dissertation Abstracts International* 45:3504A.

Render, G. F., J. M. Padilla, and H. M. Krank. (October 1987). "Assertive Discipline: A Critical Review and Analysis." Paper presented at the annual meeting of the Northern Rocky Mountain Educational Research Association, Park City, Utah.

Render, G. F., J. M. Padilla, and H. M. Krank. (In press). "Assertive Discipline: A Critical Review and Analysis." *Teachers College Record.*

Smith, S. J. (1984). "The Effects of Assertive Discipline Training on Student Teachers' Self-Perceptions and Classroom Management Skills." *Dissertation Abstracts International* 44: 2690A.

Ward, L. R. (1984). "The Effectiveness of 'Assertive Discipline' as a Means to Reduce Classroom Disruptions." *Dissertation Abstracts International* 44: 2323A–2324A.

Webb, M. M. (1984). "An Evaluation of Assertive Discipline and Its Degree of Effectiveness as Perceived by the Professional Staff in Selected School Corporations." *Dissertation Abstracts International* 44: 2324A–2325A.

Response to Render, Padilla, and Krank: But Practitioners Say It Works!

SAMMIE McCORMACK

Remember the six blind men of Indostan who went to see the elephant? They argued that it "is very like a wall . . . is very like a spear . . . is very like a snake . . . is very like a tree . . . is very like a rope." In his fable, John B. Saxe concluded that the men were "Each in his own opinion, Exceedingly stiff and strong. Though each was partly in the right, And all were in the wrong" (Saxe, "The Blind Men and the Elephant," Boston, 1852).

So also can it be said of authors who criticize the programs of others without basis. Like the blind men, Render, Padilla, and Krank are both partly in the right and partly in the wrong.

PARTLY RIGHT

I too am surprised that so little research about Assertive Discipline is available. That concern, however, is not limited to the study of Assertive Discipline; in fact, no other copyrighted classroom management program is better researched. Render, Padilla, and Krank are correct in chastising the research community for failure to compare the program's effects with other approaches to classroom management. Is that an indictment of Assertive Discipline?

Sammie McCormack is Coordinator, High Performance Schools, San Diego County Office of Education, 6401 Linda Vista Rd., San Diego, CA 92111-7399.

Does the absence of that comparison mean Assertive Discipline lacks a support base? To both questions, the answer is "no."

Other studies, beyond those examined by Render, Padilla, and Krank, indicate that from a "practitioner's perspective," Assertive Discipline achieves the outcomes that Canter and Associates promote (1976). The sample findings in Figure 1 [on page 198] come from school districts and state organizations; the publications cited are reports to their constituencies.

PARTLY WRONG

Render, Padilla, and Krank are also partially wrong in their findings. I do not choose to challenge their chart of studies, item by item. However, the information they present appears to come from a reading of abstracts rather than the complete research. I uncovered enough discrepancies to cast doubt on their conclusions. For example:

- Ersavas (1981) studied four schools. Render, Padilla, and Krank report "the school."
- Bauer (1982) studied 315 students and 23 teachers at a high school where Assertive Discipline was used, and 255 students and 45 teachers at a different high school where Assertive Discipline was not used. Render, Padilla, and Krank state "no N reported."

Location/Author	Subjects	Variables	Findings
1. Cartwright School District Phoenix, Ariz. (1982)	445 teachers All district records of behavior referrals	Tardiness Bus referrals Weapons referrals Theft Classroom management techniques	Down 54% in the district. Down 71% in the district. Down 71% in the district. Down 88% in the district. 86% of teachers felt student behavior improved.
2. Compton, Calif., School District Swanson (1984)	30 principals 241 teachers 258 parents 72 secondary students	The need for Assertive Discipline Implementation time Teaching time Program effectiveness	66% felt the program was needed. 85% felt outcomes justified the administrative implementation time. 83% of teachers felt it freed more time for instruction. Conclusion: "Program is perceived as a success. The goals and objectives of this program have been achieved to a significant extent."
3. Lennox School District Inglewood, Calif. Moffett, Jurenka, and Kovan (1982)	94 K–12 teachers (67% of district)	Student behavior	78% felt that student behavior was observably or totally improved.
4. Troy City Schools Troy, Ohio Becker (1980)	100 elementary teachers 33 teachers of grades 7–8 40 teachers of grades 9–12	Student behavior Teaching time	91% of elementary teachers, 99% of teachers of grade 7–8, and 95% of teachers of grades 9–12 felt that student behavior was observably or totally improved. 86% of elementary teachers, 99% of teachers of grades 7–8, and 90% of teachers of grades 9–12 felt more time was spent on educational experiences and less time on disruptive behavior.
5. State of Oregon Confederation of Oregon School Administrators (1980)	Random sample from over 7,800 teachers and administrators trained in Assertive Discipline (workshops sponsored by COSA) (N = not reported)	Student behavior	81% felt schoolwide student behavior was improved. 79% felt there was a decrease in classroom management problems.

FIGURE 1 **Findings from School Districts and State Organizations about Assertive Discipline**

- Henderson (1982) studied 25 teachers with Assertive Discipline training and 25 teachers without. Render, Padilla, and Krank state "no N reported."
- Crawley (1983), in summarizing his own research, states, "The research may not have been properly designed to avoid contamination from variables not controlled."

There are others. But the errors, omissions, and even value judgments that understandably result from attempting to reduce a 100-plus page research document to one or two sentences are not as important as the conclusions that Render, Padilla, and Krank draw.

AS AN ADMINISTRATOR

Would I as a site administrator let these findings guide me in the decision to train my staff in Assertive Discipline techniques? I would be interested, but my decision would be influenced by many other factors. Professional educators, unlike professional researchers, use a variety of sources from which to draw conclusions. These sources include the network of local administrators and professional organizations. I've even made phone calls to officials in districts, for example, like Irving, Texas (C. Green, personal communication, August 19, 1988), where they have just completed their eighth annual districtwide new teacher training in Assertive Discipline. Lennox School District, which is cited both in the findings of Render and his colleagues and here, also continues to report the success of its program. Assertive Discipline is now a regular part of the district's new teacher training (Moffett et al. 1987).

AS A PRINCIPAL

As a principal, did I want to know if it worked before we began the program? Certainly. My information, however, came from practitioners who told me "it works," from my observations of schools that used the program, and from the personal commitment of my faculty to employ a discipline program that would encourage students to be self-managers. I found that teachers who did not use positive recognition as part of their management system did not use Assertive Discipline (McCormack 1981). It is not necessary for research to support, as Render, Padilla, and Krank imply, that "any particular educational approach" works before an administrator makes a program decision.

NO BASIS FOR CRITICISM

My point is, if their findings supported the position that the approach did *not* work—and Render, Padilla, and Krank do *not* come to that conclusion—

there would be a reasonable reason for rejection. The findings they cite, on the other hand—improved student self-perceptions, greater teacher satisfaction, improved student behavior, fewer office referrals, reduction of classroom disruptions, improved time-on-task, better student teacher preparation, and appreciation of the program by students and staff—support the benefits of Assertive Discipline. The researchers "doth protest too much, methinks."

Author's note: I reviewed all of the following references to check Render, Padilla, and Krank's research. Not all of these references are cited in the above text.

REFERENCES

Barrett, E. R. (1987). "Assertive Discipline and Research." Unpublished manuscript.

Bauer, R. L. (1982). "A Quasi-Experimental Study of the Effects of Assertive Discipline." *Dissertation Abstracts International* 43: 25a. (University Microfilms No. 82–14316).

Becker, R. G., ed. (March 1980). *Troy Reporter.* Available from Troy Schools, 500 N. Market St., Troy, OH 45373.

Canter, L., and Associates. (1976). *Assertive Discipline: A Take-Charge Approach for Today's Educator.* Los Angeles: Canter and Associates.

Cartwright School District. (February 10, 1982). *Discipline Report,* Available from Cartwright School District, 3401 N. 67th Ave., Phoenix, AZ 85033.

Confederation of Oregon School Administrators. (April 29, 1980). Personal letter to Lee Canter.

Crawley, K. E. (1983). "Teacher and Student Perceptions with Regard to Classroom Conditions, Procedures, and Student Behavior in Classes of Teachers Trained in Assertive Discipline Methods." *Dissertation Abstracts International* 43: 2840A. (University Microfilms No. 83–01140).

Ersavas, C. M. (1981). "A Study of the Effect of Assertive Discipline at Four Elementary Schools." *Dissertation Abstracts International* 42: 0473A. (University Microfilms No. 82–09893).

Henderson, C. B. (1982) "An Analysis of Assertive Discipline Training and Implementation on Inservice Elementary Teachers' Self-Concept. Locus of Control, Pupil Control Ideology and Assertive Personality Characteristics" *Dissertation Abstracts International* 42: 4797A. (University Microfilms No. 82–09893).

Lennox School District, (1980). *Evaluation of District Assertive Discipline Program.* Available from Lennox School District. 10319 S. Firmona Ave., Inglewood. CA 90304.

Mandlebaum, L. H., S. E. Russell, J. Krouse, and M. Gonter. (1983). "Assertive Discipline: An Effective

Classroom Behavior Management Program." *Behavior Disorders Journal* 8, 4: 258–264.

McCormack, S. L, (November 1981). "To Make Discipline Work, Turn Kids into Self-Managers." *Executive Educator:* 26–27.

McCormack, S. L. (1985). "Students' Off-Task Behavior and Assertive Discipline." Doctoral diss., University of Oregon. 1986. *Dissertation Abstracts International* 46: 1880A.

McCormack, S. L. (March 1988). "Assertive Discipline: What Do We Really Know?" *Resources in Education* (ERIC Document Reproduction Service No. ED 286 618).

Moffett, K. L., D. Jurenka, and J. Kovan. (June/July/August 1982). "Assertive Discipline." *California School Board:* 24–27.

Moffett, K. L., J. St. John, and J. Isken. (February 1987). "Training and Coaching Beginning Teachers: An Antidote to Reality Shock." *Educational Leadership* 44: 34–46.

Swanson, M. Y. (Spring 1984). *Assessment of the Assertive Discipline Program.* (Available from Compton Unified School District, Compton, Calif.)

Ward, L. R. (1983). "The Effectiveness of Assertive Discipline as a Means to Reduce Classroom Disruptions." *Dissertation Abstracts International* 44: 2324A (University Microfilms No. 83–28411).

Webb, M. M. (1983). "An Evaluation of Assertive Discipline and Its Degree of Effectiveness as Perceived by the Professional Staff in Selected School Corporations." *Dissertation Abstracts International* 44: 2324A. (University Microfilms No. 83–28107).

Why Violence Prevention Programs Don't Work— and What Does

DAVID W. JOHNSON and ROGER T. JOHNSON

"Joshua was chasing Octavia. He pushed her down, and she kicked him."
"Danielle is going to beat up Amber after school. They were spitting in each other's faces and calling each other names."
"Tom shoved Cameron up against the lockers and threatened him. Cameron said he's going to bring a knife to school tomorrow to get even."

Schools are filled with conflicts. The frequency of clashes among students and the increasing severity of the ensuing violence make managing such incidents very costly in terms of time lost to instructional, administrative, and learning efforts.

If schools are to be orderly and peaceful places in which high-quality education can take place, students must learn to manage conflicts constructively without physical or verbal violence.

SIX PRINCIPLES OF CONFLICT RESOLUTION

The following six principles may be helpful to schools that are trying to accomplish this goal.

David W. Johnson is Professor of Educational Psychology, and Roger T. Johnson is Professor of Curriculum and Instruction, University of Minnesota, Cooperative Learning Center, 202 Pattee Hall, 150 Pillsbury Drive, S.E., Minneapolis, MN 55455-0298.

1. Go beyond violence prevention to conflict resolution training.

To curb violence among students, many schools have implemented violence prevention programs. Some schools focus on anger management and general social skills. Others invite guest speakers (for example, police officers) to school, employ metal detectors, or ask police to patrol the school. Still others show videotapes of violent encounters and structure discussions around how fights start and alternative ways to manage aggression.

The proliferation of such programs raises the question: Do they work? In a review of three popular violence prevention curriculums—Violence Prevention Curriculum for Adolescents, Washington [D.C.] Community Violence Prevention Program, and Positive Adolescent Choices Training—Webster (1993) found no evidence that they produce long-term changes in violent behavior or decrease the risk of victimization. The main function of such programs, Webster argues, is to provide political cover for school officials and politicians.

In their survey of 51 violence prevention programs, Wilson-Brewer and colleagues (1991) found that fewer than half of the programs even claimed to have reduced levels of violence, and few had any data to back up their claims. Tolan and Guerra (in press), after reviewing the existing research on violence prevention, concluded that (1) many schools are engaged in well-intentioned efforts without any evidence that the programs will work, and (2) some programs actually influence relatively nonviolent students to be more violence-prone.

Why don't violence prevention programs work? Here are a few possible reasons.

1. *Many programs are poorly targeted.* First, they lump together a broad range of violent behaviors and people, ignoring the fact that different people turn to violence for different reasons. Second, few programs focus on the relatively small group of children and adolescents who commit most of the acts of serious violence. In our studies of a peer mediation program in inner-city schools, for example, we found that less than 5 percent of students accounted for more than one-third of the violent incidents in the school (Johnson and Johnson 1994a).

2. *The programs provide materials but don't focus on program implementation.* Many programs assume that (a) a few hours of an educational intervention can "fix" students who engage in violent behavior, (b) a few hours of training can prepare teachers to conduct the program, and (c) no follow-up is needed to maintain the quality of the program. In other words, the programs ignore the literature on successful innovation within schools (Johnson and Johnson, in press) and, therefore, are often poorly implemented.

3. *Proponents of violence prevention programs confuse methods that work in neighborhoods with those that work in schools.* Conflicts on the street often involve macho posturing, competition for status, access to drugs, significant amounts of money, and individuals who have short-term interactions with one another. The school, on the other hand, is a cooperative setting in which conflicts involve working together, sharing resources, making decisions, and solving problems among students who are in long-term relationships. Different conflict resolution procedures are required in each setting. Street tactics should not be brought into the school, and it is naive and dangerous to assume that school tactics should be used on the street.

4. *Many programs are unrealistic about the strength of the social forces that impel children toward violence.* To change the social norms controlling street behavior requires a broad-based effort that involves families, neighbors, the mass media, employers, health care officials, schools, and government. Schools do not have the resources to guarantee health care, housing, food, parental love, and hope for the future for each child. Educators cannot eliminate the availability of guns (especially semi-automatic handguns), change the economics of the drug trade (and other types of crime), or even reduce the dangers of walking to and from school. Because there is a limit to what schools can do in reducing violence among children and adolescents outside of school, violence prevention programs should be realistic and not promise too much.

Initiating a violence prevention program will not reduce the frequency of violence in schools and in society as a whole. While violence does need to be prevented, programs that focus exclusively on violence prevention may generally be ineffective. Schools must go beyond violence prevention to conflict resolution training.

2. Don't attempt to eliminate all conflicts.

The elimination of violence does not mean the elimination of conflict. Some conflicts can have positive outcomes (Johnson and Johnson 1991, 1992). They can increase achievement, motivation to learn, higher-level reasoning, long-term retention, healthy social and cognitive development, and the fun students have in school. Conflicts can also enrich relationships, clarify personal identity, increase ego strength, promote resilience in the face of adversity, and clarify how one needs to change.

It is not the presence of conflict that is to be feared but, rather, its destructive management. Attempts to deny, suppress, repress, and ignore conflicts may, in fact, be a major contributor to the occurrence of violence in schools. Given the many positive outcomes of conflict, schools need to teach students how to manage conflicts constructively.

3. Create a cooperative context.

The best conflict resolution programs seek to do more than change individual students. Instead, they try to transform the total school environment into a learning community in which students live by a credo of nonviolence.

Two contexts for conflict are possible: cooperative and competitive (Deutsch 1973, Johnson and Johnson 1989). In a competitive context, individuals strive to win while ensuring their opponents lose. Those few who perform the best receive the rewards. In this context, competitors often misperceive one another's positions and motivations, avoid communicating with one another, are suspicious of one another, and see the situation from only their own perspective.

In a cooperative context, conflicts tend to be resolved constructively. Students have clear perceptions of one another's positions and motivation, communicate accurately and completely, trust one another, and define conflicts as mutual problems to be solved. Cooperators typically have a long-term time orientation and focus their energies both on achieving mutual goals and on maintaining good working relationships with others.

Students cannot learn to manage conflicts constructively when their school experience is competitive and individualistic. In such a context, constructive conflict resolution procedures are often ineffective and, in fact, may make the students who use them vulnerable to exploitation. Instead, schools should seek to create a cooperative context for conflict management, which is easier to do when the majority of learning situations are cooperative (Johnson and Johnson 1989, Johnson et al. 1993).

4. Decrease in-school risk factors.

Three factors place children and adolescents at risk for violent behavior. The first is academic failure. One way that schools can promote higher achievement and greater competence in using higher-level reasoning by students is to emphasize cooperative learning more than competitive or individualistic learning (Johnson and Johnson 1989). The more students know and the greater their ability to analyze situations and think through decisions, the better able they will be to envision the consequences of their actions, respect differing viewpoints, conceive of a variety of strategies for dealing with conflict, and engage in creative problem solving.

A second factor that puts children and adolescents at risk for violent and destructive behavior is alienation from schoolmates. In order to create an infrastructure of personal and academic support, schools need to encourage long-term caring and committed relationships. Two procedures for doing so are (1) using cooperative base groups that last for a number of years (Johnson et al. 1992, 1993); and (2) assigning teams of teachers to follow cohorts of students through several grades, instead of changing teachers every year (Johnson and Johnson 1994a).

Third, children and adolescents who have high levels of psychological pathology are more at risk for violent and destructive behavior than students who are psychologically well adjusted. David Hamburg, the president of Carnegie Corporation, states that reversing the trend of violence among the young depends on teaching children how to share, work cooperatively with others, and help others. The more children and adolescents work in cooperative learning groups, the greater will be their psychological health, self-esteem, social competencies, and resilience in the face of adversity and stress (Johnson and Johnson 1989).

In summary, schools must not overlook the in-school factors that place students at risk for engaging in violence and other destructive ways of managing conflicts. Anything that allows students to fail, remain apart from classmates, and be socially inept and have low self-esteem, increases the probability that students will use destructive conflict strategies.

5. Use academic controversy to increase learning.

To show students that conflicts can have positive results, schools should make academic controversies an inherent and daily part of learning situations. It is unclear whether cognitive, social, and moral development can take place in the absence of conflict. Academic *controversy* exists when one student's ideas, information, conclusions, theories, and opinions are incompatible with those of another, and the two seek to reach an agreement (Johnson and Johnson 1992).

For example, teachers can assign students to cooperative learning groups of four, divided into two pairs. One pair is assigned a pro position on an issue and the other pair, the con position. Each pair prepares a persuasive presentation (consisting of a thesis statement, rationale, and conclusion) to convince the other side of the position's validity. The two pairs then meet, and each side presents the best case possible for its position. Afterward, during an open discussion, students refute the opposing position (by discrediting the information and/or the inductive and deductive logic used) while rebutting criticisms of their position. At the same time, they try to persuade the other pair to change their minds. Next, a perspective reversal occurs in which each pair presents the best case possible for the opposing position. Finally, after trying to view the issue from both perspectives simultaneously, the students drop all advocacy and come to a consensus about their "best reasoned judgment" based on a synthesis of the two positions.

Over the past 25 years, we have conducted numerous studies on academic controversy. Similar to cooperative learning, academic controversy results in increased student achievement, critical thinking, higher-level reasoning, intrinsic motivation to learn, perspective-taking, and a number of other important educational outcomes (Johnson and Johnson 1979, 1992).

6. Teach all students how to resolve conflicts constructively.

Most of the diverse conflict resolution programs present in schools are either cadre or total student body programs. In the *cadre approach,* a small number of students are trained to serve as peer mediators for the entire school. While this approach is relatively easy and inexpensive to implement, having a few peer mediators with limited training is not likely to decrease the severity and frequency of conflicts in a school.

In the *total student body approach,* every student learns how to manage conflicts constructively by negotiating agreements and mediating their schoolmates' conflicts. The responsibility for peer mediation is rotated throughout the entire student body (or class) so that every student gains experience as a mediator. A disadvantage of this approach is the time and commitment required by the faculty. The more students who are trained how to negotiate and mediate, however, the greater the number of conflicts that will be managed constructively in the school.

An example of the total student body approach is the *Teaching Students to Be Peacemakers Program,* which we have implemented in several countries (Johnson and Johnson 1991). We conceive the training as a 12-year spiral curriculum in which each year students learn increasingly sophisticated negotiation and mediation procedures.

The negotiation procedure consists of six steps. Students in conflict: (1) define what they want, (2) describe their feelings, and (3) explain the reasons underlying those wants and feelings. Then the students: (4) reverse perspectives in order to view the conflict from both sides, (5) generate at least three optional agreements with maximum benefits for both parties, and (6) agree on the wisest course of action.

The mediation procedure consists of four steps: (1) stop the hostilities, (2) ensure that the disputants are committed to the mediation process, (3) facilitate negotiations between the disputants, and (4) formalize the agreement.

Once the students complete negotiation and mediation training, the school (or teacher) implements the Peacemakers Program by selecting two students as mediators each day. It is the actual experience of being a mediator that best teaches students how to negotiate and resolve conflicts. In addition to using the procedures, students receive additional training twice a week for the rest of the school year to expand and refine their skills.

Until recently, very little research validating the effectiveness of conflict resolution training programs in schools has existed. Over the past five years, we have conducted seven studies in six different schools in both suburban and urban settings and in two different countries (Johnson and Johnson 1994b). Students in 1st through 9th grades were involved in the studies. We found that before training, most students had daily conflicts, used destructive strategies that tended to escalate the conflict, referred the majority of their conflicts to the teacher, and did not know how to negotiate. After training, students could apply the negotiation and mediation procedures to actual conflict situations, as well as transfer them to nonclassroom and nonschool settings, such as the playground, the lunchroom, and at home. Further, they maintained their knowledge and skills throughout the school year.

Given the choice of using a "win-lose" or a "problem-solving" negotiation strategy, virtually all untrained students used the former, while trained students primarily chose the problem-solving approach. In addition, students who were taught the negotiation procedure while studying a novel during an English literature unit not only learned how to negotiate, but performed higher on an achievement test on the novel than did students in a control group, who spent their entire time studying the novel. This study represents a model of how to integrate conflict resolution training into an academic class.

After their training, students generally managed their conflicts without involving adults. The frequency of student-student conflicts teachers had to manage dropped 80 percent, and the number of conflicts referred to the principal was reduced by 95 percent. Such a dramatic reduction of referrals of conflicts to adults changed the school discipline program from arbitrating conflicts to maintaining and supporting the peer mediation process.

Knowing how to negotiate agreements and mediate schoolmates' conflicts empowers students to regulate their own behavior. Self-regulation is a central and significant hallmark of cognitive and social development. Using competencies in resolving conflicts constructively also increases a child's ability to build and maintain high-quality relationships with peers and to cope with stress and adversity.

In short, training only a small cadre of students to manage conflicts constructively and to be peer mediators will not change the way other students manage their conflicts. For this reason, schools must teach all students skills in negotiation and mediation.

MAKING THE FUTURE A BETTER PLACE

Every student needs to learn how to manage conflicts constructively. Without training, many students may never learn how to do so. Teaching every student how to negotiate and mediate will ensure that future generations are prepared to manage conflicts constructively in career, family, community, national, and international settings.

There is no reason to expect, however, that the process will be easy or quick. It took 30 years to reduce smoking in America. It took 20 years to reduce drunk driving. It may take even longer to ensure that children and adolescents can manage conflicts constructively. The more years that students spend learning and practicing the skills of peer mediation and conflict resolution, the more likely they will be to actually use those skills both in the classroom and beyond the school door.

REFERENCES

Deutsch, M. (1973). *The Resolution of Conflict.* New Haven, Conn.: Yale University Press.

Johnson, D. W., and R. Johnson. (1979). "Conflict in the Classroom: Controversy and Learning." *Review of Educational Research* 49, 1: 51–61.

Johnson, D. W., and R. Johnson. (1989). *Cooperation and Competition: Theory and Research.* Edina, Minn.: Interaction Book Company.

Johnson, D. W., and R. Johnson. (1991). *Teaching Students to Be Peacemaker.* Edina, Minn.: Interaction Book Company.

Johnson, D. W., and R. Johnson. (1992). *Creative Controversy: Intellectual Challenge in the Classroom.* Edina, Minn.: Interaction Book Company.

Johnson, D. W., and R. Johnson. (1994a). *Leading the Cooperative School.* 2nd ed. Edina, Minn.: Interaction Book Company.

Johnson, D. W., and R. Johnson. (1994b). *Teaching Students to Be Peacemakers: Results of Five Years of Research.* Minneapolis: University of Minnesota, Cooperative Learning Center.

Johnson, D. W., and R. Johnson. (In press). "Implementing Cooperative Learning: Training Sessions, Transfer to the Classroom, and Maintaining Long-Term Use." In *Staff Development for Cooperative Learning: Issues and Approaches,* edited by N. Davidson, C. Brody, and C. Cooper. New York: Teachers College Press.

Johnson, D. W., R. Johnson, and E. Holubec. (1992). *Advanced Cooperative Learning.* 2nd ed. Edina, Minn.: Interaction Book Company.

Johnson, D. W., R. Johnson, and E. Holubec. (1993). *Cooperation in the Classroom.* 6th ed. Edina, Minn.: Interaction Book Company.

Tolan, P., and N. Guerra. (In press). *What Works in Reducing Adolescent Violence: An Empirical Review of the Field.* Denver: Center for the Study of Prevention of Violence, University of Colorado.

Webster, D. (1993). "The Unconvincing Case for School-Based Conflict Resolution Programs for Adolescents." *Health Affairs* 12, 4: 126–140.

Wilson-Brewer, R., S. Cohen, L. O'Donnell, and I. Goodman. (1991). "Violence Prevention for Young Adolescents: A Survey of the State of the Art." Eric Clearinghouse, ED356442, 800-443-3742.

Chapter 13: Teaching for Learning

Memo to Constructivists: Skills Count, Too

KAREN R. HARRIS and STEVE GRAHAM

Since kindergarten, our 9-year-old daughter, Leah, has attended a "whole language/progressive education school," as the teachers there describe it. It was clear from the outset that most of them do not believe in much, if any, explicit or isolated instruction and practice in phonics, handwriting, and spelling, especially in the primary grades. No workbooks or published curriculum are used. Most weeks, for example, Leah is required to select and take a test on a number of words, but there is no instruction in spelling patterns, strategies, and word families that can make a real difference (Harris et al. 1995).

We are deeply impressed by many of the school's features—the investment in and control of curriculum that the teachers have, the students' responses to the meaningful activities that fill their days, and the thoughtful and collaborative culture. Teachers there have nurtured our daughter's creativity, thinking, and understanding, with great results.

Skills, on the other hand, have been a problem for our daughter and for other children. At the end of kindergarten, when she had not made much progress in reading, her teacher said she believed Leah had a perceptual problem or learning disability. Leah began asking what was wrong with her, because other kids were reading and she wasn't. Finally, an assessment was done. It did not indicate a learning disability, and in fact showed very strong comprehension abilities. It did, however, show that her word-attack skills were very poor.

Fortunately, we have both been reading teachers, and that summer we taught our daughter to read. We used word-attack activities that were direct, explicit, intensive, and often isolated. And guess what—we had fun! The relationship of these activities to learning to read was clear to Leah, and she was highly motivated.

Within six weeks she was reading *Bob Books*, a series of engaging little books that use phonetic word families to construct stories—authentic literature in her and our opinion. After that there was no holding her back, and Leah is now a strong reader.

This past summer, as our daughter approached 4th grade, we worked on her labored, nearly illegible handwriting and on memorizing the times tables. Leah really enjoyed working on her handwriting, which is now quite legible, but thoroughly disliked memorizing the times tables. Recently, however, she proudly told us that in a math activity, she was able to complete multiplication problems faster than the class math whiz, and that "packing the facts in your brain really helps."

Karen R. Harris and Steve Graham are Professors, Department of Special Education, University of Maryland at College Park, 1308 Benjamin Bldg., College Park, MD 20742-1121 (e-mail: kh9@umail.umd.edu).

Our next goal is to improve Leah's spelling abilities.

NEED FOR AN INTEGRATED APPROACH

For many students who face challenges in learning, behavior, and/or social and emotional development, mastering skills is clearly more difficult than it was for our daughter. These children require more extensive, structured, and explicit instruction to develop not only skills, but also processes, strategies, and understandings (Brown and Campione 1990, Harris and Graham 1996, Kronick 1990).

We strongly support integrated constructivist curriculums and authentic learning environments. For more than a decade, we have worked with local schools to advance the process approach to writing for all students. But we firmly believe that we must provide explicit, focused, and, at times, isolated instruction to the extent needed—and integrate it into the larger literacy context.

Teaching AS A DIRTY WORD

Whole language advocates—and constructivists in general—see children as inherently active, self-regulating learners who construct knowledge in developmentally appropriate ways. They believe that full participation in learning, rather than passive responding, results in deeper and richer understanding and use of knowledge.

Unfortunately, constructivists often see the teacher's role as one of simply assisting performance and the construction of powerful knowledge, rather than explicitly providing knowledge and information. To some whole language advocates, *teaching* is a dirty word. They believe it is neither necessary nor desirable (and even harmful) to teach explicitly, provide direct explanation, or require practice. This approach has serious ramifications for learners with special needs.

Consider how two whole language teachers approach spelling and handwriting in the context of reading and writing (Manning and Manning 1995). The Mannings say they schedule no separate periods for spelling or handwriting instruction, nor do they give weekly spelling tests. They might provide mini-lessons on letter formations for a group of stu-

dents experiencing problems, or note a spelling pattern while a student reads. Similarly, they teach word-attack skills only in the context of meaningful reading and writing. They do not use worksheets or other forms of practice, as these are decontextualized and isolated, and thus not meaningful.

The idea, the Mannings explain, is that children develop as spellers as they "read and discuss good literature":

> Children who are avid readers, for example, develop a strong knowledge of words, which usually leads to improved spelling. Finally, everyone must remember that spelling is not an end in itself; rather it is the communication of one's thinking (p. 53).

THE BEST OF EVERYTHING

Some whole language advocates believe that through rich social interaction and immersion in authentic learning experiences, children will come to learn all they need to know, and develop all of the skills and abilities they need, in due developmental time. This is not a question of the correct way to implement whole language instruction, but rather a fundamental issue in how to apply the philosophy of constructivism in practice (see, for example, Edelsky et al. 1991, Kronick 1990, Poplin 1988).

In successful integrated instruction, by contrast, teachers conduct ongoing assessments of each student's abilities, skills, knowledge, motivation, social characteristics, and prior experiences. They then arrange whatever support children need—from direct explanation through discovery. Children's perceptions of what they are doing and why they are doing it, and of their teacher's intentions, are critical in this integration (Harris and Graham 1994a). Further, integrated instruction is based in learning communities that are educationally purposeful, open, just, disciplined, and caring.

Although some advocates have argued that such integration is impossible and dangerously misguided, many teachers, schools, and communities are demonstrating otherwise. Our own research indicates that in some constructivist classrooms, such integration and attention to special needs learners is reaping very positive results (Graham and Harris 1994, Harris and Graham 1994b).

NO GOING BACK

We do *not* mean to suggest that we should return to a primarily skills-oriented curriculum.

We both had a taste of that when we began teaching public school in the early 1970s. One of us (Karen) taught 4th grade in a small coal mining community in the Appalachian mountains; the other (Steve) was a resource teacher for 1st through 6th graders in a small southern town.

Steeped in cognitive discovery and humanistic approaches, we were eager to facilitate discussion and inquiry, arouse awareness, stimulate problem solving, capitalize on personal interests, and facilitate discussion and inquiry. We wanted to meet the needs of individual students and to help students clarify their attitudes and values and build positive self-concepts. Unfortunately, we both ran straight into curriculums dominated by skills development and prescribed teachers' guides and workbooks.

Teachers in so many schools like these, where skills have become an end in themselves rather than a part of a larger picture, have seen, as we saw, the toll it takes on children. Recently, the mother of a student with learning disabilities and attention deficit hyperactivity disorder recalled to us the emotional and behavioral costs of the workbook approach that had been used in her son's mainstreamed elementary school classroom:

> *My son suffered so much. All day. Every day. He didn't have what it took to sit for so long and do worksheets. He could do the work. But he didn't have the organizational skills, the ability to pay attention to the teacher and get the directions. And he was punished for things he couldn't control.*

MY PARADIGM, RIGHT OR WRONG

What is the effect of whole language instruction or other constructivist approaches (such as process writing/writers' workshops) on the literacy of students with special needs? Unfortunately, the research base is insufficient to draw even the most tentative conclusions (Graham and Harris 1994). Nor can clear conclusions be drawn for other students.

In individual studies, however, researchers have observed many positive outcomes, as have teachers and parents (ourselves included). Among these outcomes: better understanding of the material and the authors' intentions; greater enjoyment of literature; an ability to produce as well as consume knowledge; and—as in our daughter's school—more positive attitudes toward school, and improved thinking and problem-solving skills.

On the other hand, problems with whole language instruction are also becoming well documented. For students who, like Leah, do not face significant problems with learning, behavior, or social/emotional development, the major issue clearly is skills—although difficulties with developing strategies and understandings have also been noted. Parents and educators have voiced concerns about the number of children who have not learned to read naturally by the 1st and 2nd grades, whose handwriting is illegible and labored in the upper elementary grades, and whose spelling remains "inventive" long past the early grades (Smith 1994, Willis 1993).

Why, given what appear to be some obvious problems with whole language approaches, are we not doing more to modify them and avoid the apparent back-to-basics backlash?

One hurdle is a lack of self-criticism. Whole language advocates often encourage teachers to inoculate themselves against criticisms of the approach, and to provide answers to frequent concerns that disavow the validity of these concerns (see, for example, Edelsky et al. 1991, Manning and Manning 1995). Donald Graves (in Newkirk 1994), one of the most influential leaders of the writing process approach, put it well in a recent interview:

> *The thing that bothers me so much about the whole language movement is that it is not self-critical. I have dire predictions for the movement. There's been terrific stuff done, and there's been a belief in teachers that has been strong. But there has to be far greater intellectual demand on the movement than we've had (p. 23).*

Some teachers conclude that if a student has problems with the whole language approach, there must be something wrong with the student. Such thinking may increase referrals to special education or tutoring services. Kronick (1990) noted that constructivism may lure some teachers into believing that individual differences are neither real nor even problematic and that difficulties will resolve themselves in due developmental time.

Then, there are those who believe that constructivism is the key to increased justice and democracy in the world (Edelsky et al. 1991). They even contend that, say, 13 years of constructivist education would lead to less crowding in our prisons and help to control the federal deficit and the drug problem (Kamil et al. 1994). We are less sanguine.

Graves (in Newkirk 1994) discussed the difficulties engendered by orthodoxies within any viewpoint, and particularly within the whole language viewpoint. When people who subscribe to one approach are incapable of examining it critically, and when their behavior is insular, they may well ignore the knowledge gained by practitioners of competing or alternative paradigms. That could have dangerous consequences.

NO ALL-PURPOSE PATH

The challenges faced by students with special needs, and indeed by all of us, are complex. No one intervention or viewpoint can address the complex nature of school failure or success, or, for that matter, of social inequalities and inequities. We, like other advocates of constructivism or whole language (Harris and Graham 1994a), believe that an integration of knowledge and successful practices is critical in today's schools.

REFERENCES

Brown, A. L., and J. C. Campione. (1990). "Interactive Learning Environments and the Teaching of Science and Mathematics." In *Toward a Scientific Practice of Science Education*, edited by M. Gardner, J. Greens, F. Reif, A. Schoenfeld, A. di Sessa, and E. Stage, pp. 111–139. Hillsdale, N. J.: Erlbaum.

Edelsky, C., B. Altwerger, and B. Flores. (1991). *Whole Language: What's the Difference?* Portsmouth, N.H.: Heinemann.

Graham, S., and K. R. Harris. (1994). "The Effects of Whole Language on Children's Writing: A Review of Literature." *Educational Psychologist* 29: 187–192.

Harris, K. R., and S. Graham. (1996). *Making the Writing Process Work: Strategies for Composition and Self-Regulation*, 2nd ed. Cambridge, Mass.: Brookline Books.

Harris, K. R., and S. Graham. (1994a). "Constructivism: Principles, Paradigms, and Integration." *Journal of Special Education* 28: 233–247.

Harris, K. R., and S. Graham. (1994b). "Implications of Constructivism for Students with Disabilities and Students at Risk: Issues and Directions." [Special issue]. *Journal of Special Education* 28.

Harris, K. R., S. Graham, J. Zutell, and R. Gentry. (1995). *Spell it - Write!* Columbus, Ohio: Zaner-Bloser Educational Publishers.

Kamil, C., F. B. Clark, and A. Dominick. (1994). "The Six National Goals: A Road to Disappointment." *Phi Delta Kappan* 75: 672–677.

Kronick, D. (1990). "Holism and Empiricism as Complementary Paradigms." *Journal of Learning Disabilities* 23: 5–8, 10.

Manning, M., and G. Manning. (1995). "Whole Language: They Say, You Say." *Teaching preK–8* 25: 50–55.

Newkirk, T., ed. (1994). *Workshop 5 by and for Teachers: The Writing Process Revisited.* Portsmouth, N.H.: Heinemann.

Perkins, D. (1992). *Smart Schools: Better Thinking and Learning for Every Child.* New York: The Free Press.

Poplin, M. S. (1988a). "Holistic/Constructivist Principles of the Teaching/Learning Process: Implications for the Field of Learning Disabilities." *Journal of Learning Disabilities* 21: 401–416.

Smith, C. B., Moderator. (1994). *Whole Language: The Debate.* Bloomington, Ind.: ERIC.

Willis, S. (November 1993). "Whole Language in the '90s." *ASCD Update*: 1, 5.

Six Myths (and Five Promising Truths) about the Uses of Educational Technology

TERRY WORONOV

Computer technology is fast becoming an almost universal presence in education. Ninety-eight percent of U.S. schools now have at least some computers. The ratio of computers to students is increasing across the country, and continued growth is expected in purchases of hardware, software, and related equipment such as videodisk players and CD-ROM technology.

The push to get more and more computers into schools has been fueled in part by the belief that their mere presence will make good things happen (and by aggressive marketing by hardware and software manufacturers). A variety of studies, however, tell us that computers in themselves do not automatically change the nature of teaching and learning; rather, it is the way teachers integrate computers into classrooms, the content of technology-aided lessons, and the quality of the software programs selected that determine whether and how computers in schools really benefit students.

Computers have proved valuable in supporting inquiry-based science teaching, inclusion of students with disabilities in regular classes, interdistrict collaboration, distance learning, and the dissemination of professional development materials (see below).

At the same time, certain myths about the magic of technology persist.

SIX WIDELY HELD BELIEFS

Six widely held beliefs, in particular, are worth examining closely:

Myth #1: Computers are here to stay, so we have to get as many of them as possible into classrooms, as quickly as possible.

Larry Cuban of Stanford University argues that computers are merely the most recent in a long line of technologies that have been promoted in schools, beginning with radio and television. As with these earlier technologies, decisions to integrate computers into education are often made without much thought about the reasons for doing so—that is, how they fit into the wider goals of education—and without a clear understanding of the benefits they are supposed to produce.

"Before technology can be used effectively," says Martha Stone Wiske of the Educational Technology Center at Harvard, "everyone involved in education—teachers, students, principals, school boards, parents, and communities—needs to think

Terry Woronov is Assistant Editor of *The Harvard Education Letter*.

carefully about why we want to use technology, and what we hope to accomplish with it."

Myth #2: Educational technology would be used more widely, and more effectively, but for resistance from technophobic teachers.

A "phobia" is an irrational fear. But there is nothing irrational about teachers being afraid of looking stupid in front of students who know more about computers than they do; similarly, the difficulties of integrating computers into daily classroom practice with no system support are not imaginary.

Blaming teachers for the failure of technology to change education is a common historical theme, says Larry Cuban. The blame usually centers on the teacher's inability to integrate the technology into classroom practice. But many teachers face formidable barriers in learning about computers. Relatively few pre-service programs for new teachers include more than a cursory introduction to technology. Neither is time generally available for in-service education about technology. Equipment and services that industry takes for granted—such as a computer and phone on every desk, access to a systems manager to help with problems and questions, and time on the job to learn new systems—generally do not exist in schools.

Robert Hannafin and Wilhelmina Savenye of Arizona State University list many other reasons why teachers may resist technology. They cite research showing that some teachers are unhappy with the poor quality of the educational software available to them, or dissatisfied with the results of using computers in their classes. For example, some English teachers feel that students use word processors simply to make their papers look good rather than to improve the quality of their writing.

Myth #3: Using and programming computers teaches children "thinking" and "problem-solving" skills.

The research jury is still out on this claim. In 1992 Aqeel Ahmed reviewed 21 empirical studies on the effects of students having learned to program computers. Each of the studies attempted to measure the students' "cognitive abilities." Ten of the 21 studies showed no effects on students' "cognition," while

the other 11 detected some benefits. But in every case, "cognitive abilities" was defined differently. Moreover, Ahmed found significant problems of methodology and reporting in all 21 studies.

Similarly, there is as yet no definitive evidence of the cognitive benefits of other uses of computers, such as multimedia, "edutainment" (computer games with nominally educational content, used at home), or hypertext (a computerized form of text that provides multiple options for calling up related texts and annotations). Indeed, researchers are still trying to determine what kinds of cognitive benefits may result from using new technologies and how to measure those benefits.

The authors of a longitudinal study of high school students enrolled in a "high access to technology" program conducted through Apple Classrooms of Tomorrow argue that, by using computers extensively in class, students acquire cognitive skills other than those measured by traditional indices. For example, they found that students had learned how to integrate graphics, animation, and hypertext into their written texts. The authors also assert that these students had improved ability to work in groups and to integrate large amounts of information, and had increased self-confidence. But did these activities and skills help the students to understand and reflect on important ideas, or to communicate clearly in speech and writing? No answer.

In another study, researchers at Purdue University looked at strategies used by college students to negotiate hypertext and found that most students wandered aimlessly through the material. Additional research is necessary to learn if hypertext reading is a skill that enhances learning, and if so, in what way.

Myth #4: Wider use of technological resources like the Internet will help remedy inequities in U.S. education.

While the Internet provides unprecedented access to information and resources around the world, only selected students currently have access to these computer tools. Henry Jay Becker's 1989–1991 study of computer use across the country found inequities based on race, gender, tracking, urban versus rural districts, and subject area. In an earlier study, Becker also found that students in lower tracks were often restricted to drill-and-practice work on computers, while "brighter" students were more frequently taught to use computers as tools for accomplishing other educational tasks.

The latest data show that the hardware gap is closing, with minimal differences in numbers of computers and student-computer ratios in schools across the country—except in Hispanic-majority schools. The new equity gap, according to Becker, is in the use of telecommunications and in computer expertise. Poorer school districts and black-majority schools have largely been "left out of the loop" when it comes to telecommunications, he says. And the need for bilingual computer-literate teachers is acute.

Gender equity is a contentious issue in educational computing, with most researchers finding that boys dominate computer use in classrooms and far outnumber girls in computer science classes. Other studies note that the majority of computer-using teachers are male; few female role models exist for young women who develop an interest in technology. Three times as many men as women currently earn degrees in computer science, according to the National Science Foundation, and the gap is growing.

Myth #5: Increased use of technology in classrooms will inevitably bring about systemic school reform.

Many advocates of educational computing claim that computer use will, by itself, cause a dramatic change in teaching and learning by promoting critical thinking and inquiry-based problem solving. But simply putting a computer in a classroom does not necessarily change anything. Computers are commonly used in traditional, unconstructive ways—for drill and practice, as electronic worksheets, and as rewards for good behavior.

Computer skills are also taught largely as ends in themselves. An advanced-level math teacher at a large public high school near Boston summarizes the problem: "I would like to have my students use the computer lab to experiment with statistical analysis, but the lab is reserved all day for teaching typing and for other vocational classes." There's nothing wrong with using computers to teach vocational skills, but that won't change the nature of teaching and learning in schools.

Some innovative schools are using technology to support efforts to re-examine the purposes and

potential of education, but it is a mistake to assume that the technology itself is driving the process of change. Michael Eisenberg, director of the ERIC Clearinghouse for Information and Technology, warns educators not to have unrealistic expectations for technology. "Schools are complex institutions," he says. "Learning and teaching are complex processes. Technology is essential because it pervades our society. But it is only a means. Technology itself will not change or reform education."

Myth #6: Kids love to use computers—so they must be learning.

Until relatively recently, most adults assumed that serious learning in school had to be unpleasant. Only in recent decades have educators come to believe that learning can and often should be fun. Computer use in schools is sometimes justified because students enjoy it. But just being engaged by computers doesn't necessarily mean that students are learning anything important from them.

FIVE PROMISING TRUTHS

Computers and new standards

New national standards in math and science call for students to engage in active, inquiry-based, hands-on learning, which can be facilitated by computer-based laboratories and simulations. (See "New Tools for Teaching Science," page 4.)

Entrepreneurial schools

A few highly technologically literate schools around the country are beginning to produce their own educational materials and distribute them to others. One project at Thayer Junior-Senior High School in Winchester, New Hampshire, produces professional development materials on videotape and distributes them via satellite to 600 schools around the country.

Elliot Washor, the program's director, says that technology is not its primary goal: "This is a restructuring project. The technology is what makes it possible." Other schools will soon be learning Thayer's video production techniques; as the technology becomes cheaper and more accessible, Washor predicts, more schools will be writing, producing, and disseminating their own materials and curricula.

Statewide initiatives

More than 40 states have set up organizations to provide telecommunication links or technology support to school districts. The Massachusetts Corporation for Educational Technology (MCET) provides courses for students of all ages, including adult education and professional development, through a national satellite network, and also operates a computer network that provides Internet access. Having a statewide mandate, with state and federal funding, gives MCET and other such organizations access to resources and expertise beyond what is usually available to individual school districts.

Like Elliot Washor, MCET staff emphasize that the technology itself is not the goal of their services to schools: "Content is at the heart of what we do," says Beverly Simon, MCET's director of communications. "What's communicated is far more important than the vehicle we use. The technology itself is of vital interest, but what is most interesting is what we can contribute to schools through technology."

Inclusion of students with disabilities

Technology has enabled students with a wide range of disabilities to participate fully in mainstream classes and to develop skills previously considered beyond their capacities. (See "Assistive Technology for Literacy," page 6.)

Distance learning

This is a broad term, encompassing technology that "extends the learning community beyond the classroom walls," says Purdue University's Ernest McDaniel. Courses offered via satellite by MCET's Mass LearnPike and Los Angeles's TEAMS project

give teachers and students access to materials and expertise not otherwise available to them.

Teachers and students are increasingly using electronic mail to communicate with peers and experts around the globe. Popular programs like National Geographic Kids Network and TERC's Global Lab enable students to share experimental data they have gathered. Growing numbers of schools are hooking into the Internet, a huge international network that provides access to a vast amount of information and resources (see box, page 8).

FOR FURTHER INFORMATION

A. Ahmed. "Learning to Program and Its Transference to Students' Cognition." Available from the ERIC Clearinghouse (ED352261, 1992); 800-443-3742.

R. Anderson (ed.). *Computers in American Schools: 1992: An Overview.* Minneapolis: University of Minnesota Department of Sociology, 1993.

L. Cuban. "Neoprogressive Visions and Organizational Realities." In *Visions for the Use of Computers in Classroom Instruction: Symposium and Response.* Cambridge, MA: Harvard Educational Review Reprint.

Educational Technology Center, Harvard Graduate School of Education, Nichols House, Appian Way, Cambridge, MA 02138.

Educational Telecommunications: The State-by-State Analysis. Hezel Associates, 1201 E. Fayette St., Syracuse, NY 13210.

C. Martin and E. Muchie-Beyma (eds.). *In Search of Gender-Free Paradigms for Computer Science Education.* International Society for Technology in Education, 1787 Agate St., Eugene, OR 97403.

MCET (and the Mass LearnPike Satellite Network), 38 Sidney St., Cambridge, MA 02139; 617-621-0290.

TEAMS Distance Learning, Los Angeles County Office of Education, 9300 Imperial Highway, Room 250, Downey, CA 90242.

TERC, 2067 Massachusetts Ave., Cambridge, MA 02140; 617-547-0430.

R. Tierney et al. *Computer Acquisition: A Longitudinal Study of the Influence of High Computer Access on Students' Thinking, Learning and Interactions.* Cupertino, CA: Apple Classrooms of Tomorrow, Report #16.

How K–12 Teachers Are Using Computer Networks

JON M. PEHA

Proponents in both government and the telecommunications industry have fueled a growing interest in connecting schools to various regional, national, and international computer networks. Educators must now determine how these networks can be integrated into classroom curricula, and how this affects school systems. Ultimately, we must also evaluate the potential benefits, and determine whether they justify the expense. While it is too soon to offer definitive answers to these difficult questions, this paper will present a few pieces of the puzzle. It will describe a wide range of promising classroom activities involving computer networks. Based on feedback from those involved and from direct observation, this paper will describe some of the apparent effects, including both potential benefits and pitfalls to be avoided. It will also discuss how school systems might provide preparation and support for teachers.

By almost any measure, the world's largest computer network is the Internet. The Internet evolved from a U.S. Defense Department communications system to become an interconnected collection of more than 46,000 independent networks, public and private, around the world (National Science Foundation 1995). Now serving millions of users worldwide, its growth is rapid and exponential. Consequently, we focus on programs that bring Internet access to schools.

Jon M. Peha is Associate Professor, Carnegie Mellon University, Department of Engineering and Public Policy, and Department of Electrical and Computer Engineering, Pittsburgh, PA 15213-3890.

In 1993, the Pittsburgh Public Schools began such a program, in partnership with the Pittsburgh Supercomputer Center and the University of Pittsburgh, and with funding from the National Science Foundation. At that time, Carnegie Mellon University began a four-month project to aid the Pittsburgh Public Schools in their new endeavor, which was known as Common Knowledge Pittsburgh.

To observe the uses of the Internet in Pittsburgh, our research group surveyed and/or interviewed approximately 45 educators in various positions throughout the school system. Of that number, 24 teachers and 4 librarians from 4 schools attended a professional development workshop on Internet use in classrooms. Of the 28, 14 completed surveys about the effectiveness of that program. We also interviewed students.

In addition, we made numerous observations in one of the four schools participating in the first year of the project, an elementary school in a low-income area of Pittsburgh. A comparable number of schools have come online each subsequent year (Carnegie Mellon University 1994).

To catalog what other teachers outside of Pittsburgh were doing with the Internet, we compiled responses from a questionnaire addressed to educators who use the Internet via relevant newsgroups and e-mail distribution lists. We received 21 responses describing 34 distinct classroom activities. Given the small sample size and a method of distributing questionnaires that naturally favors frequent Internet users, our statistics are not terribly meaningful. Our questionnaire was deliberately unstructured, however, to enable recipients to elaborate on their experiences and to share insights about using the Internet. We also conducted unstructured interviews with educators who were using the Internet. To supplement these data, we studied descriptions from the printed literature of roughly 40 classroom activities.

HOW STUDENTS ARE USING COMPUTERS

Before looking at what we found occurring in classrooms, let's define a few key terms. For many years, three types of traffic have dominated the Internet:

- With *electronic mail*, the most popular tool at all grade levels, a user can quickly send a message to any other user or specified group of users. E-mail can also reach mass audiences when used in conjunction with:

    —distribution lists, made up of e-mail addresses of people with shared interests (a list of educational distribution lists is available via anonymous FTP [see below] from nic.umass.edu); or

    —newsgroups, also called electronic bulletin boards, where any user interested in a topic may read about it much the same way one reads personal e-mail.

- *File transfers* (FTPs) allow a user to copy a file (which can contain text, software, pictures, and music) from, or to, another computer system. With a variation, anonymous FTP, a user can copy files without the need for password privileges.

- *Telnet* allows a user to log onto a remote computer as if it were in the same room. For example, one might telnet onto a system because it has capabilities that the local system lacks.

A number of important tools have also developed in recent years that facilitate the search for information on the Internet, such as Gopher, Archie, Veronica, Mosaic, and, more recently, Netscape. Obviously, such tools are useful only if the network contains useful information. (There is no way to describe all of the resources available on the Internet; the box gives five examples.)

Resources Available on the Internet: Some Examples

1. The Educational Resources Information Center (ERIC) provides information on curriculums, professional development, teaching methods, and educational materials. Telnet to acsnet. syr.edu, login: suvm, userid: suinfo. An ERIC gopher is also available.

2. The NASA Spacelink offers an interactive database with lesson plans, science activities, and NASA flight information. Telnet to spacelink. msfc.nasa.gov; username: newuser.

3. Digital images highlighting the photography of the Smithsonian Institution are available via anonymous FTP from photo1.si.edu.

4. Worldwide meteorological data (including forecasts, records, and storm warnings) are available. Telnet to hurricane.ncdc.noaa.gov, login: storm; password: research.

5. The Library of Congress Information System (LOCIS) contains more than 15 million catalog records. Telnet to locis.loc.gov; no password is necessary.

The classroom activities that we observed, that educators shared with us, or that we read about in the literature fall into the following broad categories that build on these capabilities.

1. Students send their work to some other party for evaluation or response. The network provides a high-tech postal service, but with no cost per letter, minimal hassle, and most important, a negligible time for the message to reach its destination, which enables meaningful interaction. With pen pal programs, younger students write e-mail messages about themselves and their interests to peers in distant places. There is strong motivation for students to write good letters because, as one teacher put it, "A good letter writer generally receives good letters." Older students exchange more complex material like stories and artwork, sometimes critiquing one another's work.

Other programs provide a forum to learn about distant events and different ways of life. In one example, inner-city elementary school students corresponded with Native American peers who live on a reservation. E-mail is also sometimes written in a foreign language to both motivate and help students learning that language.

The Internet makes possible communication between students and older students or professionals as well. Some students send their writing samples to professional writers for feedback; others correspond with professional engineers for help with independent science projects. Still other activities link disabled students with big brothers and sisters, for example, or connect students from schools where few go on to college with their older counterparts who are in college.

2. *Group projects enable students at different locations to collaborate on activities.* For example, students can cooperate on tasks like taking temperature and barometric measurements for a weather project or surveying garbage around their schools for an environmental project. Because many of these projects are experimental in nature, students engage in meaningful exploratory science with a large body of data. They gather information locally, and then pool data from around the world. Although they spend a relatively small amount of time collecting their part of the data, students understand how all of the data were collected, and have a sense of ownership. Other projects show students the value of working in groups, because each classroom is bound to produce ideas that improve the group's solution.

3. *Students exploit remote data sources and processing capabilities on the network.* Most often, the Internet serves as an enormous library with extraordinary search capabilities. With the growing popularity of new browsing tools, such activities are likely to become more common. The Internet's remote processing capabilities can also be valuable. For example, students can run computationally intensive scientific simulations on a powerful remote computer that cannot be run on the school's inexpensive equipment. Such simulations can also replace expensive (or dangerous) laboratory equipment in the school.

Many educators told us that the Internet allows them to tap information sources on their discipline or on teaching in general, and to correspond with other educators around the world with similar interests. As one teacher said, "When I get the information I'm seeking, I can incorporate some of the activities in my lessons, also advancing my own professionalism."

Figure 1 [p. 217] is a breakdown of activities described in responses to our questionnaire. Although these results are not statistically significant, they do dispel the myth that computers and networks are just for math and the sciences.

HOW THE INTERNET BENEFITS THE CLASSROOM

Two-thirds of the respondents to our questionnaire said that a primary benefit of the Internet is making students aware that they are part of a global community. Others commented that the Internet gives students a wide variety of resources, stimulates thinking, and improves computer literacy.

From our many observations in the inner-city elementary school in Pittsburgh, an important benefit of using this technology is enthusiasm. Whenever the Internet teacher walked into the room, students appeared hopeful that it would be their turn to use the Internet. Teachers even threatened to revoke a student's computer privileges as a punishment for disruptive behavior. As for teachers, their enthusiasm was unmistakable in both direct interviews and survey responses.

The Internet and other information technology in the classroom, of course, do much more than boost enthusiasm or expand information resources. Internet use fundamentally alters the roles of teachers and students. For example, when students write to impress a pen pal or a distant expert, the teacher is no longer the sole judge of quality, and grades are less of a motivating factor than in traditional classrooms. In addition, many activities require students to work in teams. When students spend class time browsing the Internet rather than listening to a teacher's lecture, they encounter more diverse expert opinions, work more independently, and proceed at their own pace. In fact, we observed that students experiencing computer problems were more likely to consult peers than the teacher. Throughout this process, the teacher becomes more of a facilitator, helping students find information and, more important, figure out what to do with it.

There is also potential to change the role of parents with this technology. For example, during parents' nights, students may be able to teach their parents something new about computers or networks. Doing so can greatly boost a student's self-esteem. Because familiarity with information technology can lead to jobs, schools may also want to expand their efforts to train neighborhood adults after school hours.

When parents have access to this technology at home or at work, they can become more closely involved in their children's education. Many parents already have Internet access at work. Thirty-five percent of U.S. households now have computers, and those with children are more likely to have comput-

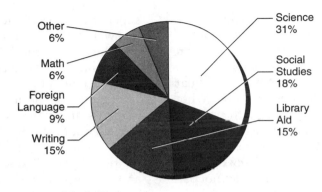

Subject Area of Activities

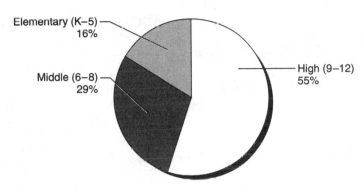

Grade Level of Activities

FIGURE 1   **How K–12 Teachers Use Computers**

ers than those without, even families on a somewhat limited budget. Of households with children and total annual incomes under $30,000, 30 percent have computers. Given that consumer spending on home computers now exceeds spending on televisions, these percentages should continue to rise quickly (Negroponte 1995). All it takes is a telephone line and a modem to connect a home computer to the network. More important, because there will always be parents without home computers, some states and municipalities are bringing network capabilities to all of their citizens. In Seattle, for example, even the homeless will be able to communicate over the network by getting an account from the city, and using it in libraries and other public buildings.

HOW TO OVERCOME DIFFICULTIES

The teachers who responded to our questionnaire offered several ways to overcome difficulties in introducing the Internet in a K–12 curriculum. Four suggestions in particular surfaced frequently:

1. *Be specific about expectations and objectives.* By providing deadlines for activities and for intermediate milestones, teachers can keep students moving in the right direction.

2. *Search the Internet yourself before asking students to.* As one teacher said, "Know what to look for in advance, so you and your students will not be disappointed."

3. *Allow ample time.* "Realize that it will take twice as much time as you have budgeted," suggested one teacher. Another offered, "Have students work in groups to speed up the process."

4. *Establish a commitment with other parties involved in an activity.* As one teacher urged, "There is nothing worse than getting a project organized or planning one into your lesson plans and then no mail arrives from your partners or people start dropping out."

Teachers also identified three difficulties not entirely within their control. First, 40- to 50-minute class periods limit students' ability to engage in unstructured tasks. Allowing time for longer activities, therefore, may require creative structuring of the school day. Second, some teachers must overcome a lack of hardware, telephone lines, or accounts. Finally, lack of time for teachers to explore the Internet is a problem. The Internet's resources are vast, and the tools change from year to year. Keeping up is not easy. Things will improve when more principals and others understand the value of the Internet, and the importance of teacher time spent exploring it.

Probably the most disturbing problem came out in direct interviews with teachers who were not part of the Pittsburgh project. Not only are rewards for innovative teachers often small, but some principals and teachers actually discourage resourceful teachers from disrupting the status quo. The reasons for such opposition may include two fears: that benefits will be small and not worth the effort, and that benefits will be great, so other teachers will be expected to keep up. Providing proper teacher incentives for innovation is critical, and may require some fundamental changes.

Although our respondents did not mention the next problem, it has the potential to seriously disrupt efforts to bring the Internet to classrooms. Students using the Internet, like students wandering the Library of Congress, may look at something their parents would prefer they not see—for example, sexually explicit material. Topics like drugs, politics, religion, abortion, and homosexuality may also stir controversy.

In June 1995, the U.S. Senate attempted to address a part of this problem by approving an amendment to the telecommunications bill that would prohibit the flow of "indecent" material (not limited to pornography) on the Internet. Aside from the serious civil rights implications of such censorship, it would not even prevent the distribution of pornography on this network of millions of users around the world, any one of whom can provide such information.

In April 1995, the Washington State legislature found a more drastic solution to protect minors from objectionable material: they made it illegal to give minors Internet access. (An even more effective solution would be to prohibit minors from learning to read.) The governor vetoed the bill.

Schools can take some precautions—for example, not carrying obviously troublesome newsgroups on local servers. And new information-filtering tools are coming. There is really no way, however, to prevent a bright, determined student from finding something he or she wants to see. Constant teacher supervision is one solution, but it is time-consuming and would deter curious exploration.

The best approach is to develop a written policy stating what does and does not constitute acceptable student usage of the Internet. In general, Internet usage should relate to coursework. Both students and parents must agree to this policy before gaining access. While such a strategy does not prevent abuse, it does make it easier to revoke the privileges of students who violate the policy, and it brings parents into the discussion from the beginning.

ABOUT TEACHER PREPARATION AND SUPPORT

Before adopting the Internet, a school system must determine how much preparation and ongoing support to provide. Two-thirds of the respondents to our questionnaire survived without any formal training, relying instead on printed literature and experimentation, or as one person described it, "blood, sweat, and tears."

Common Knowledge Pittsburgh developed a professional development workshop for teachers and librarians that participants generally found quite successful. The primary goal was to give them the problem-solving skills to become explorers of the Internet, rather than teaching them facts or rote methods. Because Internet tools and resources are constantly changing, teachers must have the ability to adapt—a view echoed by several respondents to our questionnaire.

The workshop, held in June 1993, provided 24 teachers and 4 librarians with 13 hours of instruction over two and a half days. Participants worked in pairs to promote brainstorming and to make the task less intimidating. They used a variety of tools ranging from newsgroups to Gopher, and explored resources that workshop organizers thought might be useful, like the NASA library (see box, p. 215). To test their newfound skills, they participated in a scavenger hunt for information on the Internet.

After this session, workshop organizers helped participants set up borrowed school computer equipment in their own homes to experiment during the summer. Finally, the workshop reconvened in August for 10 hours of additional instruction over a two-day period. In addition to learning more about the Internet, participants discussed possible lesson plans.

As noted earlier, 14 workshop participants responded to our survey. Every respondent agreed that the teaching methods were effective; only one person did not yet feel capable of teaching the Internet to students, with two people unsure. All found the workshop informative, and almost all would recommend it to a colleague.

Because a primary goal of this workshop was to encourage exploration, that issue deserves special consideration. After a few months into the school year, nearly half of the participants had done three or more Gopher searches in the week we surveyed them, but two people indicated that they were no longer exploring the Internet. Despite the popularity of the workshop, participants indicated that they learned only about half of the information on the Internet from workshop instructors. That finding would seem to corroborate the importance of independent exploration.

How would the Pittsburgh educators improve the workshop? They were about evenly split on the need for more step-by-step instruction time, but expressed a pressing need for more exploration time.

Because one can't afford to stop learning about the Internet, ongoing support may also be important. In answer to the questionnaire we sent to network users around the world, teachers indicated that Internet guides, newsgroups, and distribution lists are very helpful. Personal support is also needed at times.

In Pittsburgh, teachers turned to their fellow teachers most often, with the centralized support staff a close second. This finding is important because widescale adoption is possible only if teachers help one another; a centralized support staff can't be everywhere.

When asked what other kinds of ongoing technical assistance would be helpful, teachers who responded to the questionnaire most often mentioned classroom visits by Internet instructors, monthly meetings of Internet users, and online support.

THE FUTURE

Teachers have only begun to exploit existing capabilities of network technology in schools. Indeed, the majority of classroom activities that we've observed use only Internet tools that are more than two decades old, like basic e-mail. As noted, tools such as Mosaic and Netscape greatly facilitate the process of finding information on the Internet.

People are also experimenting with more interactive applications. For example, the Internet has been used for person-to-person video teleconferences, and to broadcast part of a Rolling Stones concert live.

Moreover, new networks are coming based on ATM (asynchronous transfer mode) technology. Although such things are possible to a limited degree on the Internet, ATM networks are better able to support applications where intermittent disruptions are noticeable to the user, like using a telephone, playing interactive games with a distant player, or controlling a laboratory experiment at a remote site. ATM networks can also transmit data at a rapid rate, allowing users to watch broadcast-quality video or better on demand, to quickly retrieve a series of images from the space shuttle's telescope or the complete works of Shakespeare, or to use sophisticated visualization tools to watch changing weather patterns in the area. Recently, North Carolina deployed a statewide ATM network to which schools will have access. Emerging wireless networks also offer many opportunities for education.

Although the growth of Internet use in classrooms is encouraging, schools have not been keeping up with any of the commercial sectors in adopting new information technology—so it is not clear whether technical advances alone will be beneficial for learning. An obvious obstacle is money. However, 97 percent of American schools already have some computers (Wheland 1995), and adding a low-speed Internet connection is no more expensive than adding a telephone line. Still, many of these computers are not integrated into the curriculum in a meaningful way, other than one designed specifically to teach about computers. While funding is certainly an issue—and more conclusive proof is needed that money spent on Internet access is more beneficial than money spent elsewhere—increased funding alone is unlikely to lead to productive use of information technology.

To truly exploit these advances, technology and innovation must permeate the culture of education. Teachers should be exposed to technology early in their careers, and should be actively encouraged to keep up on continual advances. To reduce installation costs, new schools should be wired for computers and networks when they are built, just as commercial office spaces are. Districts should hire staff who can help schools build and troubleshoot computer and network systems. Teachers must be given freedom and encouragement to experiment with technology.

Common Knowledge Pittsburgh, now operating in 14 schools, is currently funded through December 1997. The Pittsburgh Public Schools are showing that more teachers will choose to bring technology into the classroom when given both resources and encouragement.

Author's note: To order "The Internet in K–12 Education," send $12.40, or $16.60 from outside the U.S., to Department Receptionist, Department of Engineering and Public Policy, Carnegie Mellon University, Pittsburgh, PA 15213.

REFERENCES

Carnegie Mellon University. (1994). "The Internet in K–12 Education." Pittsburgh: Carnegie Mellon University.

National Science Foundation. (April 26, 1995). "NSF-MCI Background on the Internet/NSFnet." NSF Press Release.

Negroponte, N. (February 11, 1995). "homeless@info.hwy.net." *New York Times*, A 15.

Wheland, R. (February 1995). U.S. Department of Education, personal communications.

Chapter 14: Standardized Testing

Innovation or Enervation?

Performance Assessment in Perspective

GREGORY J. CIZEK

The first recorded performance assessment was literally a bloodbath. The interesting narrative of that event describes a truly "high stakes" examination, in which the Gilead guards "tested" fugitives from the tribe of Ephraim who tried to cross the Jordan River:

> "Are you a member of the tribe of Ephraim?" they asked. If the man replied that he was not, then they demanded, "Say Shibboleth." But if he couldn't pronounce the "H," and said "Sibboleth" instead of "Shibboleth," he was dragged away and killed. So forty-two thousand people of Ephraim died there at that time.[1]

Well, performance assessment is back. It is surely possible to overstate the parallels between the current calls for increased reliance on performance assessments and the Biblical example. Undoubtedly, the stakes involved in existing examination programs are not as momentous as those in the story. But there are similarities, not the least of which is the almost religious zealotry of some proponents of performance assessment.

Before fully embracing the doctrine of performance assessment, however, professional educators would do well to scrutinize the movement's claims, costs, and characteristics. Indeed, such scrutiny

Gregory J. Cizek is an assistant professor of educational research and measurement at the University of Toledo, Toledo, Ohio.

is a professional responsibility. Addressing a related testing controversy over a decade ago, Robert Glaser and Lloyd Bond reminded us of that responsibility:

> In the heat of the current controversy, it is especially necessary to be our own sternest critics. It is not possible to attend to every criticism, especially those that are ill-founded and well beyond the state of the knowledge of human behavior. However, it is necessary to examine the point and counterpoint in public and professional debate in order to move forward with research and development in human assessment and with analysis of institutional policy and test use. The examination should be conducted in a way that is open not only to the members of our own discipline but also the larger public that is affected by and must make decisions about tests.[2]

PERFORMANCE ASSESSMENT IN PERSPECTIVE

Performance assessment might be the answer to many social and educational problems, or so say its advocates. The recent report of the National Commission on Testing and Public Policy enthusiastically argues that this new kind of assessment must be pursued in order to halt the undermining of vital social policies and to promote greater development of the talents of all people.[3] Certainly these are worthy goals. But is performance assessment the answer? The purposes of this article are to define what is currently called *performance assessment,* to examine the goals of the advocates of performance assessment, and to offer practical and technical cautions to the makers and consumers of performance assessments.

WHAT IS PERFORMANCE ASSESSMENT?

Educational tests are, fundamentally, attempts to gauge what students know or can do. An *indirect* measure of, for example, a student's woodworking ability might be obtained through a paper-and-pencil test that asks the student to state the uses of different lathe chisels, to recognize grain patterns of different species of wood, or to identify the proper way to feed stock into a planer. Another way to gauge the student's woodworking ability would be to use a more *direct* measure. Such a test might consist of presenting the student with a block of wood and the appropriate tools and requiring the student to turn a bowl. This more direct way of assessing woodworking ability could be called a performance assessment.

Of course, this kind of direct assessment has been going on for quite some time and is not particularly new. Elementary students still solve problems in math classes, middle-schoolers go to spelling bees, high school students give speeches, education majors do their student teaching, and dentists-in-training are evaluated on their ability to fill cavities. Indeed, Walter Haney and George Madaus of the Center for the Study of Testing, Evaluation, and Educational Policy at Boston College have reminded us that performance assessment per se is not innovative: "A point worth noting about evaluation alternatives that have been suggested over the last 20 years is that many of them are not at all new. Evaluation tools such as live performances, products, teacher judgment, and school grades have a long history in education."[4]

Elsewhere, Haney recounted three trends in educational measurement that were apparent *in the 1930s:*

1. *A growing emphasis upon validity and a consequent decreasing emphasis upon reliability as the criterion for evaluating measuring instruments;*

2. *a decline of the faith in indirect measurement and an increasing emphasis upon direct measurement as a means of attaining satisfactory validity; and*
3. *a growing respect for essay examinations as instruments for measuring certain outcomes of education.*[5]

IF NOT NEW, THEN WHAT?

The three trends identified in the 1930s must certainly sound familiar to policy makers in the 1990s. They bear a remarkable resemblance to what the proponents of performance assessment are currently urging. But if the idea itself is not new, then what is original about the movement? Unfortunately, perhaps all we have up to this point is a new *name* for these activities—performance assessments. And there may not even be consensus on the name, with such aliases as genuine assessment, authentic evaluation, and practical testing—to list just a few enjoying wide circulation. But performance assessment by any other name is the same, and its advocates have yet to spell out how the current version is substantially different from its relatives.

Whatever the name, one thing is certain: performance assessment is chic. Many educational leaders, directors of state-level assessment projects, and administrators of large-scale testing programs are seriously contemplating increased reliance on performance assessment. But the push for this type of assessment should be judged on more than its current popularity. In a courageous article on educational faddism, Robert Slavin states that "education resembles such fields as fashion and design, in which change mirrors shifts in taste and social climate and is not usually thought of as true progress."[6] Slavin's article was intended to document [that] educational innovations are often funded and implemented before research on their effectiveness has taken place. The same insight should guide us in current policy considerations involving performance assessment. It is my contention that we have not yet been offered a well-conceived rationale for action, when such a rationale should be a sine qua non for widespread change and the investment of resources.[7] By my reckoning, performance assessment is flourishing somewhere between the "gee whiz" and the "hot topic" stages in Slavin's schematization of the 12 characteristic phases of the swinging education pendulum.

WHO ARE THESE PEOPLE AND WHAT DO THEY WANT?

The performance assessment bandwagon is evidently big enough to accommodate quite a crowd. Although proponents of performance assessment may not be totally sure of what they want, they know what they don't want: standardized, multiple-choice tests.

The National Education Association has encouraged the elimination of group standardized intelligence, aptitude, and achievement tests."[8] David Owen, author of a critique of the Scholastic Aptitude Test (SAT), thinks that the answer might be to "abolish the Educational Testing Service."[9] Another article accuses standardized testing of being "harmful to educational health."[10] The final report of the California Education Summit goes even farther, recommending that "all multiple-choice tests should be eliminated."[11] The recent report of the National Commission on Testing and Public Policy is more moderate, suggesting that "testing programs should be redirected from overreliance on multiple-choice tests."[12] Gerald Bracey, the director of research and evaluation for a Colorado school district, waxed philosophical about what needs to be done: "As a sociologist pointed out some years back, to make the world safe for democracy, it is not sufficient to destroy totalitarian regimes. You have to eliminate the *mentality* that produces totalitarianism. It will not be sufficient, similarly, to eliminate tests.[13]

But those touting performance assessment definitely want your money. It is highly surprising that a common complaint of testing prohibitionists is that testing is expensive. Bracey has assailed the SAT as "the $150 million redundancy."[14] The National Commission on Testing and Public Policy lodged a similar complaint, noting that "reported sales [of elementary and secondary tests and testing services] rose to over $100 million by 1986."[15] The proponents of performance assessment typically cite these figures and point out that the money could be better spent on programs for the disadvantaged, Head Start, or teachers' salaries. Certainly, education policymakers should be concerned about how limited resources are allocated. The irony is that, despite their advocates' apparent concern about cost, the vaguely defined alternative assessments will surely be costlier. For example, the National Board for Professional Teaching Standards recently requested proposals for the development

of a prototype credentialing program for "early adolescence/English language arts teachers" involving performance assessment. The estimated amount of the award for this *one* specialized program exceeds $1.4 million.[16] Another $1.4 million is expected to be awarded for the development of an "early adolescence/generalist" assessment.[17] These figures are for development only and *do not* include any printing, administrative, scoring, or reporting costs. If other performance assessments are as expensive—and surely large-scale assessments will be even more costly—the tab will be staggering.

The hidden price of increased reliance on performance assessments may be even more invidious than the actual monetary costs. For example, performance assessment advocate Ruth Mitchell of the Council for Basic Education noted in a recent interview that there is "no reliable way to compare the costs" of traditional tests and the proposed alternatives. Further, Mitchell asserts that "alternative assessment yields dividends for professional development and curriculum development. Such assessment efforts can, therefore, legitimately absorb other parts of a school district's budget."[18]

Whether such "absorption" is truly legitimate is—or should be—debatable. At minimum, Mitchell's observations should serve as a portent of future educational turf warfare if the high cost of the new assessments is balanced on the backs of other important budgetary considerations.

And what will be purchased in the rush to invest in this latest innovation? Proponents of performance assessments have offered only vague descriptions of what the new instruments will look like. For example, Mitchell has proffered that alternative assessments "can take as many forms as the imagination will allow."[19] In essence, educators are being asked to purchase this amorphous product sight unseen.

Neither is it clear that the new instruments will actually measure something different from more traditional forms of testing. Bracey, a proponent of performance assessment, contends that the new assessments will measure abilities that "are hard, if not impossible, to measure with standardized, multiple-choice tests." He goes on to say that what *should* be measured is "higher-order thinking," which is "nonalgorithmic" and "complex," "yields multiple solutions," and involves "nuanced judgment," "uncertainty," and "imposing meaning."[20] Zowie! Such fantastic claims have led education policy analyst

Chester Finn to note that performance assessment is "like 'Star Wars': the idea remains to be demonstrated as feasible."[21] Certainly, Bracey's descriptors *sound* good, but essential questions about what is actually to be measured and how these goals will be accomplished remain unanswered.

WILL PERFORMANCE ASSESSMENTS BE ANY GOOD?

I really don't mean to be a naysayer about innovation, but I do think that serious discussion about improving evaluation should not be muddied by the current euphoria surrounding performance assessment. Performance assessment advocates have built a straw person to knock down in the form of standardized, multiple-choice tests. This expenditure of energy could have been better invested elsewhere.

For example, no one claims that multiple-choice tests can solve all educational problems or that different types of measures shouldn't be matched with particular purposes. Even performance assessment zealots want whatever new measures are developed to be standardized in terms of administration and scoring. To fuss and fixate on format is to miss the point. Similarly, to intimate, as some proponents of performance assessment do, that testing may be the cause of "a palpable decrease in the quality of education" is to further obscure a troubling and enduring issue.[22]

Advocates of the new kinds of tests also frequently criticize current tests in general for being culturally biased or unfair. In bygone days it was newsworthy to discover a vocabulary test with the word *polo* or a reading selection using the word *quiche*. But real test-makers don't use quiche—anymore. Certainly, performance assessment enthusiasts would admit that impressive progress has been made toward the elimination of ethnic, gender, and socioeconomic bias. So it's difficult to comprehend why the proponents of performance assessment would now call for—I'm not kidding—more culturally biased tests. As one example, the National Commission on Testing and Public Policy reports favorably on efforts to "establish and maintain a program of research and development to provide accurate and *culturally specific* instruments" (emphasis added).[23] Educators would do well to consider seriously whether these culturally specific assessments represent a welcome advance or a misguided regression in fair testing policy.

WHAT MATTERS?

What really matters—ignoring cost for the time being—is whether performance assessment will actually be "fairer" or "better" by any reasonably rigorous and widely accepted standards. The early polls are in on this question, and the results are discouraging. It is my opinion that test-makers can develop performance assessments that rival multiple-choice tests in terms of reliability; many quite reliable performance assessments exist now. It is disconcerting, however, that standards for the new instruments are rarely discussed. One person who is concerned about the issue is Edward Haertel, who has recognized the obstacles to reliable, judgment-based measurement and who has suggested several factors to consider.[24] But such caution is not the rule. References to benchmarks such as the *Standards for Educational and Psychological Testing* or the *Code of Fair Testing Practices in Education*[25] are conspicuously absent from the discussion. What should especially trouble policy makers, educators, and testing professionals is that disciples of the performance assessment movement generally tend to ignore the question of validity.

In the first course I took on educational measurement, I recall discussing what was called "face validity." Anne Anastasi commented on the concept of face validity some time ago:

> *Face validity . . . is not validity in the technical sense; it refers, not to what the test actually measures, but to what it appears superficially to measure. Face validity pertains to whether the test "looks valid" to the subjects who take it, the administrative personnel who decide upon its use, and other technically untrained observers. Fundamentally, the question of face validity concerns rapport and public relations.*[26]

By the time I was in Robert Ebel's measurement class at Michigan State University, the professor had already penned his frequently cited sentences on validity: "Validity has long been one of the major deities in the pantheon of the psychometrician. It is universally praised, but the good works done in its name are remarkably few." Indeed, Ebel was seriously concerned about test validity, reminding test-makers that it is "the quality we have said is more important than any other."[27]

So, whither validity? In the current press for more genuine assessment, the only talk about validity that one hears—if one even hears such talk—is about face validity. My fear is that we have begun a search for genuine-*looking*, authentic-*looking*, real-*looking* assessments and have eschewed more rigorous standards of validity. It would certainly be tragic if face validity were to become the reigning deity in the psychometrician's pantheon. Bracey has gone so far as to say, "Validity, to me, is a nonissue. . . . For the new assessments, if we agree that this is what children should know or be good at, *and* we agree that the assessment strategy used represents this well, then Q.E.D., the test is valid."[28] Similarly, Dale Carlson, director of the California Assessment Program, has labeled concerns about validity "a red herring."[29] One hopes that this kind of enthusiasm represents the far point of the pendulum's arc.

CONCLUSION

By the time the pendulum completes its downswing, the current calls for more performance assessment will surely have yielded benefits. A heightened awareness of the importance of examining the match between assessment and instruction has already developed. We are—however grudgingly—acknowledging the role that social policy and ideology play in putatively objective assessment practice. When appropriate, direct assessment of certain skills and abilities will receive renewed support and resources.

But the future of performance assessment is uncertain. As sure as testing generally is not the answer to the multifaceted and complex problems facing contemporary American education, performance assessment is not the panacea either. The euphoria of its proponents should give us pause. The lowered psychometric standards to which it is currently held should cause alarm. Its cost should cause us to hide the silver under the mattress.

Slavin comments that, "as each innovation swings up and down through the arc of the pendulum, we do learn something that may be of use now or in the future."[30] While we should possibly hesitate to put all our hopes in the promise of performance assessment, it would be useful now to embark on a careful analysis of its potential, so that this innovation does not fall by the educational wayside, another cast-off quick fix in the larger school reform effort.

NOTES

1. Judg. 12:5–6, quoted in William A. Mehrens and Irvin J. Lehmann, *Measurement and Evaluation in Education and Psychology*, 3rd ed. (New York: Holt, Rinehart and Winston, 1984), p. 575.

2. Robert Glaser and Lloyd Bond, "Testing: Concepts, Policy, Practice, and Research," *American Psychologist*, October 1981, p. 997.

3. *From Gatekeeper to Gateway: Transforming Testing in America* (Chestnut Hill, Mass.: National Commission on Testing and Public Policy, 1990).

4. Walter Haney and George Madaus, "Searching for Alternatives to Standardized Tests: Whys, Whats, and Whithers," *Phi Delta Kappan*, May 1989, p. 685.

5. Walter Haney, "Validity, Vaudeville, and Values," *American Psychologist*, October 1981, p. 1023.

6. Robert E. Slavin, "PET and the Pendulum: Faddism in Education and How to Stop It," *Phi Delta Kappan*, June 1989, p. 752.

7. Gregory J. Cizek, "The 'Sloppy' Logic of Test Abolitionists," *Education Week*, 4 April 1990, p. 64.

8. Frances Quinta and Bernard McKenna, *Alternatives to Standardized Testing* (Washington, D.C.: National Education Association, 1977), p. 7.

9. David Owen, *None of the Above: Behind the Myth of Scholastic Aptitude* (Boston: Houghton Mifflin, 1985), p. 285.

10. D. Monty Neill and Noe J. Medina, "Standardized Testing: Harmful to Educational Health," *Phi Delta Kappan*, May 1989, pp. 688–97.

11. *California Education Summit Report: Meeting the Challenge* (Sacramento: California State Department of Education, 1989).

12. *From Gatekeeper to Gateway . . .* , p. 26.

13. Gerald W. Bracey, "Measurement-Integrated Instruction and Instruction-Integrated Measurement: Two of a Kind," paper presented at the Academy for the Colorado Association of School Executives, Denver, April 1990.

14. Gerald W. Bracey, "The $150 Million Redundancy," *Phi Delta Kappan*, May 1989, pp. 698–702.

15. *From Gatekeeper to Gateway . . .* , p. 16.

16. *Request for Proposals: Early Adolescence/English Language Arts* (Washington, D.C.: National Board for Professional Teaching Standards, 1990).

17. *Request for Proposals: Early Adolescence/Generalist* (Washington, D.C.: National Board for Professional Teaching Standards, 1990).

18. Scott Willis, "Transforming the Test: Experts Press for New Focus on Student Assessment," *ASCD Update*, September 1990, p. 5.

19. Ibid., p. 4.

20. Gerald W. Bracey, "Advocates of Basic Skills 'Know What Ain't So,'" *Education Week*, 5 April 1989, p. 36.

21. Chester E. Finn, Jr., quoted in Robert Rothman, "New Tests Based on Performances Raise Questions," *Education Week*, 12 September 1990, p. 1.

22. Grant Wiggins, "Reconsidering Standards and Assessment," *Education Week*, 24 January 1990, p. 36.

23. *From Gatekeeper to Gateway . . .*, p. 33.

24. Edward H. Haertel, "From Expert Opinions to Reliable Scores: Psychometrics for Judgment Based Teacher Assessment," paper presented at the annual meeting of the American Educational Research Association, Boston, April 1990.

25. American Educational Research Association, American Psychological Association, and the National Council on Measurement in Education, *Standards for Educational and Psychological Testing* (Washington, D.C.: American Psychological Association, 1985); and *Code of Fair Testing Practices in Education* (Washington, D.C.: Joint Committee on Testing Practices, 1988).

26. Anne Anastasi, *Psychological Testing*, 2nd ed. (New York: Macmillan, 1961), p. 138.

27. Robert L. Ebel. "Must All Tests Be Valid?," *American Psychologist*, May 1961, pp. 640, 646.

28. Bracey, "Measurement-Integrated Instruction . . . ," p. 21.

29. Dale Carlson, quoted in Rothman, p. 12.

30. Slavin, p. 757.

A Response to Cizek

GRANT WIGGINS

Methinks that Gregory Cizek doth protest disingenuously. How else can we explain his view that performance assessment is nothing more than a voguish fad—"chic"—situated somewhere near the margin of sound assessment principles and practice? Why does he not cite the many performance assessments long in place in this country or the extensive and long-established body of writing calling for the need to get beyond proxy tests?

Let us note, for example, a test publisher's introductory comments to a proposed performance assessment:

> *The acquisition of specific facts and concepts is important, but not the only important outcome. . . . At least equally important is the acquisition of the ability to apply specific facts and concepts in work, family, and community roles. . . . Since the outcomes described stress the application of knowledge in real life rather than merely recalling it or engaging in mental exercises, [our test] emphasizes a variety of measurement techniques and procedures other than the usual multiple-choice tests.*
>
> *[The test] is a series of fifteen simulation activities based on realistic materials drawn from the adult public domain, in six outcome areas: Communicating, Solving Problems, Clarifying Values, Functioning Within Social Institutions, Using Science and Technology, and Using the*

Arts. . . . Student responses are judged by faculty raters using standardized rating scales.

Is this a description of a naive, unvalidated assessment from an unknown vendor trying to cash in on the latest trend? No, I am quoting from a technical report produced a decade ago by Cizek's own employer, American College Testing. The excerpt summarizes the rationale behind the development of COMP, the College Outcome Measures Project, a battery of assessments that have been used for 10 years to evaluate the results of a liberal arts education. The tasks it requires range from preparing a report on the appropriateness of a piece of artwork for a public space to giving an oral presentation that will demonstrate speaking effectiveness.

Technical soundness? Contained in the COMP report are summaries of technical studies that conclude that the performance tests are both valid and reliable and that the objective "proxies"—their word—are not adequate replacements since the "performance tests measure certain abilities not tested by the multiple-choice format."[1]

Surely something more than trendiness is at work in the current push for assessment reform. Has Cizek failed to note the soul-searching that has gone on for years throughout the measurement community—as evidenced by the insightful criticism of conventional testing provided years ago by Norm

Grant Wiggins is director of research and development for Consultants on Learning, Assessment, and School Structure (CLASS), Rochester, N.Y.

[1]Aubrey Forrest and Joe Steele, *Defining and Measuring General Education Knowledge and Skills* (Iowa City, IA: American College Testing, College Outcome Measures Project, Technical Report No. 1976–81, 1982).

Frederiksen of the Educational Testing Service (ETS) and David McClelland of Harvard?[2] Why would test companies be willing to develop performance measures, at the seeming expense of their other products, if there were not a need? For example, ETS, in its publication highlighting the results of the hands-on science test it developed and implemented for the National Assessment of Educational Progress (NAEP), states:

> We should recognize that schools teach what is tested. In conjunction with improving science and mathematics curricula, we must provide for both instruction [in] and assessment of higher-order thinking skills. The use of hands-on assessment techniques will guide instruction in more beneficial directions as well as provide better information about students' understandings of the concepts underlying science and mathematics.[3]

Note the subtle criticism here of multiple-choice measures, including, presumably, those produced by ETS: higher-order understandings are implicitly not well-assessed by conventional tests.

Chic? The simple fact is that state departments of education, test companies, and ministries of education in other countries have been using direct, nonproxy measures of academic performance for years, even decades. The following list represents just a sample of state and national activity:

- Advanced Placement exams, including not only essays in most subjects but 15 years of experience with the Art Portfolio;
- ACTFL (American Council on the Teaching of Foreign Languages) foreign language proficiency exams;
- statewide writing assessments in over two dozen states;
- hands-on assessment in vocational programs in most states;
- NAEP performance assessments in science, writing, history, and reading;
- New York Regents Examinations;

- High School International Baccalaureate;
- Assessment of Performance Unit (APU) national studies in Great Britain (performance assessments in science, mathematics, reading, speaking, listening, and writing); and
- GCSE (General Certificate for Secondary Education) exams in Great Britain (and their equivalents in Australia and New Zealand).

Of course, most of the world has long been assessing student performance directly—even in high-stakes settings. Alas, as Daniel Resnick and Lauren Resnick put it years ago, American students remain the most tested but least examined in the world.[4] The Canadians, British, Australians, French, Italians, Germans, Russians, and Dutch (to name a few) all routinely demand of their students the production of high-quality documents and oral performances—even in mathematics, as Tom Romberg and Lynn Steen have recently pointed out.[5]

Cizek conveniently ignores a vast literature on direct assessment. Where is mention of the work of Ronald Berk, George Madaus, Richard Shavelson, Howard Gardner, and Edward Chittenden? What about the 10 years that went into researching and implementing the British APU? What about the ETS work in portfolios and performance assessment, the competency-based work at the college level, and the judgment-based instruments and studies available in professional fields such as medicine and music? When citing me, Cizek chose to ignore half a dozen published articles, focusing instead on one sentence taken out of context from an *Education Week* "Commentary." (It was hardly my aim to "further obscure" the issue of the relation between education and testing. I began a discussion of local quality control by posing a few rhetorical questions, one of which asked, "Is it too cranky to suggest that the decline of educational performance coincides with a massive increase in testing?" This hardly obscures the issue, since there is such a correlation, and the implication is plausible.)

Ah, but then we are taken to task for reinventing the testing wheel. Cizek cannot have it both

---

[2]Norm Frederiksen, "The Real Test Bias: Influences of Testing on Teaching and Learning," *American Psychologist*, March 1984, pp. 193–202; and David McClelland, "Testing for Competence Rather Than for 'Intelligence,'" *American Psychologist*, January 1973, pp. 1–14.

[3]*Learning by Doing: A Manual for Teaching and Assessing Higher-Order Thinking in Science and Mathematics* (Princeton, N.J.: Educational Testing Service, 1987), p. 31.

[4]Daniel P. Resnick and Lauren B. Resnick, "Standards, Curriculum, and Performance: A Historical and Comparative Perspective," *Educational Researcher*, April 1985, pp. 5–21.

[5]Tom Romberg, "Problematic Features of the School Mathematics Curriculum," in Philip Jackson, ed., *Handbook of Research on Curriculum* (New York: Macmillan, forthcoming); and Lynn Arthur Steen, "Mathematics in the Soviet Union," *Educational Leadership*, February 1991, pp, 26–27.

ways, at one moment decrying the trendiness of this idea and at another reminding us that the idea has a lineage that runs back at least through the Thirties.[6] Whoever claimed that this idea was new? Certainly not any of us who have written on the subject. Our point is the opposite: we bemoan the repeated rejection of *established* common sense when fundamental pedagogical and policy decisions are based on superficial, proxy, norm-referenced data.

The essential question, then, is not, "But if the idea is not new, then what is original about the movement?"—a question Cizek begs, by the way—but rather, "Why has education been driven by indirect measures that cannot provide, in principle, direct feedback for improving local schools?" Why have local and state policy makers consistently resisted using direct instead of proxy measures? Is it cost? A mistrust of teachers? An "audience" for such data that consists of boards and legislators—not practitioners with different needs but no clout? (Is Cizek really unconcerned about the dangers to quality and integrity implied by the Lake Wobegon effect of recent years?)

Instead of trying to explore *why* at this time in our history a clearly commonsensical old idea has resurfaced, we are given a glib, somewhat slyly ad hominem proposition: "By my reckoning, performance assessment is flourishing somewhere between the "gee whiz" and "hot topic" stages. . . . Although proponents of performance assessment may not be totally sure of what they want, they know what they don't want: standardized, multiple-choice tests."

Enough obstructionism. Let's quickly remind ourselves why assessment reform is essential, why spending less than a penny per student on the "objective" scoring of student work via Scantrons is a profound mistake—if our aim is to exemplify, measure, *and* evoke high-quality performance. Conventional forms of standardized testing, in Cizek's own words, offer only "indirect" ways of measuring performance. Instead of setting standards for quality performance, they merely audit those abilities in an indirect, superficial way.

As Cizek notes, direct assessment is typically found in use at the classroom level. What he conveniently fails to mention, however, is that, until recently, direct forms of assessment have rarely been used on a large scale at either the school, the district, or the state level. We have had a long and unfortunate tradition in public schooling in America of testing cheaply what can easily be scored "objectively" and quickly, not of testing rigorously what we value as intellectual accomplishment—a very different approach from that used by other countries at the K–12 level and by all our colleges and professions.

Are typical tests being criticized as "invalid"? Not in any technical sense. But predictive or correlative validity for large samples of students should never be the *essential* aim of any testing program. At stake is feedback to local educators and students—genuinely insightful, useful information. Cizek apparently feels little responsibility for the impact of traditional forms of testing on teaching, learning, policy making, and expenditures what has recently been called "systemic validity."[7] Why should we not finally begin to assess the assessments in terms of their benefit to schooling? Consider the obvious drawbacks of steady doses of multiple-choice tests, apparent to anyone who spends time in schools:

- The generic nature of the test cannot possibly align with all the instructional aims of a given school or district.
- The simplistic and "closed" nature of the questions ensures that students never have adequate access to more realistic, ill-structured tasks and questions.
- Students receive the anti-intellectual message that a "test" involves choosing the sanctioned, orthodox answer instead of being challenged and allowed to justify one's answers.
- One-shot, end-of-year testing that yields only norm-referenced data can have no direct impact on teaching and learning; the feedback is not useful.
- Tests that require students merely to point to answers can never tell us whether students are capable of using knowledge to fashion high-quality products or performances.
- The "security" required for ensuring the validity of such tests disempowers both teachers and students, making it impossible for three essential

---

[6]Cizek's view of history seems limited: the reform urge in the Thirties was spearheaded by the Progressives in the Eight-Year Study, with performance measures developed by a young Ralph Tyler and his staff. This was in response to the dreadful excesses of the I.Q., "efficiency scales," and Army standardized testing, which led to a highly reductionist view of teaching, learning, and testing in schools—from which we still suffer.

[7]John Frederiksen and Allan Collins, "A Systems Approach to Educational Testing," *Educational Researcher*, December 1989, pp. 27–32.

elements of real-world learning to occur: appropriate rehearsal, intelligent use of available resources, and increased self-assessment.

- The routine reliance on outside assessors ensures that both the quality of and the faith in local assessment will decrease—despite the fact that it is local assessment that will ultimately determine whether students are held to high standards.

- Finally, the tests have a debilitating effect on students who are below the norm and will likely remain so, given the nature of test design and norming processes that deliberately exaggerate differences.

Neither I nor anyone else has proposed that validity and reliability are not central to assessment design and execution. (To intimate that Dale Carlson, the head of California's Assessment Program, does not care about validity is outrageous, given his job and distinguished record in assessment.) What we who have criticized current policy in testing have insistently claimed is that the failure to demand "authenticity" or better "systemic validity" from our large-scale testing has impoverished instruction and lowered local standard-setting. "Teaching to the test" is inevitably impoverishing when the multiple-choice test is, by design, a simplistic proxy.

Nor is reliability in direct assessment the overwhelming problem that critics of performance assessment make it out to be. Yes, we must be vigilant about making sure it does not fall below a *tolerable* minimum. But recent technical reports from the NAEP note that interrater reliability is 90% or better on the scoring of essays now used in various NAEP subject-area tests. Similar data exist for the writing assessments required by some states and for those used in other countries. It is worth noting an irony about reliability, however: such established and well-regarded tests as the New York Regents Examinations admit of far less reliability than test and policy makers claim is required for accountability (since the tests are scored by each classroom teacher, and only small samples are audited by the state). Yet these exams retain their reputation and integrity.

Yes, to ensure fairness, we must have reliability; on that we all agree. The best way to ensure fairness, however, is to demystify testing and to have oversight and audit practices—"sunshine" laws. The current proprietary and validity-required secrecy of the design and administration of tests makes fairness far less likely; local students and teachers are routinely prevented from fully grasping their de facto obligations (or challenging the test design or answer key).

Cizek thus misses the point about the need for greater face validity. Does he seriously believe that the form of the assessment (think of the simplistic tasks students repeatedly encounter) has no impact on local instruction and assessment—on our view as to what intellectual challenges are about? Can he be serious in suggesting that face validity is of little importance to students and teachers? Does he seriously believe that a third grade reading test that bores the student and angers the teacher by its dopey questions is in any vital sense of the term "valid"?

The aim is not the *semblance* of realism but the educative and motivational power that comes from tests built out of exemplary and vital challenges and from the model performances from which we learn and are inspired.

The word *performance* in performance assessment is thus not idly used. How would pilots, musicians, engineers, or athletes learn to perform adequately if they were tested only through multiple-choice tests? Are we to believe that the constant essay, oral, and hands-on tests I have seen regularly used in other countries are not likely to lead to better local learning, instruction, and assessment? If Cizek demands an "original" perspective on direct assessment, let it be this one: it is time that test designers gave up the medieval view implied in their work and realized that "knowledge that" something is the case is *not* a prerequisite for or indicator of masterly "knowhow." While not very original for anyone with a knowledge of learning theory or of the history of ideas, this notion appears truly novel when one does an item analysis of conventional tests that purport to meet acceptable standards of construct and content validity.

The result of the ubiquity of multiple-choice tests is, sadly, writ large all over America's classrooms: a school "test" in this country is, de facto, a secret, simplistic instrument for "objectively" scoring student answers on a curve. No matter that a curve is indefensible on such a small scale; no matter that validity is assumed, not proven; no matter that unending secrecy and one-shot testing in assessment are counterproductive to mastery even if they work for audit accountability—*our teachers have internalized the form of standardized testing because it is the only, sanctioned kind of assessment mandated in their districts and in the education courses they once took.*

Another way to look at the effects of the form of the assessment is to consider the positive trends: California's first-class writing assessment and New York's hands-on science assessment for fourth graders have had just the result we would hope for: an increase in more focused instruction on (and thus performances of) writing and experimenting.

We are in a vicious cycle: the more we have relied on externally designed multiple-choice tests for accountability, the more local assessment practices have deteriorated; the more they deteriorate, the more the public and school officials do not trust teachers to bear the primary burden for assessing students. Yet we know from the experience of other countries that adequate reliability is eminently possible in local assessment when proper procedures are followed for administration and oversight (as in the British moderation process or as in our state-wide writing assessments). More to the point, school reform built on the entrepreneurial efforts of local educators is impossible without reliable, usable data from the measures and standards by which we agree to abide.[8] At issue is not some quaint view of "face validity" but the proper demand for credible, rich, direct measures that admit of no excuses when the results are poor.

[8] Grant Wiggins, "Standards, Not Standardization: Evoking Quality Student Work," *Educational Leadership*, February 1991, pp. 18–25.

For those of us concerned with school improvement, that last point is vital. We will not improve schools until local teachers and administrators have complete faith that the assessment system will adequately represent their students' (and thus, indirectly, their own) achievements. Such a view is not merely commonsensical; it is the only moral position we can take. Does Cizek want his salary tied to a "secure" proxy test imposed on him by his employer—when he has no say in or adequate prior knowledge of that test's content? Are hypocritical policy makers prepared to be held accountable for measures and standards of which they know little or nothing in advance—as they expect teachers to be?

So please, Gregory Cizek, give up the coy and disingenuous rhetoric about the "faddishness" of direct assessment. Yes, we have to be sure that the performances assessed do justice to the whole knowledge domain; yes, we have to ensure a lack of bias, drift, and other sources of error in judgment-based assessing. Let us then have a more constructive debate about the pressing issues of costs versus benefits, about the place of face validity in assessment design, about the differing needs in reporting of assessment data, and about what kinds of assessment and standard setting actually *improve* schools (as opposed to merely auditing, in a simplistic way, their current performance). We must begin at last to assess our assessments from a "performance-based" point of view: to judge them by their measurable *effect* on teaching and learning.

Confusion Effusion: A Rejoinder to Wiggins

GREGORY J. CIZEK

No, Grant Wiggins, I'd prefer not to have my salary tied to a secure proxy test imposed on me by my employer. I'd much rather have it tied to an index of euphoria about performance assessment. The euphoria grows despite a number of troubling issues that I (and others) have raised but that continue to be ignored or insufficiently addressed by proponents of an increased reliance on performance assessment.

In his rebuttal to my article on performance assessment, which appeared in the May 1991 *Kappan*, Wiggins seems to put forth more confusion than resolution.[1] In this rejoinder, I respond to his criticisms and suggest that it would be useful for all concerned to examine more carefully the following areas of controversy.

MEASUREMENT-DRIVEN INSTRUCTION

Almost without exception, proponents of performance assessment bemoan the purported hegemony of multiple-choice examinations. With remarkable speed, the rhetoric has progressed, from Wiggins' contention that multiple-choice testing "may have caused a palpable decrease in the quality of education"[2] to Monty Neill's statement of "fact" that "or-

Gregory J. Cizek is an assistant professor of educational research and measurement at the University of Toledo, Toledo, Ohio.

ganizing schooling around multiple-choice tests has been convincingly shown to do great damage to curriculum and instruction."[3] Frequently invoked are images of teacher-automatons mechanically force-feeding their students only that content found on mandated tests. The mere mention of alignment between curricular objectives and assessment specifications is enough to incite the enthusiasts to flail about en masse.

Given this seeming unanimity of opinion about the destruction wreaked by multiple-choice examinations, it is surprising to see the proponents of performance assessment strenuously arguing the other side of the coin, as well. For example, while the complaint persists that multiple-choice examinations are too closely aligned with the curriculum, Wiggins also faults the tests because they "cannot possibly align with all of the instructional aims of a given school or district." Wiggins goes further: "One-shot, end-of-year testing that yields only norm-referenced data *can have no direct impact on teaching and learning*" (emphasis added).[4]

So which way is it? How are concerned educators to decide on the truth of the matter in the face of the obviously contradictory claims? If Wiggins really wants a test that matches all our educational objectives, a much greater degree of curricular and instructional uniformity will need to be enforced. For accountability or comparison purposes, that suggests a move toward a standardized—possibly national—curriculum. But are we convinced that a match between a nascent national curriculum and some mother-of-all-performance-assessments is what we really want? Judging by the reactions of many scholars in the area of education policy to the current calls for expansion of the National Assessment of Educational Progress (NAEP), there is clearly a lack of consensus regarding the wisdom of that proposal. And, assuredly, the goals that Wiggins advocates—replacing norm-referenced tests with performance assessments for purposes of accountability and liberating school-level personnel to affect the design of assessment—are at odds.

And what about "teaching to the test" as the worst corruption of measurement-driven instruction? Does Wiggins really think that the practice will disappear if more performance assessments are implemented? Would coaching, teaching to the test, and the "Lake Wobegon" effect become mere memories? Probably not.

In his rebuttal, Wiggins points proudly to what works in performance assessment and mentions several examples, including performance assessments for pilots, writing assessments, and the New York Regents Examinations. However, these assessments suffer from the same problems that Wiggins and others incorrectly assert emanate only from paper-and-pencil tests. For example, a recent investigation of testing procedures for pilots uncovered serious flaws in the performance-based system. Evidently, because the in-flight, practical portion of the pilots examination is administered on a one-to-one basis, examiners have an incentive to give easy, cursory tests that fail to identify incompetent pilots. The incentive arises because the higher the proportion of examinees an examiner passes, the more he or she is sought out by other examinees, which generates more income. One examiner has apparently even awarded licenses without testing candidates in the air.[5]

In the area of essay testing, George Madaus reports a revealing complaint from the head of an English department regarding the Georgia Regents Testing Program:

> Because we are now devoting our best efforts to getting the largest number of students past the essay exam . . . , we are teaching to the exam. . . . Because the Regents Test is primarily designed to establish a minimal level of literacy, our teaching to this test, which its importance forces us to

do, tends to make the minimal acceptable competency the goal of our institution, a circumstance that guarantees mediocrity.[6]

Finally, Robert Linn, Eva Baker, and Stephen Dunbar relate the case of a geometry teacher from New York who had been recognized for excellence in teaching, based on his students' performance on the Regents geometry examination. However, it was learned that the students' outstanding performance was achieved largely because they were encouraged to memorize the 12 proofs that were likely to appear on the examination.[7]

In citing these examples, I am *not* suggesting that Wiggins is wrong in concluding that traditional measures are susceptible to the corrupting influences he cites. However, I am suggesting that he and other proponents of performance assessment should remove their rose-colored glasses: the shortcomings they perceive in multiple-choice tests will surely crop up in performance assessments as well. It *is* wrong to promote the false notion that simply changing the form of the assessment will ensure better classroom instruction or make assessments immune to the corruption we wish to avoid. As Madaus has pointed out, just because performance assessments are labeled "authentic" doesn't mean that they aren't "just as corruptible as multiple-choice tests."[8]

VALIDITY

I take no issue with Wiggins' hope that greater face validity will spawn greater enthusiasm for testing on the part of students and teachers. However, this is clearly an example of misdirected emphasis. Can he be seriously suggesting that face validity is of *primary* importance? Apparently so. Despite Wiggins' protestations, "a third-grade reading test that bores the student and angers the teacher by its dopey questions"[9] *can* be valid. (To my knowledge there is no strong evidence that relates his hypothetical "perceived dopiness quotient" to what a test can adequately assess.) In any case, a repeated finding concerning attitudes toward testing does not reveal the ennui and hostility that Wiggins asserts. For example, the May 1981 issue of the *Kappan* contains the reports of several researchers who concluded that many educators actually perceive testing as rather innocuous.[10]

Where Wiggins and I disagree on the validity issue could not be clearer: he would apparently adopt face validity as a necessary and nearly sufficient condition for receipt of his psychometric imprimatur; I see it as a nice accouterment, never to be purchased at the expense of any other form of validity that contributes to the accuracy of inferences made on the basis of test scores. And, while he invokes some new form of validity—"systemic validity"[11]—to validate the newfound enthusiasm for performance assessments, many of us in education are still not sure what "systemic validity" really is.[12] We could, of course, continue to invent more and more kinds of validity until everyone would have his or her own special conception of validity, and the term would lose all its meaning. Personally, I'll cling to the hope that the trend will abate with "instructional validity"[13] and that we will begin to concentrate more on ensuring and reporting on validity than on increasing its forms.

Two other concerns about validity separate me and Wiggins. First, I wish to reassure him that, having spent five years as an elementary teacher, I do care about students and teachers. However, I also care about school administrators, school boards, and school districts. It is the latter groups that will surely suffer under the face-validity emphasis that Wiggins promotes. Does he forget the tortuous court battles of the Seventies and Eighties in which school districts and state departments of education were forced to defend themselves—often unsuccessfully—against charges of inadequate evidence of validity in the teacher certification and student competency tests? (And many of those tests were developed according to much more stringent standards than those currently endorsed by advocates of performance assessment.) The face-valid performance assessments that might please Wiggins would undoubtedly fail to satisfy the courts.

Second, Wiggins' comments about "dopiness" are essentially content-validity concerns. He has apparently been seduced by the chorus of the antitesting faithful, chanting their litany of complaints: "Multiple-choice questions are trivial!" they say; "They are lower-order and simplistic!" they intone; and so on. Indeed, some poorly constructed multiple-choice tests are simplistic and fail to address higher-order skills. That is not to say that poorly constructed performance tests would not be the same. Nor does Wiggins note that many well-constructed multiple-choice tests *do* assess complex, higher-order skills. Has he never looked at a

copy of the *Iowa Tests of Basic Skills* or the *Iowa Tests of Educational Development*,[14] to name just two? A quote from the historian Jeremy Jackson comes to mind: Wiggins seems "innocent of any careful appraisal of his conjectures in the light of the documents he purport[s] to criticize."[15]

RELIABILITY

It is rather disconcerting to hear reliability being damned with such faint praise. Calling reliability "not the overwhelming problem that critics of performance assessment make it out to be," Wiggins advises us to be "vigilant about making sure it does not fall below a *tolerable* minimum."[16] That is surely the weakest admonition to adhere to rigorous testing standards that I've ever heard. And surprisingly, this comes from the same Grant Wiggins who has of late been banging the drum for higher, more rigorous standards in education generally.[17]

Wiggins is apparently pleased to settle for only cursory investigations of reliability, citing an NAEP report of interrater reliability of 90% or better on NAEP subject-area essay tests.[18] He ought to know better. No one disputes the possibility that human raters can be trained to agree on a score for a single sample of a student's work. Maybe some invertebrates could be similarly trained. However, the more crucial issue is the extent to which *broad sampling* of the student's work produces accurate estimates of a student's true ability. When looked at in *this* context, reliability is typically much lower. In a thorough analysis of performance-based assessments, Linn, Baker, and Dunbar restated the findings of much previous research:

> 1) experience with performance assessments in other contexts . . . suggest[s] that there is likely substantial variability due to task; and 2) the limited generalizability from task to task is consistent with research in learning and cognition . . . that emphasizes the situation and context specific nature of thinking.[19]

Although Wiggins might call such discrepant information "credible" and "rich,"[20] the overwhelming majority of those interested in fair and accurate measurement would call it by another name: error.

What I tried to point out in my article, and what Wiggins apparently missed, is that, for the new performance measures to be truly useful, they must be held to the same high standards we have come to demand of existing paper-and-pencil assessments. Wiggins' quote from the technical manual of the College Outcome Measures Project (COMP)[21] only illustrates my point. The fact that the publisher of the COMP assessments produced "summaries of technical studies that conclude that the [COMP] performance tests are both valid and reliable"[22] is a credit to the publisher and is *precisely what I am calling on all producers of performance assessments to provide.* And this is what consumers of performance assessments should demand before a new instrument is used for any important educational decision.

But it doesn't look as if this is currently the case. To borrow Wiggins' words, there *are* "naive, unvalidated assessment[s] from unknown vendor[s] trying to cash in on the latest trend"[23] out there. They're selling unproven instruments, hawking whizz-bang video how-to's, and biting off a big piece of the in-service training pie. All I'm asking for is the educational equivalent of "truth in lending" so that consumers of these new instruments are made aware of the extent to which the instruments have—or have not—been critically examined for psychometric propriety.

REINVENTION

Wiggins objects to being "taken to task for reinventing the testing wheel." He also contends that I cannot "have it both ways, at one moment decrying the trendiness of [performance assessment] and at another reminding us [of its age]."[24] It is ironic that Wiggins claims I have begged the question concerning what new ideas are being put forth in current calls for more reliance on performance assessments. The clear implication of my article was that so far nothing terribly substantial has been provided by the enthusiasts—mostly we have gotten jargon-filled pronouncements. How can Wiggins, with a straight face, chastise me for not supplying some original justification for his movement?

And, by the way, one *can* have it both ways. To say that something is old but trendy is not at all contradictory. Perhaps Wiggins doesn't wear a paisley tie, but maybe he has noticed a few of the fashion-conscious folks in Rochester, New York, sporting knee-length shorts, horn-rimmed glasses, or fountain pens.

REFORMATION

There is surely one larger issue about which Wiggins and I are in agreement: the need for reform of the education system. However, it is revealing that the topic of assessment has brought to light so precisely the critical difference we have in *approach* to the problem of reform.

Wiggins (and others before him) have suffered from a simplistic, "univariate" view of education reform. He states: "We will not improve schools until local teachers and administrators have complete faith that the assessment system will adequately represent their students' . . . achievements."[25] Others of us see many complex and interrelated factors that work against the quick-fix reform of education using single-variable solutions. If "complete faith" is all it takes to reform education, then perhaps we were reformed decades ago when our faith was greater—and we just didn't realize it.

No, it's going to take more than faith. And it will take more than superficial fussing with the form of assessment tools we use. As a single variable in the complex process of education reform, performance assessment cannot possibly accomplish all that its enthusiasts have, sadly, led many to believe that it will. As Robert Travers has noted: "Amateur reformers in the field of education would probably drop most of their plans for the remodeling of public education if they had a better understanding of the failures of the past."[26]

WHAT MATTERS

As Wiggins correctly notes, a constructive debate is surely needed, but it must go beyond short-sighted fix-all fads. Some bold new plans proposing more comprehensive strategies for assessment reform[27] and far-reaching conceptualizations that address the complexity of school reform[28] have been advanced; others should be developed and tested. The true reform of American education—if that is what we are willing to work toward—will undoubtedly be evidenced by something more substantial than pocket folders bulging with student work. Performance assessment does have the potential to make a positive contribution to reform efforts by providing unique information about student ability that complements the kinds of data currently gathered. It should not be promoted as a replacement for other assessments or, worse, as *the* cure for what ails us.

NOTES

1. See Gregory J. Cizek, "Innovation or Enervation? Performance Assessment in Perspective," *Phi Delta Kappan,* May 1991, pp. 695–99; and Grant Wiggins, "A Response to Cizek," *Phi Delta Kappan,* May 1991, pp. 700–703.

2. Grant Wiggins, "Reconsidering Standards and Assessment," *Education Week,* 24 January 1990, p. 36. Although Wiggins' causal assertion is nearly untenable, others have gone beyond credibility. For example, Martin Solomon has publicly wondered whether the "bland" 1988 Presidential campaign was "perhaps a byproduct of 30 years of a different [multiple-choice] system of testing in education" (*Education Week,* 30 January 1991, p. 34). Apparently, critics of multiple-choice testing can now attribute the occurrence of any undesirable phenomenon to the test!

3. Monty Neill, "Do We Need a National Achievement Exam?," *Education Week,* 24 April 1991, p. 36.

4. Wiggins, "A Response," p. 702.

5. "Systematic Flaws Found in Pilot Testing," *NOCA Professional Regulation News,* December 1990, p. 3.

6. George F. Madaus, "The Influence of Testing on the Curriculum," in Laurel N. Tanner, ed., *Critical Issues in Curriculum: 87th NSSE Yearbook* (Chicago: National Society for the Study of Education, University of Chicago Press, 1988), p. 96.

7. Robert L. Linn, Eva L. Baker, and Stephen B. Dunbar, "Complex Performance-Based Assessment: Expectations and Validation Criteria," *Educational Researcher,* in press.

8. George F. Madaus, quoted in Robert Rothman, "Researchers Say Emphasis on Testing Too Narrow, Could Set Back Reform," *Education Week,* 12 June 1991, p. 25.

9. Wiggins, "A Response," p. 702.

10. See, for example, the following articles in the May 1981 *Phi Delta Kappan:* Lee Sproull and David Zubrow, "Standardized Testing from the Administrative Perspective," pp. 628–31; Leslie Salmon-Cox," Teachers and Standardized Achievement Tests: What's Really Happening?," pp. 631–34; and George F. Madaus, "Reactions to the 'Pittsburgh Papers,' " pp. 634–36.

11. Wiggins, "A Response," p. 702.

12. Obviously, just because a name for something is popularized doesn't mean that it exists. That belief, called *reification,* is described—ironically—in Steven J. Gould's criticism of intelligence testing, *The Mismeasure of Man* (New York: Norton, 1981).

13. *Debra P. v. Turlington,* 474 F. Supp. 244 (M. D. Fla., 1979).

14. Albert N. Hieronymous and Hiram D. Hoover, *Manual for School Administrators, Iowa Tests of Basic Skills, Forms G/H* (Chicago: Riverside, 1986); and Leonard S. Feldt, Robert A. Forsythe, and Stephanie D. Alnot, *Teacher, Administrator, and Counselor Manual, Iowa Tests of Educational Development, Forms X-8 and Y-8* (Chicago: Riverside, 1989).

15. Jeremy C. Jackson, *No Other Foundation: The Church Through Twenty Centuries* (Westchester, Ill.: Crossway Books, 1980), p. 223.

16. Wiggins, "A Response," p. 702.

17. See, for example, Wiggins, "Reconsidering Standards"; and Grant Wiggins, "Standards, Not Standardization: Evoking Quality Student Work," *Educational Leadership,* February 1991, pp. 18–25.

18. Wiggins, "A Response," p. 702.

19. Linn, Baker, and Dunbar, op. cit.

20. Wiggins, "A Response," p. 703.

21. Aubrey Forrest and Joe Steele, *Defining and Measuring General Education Knowledge and Skills* (Iowa City, Ia.: American College Testing, College Outcome Measures Project, Technical Report No. 1976–81, 1982).

22. Wiggins, "A Response," p. 701.

23. Ibid.

24. Ibid.

25. Ibid., p. 703.

26. Robert M. W. Travers, *An Introduction to Educational Research,* 2nd ed. (New York: Macmillan, 1964), p. 127.

27. See, for example, John R. Hills, "Apathy Concerning Grading and Testing," *Phi Delta Kappan,* March 1991, pp. 540–45; and Richard J. Stiggins, "Assessment Literacy," *Phi Delta Kappan,* March 1991, pp. 534–39.

28. John E. Chubb and Terry M. Moe, *Politics, Markets, and America's Schools* (Washington, D.C.: Brookings Institution, 1990).

Parents' Thinking about Standardized Tests and Performance Assessments

LORRIE A. SHEPARD and CARRIBETH L. BLIEM

In Palo Alto recently, a group of high-tech parents organized to oppose the new "fuzzy math" curriculum introduced by the California Mathematics Framework. The group wants to restore the teaching of "math basics" and computational skills instead of what one parent called "no-correct-answer math." In Littleton, Colorado, new school board members elected on a "back-to-basics" antireform platform promised to eliminate performance-based high-school proficiency requirements. Opposition to the newly instituted reform reflected a variety of concerns: too much emphasis on self-esteem, too little attention to skills in whole-language instruction, fear that students would be ill prepared for the SAT, and one board member's worry that school-developed performance assessments lacked sufficient reliability and validity evidence to make high-stakes graduation decisions.

Instances such as these are part of a backlash against standards-based reform and new forms of assessment that have arisen nationally, in most cases before reform efforts have gotten off the ground. On the surface, the controversy seems perplexing. Who could be against the rhetoric of the reform—setting high academic standards for all students, developing challenging assessments to reflect the standards, creating the conditions necessary to ensure student learning? Indeed, each side in this many-sided debate claims to be working to ensure academic excellence.

The effort to set standards raises fundamental questions, however, about what students should know, about the nature of subject matter, how best to support learning, and how to measure what has been learned. Most reformers envision a curriculum that fosters thinking and depth of understanding, where the "big ideas" in a discipline are emphasized and skills are learned and applied in authentic contexts. Nonetheless, some standards efforts have produced exhaustive lists of content that could not possibly be taught within the constraints of a normal school year. Some business leaders see the need to broaden school curricula to develop students' communication skills, their abilities to work in groups, to use technology, and so forth. In contrast, many parents and other citizen groups see teaching practices that diverge from their own school experiences as an abandonment of academic rigor. Their fears are sometimes exacerbated by poorly implemented versions of reform. Some groups see the emphasis on thinking per se to be a threat to authority and to a basic-skills definition of achievement. These themes are familiar, but how the lines of dispute are drawn may vary from one community to the next.

237

INTEREST IN PARENTS' THINKING ABOUT ASSESSMENT

Three years ago, a team of researchers from the University of Colorado at Boulder began working with third-grade teachers in three schools to develop classroom-based performance assessments in reading and mathematics. From the beginning of the project, we were interested—along with district leaders—in parents' views about performance assessments, particularly in contrast to their views regarding more familiar standardized tests. Our concern about parent acceptance and support of new forms of assessment had both classroom- and district-level implications. At the classroom level, we had often heard teachers refer to parents' expectations as the justification for classroom-assessment practices. For example, teachers might give timed tests on math facts because "parents expect it" or might use chapter pre- and posttests to be able "to defend" grades to parents. Therefore, teachers' willingness to try new forms of assessment in their classrooms could very likely be influenced by anticipated and real parent reactions. At the district level, curriculum specialists were developing their own performance assessments to be used along with standardized tests. Although there was not the same dissention that arose the next year in neighboring Littleton, enough questions had been raised about curriculum changes to make district leaders wary that controversy might suddenly erupt if assessment changes were perceived as radical. For example, sympathetic members of the district accountability committee asked that we stop using the term *alternative* assessment because it connoted lack of standards and rigor. We agreed thereafter to refer to the assessments we were developing as *performance assessments*.

THE STUDY

In the context of our work with teachers we used the terms *performance assessments, authentic assessments,* and *direct assessments* interchangeably, the idea being to judge what students can do in terms of the actual tasks and end performances that are the goals of instruction. In reading this meant evaluating fluency during oral reading and measuring comprehension by having students talk and write about what they had read. In mathematics, newly adopted district frameworks emphasizing problem solving and communicating mathematically, and introducing new topics such as geometry and probability, implied a shift in content as well as in the mode of assessment.

In planning a collateral study to collect data from parents, our purpose was to examine systematically the attitudes and thinking about testing sometimes ascribed to parents. Is it the case, for example, that parents disdain the use of performance assessments as less rigorous or objective? We especially wanted to focus parent attention on the content and form of these two types of measures by showing them examples of questions from each measure. By means of both questionnaire surveys and extended interviews, we wanted to learn specifically how parents evaluate the usefulness of standardized tests compared to less formal types of information such as report cards, talking to the teacher, or seeing samples of their child's work. Do parents value different types of information when judging the quality of the school instead of learning about their own child's progress? We also wanted to analyze interview data in sufficient detail to understand the reasons behind parent preferences for standardized tests or performance assessments and to see if their preferences vary depending on whether the purpose of testing is for classroom instruction or district accountability purposes.

Interview and questionnaire data were collected in the fall and spring of the first project year using non-overlapping random samples. A total of 60 interviews were conducted with individual parents or parent dyads following regularly scheduled parent-teacher conferences. Questionnaires were also administered in control schools. Detailed analyses of results are provided in technical papers by Shepard and Bliem (1993, 1994). In this article we focus on the most important insights gained from talking to parents that might be applicable to other settings where assessment reforms are contemplated. Fall data are emphasized because this was the time when parents were least familiar with the assessment project; therefore, their reactions were more analogous to what first-time encounters with performance assessments might be like in other districts.

WHAT PARENTS WANT TO KNOW ABOUT THEIR CHILD'S PROGRESS IN SCHOOL

We wanted to ask parents questions about testing and assessment in the context of other sources of

TABLE 1 **Parent Questionnaire Ratings of the Usefulness of Different Types of Information for Learning about Their Child's Progress in School (n = 105)**

	How useful					
Type of Information	Not at all				Very	Blank/ missing
	1	2	3	4	5	
Report cards	2%	2%	20%	33%	43%	
My child's teacher talking about his/her progress	0	2%	4%	17%	77%	
Standardized tests	6%	15%	41%	22%	14%	2%
Seeing graded samples of my child's work	0	0	10%	30%	60%	

information used to follow their child's progress or judge the quality of their child's school. An example of one question set from the questionnaire is shown in Table 1 with data from the fall. Overwhelmingly, parents indicated that they learn the most about their child's progress by talking with the teacher; 77% rated this source of information as very useful. Results were highly consistent, across project schools and control schools, and between survey and interview responses—except that interview data collected just after parent conferences showed an even more "euphoric" endorsement of the value of talking to their child's teacher.

Given our prior, framing set of issues regarding the need for external and objective measures, we were surprised that parents rated informal sources of information—talking to the teacher and seeing graded samples of their child's work—as more useful than standardized tests for learning about their "child's progress in school" and even for judging the "quality of education provided at their child's school." Note that we do not promote these findings as an all-time plebiscite for or against traditional standardized tests. A sample of third-grade parents is not likely to respond in the same way as high-school parents; and we confirmed, based on Gallup Poll questions embedded in the survey, that our sample was less favorably disposed toward standardized tests than the national sample. Nonetheless, the pattern of preferences reported here was true even for the subsample who strongly endorsed standardized tests on the Gallup questions. Therefore, what is most important for us to understand is the reasoning behind parents' valuing of informal sources of information.

In support of their ratings parents offered comments that emphasized the value of receiving specific information about their child's strengths and weaknesses.

Talking with my child's teacher is most helpful because I learn firsthand what progress is being made in class, where the shortcomings are, and how I can best help at home.

This way I can see the actual work, the teacher's response, and evaluate what I understand the child's level of learning to be.

When the questions were changed to focus on information used to "evaluate the quality of education provided at your child's school," the percentage of parents who considered standardized tests to be useful increased (from 36% to 45% in the corresponding fall questionnaire sample). Approximately one third of the interview sample elaborated that it was the normative or comparative information provided by such tests that made them useful for this second purpose.

That is one of the reasons I like the standardized tests, because to me if you have a national standard test for third graders, it shows you where your kid is against national standards. Which doesn't necessarily say anything about your kid, but it might point out there is a problem here . . . [at this school]

Even for the purpose of evaluating the school, however, parents found talking to the teacher and seeing graded samples of work to be more useful than standardized tests. Moreover, in follow-up comments parents gave justifications that showed they understood the accountability purpose of this second set of questions. Parents explained that these informal sources help them learn about the quality of education by giving them first-hand information about the school curriculum, what expectations were being set, and how caring the teacher is with students. In particular, parents said that seeing the actual work that students brought home let them judge whether what was being taught was worthwhile.

> *I can see what kind of work the teacher is handing out. The teacher is the one that's in there quarterbacking the classroom. You know, if she's handing out pretty basic stuff to the kids to work on, then that's pretty boring, you know, 'get-me-through-the-school-day' type of activities as far as I'm concerned. But if she's handing out stuff that will keep their interest and get their initiative going as far as keeping them active in school, and wanting to learn, that pretty much sets the tone for the school year and gives me an indication of what kind of quality teachers there are, and what kind of quality programs are here at this school.*

Given the arguments for external, accountability testing, two things surprised us about parent responses to this series of questions. First, parents seemed consistently to trust teachers and to have confidence in teachers' professional judgment.

> *She's the trained professional, she knows what to look for if something should come up that we should be aware of . . . To be able to talk with somebody who can see their development and be there at all times is very important.*

Parents' reported trust in teachers' first-hand knowledge and ability to judge their child's progress was especially striking given teachers' worries throughout our project that they needed to justify and objectify their evaluations to satisfy parents. Second, many parents expressed a need for what we would call normative data but felt that this need was met if teachers could tell them how their child was doing in relation to grade-level expectations. This suggests that parents would value even locally developed benchmarks or performance standards. As an example in our own project, teachers developed a grade-level continuum with benchmark examples to evaluate the text difficulty of chapter books being used in their classrooms. This helped parents see not only whether their child was reading with under-

standing but also whether he or she could handle grade-level material.

PARENTS' EVALUATIONS OF STANDARDIZED TESTS AND PERFORMANCE ASSESSMENTS

On the questionnaire, parents were provided with displays showing multiple-choice questions in reading and mathematics like those on the standardized test used by the district and a sample of more open-ended questions used in performance assessments. Parents were asked to rate their approval or disapproval of each type of measure but were not forced to choose one type of measure over the other. Although the majority of parents approved of both types of measures, performance assessments had higher approval ratings than did standardized tests. For example, in mathematics 18% strongly approved of standardized tests, [and] 31% strongly approved of the use of performance assessments.

Although the quantitative questionnaire data give a systematic summary of parent reactions from both participating and control schools, interview data provided a much richer and elaborated account of parent responses to the two types of measures. Interviews were conducted with sample assessments and test questions on the table as prompts. Figures 1 and 2 [on pages 241 and 242] show some of the examples provided in mathematics for multiple-choice and performance-assessment questions, respectively. In reading, the standardized test examples included vocabulary items, a reading passage, and comprehension questions. The performance assessment in reading included a 15-page booklet with a complete story and attractive line drawings; open-ended questions with multiple formats were used where students completed a chart, drew a picture, and wrote about why things happened in the story. Parents were asked to indicate whether they approved or disapproved of each type of measure and then to say what they thought were "the advantages and disadvantages of using tests (or performance assessments) with questions like these." After parents discussed both types of measures in both reading and mathematics, they were then asked one final pair of questions about which they would prefer to see used in classrooms for instructional purposes.

Apart from insights gained from the data, conducting these interviews was a valuable learning ex-

Computation

Add.

1.

```
   3842
 + 4104
```

- O 7946
- O 7746
- O 7906
- O 7942
- O None of these

Subtract.

2. 82 - 3 =

- O 89
- O 79
- O 81
- O 52
- O None of these

Multiply.

3.

```
    6
 x  9
```

- O 63
- O 48
- O 54
- O 69
- O None of these

Divide.

4. 8) 16

- O 2
- O 24
- O 20
- O 8
- O None of these

Concepts and Applications

1. What is 763 rounded to the nearest hundred?

- O 700
- O 750
- O 760
- O 800

2. How much change will you get if you have $6.55 and spend $4.32?

- O $2.23
- O $2.43
- O $3.23
- O $10.87

3. What is the perimeter of this shape?

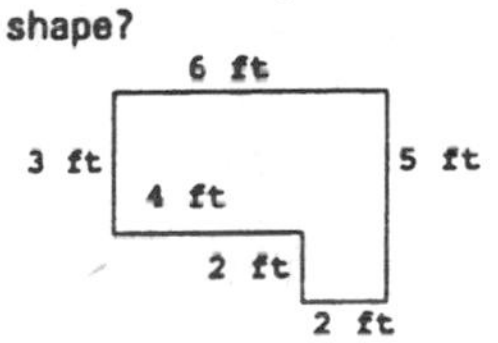

- O 20 ft
- O 21 ft
- O 22 ft
- O 23 ft

FIGURE 1 **Examples of questions on third-grade standardized achievement tests in mathematics.**

perience for the team of 10 faculty and graduate students. Whereas beforehand we had been mindful of not taking too much of parents' time, it was our impression that almost all parents were intrigued by the opportunity to have a close look at both standardized test questions and performance assessments for third graders. Despite being presented with these examples near the end of the interview, most parents took time to look through the materials carefully. They "got into it." They worked through the problems, asked questions about how they were administered typically, and occasionally asked how to do a particular problem (such as the "dot" problem).

The sample interview segment in Figure 3 [on page 243] gives the flavor of how parents talked as they looked through the examples and gave their reactions, often pointing to specific items. We created a notational system to make it clear which structured question had just been asked and how each measure was rated. For example, the transcript segment in Figure 3 begins in response to the question about approval or disapproval of performance assessments in reading. The respondent previously indicated approval of standardized tests in reading (STreading+) and strongly approved of performance assessments in reading (PAreading++). The parenthetical notations (ST) and (PA) are used whenever parents pointed to one of the examples in front of them.

Qualitative analysis was used to develop categories representing different positions. Entire transcript segments from this portion of the interview were read and sorted into categories resulting in the final categorization scheme shown in Table 2.

1. Bus Ride -- A friend of yours, who just moved to the United States, must ride the bus to and from school each day. The bus ride costs 50 cents. Your friend must have exact change and must use only nickels, dimes, and quarters. Your friend has a problem because she does not yet understand our money, and she does not know how to count our money.

Help your friend find the right coins to give to the bus driver. Draw and write something on a whole sheet of paper that can help her. She needs a sheet of paper that can show which combinations of coins can be used to pay for the 50-cent bus ride.

Sample Student Answer 1

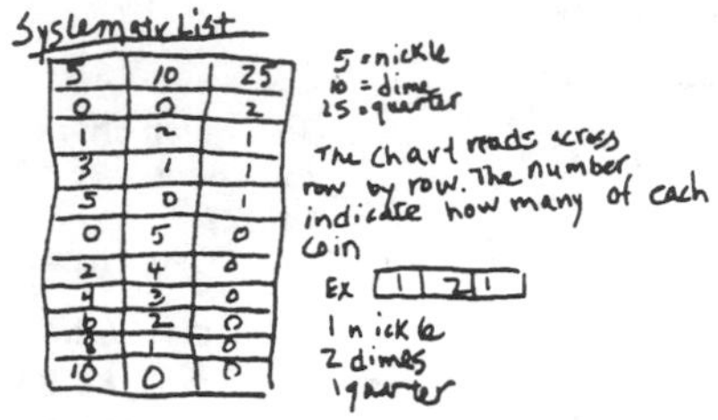

Sample Student Answer 2

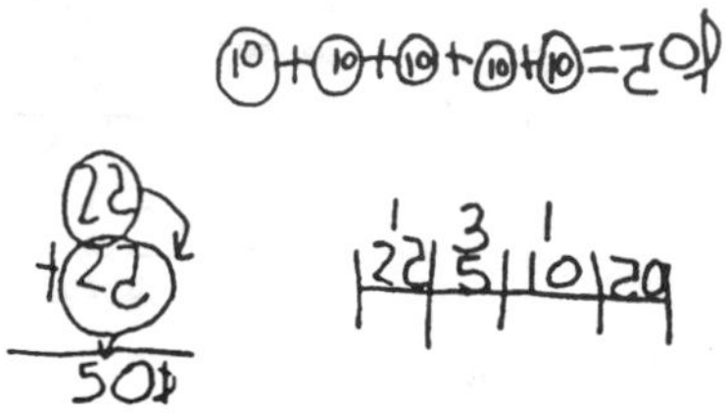

2.

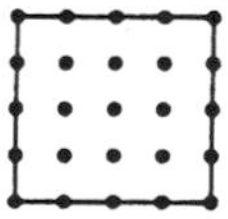

For the figure at left, show 1/2 in as many ways as you can. You may draw more figures, if necessary. For each way you find, explain how you know you have 1/2.

3. Suppose you couldn't remember what 8 x 7 is. How could you figure it out?

4. Our class of 26 students is going to the Denver Art Museum. How many cars do we need if 4 students can go in each car? How many do we need if only 3 students can go in each car?

5. Adam says that 4 + 52 is 452. Is he right or wrong? What would you tell Adam?

6. Put 4 different one-digit numbers in the boxes to make the largest possible answer.

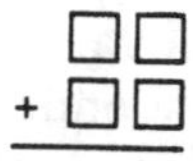

How did you know what to choose?

FIGURE 2   **Examples of third-grade performance assessment questions in mathematics.**

Note: The first two examples are reproduced with permission from Pandey, T. (1991). *A sampler of mathematics assessment.* Sacramento, CA: California Department of Education.

(STreading +) (PAreading + +) Actually I'd like to see them have this type of test but you have to start really young with them, showing them how to communicate and how to really write that out, bring it out of themselves. . . . I would go with this one (PA). I would strongly approve of this type. I want my son to learn how to write more, communicate better. . . . This seems the faster way (ST) as far as a test time goes, but this (PA) looks like they've really worked out the problem. They've had to sit there and think about it and take the time to do it.

(STmath +) I'm comfortable with these still, so I approve of them.

(PAmath +) This would be interesting. I'd like to see them start working some of these into the program.

(Instruction) I would like to see them use these (PA), because as I'm looking at this, you're reading it and it's asking you, and it's almost as though you're talking to the teacher one on one. As you're looking at this (ST), you say 4 times 8, what is that? Well, this one (PA) is giving you a little bit more challenge. It's kind of almost speaking, you say OK, now you figure this out. "Suppose you couldn't remember what 8 x 7 is. How could you figure it out?" It seems like this is better communicated this way.

FIGURE 3   **Sample interview segment illustrating the "Prefers performance assessment (likes both)" category.**

Note. Notations in parentheses indicate approval ratings of standardized tests (ST) and performance assessments (PA) from strong approval (++) to strong disapproval (−−). Notations help keep track of the question being responded to in these shortened excerpts; ST and PA abbreviations are also used when respondents point to a test or assessment sample.

The counts in Table 2 are for the fall interviews. Only 3 of the 33 fall parents or parent dyads preferred the use of standardized tests for both district and instructional purposes. Respondents in this category saw standardized tests as more cut and dried, more aligned to instruction, easier, and providing more support (because having the answers there made it clear what was expected). Figure 4 [on page 244] provides an excerpt representative of responses in this category.

By far the majority of respondents preferred performance assessments. Twelve interview segments were placed in the category "Prefers performance assessments (likes both)" and another 11 responses were in the "Strongly prefers performance assessments" category illustrated by the interview segment in Figure 5 [on page 245]. Although the "Prefers PA (likes both)" category was heterogeneous, the dominant response was to approve of both kinds of measures being used for district purposes but to prefer

TABLE 2   **Parent Interview Categories: Preferences for Standardized Tests or Performance Assessments (*n* = 33 Parents or Parent Dyads)**

Preference category	*n*
Strongly prefers standardized tests	2
Prefers standardized tests (likes both)	1
Standardized tests math/performance assessments reading	4
Standardized tests reading/performance assessments math	1
Both: likes both, wants both in instruction	2
Prefers performance assessments (likes both)	12
Strongly prefers performance assessments	11

(STreading + +) Well, I think it's really clear cut what is expected of these kids. It's easy for them to understand, it's easy for them to answer it.

(PAreading-) Well, the disadvantages of it are that there are too many right or wrong answers. I think that is kind of hard for kids that age to comprehend all this. Maybe the advantage of it would be they are more able to use their imagination.

(PAmath-) For one thing, the child might understand how to do something like this but they don't know how to explain it. They have trouble with words. . . .
Just that a test like this might be useful again to get an idea of how they are at comprehending different things but it wouldn't really be fair to grade their learning on this.

(Instruction) Oh. Standardized. Because I feel that that is easier to teach and easier for the kids to learn and easier to grade them on it.

FIGURE 4 **Sample interview segment illustrating the "Strongly prefers standardized tests" category.**

Note. Notations in parentheses indicate approval ratings of standardized tests (ST) and performance assessments (PA) from strong approval (++) to strong disapproval (−−). Notations help keep track of the question being responded to in these shortened excerpts; ST and PA abbreviations are also used when respondents point to a test or assessment sample.

that performance assessments be used for classroom instruction. Across responses in all categories the most frequently mentioned feature of performance assessments is that they make children think.

I like the idea that they read the story, and they really have to get into it, and have to answer some questions and think about it a little harder than the standardized one. I think it would make them comprehend it a little more.

Strongly approve. I mean they make the child think. They have to think about what they read. They have to think about what they're going to write. It helps with their work on their writing skills even. This (ST) is just coloring in a box, you know.

F: Again I think it gives them a broader understanding of what they're doing, rather than just A + B = C. . . . It's like, well how did you get it? Use logic rather than just being told this is the answer. Use your logic, use your mind, picture. . . . M: It's not just memorization. . . . F: Yeah exactly, there you go. Be able to work it out instead of just memorizing.

I think in order to learn any kind of subject you have to have concepts down, and I think number 2 (PA) is going to show how to develop the concepts better. . . . You need to get those basics. . . .

But I do think this (PA) is going to make them think more.

Even respondents who preferred standardized tests for other reasons often noted that performance assessments would stimulate children's imagination or make them have to think.

Beyond their overall evaluations of the two types of measures, parents demonstrated remarkable sophistication in their analysis of the strengths and weaknesses of standardized tests and performance assessments, in many cases anticipating issues of concern to measurement experts. We developed a "key features" coding system to represent issues as they arose in the data. The codes are shown in Table 3 [on page 246] along with response frequencies for the fall interviews. Parents tended to agree on these characterizations regardless of which type of measure they preferred. For example, parents at both ends of the preference continuum noted that standardized tests have clear-cut right or wrong answers (the Yes/No code) and are more objective. They also seemed easier to a number of parents than performance assessments. Less frequently, parents commented that standardized tests are important because they give you normative information. Only parents who preferred standardized tests commented that they measure what you really need to know in real life, especially math skills. In contrast, a num-

(STreading-) M: It doesn't really force you to think, I mean, the answers are right there. . . . F: It makes you have one of their choices instead of one of your own choices.

(PAreading +) M: This one has you also explain. Like right here (ST) you don't really have to think too much about it, and this one (PA) you really have to kind of pull it all together and reason it out. . . . The only problem I see with this is if they were at a lower level of third grade reading, you know, they probably couldn't grasp some of this.

(STmath-) (PAmath + +) F: If I had the option, something like this (PA) would be a little bit better . . . M: Yeah. I think this would make them, if they were to teach, obviously they'd have to teach this to take these tests. We'd probably get better quality in teaching. Things would probably stick with them a little bit more. . . . I think you can probably guess more on (ST). On these (PA) you can't really guess, you kind of have to think about it. F: Plus, I think this (PA) makes it a little bit more interesting for the kids. This (ST) is pretty cut and dried.

(Instruction) F: Well, like we said, this one (PA). This one, I think. The kids could relate to this. . . . M: It's more practical. You can apply it; it stresses more of life skills.

FIGURE 5   **Sample interview segment illustrating the "Strongly prefers performance assessments" category.**

Note. Notations in parentheses indicate approval ratings of standardized tests (ST) and performance assessments (PA) from strong approval (++) to strong disapproval (--). Notations help keep track of the question being responded to in these shortened excerpts; ST and PA abbreviations are also used when respondents point to a test or assessment sample. The abbreviations F and M stand for father and mother, respectively.

ber of parents noted that standardized tests allow students to get the right answer by guessing, but this characterization was made by parents who preferred performance assessments.

As stated previously, making kids "think" was the most frequently cited feature of performance assessments. In addition nearly half of parents also explained that performance assessments could be used "diagnostically" by teachers because the way children answered would reveal their thought process.

The other tests (PA math) kind of makes them tell you the concept, not just the right answer. I like the "explain your choice," or "what would you tell Adam" type questions . . . This would give a teacher more information to think about, especially on the concepts that they haven't quite grasped yet.

Parents commented that performance assessments allow students to use their "imagination" and be creative. Performance assessments appear to be harder, prompting several parents to ask if this was really third-grade work, and they were perceived by a number of parents to be potentially "unfair" particularly to the low kids in the class or for kids who have trouble writing. Although reading level and writing demand were mentioned as problems to be resolved, for the most part they did not appear to affect parents' enthusiasm for using performance assessments in instruction. For some parents in the Prefers PA (likes both) category, however, these features were cited specifically as the reason that both types of tests should be used at least for district purposes. "Different children learn in different ways." Some children, especially those who "are not good with words," would be helped by having the answers there so they could show that they understood.

Nine of 33 parents or parent dyads commented on the issue of instructional "alignment" (our term, not theirs) for performance assessments. They

TABLE 3   **Key Features of Standardized Tests and Performance Assessments Mentioned by Parents in Interview Responses (*n* = 33)**

Standardized tests		Performance assessments	
Code	*n*	**Code**	*n*
Guess	16	Think	24
Yes/No	15	Imagination	18
Easy	8	Diagnostic	16
Objective	8	Hard	10
Support	6	Unfair	10
Know	4	Know	10
Real life	3	Aligned	9
Norm	3	Subjective	8
		Real life	6

insisted that it would not be fair to test children with these kinds of assessments unless teachers also taught using the same kinds of problems.

> *I'm assuming that if they were going to be testing this way they would be doing, of course, more papers this way in the first place to get them ready for it.*

Parents recognized that performance assessments are more "subjective" and therefore more difficult to score, but some said that this was how good teachers should spend their time. Less frequently (but in greater numbers than for standardized tests) parents said things like "performance assessments would really tell what students 'know'" and "this kind of problem is what kids need to know in 'real life.'"

PARENTS' CONCEPTIONS OF SUBJECT MATTER

For some parents, attitudes toward performance assessments and standardized tests appeared to be related to beliefs about subject matter. A distinct subgroup of parents preferred standardized tests for mathematics instruction because "in math there is only one right answer." We noted in the questionnaire responses that the proportion of parents favoring the use of performance assessments in reading was much larger than in math. In reading, 58% favored performance assessments compared to 21% preferring standardized tests; in mathematics the margin was much narrower, with 44% favoring performance assessments versus 31% for standard-

ized tests. The same pattern emerged in interview ratings but with collateral parent talk explaining or revealing reasons behind their preferences. As shown in Table 2, a category was created for 4 of 33 parent interviews who favored standardized tests for math and performance assessments for reading. We think this category warrants interpretation, not only because the same preference occurred several times, but also because the reasoning expressed was highly similar and recurred again in spring cases.

For this subgroup of parents, the difference in preference for the two types of measures was associated with differences in their views about the nature of reading and the nature of mathematics or how mathematics is taught in school. Doing well in reading (and writing) allows for individual expression, whereas for mathematics, it is important to know the one correct way:

> *(Instruction?)(PA reading+) In mathematics, I think this type (ST) is probably the best . . . because math is pretty basic as far as having the right answer, and you have to have the right answer. With this (PA reading) they can use their imagination and they can tell you a story the way they see it rather than, you know, it doesn't always have to be one way.*

> *(Instruction?) I'd say the performance assessments (in reading) because it still does give him a chance to tell his part. (In math?) I would have to say I prefer the standardized because that's not an option, there's only one answer, you know.*

This same type of response occurred again in spring interviews, but interestingly some of the parents who commented "math is black and white" were willing in the spring to suggest using both types of measures rather than only standardized tests for mathematics. Unfortunately, numbers are too small to claim that this change was reliable, but it is possible that parents were more accepting of open-ended math problems after seeing them used in their child's classroom during the school year.

CONCLUSIONS

The purpose of the study was to examine parent opinions about standardized tests and new performance assessments in greater depth than can be understood from national survey data. The classic Gallup Poll question showing a high percentage of citizens and public school parents in favor of standardized national tests (Elam, Rose, & Gallup, 1992) is often interpreted as a mandate for external, machine-scorable, accountability measures. What was discovered in this study is that parents' favorable ratings of standardized national tests do not imply a preference for such measures over other less formal sources of information for monitoring their child's academic progress or for judging the quality of education provided at their local school. Approval of standardized tests likewise does not imply disapproval of performance assessments.

In this study, third-grade parents considered report cards, hearing from the teacher, and seeing graded samples of student work to be much more useful in learning about their child's progress than standardized tests. Though in interview data parents often mentioned the need for comparative information to know how to interpret their own child's progress, they trust the teacher to tell them how their child is doing in relation to grade-level expectations or to other children in the class. These parents of early elementary school children rarely mentioned the need for comparison to external or national norms. Even for accountability purposes, the usefulness ratings for standardized tests increased but did not equal parents' high ratings for talking to the teacher and seeing student work. According to parents, seeing graded samples of student work is an important indicator of school quality because it shows them what is being taught and what expectations are set by the classroom teacher.

When parents were provided with specific examples of the types of questions used on standardized tests and on performance assessments, the majority of parents approved of both types of measures, giving stronger approval ratings to performance assessments. Recurring themes in parent interviews were that performance assessment problems "make children think" and that they are likely to give teachers better insights about what children are understanding and where they are struggling. Parents commented frequently about the desirability of having children explain their answers in mathematics and being encouraged to express themselves in response to stories they read. Standardized tests were seen as easier and more supportive by some parents because having answer choices communicates what's expected and allows children who aren't very verbal to show what they know; at the same time, parents complained frequently that multiple-choice questions allow children to guess the right answer "25% of the time."

In the context of controversy surrounding educational reform and the development of new forms of assessment, our surveys of parent opinions and extended interviews were remarkably noncontroversial. We do not think it was because this lower and middle-class district has such an unusual population of parents; for example, the religious right is well represented and has been vocal on curricular matters; in our project some parents asked for and took advantage of the opportunity to review "secure" assessments used as end-of-project outcome measures because they wanted to be sure there was no objectionable content.

We attribute the generally favorable response and the absence of any angry or disruptive reactions to two factors that may be replicable and useful elsewhere. First, the changes being proposed were not radical, wholesale changes. It was the climate of the district, and the tone of our questions, such that use of performance assessments did not imply throwing out standardized tests. Second, parents were able to look closely at performance assessment problems, the "stuff" of the reform, before it had been characterized pejoratively in the local media. When given the chance, parents seemed intrigued with the opportunity to examine in detail questions from both standardized tests and performance assessments. Although nearly all indicated that what they saw on the performance assessments was different from their own test-taking experiences, most were satisfied that the material was challenging and worth learning.

Parents are essential to any educational reform effort. Individually they support their children's learning, and collectively they can unseat professionally developed, research-based curriculum and assessment changes, as has been demonstrated in several states and local districts. It is important to understand parent perspectives on academic standards and what they think is important for students to learn, not so that past curricular practices will always dictate future curriculum but so that points of agreement can be identified. For example, many parents fear the abandonment of basic skills. Our experience suggests that parents are more likely to be reassured if they see problems like "If you couldn't remember what 8 x 7 is, how could you figure it out?" or "How would you pick four digits to make the largest sum?" than if reformers lead with calculator use in the early grades. Even considering all the contending views of what it means to achieve academic excellence, there is a large common ground on which to build support for reform.

REFERENCES

Elam, S. M., Rose, L. C., & Gallup, A. M. (1992). The 24th annual Gallup-Phi Delta Kappan Poll of the public's attitudes toward the public schools. *Phi Delta Kappan, 74,* 41–53.

Pandey, T. (1991). *A sampler of mathematics assessment.* Sacramento, CA: California Department of Education.

Shepard, L. A., & Bliem, C. L. (1993, April). *Parent opinions about standardized tests, teacher's information, and performance assessments.* Paper presented at the Annual Meeting of the American Educational Research Association, Atlanta.

Shepard, L. A., & Bliem, C. L. (1994). *An analysis of parent opinions and changes in opinions regarding standardized tests, teacher's information, and performance assessments* (Tech. Rep.). Los Angeles: Center for Research on Evaluation, Standards, and Student Testing.

Chapter 15: Classroom Assessment and Grading

Synthesis of Research on Reviews and Tests

FRANK N. DEMPSTER

"Practice makes perfect" in itself is hardly a reliable guide to successful learning. Mere repetition over the course of days or even weeks is no guarantee of long-term learning. How many Americans, despite weeks of concentrated practice, can recall more than the opening phrase of the preamble to *The Constitution*, which has just 52 words? Yet most of us can still remember the "Pledge of Allegiance" or an evening prayer we once recited daily for years.

When, then, is practice most effective? Answers from learning research show that the effectiveness of repetition depends on a number of factors, including the time interval between repetitions, the frequency of repetitions, and even the form of the repetition, that is, whether it is in the form of a review or a test. The effects of these factors are currently being explained in terms of *constructive* processing. My purpose here is to review research and theory relating to effective practice and to suggest implications for classrooms.

RESEARCH ON REVIEWS

Several findings concerning the effects of reviews deserve special attention. First, with total study time constant, two or more opportunities to study the same material are more effective than a single oppor-

tunity. For example, in a study conducted early in the century, Edwards (1917) had one group of elementary school children study a history or arithmetic lesson for six-and-one-half minutes continuously and another group for four minutes on one occasion and for two-and-one-half minutes several days later. Overall, the group given the opportunity to study the material twice performed about 30 percent better on the achievement measure than the group that did not receive a review.

More recent research has found that an opportunity to review previously presented material may affect not only the quantity of what is learned but also the quality. For example, Mayer (1983) found that repeated presentations of a science passage resulted in a hefty increase in recall of conceptual principles but did little to promote the recall of technical details. Thus, reviews may do more than simply increase the amount learned; they may shift the learner's attention away from the verbatim details of the material being studied to its deeper conceptual structure.

Another important finding about reviews is that the amount of learning following two reviews that occur close together in time (massed) often is only slightly better than that following a single study opportunity. Thus, massed reviews, such as reviews that occur just a few hours apart, may be entirely uneconomical when evaluated in terms of additional learning. Much more effective are reviews that are spread out or distributed over lengthier periods of time. This phenomenon—known as the "spacing

Frank N. Dempster is Professor, University of Nevada, Las Vegas, Department of Educational Psychology, 4505 Maryland Pkwy., Las Vegas, NV 89154–3003.

effect"—is one of the most robust and dependable phenomena yet documented by psychologists (Dempster 1988, Hintzman 1974, Melton 1970). In fact, two spaced presentations are often about twice as effective as two massed presentations, and this advantage tends to increase as the frequency of review increases. In a recent study of vocabulary learning, for example, a surprise retention test was administered to 35 adults who had studied Spanish vocabulary words at 30-day intervals, 24-hour intervals, or all in one day, in an experiment conducted eight years earlier (Bahrick and Phelps 1987). At the end of the experiment, each of the subjects had achieved a high level of initial learning. On the retention test, however, only the subjects who had received reviews at 30-day intervals remembered a respectable number of definitions. For subjects in the other spacing conditions, even words reviewed seven times or more were almost always forgotten eight years later.

The spacing effect also is remarkable in the scope of its application: with students of all ages and ability levels, in all sorts of situations, and with a wide variety of materials and procedures. Spacing effects have been found in a variety of instructional modes, including learning from text (for example, Dempster 1986, English et al. 1934), lecture presentations (Glover and Corkill 1987), and computer-assisted instruction (Gay 1973). Subject matter has included historical facts (Edwards 1917), arithmetical rules (Gay 1973), addition facts (Pyle 1913), science concepts (Reynolds and Glaser 1964), and vocabulary (Bahrick and Phelps 1987, Dempster 1987).

RESEARCH ON TESTS

One of the complexities of research is that the act of measurement often has an effect on what is measured. In physics, for example, procedures designed to pinpoint the location of a single quantum of light may actually alter its behavior. Memory is no exception; it is affected not only by additional study opportunities but also by tests—even though they may be designed simply to assess the individual's state of knowledge about a subject. As Lachman and Laughery (1968) put it, "Test[s] . . . though they be designed to measure changes in the state of the human memory system have profound and perhaps residual effects on the state of that system" (p. 40).

Research on learning—specifically research on the effectiveness of tests—has found consistently that tests do more than simply test; they also promote learning (for example, Jones 1923–24, Nungester and Duchastel 1982, Rea and Modigliani 1985, Slamecka and Katsaiti 1988). In many cases, the effect has been strong. For example, Jones (1923–24) found that the retention test scores of previously tested students were twice that of untested students. In other words, taking a test can confer substantial benefits on the retention of the same material tested at a later date, even when no corrective feedback is provided and when there are no further study opportunities. Moreover, testing may be more productive than an additional review, especially if the student has achieved a high level of initial learning (Nungester and Duchastel 1982).

As with reviews, however, the most effective tests are those that come at spaced intervals, especially if the intervals are of an expanding nature (Landauer and Bjork 1978, Rea and Modigliani 1985). This means that three or more tests covering the same educational objectives are likely to result in more learning if there is a progressive increase in the interval between each of the successive tests (for example, 1 day, 3 days, 6 days), than if the interval between the tests is the same.

Research on testing has revealed a number of other conditions that either lengthen or diminish the effects of tests, whether massed or spaced. First, tests are most effective if the material to be learned is first tested relatively soon after its presentation. The importance of early testing is nicely illustrated in a study by Spitzer (1939), who tested the entire 6th grade population of 91 elementary schools in Iowa. Each child read a highly factual article and was then tested one or more times at various intervals. An especially noteworthy outcome was that students whose initial test occurred either 1 day or 7 days after reading scored 15 to 30 percent higher on a final test two weeks later than did students whose initial test occurred either 14 or 21 days following reading.

Second, information tested but not remembered at the first opportunity is not as likely to be remembered later as is information that was successfully negotiated on the first test (for example, Jones 1923–24, Modigliani 1976, Runquist 1986). Thus, the facilitating effect of tests applies mainly to questions with successful outcomes. Third, the effects of testing are greater for repeated questions than for new items (Anderson and Biddle 1975, Nungester and Duchastel 1982, Runquist 1986, Sones and Stroud 1940). For example, Rothkopf (1966) had students study a lengthy selection from a book on marine biology, followed by a quiz on the passage. On a later test, these students performed substantially better than a control group on repeated items and modestly better on new items (an indirect effect), even though knowing the answer to one question should not have given the answer to another. However, as Anderson and Biddle (1975) noted, the aggregate indirect benefit is likely to be greater than the direct benefit: "Only the points of information about which . . . questions are asked could be directly affected, whereas presumably every point in the text could be indirectly influenced" (p. 92).

Finally, research has demonstrated that frequent cumulative tests result in higher levels of achievement than do infrequent tests or tests related only to content since the last test. For example, Fitch et al. (1951) found that students who received weekly quizzes followed by cumulative monthly quizzes had significantly higher final exam scores than did students who had only the monthly quizzes. Similarly, 5th graders tested daily performed better on cumulative weekly spelling tests than did students who received only the weekly tests (Reith et al. 1974). However, even quizzes that contain just one or two questions covering previously tested material can be helpful, so long as the quizzes are frequent (Burns 1970, MacDonald 1984).

SPACED VS. MASSED REPETITIONS

Psychologists have attempted to understand the relation between practice and learning for nearly a century. Yet for many years, the theoretical picture surrounding spacing effects was confused and uncertain, despite numerous attempts at clarification. Recently, however, the "reconstruction" or "accessibility" hypothesis has emerged as the single most compelling explanation of spacing effects (for example, Dempster 1988, Rea and Modigliani 1987).

The basic idea is that when an individual is confronted with a repetition, he or she makes an attempt to remember, that is, to "retrieve" or "access" the previous experience with the repeated information. If the spacing between occurrences is relatively short, memory of the previous encounter will be more accessible than if the spacing between repetitions is relatively lengthy. Thus, the individual will need to devote more attention or processing effort to spaced repetitions than to massed repetitions. In

general terms, the assumption is that repetitions are effective to the extent that they engender successful retrieval of the results of earlier processing and that the effort involved in a successful retrieval operation, and thus the additional learning, increases with spacing.

One bit of evidence favoring the reconstruction hypothesis is that spaced reviews and tests have been found to be more attention-grabbing than similar massed events (Dempster 1986, Magliero 1983, Zechmeister and Shaughnessy 1980). Massed repetitions, because there is not much time between them, tend to inspire a false sense of knowing or confidence (Zechmeister and Shaughnessy 1980). Thus, they receive relatively little attention ("Since I remember it so well, why pay much more attention to it?"). In short, massed repetitions are likely to encourage superficial rote processing. Spaced repetitions, on the other hand, are likely to encourage exactly the kinds of constructive mental processes, founded on effort and concentration, that teachers hope to foster.

Another finding congruent with the reconstructive hypothesis is that research subjects have consistently reported that spaced repetitions are more interesting and enjoyable than either massed repetitions or single presentations (for example, Burns 1970, Dempster 1986, Elmes et al. 1983). Massed repetitions, in fact, are perceived as "boring" and unnecessarily repetitive (Dempster 1986).

THE USE OF REVIEWS AND TESTS IN CLASSROOMS

Reviews and tests are currently underutilized in terms of their potential for improving classroom learning. First, we'll look at teachers' use of reviews. In a study of the effectiveness of an experimental mathematics teaching program, the teachers summarized the previous day's lessons only about 25 percent of the time, and homework was checked or reviewed only about 50 percent of the time (Good and Grouws 1979). Many topics are presented just once (for example, Armbruster and Anderson 1984). In their synthesis of research on classroom instruction, Rosenshine and Stevens (1986) noted that review is a teaching function that could be done more frequently in most classrooms. Unfortunately, textbooks do not help much. In surveys of mathematics texts, for example, the use of a distributed method of presentation, with frequent use of spaced review, is clearly the exception rather than the rule (Saxon 1982, Stigler et al. 1986). Clearly, review—and certainly *spaced* review—is not a common practice in the classroom.

As to the use of tests in the classroom, many, if not most, courses of instruction offer far less than optimal testing patterns. For example, tests are rarely as frequent as they could be. They do not appear to be an integral part of teachers' regular instruction at the elementary level, even though a particular subject may be taught three to five times a week. In one survey, 4th and 6th grade mathematics teachers reported having administered an average of about 18 curriculum-embedded tests per year, or approximately one test every two weeks (Burry et al. 1982). Research also suggests that teachers test more frequently in mathematics than in reading and that grade level and amount of testing are inversely related (Yeh 1978).

There appear to be two primary reasons for this state of affairs. First, there is no evidence of any serious effort to disseminate the results of research on reviews and tests to the educational community. In a recent sampling of practitioner-oriented textbooks suitable for use in teacher education programs (for example, Good and Brophy 1986, Kim and Kellough 1987, Maver 1987, Slavin 1988, Woolfolk 1987), I found very little mention of spacing effects and no mention of the relation between testing and learning. Tests are regarded as instruments for making decisions about grading and pacing, not as vehicles for promoting learning (Kuhs et al. 1985).

Second, spacing effects are not intuitively obvious. Students tend to be more confident they will remember material presented under massed conditions than under spaced conditions (Zechmeister and Shaughnessy 1980). Thus, it is not surprising that cramming—"a heavy burst of studying immediately before an exam following a long period of neglect"—is the rule rather than the exception among students (Sommer 1968). Even experienced educators, when judging the instructional effectiveness of text passages, tend to rate prose in which the repetition of information is massed as better than prose in which it is spaced (Rothkopf 1963).

IMPLICATIONS FOR EDUCATORS

With relatively little difficulty, teachers can incorporate spaced reviews and tests into a variety of their existing instructional activities. For example, they can ask questions about concepts and skills taught in previous lessons, assign and check homework, and provide feedback (a form of review) on quizzes covering material from previous lessons. Discussion, too, can be an occasion for spaced review. DiVesta and Smith (1979), for example, showed that spaced discussions of a topic interspersed during a lecture facilitated learning more than did massed discussions.

Teachers can organize lessons by setting aside a brief period of time each day for reviewing the main points of the previous day's lessons. Once or twice a month, they can set aside a longer period of time for a more comprehensive review covering the main points of all previously presented material. To make the most efficient use of these review sessions, teachers can interweave related new material with old material expressed in paraphrased form. To be effective, reviews need not consist of verbatim repetitions of previously presented material (for example, Rothkopf and Coke 1966).

Saxon (1982) demonstrated that textbooks also can be designed to make use of spaced practice. In his algebra text, each lesson contains a set of problems in much the same fashion as most other mathematics texts. However, of the two dozen or so problems contained within each problem set, only a few deal with the most recently-presented topic; the remaining problems are review questions containing elements of all previously presented topics. Notably, this text has fared very well in comparisons with standard algebra texts in terms of achievement gains, at least when the students have been of low and average ability (Johnson and Smith 1987, Klingele and Reed 1984, Saxon 1982).

Ideally, tests should be cumulative and administered according to a pattern of increasing intervals between successive tests. A test administered soon after the material is introduced is likely to have a successful outcome, engender feelings of success and accomplishment, and strengthen the information in memory sufficiently to survive a somewhat longer interval. A recent example of this sort of application has been provided by Siegel and Misselt (1984), who conducted a study in which students [learned] foreign language vocabulary using a computer-assisted instruction program. When a student made an error, he or she received corrective feedback, and the missed word was programmed to reappear according to an expanded ratio practice schedule. For example, the first retesting of a missed word might occur after an interval of three intervening items; if that test

---

Highlights of Research on Reviews and Tests

- With total study time equated, two or more opportunities to study the same material are much more effective than a single opportunity.
- Achievement following two massed study opportunities often is only slightly higher than that following a single study opportunity.
- Spaced reviews yield significantly better learning than do massed reviews.
- The effectiveness of spaced review, relative to massed review, tends to increase as the frequency of review increases.

- Tests promote learning, especially if the material to be learned is first tested relatively soon after its introduction.
- Spaced tests are more effective than massed tests, especially if the inter-test intervals are of an expanding nature.
- Frequent spaced testing results in higher levels of achievement than relatively infrequent testing.
- The use of cumulative questions on tests is one of the keys to effective learning.

—Frank N. Dempster

---

had a successful outcome, the third test would occur after an interval of six intervening items, and so forth. Clearly this technique could be expanded to guide instruction in a variety of areas, including spelling, arithmetic, history, English, and science.

In addition, tests, as well as informal recitation questions, should be frequent. Process-outcome research (reviewed in Brophy and Good 1985) indicates a positive relationship between frequency of academic questions addressed to students and size of gain in student achievement. Moreover, the largest gains are seen in classes where most, perhaps 75 percent, of the teachers' questions are answered correctly (Brophy and Evertson 1976), just as the results of research on testing would predict.

conscious processing, whereas a massed repetition or a single presentation tends to evoke shallow, effortless processing—which, though it involves "no pain," results in little or "no gain."

Obviously, frequent spaced practice requires a precious classroom resource—namely, time, which otherwise could be devoted to the presentation of new material. However, schools are already exposing students to too many topics, a high percentage of which are taught only briefly and thus superficially (see, for example, Armbruster and Anderson 1984, Porter 1989). The alternative is to expose students to relatively few, but important, ideas (Porter 1989) and—with the aid of principles of distributed practice—attempt to teach them thoroughly.

THE BENEFITS OF FREQUENT SPACED PRACTICE

To summarize, more frequent use of properly spaced reviews and tests in the classroom can dramatically improve classroom learning and retention. In addition, research suggests that spaced repetitions can foster time-on-task and help students develop and sustain positive attitudes toward school and learning.

Another potential benefit hinges on recent theoretical developments (that is, the reconstruction hypothesis), which suggest that spaced repetitions encourage highly constructive thinking. Exactly how this works is still a mystery, but there is reason to believe that spaced repetitions result in a richer, more elaborate understanding of the topic (McDaniel and Masson 1985). The point is that spaced repetitions require the student to engage in active,

REFERENCES

Anderson, R. C., and W. B. Biddle (1975). "On Asking People Questions about What They Are Reading." In *The Psychology of Learning and Motivation*, Vol. 9, pp. 90–132, edited by G. H. Bower. New York: Academic Press.

Armbruster, B. B., and T. H. Anderson. (1984). "Structures of Explanation in History Textbooks, or So What If Governor Stanford Missed the Spike and Hit the Rail?" *Journal of Curriculum Studies* 16: 181–194.

Bahrick, H. P., and E. Phelps. (1987). "Retention of Spanish Vocabulary over Eight Years." *Journal of Experimental Psychology: Learning, Memory, and Cognition* 13: 344–349.

Brophy, J., and C. Evertson. (1976). *Learning from Teaching: A Developmental Perspective.* Boston: Allyn and Bacon.

Brophy, J., and T. Good. (1985). "Teacher Effects." In *Handbook of Research on Teaching*, 3rd ed., p. 372, edited by M. C. Wittrock. New York: Macmillan.

Burns, P. C. (1970). "Intensive Review as a Procedure in Teaching Arithmetic." *Elementary School Journal* 60: 205–211.

Burry, J., J. Catteral, B. Choppin, and D. Dorr-Bremme. (1982). *Testing in the Nation's Schools and Districts. How Much? What Kinds? To What Ends? At What Costs?* (CSE Report No. 194). Los Angeles: Center for the Study of Evaluation, University of California.

Dempster, F. N. (1986). "Spacing Effects in Text Recall: An Extrapolation from the Laboratory to the Classroom." Manuscript submitted for publication.

Dempster, F. N. (1987). "Effects of Variable Encoding and Spaced Presentations on Vocabulary Learning." *Journal of Educational Psychology* 79: 162–170.

Dempster, F. N. (1988). "The Spacing Effect: A Case Study in the Failure to Apply the Results of Psychological Research." *American Psychologist* 43: 627–634.

DiVesta, F. J., and D. A. Smith. (1979). "The Pausing Principle: Increasing the Efficiency of Memory for Ongoing Events." *Contemporary Educational Psychology* 4: 288–296.

Edwards, A. S. (1917). "The Distribution of Time in Learning Small Amounts of Material." In *Studies in Psychology: Titchener Commemorative Volume*, pp. 209–213. Worcester, Mass.: Wilson.

Elmes, D. G., C. J. Dye, and N. J. Herdelin. (1983). "What Is the Role of Affect in the Spacing Effect?" *Memory and Cognition* 11: 144–151.

English, H. B., E. L. Wellborn, and C. D. Killian. (1934). "Studies in Substance Memorization." *Journal of General Psychology* 11: 233–260.

Fitch, M. L., A. J. Drucker, and J. A. Norton, Jr. (1951). "Frequent Testing as a Motivating Factor in Large Lecture Courses," *Journal of Educational Psychology* 42: 1–20.

Gay, L. R. (1973). "Temporal Position of Reviews and Its Effect on the Retention of Mathematical Rules." *Journal of Educational Psychology* 64: 171–182.

Glover, J. A., and A. J. Corkill. (1987). "Influence of Paraphrased Repetitions on the Spacing Effect." *Journal of Educational Psychology* 79: 198–199.

Good, T. L., and J. E. Brophy. (1986). *Educational Psychology*, 3rd ed. New York: Longman.

Good, T. L., and D. A. Grouws. (1979). "The Missouri Mathematics Effectiveness Project: An Experimental Study in Fourth-Grade Classrooms." *Journal of Educational Psychology* 71: 355–362.

Hintzman, D. L. (1974). "Theoretical Implications of the Spacing Effect." In *Theories in Cognitive Psychology: The Loyola Symposium*, pp. 77–99, edited by R. L. Solso. Potomac, Md.: Erlbaum.

Johnson, D. M., and B. Smith (1987). "An Evaluation of Saxon's Algebra Text." *Journal of Educational Research* 81: 97–102.

Jones, H. E. (1923–24). "The Effects of Examination on Permanence of Learning." *Archives of Psychology* 10: 21–70.

Kim, E. C., and R. D. Kellough. (1987). *A Resource Guide for Secondary School Teaching*. 4th ed. New York: Macmillan.

Klingele, W. E., and B. W. Reed. (1984). "An Examination of an Incremental Approach to Mathematics." *Phi Delta Kappan* 65: 712–713.

Kuhs, T., A. Porter, R. Floden, D. Freeman, W. Schmidt, and J. Schwille. (1985). "Differences among Teachers in Their Use of Curriculum-Embedded Tests." *The Elementary School Journal* 86: 141–153.

Lachman, R., and R. R. Laughery. (1968). "Is a Test Trial a Training Trial in Free Recall Learning?" *Journal of Experimental Psychology* 76: 40–50.

Landauer, T., and R. Bjork. (1978). "Optimum Rehearsal Patterns and Name Learning." In *Practical Aspects of Memory*, pp. 625–632, edited by M. M. Gruneberg, P. E. Morris, and R. N. Sykes. New York: Academic Press.

MacDonald, C. J., II. (1984). "A Comparison of Three Methods of Utilizing Homework in a Precalculus College Algebra Course." Doctoral diss., Ohio State University, 1984. *Dissertation Abstracts International* 45: 1674-A.

Magliero, A. (1983). "Pupil Dilations Following Pairs of Identical Words and Related To-Be-Remembered Words." *Memory and Cognition* 11: 609–615.

Mayer, R. E. (1983). "Can You Repeat That? Qualitative Effects of Repetition and Advanced Organizers on Learning from Science Prose." *Journal of Educational Psychology* 75: 40–49.

Mayer, R. E. (1987). *Educational Psychology: A Cognitive Approach*. Boston: Little, Brown.

McDaniel, M. A., and M. E. J. Masson. (1985). "Altering Memory Representations through Retrieval." *Journal of Experimental Psychology: Learning, Memory, and Cognition* 11: 371–385.

Melton, A. W. (1970). "The Situation with Respect to the Spacing of Repetitions and Memory." *Journal of Verbal Learning and Verbal Behavior* 9: 596–606.

Modigliani, V. (1976). "Effects on a Later Recall by Delaying Initial Recall." *Journal of Experimental Psychology: Human Learning and Memory* 2: 609–622.

Nungester, R. J., and P. C. Duchastel. (1982). "Testing Versus Review: Effects on Retention." *Journal of Educational Psychology* 74: 18–22.

Porter, A. (1989). "A Curriculum Out of Balance: The Case of Elementary School Mathematics." *Educational Researcher* 18: 9–15.

Pyle, W. H. (1913). "Economical Learning." *Journal of Educational Psychology* 3: 148–158.

Rea, C. P., and V. Modigliani. (1985). "The Effect of Expanded Versus Massed Practice on the Retention of Multiplication Facts and Spelling Lists." *Human Learning* 4: 11–18.

Rea, C. P., and V. Modigliani. (1987). "The Spacing Effect in 4- to 9-Year-Old Children." *Memory and Cognition* 15: 436–443.

Reith, H., S. Axelrod, R. Anderson, F. Hathaway, K. Wood, and C. Fitzgerald. (1974). "Influence of Distributed Practice and Daily Testing on Weekly Spelling Tests." *Journal of Educational Research* 68: 73–77.

Reynolds, J. H., and R. Glaser. (1964). "Effects of Repetition and Spaced Review upon Retention of a Complex Learning Task." *Journal of Educational Psychology* 55: 297–308.

Rosenshine, B., and R. Stevens. (1986). "Teaching Functions." In *Handbook of Research on Teaching*, 3rd ed., pp. 376–391, edited by M. C. Wittrock. New York: Macmillan.

Rothkopf, E. Z. (1963). "Some Observations on Predicting Instructional Effectiveness by Simple Inspection." *Journal of Programmed Instruction* 3: 19–20.

Rothkopf, E. Z. (1966). "Learning from Written Instructive Materials: An Exploration of the Control of Inspection Behavior by Test-Like Events." *American Educational Research Journal* 3: 241–249.

Rothkopf, E. Z., and E. V. Coke. (1966). "Variations in Phrasing and Repetition Interval and the Recall of Sentence Materials." *Journal of Verbal Learning and Verbal Behavior* 5: 86–91.

Runquist, W. N. (1986). "The Effect of Testing on the Forgetting of Related and Unrelated Associates." *Canadian Journal of Psychology* 40: 65–76.

Saxon, J. (1982). "Incremental Development: A Breakthrough in Mathematics." *Phi Delta Kappan* 63: 482–484.

Siegel, M. A., and A. L. Misselt. (1984). "Adaptive Feedback and Review Paradigm for Computer-Based Drills." *Journal of Educational Psychology* 76: 310–317.

Slamecka, N. J., and L. T. Katsaiti. (1988). "Normal Forgetting of Verbal Lists as a Function of Prior Testing." *Journal of Experimental Psychology: Learning, Memory, and Cognition* 14: 716–727.

Slavin, R. E. (1988). *Educational Psychology: Theory into Practice*. 2nd ed. Englewood Cliffs, N.J.: Prentice-Hall.

Sommer, R. (1968). "The Social Psychology of Cramming." *Personnel and Guidance Journal* 9: 104–109.

Sones, A. M., and J. B. Stroud. (1940). "Review with Special Reference to Temporal Position." *Journal of Educational Psychology* 31: 665–676.

Spitzer, J. F. (1939). "Studies in Retention." *Journal of Educational Psychology* 30: 641–656.

Stigler, J. W., K. C. Fuson, M. Ham, and M. S. Kim. (1986). "An Analysis of Addition and Subtraction Word Problems in American and Soviet Elementary Mathematics Textbooks." *Cognition and Instruction* 3: 153–171.

Woolfolk, A. E. (1987). *Educational Psychology*. 3rd ed. Englewood Cliffs, N.J.: Prentice-Hall.

Yeh, J. P. (1978). *Test Use in Schools*. Washington, D.C.: National Institute of Education, U.S. Department of Health, Education, and Welfare.

Zachmeister, E. B., and J. J. Schaughnessy. (1980). "When You Know That You Know and When You Think That You Know But You Don't." *Bulletin of the Psychonomic Society* 15: 41–44.

Understanding Rubrics

HEIDI GOODRICH

Every time I introduce rubrics to a group of teachers, the reaction is the same—instant appeal ("Yes, this is what I need!") followed closely by panic ("Good grief, how can I be expected to develop a rubric for everything?"). When you learn what rubrics do—and why—you can create and use them to support and assess student learning without losing your sanity.

WHAT IS A RUBRIC?

A rubric is a scoring tool that lists the criteria for a piece of work, or "what counts" (for example, purpose, organization, details, voice, and mechanics are often what count in a piece of writing); it also articulates gradations of quality for each criterion, from excellent to poor. The term defies a dictionary definition, but it seems to have established itself, so I continue to use it.

The example in Figure 1 (adapted from Perkins et al. 1994) lists the criteria and gradations of quality for verbal, written, or graphic reports on student inventions—for instance, inventions designed to ease the Westward journey for 19th century pioneers, or to solve a local environmental problem, or to represent an imaginary culture and its inhabitants, or anything else students might invent.

This rubric lists the criteria in the column on the left: The report must explain (1) the purposes of

Heidi Goodrich is a Research Associate at the Harvard Graduate School of Education, Longfellow Hall—Project Zero, Cambridge, MA 02138 (e-mail: heidi@pz.harvard.edu).

the invention, (2) the features or parts of the invention and how they help it serve its purposes, (3) the pros and cons of the design, and (4) how the design connects to other things past, present, and future. The rubric could easily include criteria related to presentation style and effectiveness, the mechanics of written pieces, and the quality of the invention itself.

The four columns to the right of the criteria describe varying degrees of quality, from excellent to poor. As concisely as possible, these columns explain what makes a good piece of work good and a bad one bad.

WHY USE RUBRICS?

Rubrics appeal to teachers and students for many reasons. First, they are powerful tools for both teaching and assessment. Rubrics can improve student performance, as well as monitor it, by making teachers' expectations clear and by showing students how to meet these expectations. The result is often marked improvements in the quality of student work and in learning. Thus, the most common argument for using rubrics is that they help define "quality." One student actually *didn't* like rubrics for this very reason: "If you get something wrong," she said, "your teacher can prove you knew what you were supposed to do!" (Marcus 1995).

A second reason that rubrics are useful is that they help students become more thoughtful judges of the quality of their own and others' work. When rubrics are used to guide self- and peer assessment,

Criteria	Quality			
Purposes	The report explains the key purposes of the invention and points out less obvious ones as well.	The report explains all the key purposes of the invention.	The report explains some of the purposes of the invention but misses key purposes.	The report does not refer to the purposes of the invention.
Features	The report details both key and hidden features of the invention and explains how they serve several purposes.	The reports details the key features of the invention and explains the purposes they serve.	The report neglects some features of the invention or the purposes they serve.	The report does not detail the features of the invention or the purposes they serve.
Critique	The report discusses the strengths and weaknesses of the invention and suggests ways in which it can be improved.	The report discusses the strengths and weaknesses of the invention.	The report discusses either the strengths or weaknesses of the invention but not both.	The report does not mention the strengths or the weaknesses of the invention.
Connections	The report makes appropriate connections between the purposes and features of the invention and many different kinds of phenomena.	The report makes appropriate connections between the purposes and features of the invention and one or two phenomena.	The report makes unclear or inappropriate connections between the invention and other phenomena.	The report makes no connections between the invention and other things.

FIGURE 1 **Rubric for an Invention Report**

students become increasingly able to spot and solve problems in their own and one another's work. Repeated practice with peer assessment, and especially self-assessment, increases students' sense of responsibility for their own work and cuts down on the number of "Am I done yet?" questions.

Third, rubrics reduce the amount of time teachers spend evaluating student work. Teachers tend to find that by the time a piece has been self- and peer-assessed according to a rubric, they have little left to say about it. When they do have something to say, they can often simply circle an item in the rubric, rather than struggling to explain the flaw or strength they have noticed and figuring out what to suggest in terms of improvements. Rubrics provide students with more informative feedback about their strengths and areas in need of improvement.

Fourth, teachers appreciate rubrics because their "accordion" nature allows them to accommodate heterogeneous classes. The examples here have three or four gradations of quality, but there is no reason they can't be "stretched" to reflect the work of both gifted students and those with learning disabilities.

Finally, rubrics are easy to use and explain. Christine Hall, a 4th grade teacher, reflected on how both students and parents responded to her use of rubrics:

Students were able to articulate what they had learned, and by the end of the year could be accurate with their evaluations. Parents were very excited about the use of rubrics. During parent conferences, I used sample rubrics to explain to parents their purpose, and how they were used in class. The reaction of parents was very encouraging. They knew exactly what their child needed to do to be successful.

HOW DO YOU CREATE RUBRICS?

Rubrics are becoming increasingly popular, with educators moving toward more authentic, performance-based assessments. Recent publications contain some rubrics (Brewer 1996; Marzano et al. 1993). Chances are, however, that you will have to develop a few to reflect your own curriculum and teaching style. To boost the learning leverage of rubrics, the rubric design process should engage students in the following steps:

1. *Look at models:* Show students examples of good and not-so-good work. Identify the characteristics that make the good ones good and the bad ones bad.

2. *List criteria:* Use the discussion of models to begin a list of what counts in quality work.

3. *Articulate gradations of quality:* Describe the best and worst levels of quality, then fill in the middle levels based on your knowledge of common problems and the discussion of not-so-good work.

4. *Practice on models:* Have students use the rubrics to evaluate the models you gave them in Step 1.

5. *Use self- and peer-assessment:* Give students their task. As they work, stop them occasionally for self- and peer-assessment.

6. *Revise:* Always give students time to revise their work based on the feedback they get in Step 5.

7. *Use teacher assessment:* Use the same rubric students used to assess their work yourself.

Step 1 may be necessary only when you are asking students to engage in a task with which they are unfamiliar. Steps 3 and 4 are useful but time-consuming; you can do these on your own, especially when you've been using rubrics for a while. A class experienced in rubric-based assessment can streamline the process so that it begins with listing criteria, after which the teacher writes out the gradations of quality, checks them with the students, makes revisions, then uses the rubric for self-, peer-, and teacher assessment.

Ann Tanona, a 2nd grade teacher, went through the seven-step process with her students. The result was a rubric for assessing videotaped *Reading Rainbow*-style "book talks" (fig. 2).

TIPS ON DESIGNING RUBRICS

Ann's rubric is powerful because it articulates the characteristics of a good "book talk" in students' own words. It also demonstrates some of the difficulties of designing a good rubric.

Perhaps the most common challenge is avoiding unclear language, such as "creative beginning." If a rubric is to teach as well as evaluate, terms like

Criteria	Quality		
Did I get my audience's attention?	Creative beginning	Boring beginning	No beginning
Did I tell what kind of book?	Tells exactly what type of book it is	Not sure, not clear	Didn't mention it
Did I tell something about the main character?	Included facts about each character	Slid over character	Did not tell anything about main character
Did I mention the setting?	Tells when and where story takes place	Not sure, not clear	Didn't mention setting
Did I tell one interesting part?	Made it sound interesting—I want to buy it!	Told part and skipped on to something else	Forgot to do it
Did I tell who might like the book?	Did tell	Skipped over it	Forgot to tell
How did I look?	Hair combed, neat, clean clothes, smiled, looked up, happy	Lazy look	Just-got-out-of-bed look, head down
How did I sound?	Clear, strong, cheerful voice	No expression in voice	Difficult to understand—6-inch voice or screeching

FIGURE 2 **Book Talk Rubric**

Criterion	Quality			
Gains attention of audience.	Gives details or an amusing fact, a series of questions, a short demonstration, a colorful visual, or a personal reason why they picked this topic.	Does a two-sentence introduction, then starts speech. Gives a one-sentence introduction, then starts speech.		Does not attempt to gain attention of audience, just starts speech.

FIGURE 3   **Rubric for an Oral Presentation**

these must be defined for students. Admittedly, *creative* is a difficult word to define. Ann handled this problem by having a discussion of what the term "creative beginning" meant in book talks. Patricia Crosby and Pamela Heinz, both 7th grade teachers, solved the same problem in a rubric for oral presentations by actually listing ways in which students could meet the criterion (fig. 3). This approach provides valuable information to students on how to begin a talk and avoids the need to define elusive terms like *creative*.

A second challenge in rubric design is avoiding unnecessarily negative language. The excerpt from the rubric in Figure 3 avoids words like *boring* by describing what was done during a so-so beginning of a talk and implicitly comparing it with the highest level of quality. Thus, students know exactly what they did wrong and how they can do better next time, not just that the opening to their talk was boring.

Articulating gradations of quality is often a challenge. It helps if you spend a lot of time thinking about criteria and how best to chunk them before going on to define the levels of quality. You might also try a clever technique I borrowed from a 5th grade teacher in Gloucester, Massachusetts. She describes gradations of quality as "Yes," "Yes but," "No but," and "No." For example, Figure 4 shows part of a rubric for evaluating a scrapbook that documents a story. This approach tends to work well, as long as you aren't too rigid about it. Rigidity can

have amusing results: One student wrote out the lowest level of quality for the criterion, "Is it anachronism free?" this way: "No, I did not remember to not use anachronism"!

WHAT TO DO ONCE YOU'VE CREATED RUBRICS

Creating rubrics is the hard part—using them is relatively easy. Once you've created a rubric, give copies to students and ask them to assess their own progress on a task or project. Their assessments should not count toward a grade. The point is for the rubric to help students learn more and produce better final products, so including self-assessments in grades is unnecessary and can compromise students' honesty.

Always give students time to revise their work after assessing themselves, and then have them assess one another's work. Peer assessment takes some getting used to. Emphasize the fact that peer assessment, like self-assessment, is intended to help everyone do better work. You may need to hold students accountable for their assessments of a classmate's work by having them sign off on the rubric they use. You can then see how fair and accurate their feedback is, and you can ask for evidence that supports their opinions when their assessments don't match yours. Again, giving time for revision after peer assessment is crucial.

Criterion	Quality			
Gives enough details.	Yes, I put in enough details to give the reader a sense of time, place, and events.	Yes, I put in some details, but some key details are missing.	No, I didn't put in enough details, but I did include a few.	No, I had almost no details.

FIGURE 4   **Rubric for Evaluating a Scrapbook**

Parents can use rubrics to help their children with their homework. Finally, when you assess student work, use the same rubric that was used for self- and peer assessment. When you hand the marked rubric back with the students' work, they'll know what they did well and what they need to work on in the future.

Grading (if you must) is also relatively easy with rubrics. A piece of work that reflects the highest level of quality for each criterion obviously deserves an *A*, one that consistently falls in the lowest level deserves a *D* or *F*, and so on. Because one piece of work rarely falls in only one level of quality, many teachers average out the levels of quality, either formally or informally.

Rubrics can also be included in portfolios. However you use them, the idea is to support and evaluate student learning. Students, as well as teachers, should respond to the use of rubrics by thinking, "Yes, this is what I need!"

REFERENCES

Brewer, R. (1996). *Exemplars: A Teacher's Solution*. Underhill, Vt.: Exemplars.

Marcus, J. (1995). "Data on the Impact of Alternative Assessment on Students." Unpublished manuscript. The Education Cooperative Wellesley, Mass.

Marzano, R., D. Pickering, and J. McTighe (1993). *Assessing Student Outcomes: Performance Assessment Using the Dimensions of Learning Model*. Alexandria, Va.: ASCD.

Perkins, D., H. Goodrich, S. Tishman, and J. Mirman Owen. (1994). *Thinking Connections: Learning to Think and Thinking to Learn*. Reading, Mass.: Addison-Wesley.

Competitive Grading Sabotages Good Teaching

JOHN D. KRUMBOLTZ and CHRISTINE J. YEH

Professor Jones took great pride in the bell-shaped curve generated from students' scores on his final exam. He was able to assign grades of A, B, C, D, and F with precision, simply by marking off segments of that normal curve. He told a colleague, "One semester I experimented with a new method of teaching in which I used more examples and explained the material more clearly. It was a disaster! My normal curve was hopelessly skewed. Too many students received high scores. So now I am deliberately more ambiguous in my lectures, I use fewer examples, and I am gratified to find that my exams produce normally distributed scores once again."

In other words, Professor Jones intentionally taught in a way that inhibited student learning. He chose this approach because of the need to assign grades. Clearly, competitive grading can redefine and distort the underlying purpose of education, which is to help every student learn.[1]

To date, arguments against the current grading system have focused on ways in which competitive grading victimizes students, but teachers are negatively affected as well. Assigning competitive grades affects teachers' behavior in five basic ways: 1) it turns teachers into students' opponents, 2) it justifies inadequate teaching methods and styles, 3) it trivializes course content, 4) it encourages methods of evaluation that misdirect and inhibit student learning, and 5) it rewards teachers for punishing students.

TEACHERS BECOME OPPONENTS

Many educators justify a differential grading system as a means of sorting students according to their performance. Unfortunately, sorting and ranking students inevitably creates a contentious relationship between students and their teachers. Imagine the following scenario.

Ms. Smith, an 11th-grade English teacher, has a pile of student papers to grade. The topics vary tremendously, and she must assign a letter grade to each paper. Since everyone cannot receive the same grade, Ms. Smith must find reasons to give some papers lower grades than others. As she reads the papers, she looks for flaws—awkward sentences, factual errors, incorrect interpretations—and marks each one in red ink. She concentrates on the negative, carefully counting errors. If a student complains about his or her grade, those errors will be her defense. But what about the student? Is he or she encouraged to write more or look for ways to improve the paper? More likely, the student will feel discouraged, defeated, and humiliated.

---

[1] All subsequent references to "grading" or "grades" pertain to competitive grading practices, in which student accomplishments are compared with one another for the purpose of assigning marks indicating their relative merit.

John D. Krumboltz is a professor of education and psychology in the School of Education at Stanford University, Stanford, Calif., where Christine J. Yeh is a postdoctoral fellow at the Stanford Center on Adolescence.

Now imagine the same scenario with one difference: no grades are expected or allowed. Ms. Smith's sole purpose is to motivate all the students to learn and to improve their work. Does she read and respond to the papers differently? Most certainly. Now she points out the strengths of the writing—the apt phrase, the persuasive argument, the clever use of alliteration. She considers and appreciates students' ideas and their individual learning styles. She is constantly looking for improvement.

To assign grades, teachers must become critics whose focus is negative, always seeking errors and finding fault with students' work. Moreover, students must be compared with one another, because there is no accepted standard for a given letter grade. A performance that earns an A in one classroom could earn a C in another classroom because of differences in the teachers' standards or in the composition of the two classes.

When judging the relative merit of students' performances takes precedence over improving their skills, few students can feel good about their accomplishments. Only one student can be the best; the rest are clearly identified as less able. Comparative grading ensures that, unlike children in Lake Wobegon, half of the students will be below average.

It could be argued that, despite the drawbacks, grading is necessary in order to sort people. Colleges demand high school grades, for example, to help them decide which applicants to admit. But high schools should never compromise their central mission in order to satisfy the demands of colleges for student rankings.

What would colleges do if high schools refused to employ a competitive grading system? Colleges would find some other method of deciding whom they wished to admit. High schools have no responsibility to serve colleges by performing the sorting function for them. Since mandatory sorting undermines student learning, colleges have no right to demand competitive grades from high schools. High schools cannot serve two masters.

GRADING JUSTIFIES INADEQUATE METHODS OF TEACHING

When students fail to achieve course objectives, whose responsibility is it—the teachers' or the students'? Current grading practices put the onus squarely on the students. Teachers can use the most slipshod of teaching methods, discover that many students do not understand the material, and then assign grades accordingly. Current grading practices do not encourage teachers to help students improve, because only the students are blamed when they fail to learn.

If every student achieved all the objectives of a given course, every student would earn an A—an unacceptable state of affairs in the current view. Thus teachers are reinforced for using methods that ensure that some students will not succeed. For example, instruction is often provided in a unidirectional manner, as in a lecture, and interaction between the lecturer and the students is discouraged. Moreover, teachers often create conditions that inhibit students from challenging them or asking questions. Most people find it difficult to sit and listen to someone else talk for long periods of time. Those students who can tolerate that situation best will tend to receive higher grades.

In developing examinations, many teachers tend to focus on objective information that cannot be disputed. By emphasizing the memorization of facts, however, such teachers discourage debate, inhibit the expression of opinion, minimize teamwork and cooperation, and force students to listen passively—the very worst way to learn. An emphasis on memorization deprives students of opportunities to ponder their ideas critically or discuss their ideas publicly. Students have to remember the facts only long enough to pass the next exam.

Meanwhile, teachers find it easy to dispense, and then test for, factual information. Unidirectional teaching gives them a safety net. If students are unable to demonstrate comprehension of the material covered in lectures, they are presumed to have been inattentive and thus are blamed for their poor performance.

Teachers who rush to cover all the material in a course syllabus are really trying to cover their behinds. If a student fails to understand the material, such a teacher can say, "I did my job. I covered it in class."

GRADES TRIVIALIZE COURSE CONTENT

Which of the following questions is more challenging to a student?

- When was the Declaration of Independence signed?

- Would you have signed the Declaration of Independence if you had lived in 1776? Why or why not?

The answer seems clear. The first question requires students to memorize a date. The second question requires them to think—to imagine themselves in another time and place and then to justify an action that would profoundly affect their own lives and the lives of others. However, many teachers might hesitate to include such thought-provoking questions on a test. Grading students' responses would be time-consuming and laborious, requiring subjective judgments that would be hard to justify to students and their parents.

If assigning grades were not required, teachers might opt for the second question. Thus course content is determined, at least partly, by the need to grade students. Teachers would be liberated to teach toward more consequential goals if they were not obligated to assign grades.

GRADING INHIBITS CONSTRUCTIVE EVALUATION

Evaluation of student performance is essential, but it should serve to promote student learning. Ideally, the evaluation process would help students discover how to improve their achievement of important goals. Grading defeats this purpose by discouraging the vast majority of students, who receive below-average grades, and by not challenging students who could improve on what they have already learned. Constructive evaluation encourages students to exert maximum effort by emphasizing their strengths, identifying concrete ways for them to improve, and providing them with positive reinforcement for progress.

Mandatory grading encourages teachers to evaluate their students in ways that do not promote critical thinking and long-term retention. For example, teachers of large classes may assign grades based on students' ability to memorize facts. Tests based on factual information are simple and quick to score, but they do not foster critical thinking.

Pressure to perform well often causes students to attend only to "material that will be on the final." Their behavior in preparing for a test depends on the nature of the test. If they believe that the test will require knowledge of isolated facts, most students will try to memorize isolated facts (which will quickly be forgotten). Students develop learning styles that they expect to yield good grades. They quickly learn that the operational definition of a course objective is "what appears on the final exam."

TEACHERS CAN TAKE PRIDE IN FAILURE

Some teachers feel proud when a high percentage of their students fail. They want others to believe that a high failure rate signifies a difficult course and an intelligent teacher. To a large extent, they succeed.

There is a common assumption that taking a "tough" course is more prestigious than taking a "Mickey Mouse" course. Some teachers believe that giving students low grades adds luster to their own reputations. Such teachers may choose to include excessively difficult material in their courses simply to enhance their own self-importance.

One way of guaranteeing a high failure rate is to present material that is too difficult for most of the class to comprehend. But the inclusion of material for this purpose stands education on its head. Teachers deserve shame, not praise, if their students fail to achieve.

Teachers who take pride in giving low grades blame the students, not themselves, when course material is not mastered as quickly as it is presented. They expect every student to learn the same material in the same amount of time. The few students who master the material are "proof" that this expectation is realistic. Although the system is rigged so that some students fail, the teacher can always point to the few high achievers and say, "They understood. Why didn't you?" The students who fail are blamed undeservedly, and the teachers who fail them are esteemed undeservedly—but the real culprit is the grading system.

Competitive grades turn educational priorities on their head. Classes in which most of the students master the material are perceived as unchallenging. High grades are often dismissed as "grade inflation," not as a sign that the teacher and the students have successfully achieved their mutual objectives. Meanwhile, prestige is accorded to teachers who are unable to help most of their students learn the material. The situation is ridiculous.

Teachers and students are all victims of a competitive grading system. Competitive grading creates a conflict of interest for teachers: improving students' learning versus judging the relative merit of their academic performance. As long as teachers are forced to make comparative judgments, they cannot focus single-mindedly on the improvement of students' learning. Indeed, under the competitive grading system, teachers are not required to help every student learn, but they *are* required to judge every student. Judgment is mandatory; improvement is optional.

Teachers may not realize how much of their job frustration stems from this inherent conflict. By definition, half of all students must receive below-aver-

age grades. Student reactions to negative evaluations range from passive resistance to active rebellion. The resultant hostile interactions between students and teachers leave many teachers feeling apprehensive much of the time.

Competitive grading deemphasizes learning in favor of judging. Learning becomes a secondary goal of education. Clearly, then, the need to grade students undermines the motive—to help students learn—that brought most of us into the profession.

CREDITS *(Continued)*

7. Scherer, M. (April 1996). On our changing family values: A conversation with David Elkind. *Educational Leadership, 53*(7), 4–9. Reprinted with permission of the Association for Supervision and Curriculum Development. Copyright 1996 by ASCD. All rights reserved.

8. Noddings, N. (1995). Teaching themes of care. *Phi Delta Kappan, 76,* 675–679. Reprinted by permission of Nel Noddings, Lee Jacks Professor of Education, Stanford University.

9. Sternberg, R. J. (1996). Myths, countermyths, and truths about intelligence. *Educational Researcher, 25*(2), 11–16. Copyright 1996 by the American Educational Research Association. Reprinted by permission of the publisher.

10. Gardner, H. (1995). Reflections on multiple intelligences: Myths and messages. *Phi Delta Kappan, 77,* 200–209. Copyright 1995 by Howard Gardner.

11. Fachin, K. (1996). Teaching Tommy: A second-grader with Attention Deficit Hyperactivity Disorder. *Phi Delta Kappan, 77,* 437–441. Reprinted by permission of Katharina M. Fachin.

12. Means, B. & Knapp, M. S. (1992). Cognitive approaches to teaching advanced skills to educationally disadvantaged students. *Phi Delta Kappan, 73,* 282–289. Adapted with permission from Barbara Means, Carol Chelemer, and Michael S. Knapp (Eds.), *Teaching advanced skills to at-risk students: Views from research and practice.* Copyright 1991, Jossey-Bass Inc.

13. Bailey, S. M. (1996). Shortchanging girls and boys. *Educational Leadership, 53*(8), 75–79. Copyright 1996 by Susan McGee Bailey. Reprinted by permission of Susan McGee Bailey.

14. Goldenberg, C. (1996). The education of language-minority students: Where are we, and where do we need to go? *The Elementary School Journal, 96*(3), 353–361. Copyright 1996 The University of Chicago. All rights reserved. Reprinted by permission of The University of Chicago Press and Claude Goldenberg.

15. O'Leary, S. G. (1995). Parental discipline mistakes. *Current Directions in Psychological Science, 4*(1), 11–13. Reprinted by permission of Susan G. O'Leary.

16. Cameron, J. & Pierce, W. D. (1996). The debate about rewards and intrinsic motivation: Protests and accusations do not alter the results. *Review of Educational Research, 66*(1), 39–51. Copyright 1996 by the American Educational Research Association. Reprinted by permission of the publisher.

17. Derry, S. J. (Dec. 1988/Jan. 1989). Putting learning strategies to work. *Educational Leadership, 46*(4), 4–10. Reprinted with permission of the Association for Supervision and Curriculum Development. Copyright 1989 by ASCD. All rights reserved.

18. Greeno, J. G. & Hall, R. P. (1997). Practicing representation: Learning with and about representational forms. *Phi Delta Kappan, 78,* 361–367. Reprinted by permission of James G. Greeno.

19. Tishman, S. & Perkins, D. (1997). The language of thinking. *Phi Delta Kappan, 78,* 368–374. Reprinted by permission of David Perkins.

20. Gardner, H. & Boix-Mansilla, V. (Feb. 1994). Teaching for understanding—within and across the disciplines. *Educational Leadership, 51*(5), 14–18. Reprinted with permission of the Association for Supervision and Curriculum Development. Copyright 1994 by ASCD. All rights reserved.

21. Rosenshine, B. & Meister, C. (April 1992). The use of scaffolds for teaching higher-level cognitive strategies. *Educational Leadership, 49*(7), 26–33. Reprinted with permission of the Association for Supervision and Curriculum Development. Copyright 1992 by ASCD. All rights reserved.

22. Fielding, L. G. & Pearson, P. D. (Feb. 1994). Reading comprehension: What works. *Educational Leadership, 51*(5), 62–67. Reprinted with permission of the Association for Supervision and Curriculum Development. Copyright 1994 by ASCD. All rights reserved.

23. Airasian, P. W. & Walsh, M. E. (1997). Constructivist cautions. *Phi Delta Kappan, 78,* 444–449. Reprinted by permission of Peter W. Airasian and Mary E. Walsh.

24. Beane, J. (Sept. 1991). Sorting out the self-esteem controversy. *Educational Leadership, 49*(1), 25–30. Reprinted with permission of the Association for Supervision and Curriculum Development. Copyright 1991 by ASCD. All rights reserved.

25. Clifford, M. (Sept. 1990). Students need challenge, not easy success. *Educational Leadership, 48*(1), 22–26. Reprinted with permission of the Association for Supervision and Curriculum Development. Copyright 1990 by ASCD. All rights reserved.

26. Weiner, B. (1990). History of motivational research in education. *Journal of Educational Psychology, 82,* 616–622. Copyright 1990 by the American Psychological Association. Reprinted with permission from the publisher and Bernard Weiner.

27. Blumenfield, P. C., Marx, R. W., Soloway, E., & Krajcik, J. (1996). Learning with peers: From small group cooperation to collaborative communities. *Educational Researcher, 25*(8), 37–40. Copyright 1996 by the American Educational Research Association. Reprinted by permission of the publisher.

28. Strong, R., Silver, H. F., & Robinson, A. (Sept. 1995). What do students want (and what really motivates them)? *Educational Leadership, 53*(1), 8–12. Reprinted with permission of the Association for Supervision and Curriculum Development. Copyright 1995 by ASCD. All rights reserved.

29. Render, G. F., Padilla, N., & Krank, H. M. (March 1989). What research really shows about assertive discipline. *Educational Leadership, 46*(6), 72–75. Reprinted with permission of the Association for Supervision and Curriculum Development. Copyright 1989 by ASCD. All rights reserved.

30. McCormack, S. (March 1989). Responses to Render, Padilla, and Krank: But practitioners say it works! *Educational Leadership, 46*(6), 77–79. Reprinted with permission of the Association for Supervision and Curriculum Development. Copyright 1989 by ASCD. All rights reserved.

31. Johnson, D. W. & Johnson, R. T. (Feb. 1995). Why violence prevention programs don't work—and what does. *Educational Leadership, 52*(5), 63–68. Reprinted with permission of the Association for Supervision and Curriculum Development. Copyright 1995 by ASCD. All rights reserved.

32. Harris, K. R. & Graham, S. (Feb. 1996). Memo to constructivists: Skills count, too. *Educational Leadership, 53*(5), 26–29. Reprinted with permission of the Association for Supervision and Curriculum Development. Copyright 1996 by ASCD. All rights reserved.

33. Woronov, T. (Sept./Oct. 1994). Six myths (and five promising truths) about the uses of educational technology. *The Harvard Education Letter, 10*(5), 1–3. Reprinted with permission from *The Harvard Education Letter.* Copyright 1994 by the President and Fellows of Harvard College. All rights reserved.

34. Peha, J. M. (Oct. 1995). How K–12 teachers are using computer networks. *Educational Leadership, 53*(2), 18–25. Reprinted with permission of the Association for Supervision and Curriculum Development, with adaptations requested by the author. Copyright 1995 by ASCD. All rights reserved.

35. Cizek, G. J. (1991). Innovation or enervation? Performance assessment in perspective. *Phi Delta Kappan, 72*(9), 695–699. Used with permission of Gregory J. Cizek, Associate Professor of Educational Research and Measurement, 350 Snyder Hall, University of Toledo, Toledo, OH 43606-3390.

36. Wiggins, G. (1991). A response to Cizek. *Phi Delta Kappan, 72*(9), 700–703. Reprinted by permission of Grant Wiggins.

37. Cizek, G. J. (1991). Confusion effusion: A rejoinder to Wiggins. *Phi Delta Kappan, 73*(2), 150–153. Used with permission of Gregory J. Cizek, Associate Professor of Educational Research and Measurement, 350 Snyder Hall, University of Toledo, Toledo, OH 43606-3390.

38. Shepard, L. A. & Bliem, C. L. (1995). Parents' thinking about standardized tests and performance assessments. *Educational Researcher, 24*(8), 25–32. Copyright 1995 by the American Educational Research Association. Reprinted by permission of the publisher.

39. Dempster, F. N.(April 1991). Synthesis of research on reviews and tests. *Educational Leadership, 48*(7), 71–76. Reprinted with permission of the Association for Supervision and Curriculum Development. Copyright 1991 by ASCD. All rights reserved.

40. Goodrich, H. (1997). Understanding rubrics. *Educational Leadership, 54*(4), 14–17. Reprinted by permission of Heidi Goodrich.

41. Krumboltz, J. D. & Yeh, C. J. (1996). Competitive grading sabotages good teaching. *Phi Delta Kappan, 78,* 324–326. Reprinted by permission of John D. Krumboltz.